Your Fatwa Does Not Apply Here

Your Fatwa Does Not Apply Here

UNTOLD STORIES FROM THE FIGHT AGAINST
MUSLIM FUNDAMENTALISM

KARIMA BENNOUNE

W. W. NORTON & COMPANY

NEW YORK | LONDON

Lyrics from "Let it Be" © 1970 Sony/ATV Music Publishing LLC. All Rights administered by Sony/ATV Music Publishing LLC, 8 Music Square West, Nashville, TN 37203. All rights reserved. Used by permission.

Excerpt from *The Last Summer of Reason: A Novel* by Tahar Djaout, translated by Marjolijn de Jager, by permission of the University of Nebraska Press. Originally published as *Le Dernier été de la raison*, copyright 1999 Éditions du Seuil. English translation copyright 2001 by Marjolijn de Jager.

For information about permission to reproduce selections from this book, write to Permissions, W. W. Norton & Company, Inc., 500 Fifth Avenue, New York, NY 10110

For information about special discounts for bulk purchases, please contact W. W. Norton Special Sales at specialsales@wwnorton.com or 800-233-4830

Manufacturing by RR Donnelley, Harrisonburg
Book design by Barbara Bachman
Production manager: Devon Zahn

ISBN 978-0-393-08158-9

W. W. Norton & Company, Inc.
500 Fifth Avenue, New York, N.Y. 10110
www.wwnorton.com

W. W. Norton & Company Ltd.
Castle House, 75/76 Wells Street, London W1T 3QT

1 2 3 4 5 6 7 8 9 0

Boualem Yekker was one of those who had decided to resist, those who had become aware that when the hordes confronting them had managed to spread their fear and impose silence they would have won.

—TAHAR DJAOUT (1954–1993),
The Last Summer of Reason

For Leila and Mohamed Redha Kheddar,
     Abdorrahman Boroumand, and Ahmad Reshad
     Mosadiq, who live on in the unquenchable human
     rights struggles of those who love them.

For Amel Zenoune-Zouani, an Algerian law student.
     For the lawyer she could have been, and the
     free woman she was.

For Lakhdar Bennoune, my grandfather, who died
     defeating colonialism that his descendants might be free.

For all the Boualem Yekkers—female and male—
     still resisting.

CONTENTS

Your Fatwa Does Not Apply Here

Everything Looks Different Once You Have Seen "Death To" Before Your Name

----

Could I defend my father from the Armed Islamic Group with a paring knife?

This was the question I pondered on Tuesday June 29, 1993. That day I woke up early in Dad's apartment, on the outskirts of Algiers, Algeria, to an unrelenting pounding on the front door. It had been exactly two weeks since the murder of Dr. Mahfoud Boucebsi, the country's leading psychiatrist, and one week since the assassination of Mohamed Boukhobza, a sociologist and former colleague of my father's at the University of Algiers. As a local newspaper described the season, "at the time, every Tuesday a scholar fell to the bullets of . . . fundamentalist assassins."[1] Boucebsi and Boukhobza, and others, had been killed that year by the Muslim fundamentalist armed groups that plagued Algeria's predominantly Muslim population. The learned Dr. Boukhobza was tied up in front of his daughter and had his throat cut.

One Tuesday later, and at the same time of day, unwanted visitors were outside the entrance to the home of Mahfoud Bennoune, professor and outspoken critic of successive Algerian governments and the armed fundamentalists who opposed them. My father's teaching of Darwin had already provoked a classroom visit from the head of the Islamic Salvation Front, who denounced him as an advocate of "biologism" before Dad ejected the man. Now, whoever was pounding on the door would neither identify himself nor go away. We tried to ascertain who might be outside with him. Inside the apartment, my father was not frightened for himself, but visibly worried for me, then a law student visiting for the summer break. He tried repeatedly to phone the police. Perhaps terrified themselves by the rising tide of armed extremism that had already claimed the lives of many Algerian officers, the local police station did not even answer. We were alone to face whoever was on the other side of the door.

That was when I went to the kitchen, found a paring knife, and took up a position inside the entryway. What happened to Dr. Boukhobza was not going to happen again here, I told myself. I don't know what I was thinking: I am not exactly the combatant type. My father looked at me and rolled his eyes. But I could not come up with anything else to do. So there I stood.

That moment set me on the path to writing this book.

It was the very beginning of a journey that would eventually lead me to interview about 286 people of Muslim heritage from twenty-six countries to find out how they fought fundamentalism like my father did, and how they coped with the attendant risks. My hope is that telling the stories of those who have truly faced the fire to battle extremism will be a far more useful contribution than my attempt to deploy a kitchen utensil was.

Fortunately, on June 29, 1993, the unwanted and unidentified visitors eventually departed. We never knew why, or exactly who they were. Perhaps they were deterred by watching neighbors or by the industrial-strength metal frame my dad had just installed over the frail wooden portal to his apartment. Whatever made them go away, someone would return a few months later, leaving a note on the kitchen table: "Consider yourself dead." They would scrawl "death to" on the mailbox, tragicomically misspelling it in French (*mor a Bennoune*). The world looks very different once you have seen "death to" before your name.

Subsequently, Algerian fundamentalists would add Mahfoud Bennoune's name to "kill lists" posted in extremist-controlled mosques in Algiers, along with the names of so many others—journalists, intellectuals, trade unionists, women's rights activists. They would murder more of my father's colleagues, his friends and relatives, and as many as two hundred thousand Algerians during what came to be known as "the dark decade." No matter how awful things became, the international community largely ignored these events. Like the local police who would not even answer our urgent calls in June 1993, the world would leave all those victims to fend for themselves.

Finally, my father, an Algerian peasant's son turned professor who had spent his entire life building the young country, would be forced to flee his apartment and give up teaching at the university. Life in Algeria as we had known it during my regular visits—in an ordinary apartment in a *cité* in a then-quiet suburb of Algiers—was over.

EAT, PRAY, HATE

My father's country showed me in those grim years of the 1990s that the struggle waged in Muslim majority societies against extremism is one of the most important—and overlooked—human rights struggles in the world. This remains true twenty years later. In this book, I will describe as much of this antifundamentalist engagement as I can, and tell the stories of those who make it, because they deserve to be known and remembered.

This is a very personal account of my peregrinations there and back again, across every kind of border, to record these oral histories. I sometimes joked to myself that I was writing, *Eat, Pray, Hate*. Or perhaps *Fast, Pray, Hate*.

I hope that readers will come along on my trip, and view the landscape through my eyes. My perspective—that of a secular person of Muslim heritage concerned with both rising fundamentalism and increasing discrimination against Muslims—is rarely heard in the West. In the post-9/11 era, this is all contentious subject matter often seen only through right- or left-wing versions of the so-called clash of civilizations, a set of paradigms I reject. For me, the clashes *within* civilizations, like those between fundamentalists and their opponents everywhere, are much more defining today.

Nevertheless, writing about Muslim fundamentalism in this era for an American audience feels like dancing on a minefield. I have decided to do it anyway, given that what I face is merely a metaphorical minefield, while many of those you will meet in this book confront something rather more like the real thing and continue to speak out anyway. They sing and dance and write and joke and bare their heads and speak their minds and claim equality and the right to be themselves when all these things are forbidden by fundamentalists, sometimes on pain of death.

I think about a Pakistani woman I interviewed in December 2010 who with considerable courage, sitting in a crowded place near where a militant's bomb—and the militant himself—had exploded some two weeks earlier, looked at me and said, "Personally, I am an atheist." She does not stop there. "In the sixties and seventies, I could openly stand in public and say, 'I am an atheist.' Today, dare I say it? I would be killed." But here she was saying it to me in public nonetheless, without lowering her voice.

This reminds me of my father's threat throughout the nineties that he would write a book called *Why I Became an Apostate*. As a concerned daughter, I repeatedly urged him not to. Of course, he was right to denounce those who declared him and so many others excluded from the culture of their birth because they dared to think and speak freely. Despite bombers and assassins, both Mahfoud Bennoune and the Pakistani atheist continued to express themselves openly about fundamentalism, and to do so whether or not the world dared to listen.

As you will see, they are not alone, though they sometimes have felt alone, given the indifference of so many who should be their allies. Algerian psychologist and women's rights advocate Cherifa Bouatta says there is still tremendous anger at those internationally—the Left, human rights advocates—who could have been the allies of progressive antifundamentalists but were not. "No one said, 'We are with you.'"

Even as I hope to bring people like them more support, I am also aware that I write this book, about people of Muslim heritage fighting fundamentalism, in English in the West in troubled times. Switzerland has banned minarets. President Obama is falsely accused of being a Muslim, which has somehow become an offense. Remote U.S. states are lining up to pass resolutions against the application of "Sharia law"—in places such as Oklahoma where this is about as likely as Saudi Arabia's future use of the Talmud. Moreover, they are adopting these bans for rather different reasons than I have for criticizing recourse to what is called Sharia.

This tome in no way justifies discrimination against Muslims or unlawful violence against anyone, including those alleged to be Muslim fundamentalists or merely confused with them. It is not an apology for the Iraq War or waterboarding. It offers no comfort to right-wing anti-Muslim demagogues (the Pamela Gellers of the world) or the supporters of the policies of the Israeli government or George W. Bush, though undoubtedly some critics may claim it does. Criticizing Muslim fundamentalists is mistakenly equated with support for the actions of Western governments that claim to be their opponents. This is just wrong, and it entirely overlooks the fact that not everything is about the West.

Nor, as everyone knows now, was the problem swept away in the revolutionary euphoria of 2011. In fact, it is getting worse, as Islamist electoral victories crisscross North Africa, from Cairo to Casablanca. On October 23, 2011, Tunisians elected eighty-nine members of the fundamentalist party Ennahda to their 217-member Constituent Assembly, the body charged with drafting the country's new constitution. This happened on the same day that neighboring Libya declared the application of "Sharia law" and abrogation of the ban on polygamy. Meanwhile, in revolutionary Egypt, fundamentalist parties have claimed 75 percent of the seats in the lower house of the first parliament and even the presidency. The new Egyptian constitution they drafted subverts rights to religious rules, deems the family to be "founded on religion," bans insulting the Prophet, and may create the architecture of an Islamic-Republic-on-the-Nile. In this environment, some of the newly ascendant mullahs[2] advocate female genital mutilation, polygamy, theocracy. Salafi violence and pressure aimed at women and freethinkers accelerates unchecked. North Africans call this regional dynamic "the Green Wave," the color being associated in this region with Islamist political parties. It does not bode well for secular, liberal, leftist, artistic, female, and gay sectors of these countries' populations on whom the wave's force has already begun to crash.

When U.S. ambassador Christopher Stevens, who loved North Africa, was killed by Al Qaeda in Benghazi, Libya, on September 11, 2012, along with ten Libyans protecting the consulate, it seemed as though the jihadists were trying to kill any hope of a different future for the region along with them. Many Libyans wept for "Chris," as they called him, but also for the Libya of their dreams, which they feared was being asphyxiated too. The proliferating displays of hysteria that followed, engineered by fundamentalists from Indonesia to Sudan in the name of outrage over a so-called film that no one in the United States had seen until they protested it, and that many who protested had not seen, suggests that the place I try not to call "the Muslim world" is now acutely vulnerable to fundamentalist manipulation. Given that fundamentalists themselves had some two weeks earlier desecrated several Muslim holy sites in Libya not in keeping with their own dogma, eliciting barely a whiff of protest, it was hard to take their sensitivities too seriously, however appalling the *Innocence of Muslims* was.[3]

It was a clash of right wings, not a clash of civilizations. In my U.S. home district, some called their congressman, demanding to know when we were going to invade somewhere, while in some Arab streets anything with the word *American* in it seemed to become an appropriate target. The American Cooperative School of Tunis, largely educating children of African Development Bank staff, was torched.[4] As usual, many of our commentators failed us. On Fox News, one suggested, "*The Muslims* attacked us," while on CNN another tried to explain sympathetically that Muslims are simply too sensitive to tolerate any insult to their Prophet and unable to understand Western notions of freedom of expression. The question asked by some U.S. commentators yet again was, "Why don't the Muslims speak out?" But almost no one was listening to those who did.

Sensible, self-critical voices more concerned with the responsibility of Muslims than the "Innocence of Muslims" were rarely transmitted, such as that of the imam of Al Badr Mosque in Algiers, who encouraged his congregation in strong terms not to protest the movie: "So Americans produce a film against Islam. Who cares? It is up to us to make films defending our religion. . . . None of us behaves in a civilized manner. And afterwards we complain about a film made overseas."[5] The Algerian writer Yasmina Khadra, saying that Muslim outrage was being ideologically exploited, urged Muslims "not to allow themselves to be manipulated or to react with violence. What we have to prove to the world, we must prove with work, talent and ambition."[6]

The problem, of course, is not unique to the Maghreb. In West Africa, northern Mali became Al Qaedastan in 2012, with ruling jihadist groups like Ansar Dine (Protectors of the Faith) destroying centuries-old Muslim holy sites in Timbuktu yet provoking nowhere near the global Muslim outrage as Terry Jones's pathetic attempts at Qur'an burning.[7] The young militants reportedly screamed, "*Allahu Akbar*" (God is Great) while descending on the remains of Sufi saints. In October 2012, reports surfaced at the United Nations that Islamist groups were "compiling lists of unmarried mothers," suggesting that these women were at risk of stoning or flogging.[8] The chief prosecutor of the International Criminal Court, Fatou Bensouda, herself of Muslim heritage, denounced the actions of Ansar Dine as possible war crimes.[9] A Malian academic calls his country the "testing ground" of Al Qaeda's strategy for the region.[10] Until French, African, and Malian troops intervened in January 2013, Afghan, Pakistani, and Algerian jihadis reportedly flocked to this safe haven while the international community watched.[11] Meanwhile, unarmed sectors of the local populace protested regularly, receiving little international attention.

In Afghanistan, the Taliban are again gaining ground, despite the hatred felt toward them by large swaths of the population. They have renewed their deliberate killings of women, demonstrated by the filmed machine-gunning of a twenty-two-year-old named Najiba for adultery to the sound of Qur'anic recitation in late June 2012, and the car bomb execution of Hanifa Safi, regional head of women's affairs in eastern Laghman Province in July 2012, most likely attributable to the Taliban.[12] During the first months of 2012, until the Taliban broke off the talks, the United States negotiated avidly with this force that once imposed—and has not renounced—gender apartheid. As Hanifa Safi herself said to the *Christian Science Monitor* a year before she was killed, "When the foreigners go, they are putting us in the mouth of a lion."[13] The Carnegie Endowment for International Peace, in a report that never once uses the word *women*, coolly predicted that the Taliban will retake Afghanistan in 2014,[14] while the peace movement ceaselessly lobbies for an end to international action against the Talibs, even assuring anyone who would listen—as the campaign of 2 Million Friends for Peace in Afghanistan did—that there are no "extremists" in the country.[15]

In neighboring Pakistan, standing against the creep of fundamentalism has become a life-threatening enterprise. Zarteef Afridi, a Pakistani school headmaster in Jamrud, Khyber Agency, who campaigned for the franchise of tribal women and organized tribal elders against terrorism, was gunned down walking to his school on December 8, 2011.[16] As his friend Salman Rashid wrote of him, "Not one of the boys who passed under [his] tutelage . . . turned to that so-called holy war. . . . He stood for the liberation of the human soul through education and enlightenment."[17]

Even children are not immune. On October 9, 2012, now-famous fifteen-year-old Malala Yousafzai, who had blogged in anguish back in 2009 about being excluded from school by the Taliban, was shot in the head by that same group on her way home from class in the Swat Valley. As she lay in the hospital fighting for her life, a spokesman for Tehreek-i-Taliban Pakistan said they would target her again if she survives, "because she was a 'secular-minded lady.' "[18] "Whoever criticizes the Taliban will suffer the same fate," the spokesman declared.[19] The Human Rights Commission of Pakistan inveighed against the crime in unequivocal terms and demanded an urgent response. "Words cannot begin to express the condemnation that this merits. This is a new low even for the Taliban. . . . It is also a wake up call, if another one was needed, for those pining to appease the extremists. . . . [A]ll conscious citizens . . . should show through words and actions their contempt for the blind hate . . . that the Taliban stand for." What else but blind hate could lead them to assassinate health workers fighting the polio that can paralyze Muslim children, as they did repeatedly in 2012?

Meanwhile, Saudi Arabia, Sudan, and Iran continue to use state structures to consolidate extremism as the law of the land, and to export these catastrophic models. Qatar now joins them in promoting fundamentalists across the regions with its money and its media.[20] From the Sahel to the Caucasus, a creeping "Islamization" narrows social space, assaults women's rights, and transfigures lifestyles. Everywhere—from Montreal to Dearborn to Paris to Grozny to East Jerusalem—women of Muslim heritage are under pressure to cover more and more of their skin, their hair, their very beings. To disappear. The mere physical manifestation of their existence is now a provocation. After the 2012

London Summer Olympics, Tunisian fundamentalists used social media to call for the first Tunisian woman ever to win a medal, Habiba Ghribi, to be stripped of her citizenship for being a "naked, shameless woman."[21] (She raced in the same shorts and midriff-baring top worn today by most women runners.)

In such a global environment, one must speak out against Muslim fundamentalists for the sake of basic human rights. It is a moral imperative. But, when doing so in the United States, one must also try to do this in a way that will not be hijacked by those with anti-Muslim agendas.

Islam and Islamism are not the same thing. The three extra letters make a huge difference. Being a devout believer has nothing to do with purveying political Islam. The vast majority of Muslims are not fundamentalists, though of course too many are. The goal of this book is to rebroadcast the words of those who in fact do the most to dissipate discrimination against Muslims. Whether believers, agnostics, freethinkers, or atheists, they do this by representing some of the Muslim traditions' greatest values—mercy, compassion, peace, tolerance, study, creativity, openness. They do this not by mouthing platitudes about "Islam-religion-of-peace" but in many cases by putting their lives on the line to fight fundamentalism.

THE LONG JOURNEY OF THE "APOSTATE'S" DAUGHTER

Passions are so intense and suspicions so rife around this subject that I know some will question my motives and my methodology. Now that I have explained why I wrote this book, let me be candid about how it was written. I took two semesters of research leave, collected my modest book advance, and traveled around the world talking to people in Muslim majority countries, or in diaspora populations of Muslim heritage, about their experiences with fundamentalism. I crossed the ocean repeatedly with my laptop computer, a digital recorder, and a pile of notebooks. I went as far as possible with the money and time I had, though I am the first to concede there are many places I did not go but should have, people I wanted to interview but could not. I still ended up with enough material for several books, and I regret that I had to leave out many accounts I heard.

On a series of eight trips between September 2010 and December 2012, I went—in chronological order—to France, Algeria (five times), Niger, Pakistan, Turkey (briefly), Russia (to interview people from Azerbaijan, Chechnya, Dagestan, Tajikistan, and Tatarstan), Palestine/Israel, post-revolutionary Egypt and Tunisia (twice), Senegal (where I also interviewed women from Gambia and Nigeria), Afghanistan, Canada, and Mali. I met with Somali and Iranian refugees in the United States and in Europe. I Skyped women activists in Saudi Arabia and Sudan and consulted visitors from Iraq, Turkey, and Malaysia. I had already done some other relevant interviews with people of Muslim heritage in places as disparate as Fiji and France.

Given this geographic range, I do not attempt to relate the entire situation in any of the countries I cover. Moreover, as a human rights lawyer, I am conscious of the strengths and weaknesses of using firsthand witness statements. I have tried to corroborate these where necessary and possible. Otherwise, just as with many human rights reports, I am reflecting what I have been told by people whom I had good reason to believe, and what I observed myself.

One worry I had, given my format and itinerary, is that I would be shadowing the fundamentalist logic that there is a monolithic *umma* of Muslims, 1.5 billion people who are all alike, who are all simply Muslims. I do not wish to confirm either the *umma* of the fundamentalist universe or the *umma* of the Western imagination. While some things followed me most of the way—the call to prayer (*ithan*), the direction faced by those who choose to pray, mosques, a sense of hospitality, and the challenge of fundamentalism—every single one of these contexts was unique and the people I interviewed tremendously diverse. They were as different as they were alike, just as one would expect when traveling to the Philippines and Italy because both have Christian majority populations. In fact, these people would not all agree with each other about everything, nor should the totality of views expressed here (especially my own) be imputed to any one of them.

In light of such diversities, I have tried to be careful how I describe the people I met. Lately, we call everyone "Muslim," whether they are practicing or not. Muslims are not a trope that exist to provide non-Muslims with diversity by being a monolithic "other." They have their own diversities. *The Muslim World* is the unhelpful term used nowadays to describe collectively many of the places I went. It would make my life easier to employ it because everyone thinks they know what it means. But that is precisely what worries me. In fact, the people who inhabit that presumed "world" may have a whole range of relationships with the Muslim religion. They may practice or not, they may believe or not, they may assume this to be a key component of their identity or not, all across a continuum, just like people born into other religious traditions. They are citizens of countries, they have genders, ethnicities, social-class memberships, regional identities, and on and on, and each of these may be more or equally defining for them.

That is why I have chosen to use the more cumbersome terms *Muslim majority societies* and *people of Muslim heritage or culture* instead. I know these phrases are less neat, but that is the point. They leave more space for the messy lived realities I observed repeatedly during this odyssey.

The people I encountered were multifarious, to say the least. I met journalists, writers, medical doctors, nurses, lawyers (lots of lawyers!), psychologists, concert promoters, TV producers, TV presenters, trade unionists, workers, drivers, dancers, poets, academics, students, museum directors, imams (and their daughters), women's rights activists, housewives, grandmothers, sexual rights activists, activists in wheelchairs, businesswomen, members of the Muslim Brotherhood and Ennahda, sheikhs, bloggers, politicians, filmmakers, artists, former prisoners, former hostages, victims of terrorism, judges, teachers, schoolchildren, community organizers, young and old revolutionaries, people who prayed in the middle of interviews, and others who drank wine when I met them on the Prophet Muhammad's birthday.

I froze in Russia meeting Chechen men, sweltered in Senegal meeting Nigerian and Gambian women, got cultural whiplash when I transited from Karachi to Moscow via Antalya or from Algiers to Lahore via London. I followed an itinerary I will never be able to match again. I spent New Year's Eve at a Palestinian party in East Jerusalem on a dance floor with both a woman in a headscarf and Santa Claus, and then toasted all whom I had met on the hillside above the Haram al-Sharif, Islam's third-holiest site. I went to Mohamed Bouazizi's neighborhood, where the man who set himself on fire and launched a regional revolution lived his modest Tunisian youth, to Cairo cafés filled with women freely smoking water pipes, to Internet cafés full of young people Skyping for love. I had days that began in the Old City of Hebron, observing Jewish settler destruction of Palestinian homes and businesses, and ended in a Tel Aviv bistro, talking to progressive Israeli feminists. In Algeria, I drank vodka with residents in the slums of Bab el Oued and watched women protesters scraped off the sidewalk by policewomen in First of May Square. In Afghanistan, I carried out some interviews under the watchful eye of the interviewees' bodyguards. I saw little girls sing on stage bareheaded in Pakistan and observed Tunisian women count ballots.

I stood in Kabul Stadium, site of Taliban stonings, where I could still feel the unevaporated pain in the air, and I also stood in immediate post-revolutionary Tahrir Square, where a liberal imam preached unity between Christians and Muslims and I could still feel the hope. I listened to Cheikh Imam sung by young Tunisians, to Leonard Cohen sung by young Pakistanis, and to Nusrat Fateh Ali Khan on my iPod. I met people in tight jeans, low-cut tops, peasant clothes, Western clothes, business suits, gondouras, jellabas, boubous, burqas, miniskirts, saris, shalwar kameezes, headscarves, jilbabs, and chadors. They honored me with their time and trust. It was an indescribable pilgrimage from which I will never quite come home.

Another kind of diversity I encountered among people I met was a Babel of languages—various dialects of Arabic, Tamazight, Hausa and Zarma/Songhai, Bamanankan, Urdu, Russian, Wolof, Dari, Persian, Pashto, Somali, and French, just to name a few. Many of the interviews were done through second languages or translators. Sometimes I translated them myself. I also excerpted the interviews and edited them for readability, and occasionally for security reasons. I made a good-faith effort to be as true to the spirit of the original conversations as I could, even through all these filters. I cannot speak *for* any of those I interviewed, but I will do my best to recount what I heard them say.

Though the people I talked to in all these ways were distinct, rising tides of Muslim fundamentalism were constraining their lives in every locale. They generally feared it might get worse before it gets better. I was continually reminded of the words a young woman journalist had said to me in Algeria in 1994 as the savagery of armed fundamentalism gripped the country: "I believe other people were told, elsewhere in other times that the evil and fear around them would pass. As far as I know, it did not pass. It got worse. I believe it will get worse unless someone hears us."[22] That was the thought that drove me onward.

Iranian sociologist Chahla Chafiq would tell me, "There is a political war that divides Muslims." This book is about the people on one side of that "political war," the people you are less likely to have heard about. They are themselves politically diverse, coming from the center as well as from a range of liberal and left-wing perspectives. Chafiq's metaphoric "political war," in which they are engaged, is mostly not a war in the literal sense. It is, however, a long, pervasive, and sometimes violent struggle (the vast majority of the violence being on the fundamentalist side), and one that will determine the fates of more than a billion people around the world. On the antifundamentalist side, the "war" largely consists of political opposition; on the fundamentalist side, it is often carried out through everything from death threats to beheadings.

For their part, those I met were engaged in peaceful resistance to extremism, and their efforts constitute a far superior way of defeating it than the phenomenon formerly known as the "War on Terror." I do not dispute that the use of force is sometimes necessary to combat some manifestations of armed *Salafi jihadism*. Too many Western liberals and leftists do not recognize this. But treating this mainly as a literal war, and especially as one without rules, as many on the right have, has done more harm than good. It has undermined the people in this book. Actually listening to the concerns and perspectives of these individuals and those they represent would force us to radically reconfigure how we combat jihadist terrorism.

Ultimately, however, Muslim fundamentalism is not essentially a security question for Westerners. At its very core, it is a basic question of human rights for hundreds of millions of people who live in Muslim majority countries and populations around the world. In Algiers, Cherifa Bouatta tells me that Muslim fundamentalism "is a deadly ideology which stands against choice, hope, change and humanity. It represents the breaking of our countries." Franco-Algerian community organizer Mimouna Hadjam wants to remind Westerners, "Islamism is a danger for the Muslim population. It is a danger for us."

WHAT IS MUSLIM FUNDAMENTALISM?

Even the words I use are fraught with controversy. I prefer *Muslim fundamentalism* to such alternatives as *Islamism* and *radicalism*, though I may use them occasionally for variety or in quotations. The reason I prefer *fundamentalism* is that it applies across religious boundaries to contemporary movements within all of the world's great religious traditions—not just Islam, but also Christianity, Hinduism, Judaism, and others. These movements are increasingly powerful and pose a variety of human rights problems. Muslim fundamentalism also has its own specificities. It is one of the most truly transnational fundamentalisms, notable for the ubiquity of its adherents and the sophistication and reach of its vicious armed groups.

Marieme Hélie-Lucas, an Algerian sociologist who founded the network of Women Living Under Muslim Laws (WLUML), defined fundamentalisms generally as "political movements of the extreme right, which in a context of globalization. . . manipulate religion. . . in order to achieve their political aims."[23] This way of understanding the phenomenon underlines the fact that these movements are primarily political rather than spiritual. Similarly, Chahla Chafiq told me that she uses the term *Islamism* to describe an Islam that ideologizes religion to create a totalitarian political platform. This is not an inherently Muslim approach or one to which Muslim majority societies naturally tend. There are many other Islams, as this book indicates.

Some Western observers see Muslim fundamentalists as the stalwart representatives of the local standing up to the global, the Jihad versus McWorld scenario. That is not how they are often seen on the ground. Women in Niger complained bitterly to me that fundamentalists were trying to replace the wonderfully colorful local dress—the boubou—with dour veils worn by some in the Arabian Peninsula, to de-Africanize their lived Islams. Moroccan anthropologist Hassan Rachik had explained this dynamic when he wrote that Muslim majority societies currently face two kinds of globalization, "Western global-ization" and "Islamic globalization," by which he meant transnational Muslim fundamentalist networks and ideology.[24] In other words, Jihad *is* McWorld, just a different version of it.

Some of those I would meet would emphasize still other aspects of fundamentalism—the way it embraces absolutism and refuses to accept questioning. It denies the possibility of interpretation and reinter-pretation even while its own adherents engage in both. As an Iranian lawyer still practicing in Tehran would tell me, fundamentalism "says it is Islam and you cannot question it." In Algeria, one expert would describe Muslim fundamentalism to me as being based on "absolute truth," and the idea that its social model "is the only one that can exist."

These ideologies and movements that I characterize as "fundamen-talist" are varied, and I want to avoid conflating them. I place them along the far right of the broader political spectrum among people of Muslim heritage who, it bears repeating these days, are just as polit-ically diverse as anyone else. The people we call Muslims do not all have the same politics. This is also true for the people I call Muslim fundamentalists.

There is no question that there are significant commonalities among the fundamentalists, however. They believe in the imposition of "God's law," something called *the* Sharia—their version of it rather than others'—on Muslims everywhere, and in the creation of what they deem to be Islamic states or disciplined diasporic communities ruled by these laws. (I prefer the concept of "Muslim laws" to "Sharia," because, as the network of Women Living Under Muslim Laws asserts, this term "consciously reflects the diversity of such laws and . . . dis-pel[s] the myth that there is a monolithic system of . . . Islamic law."[25]

Beyond the law, fundamentalists denounce secularists and seek to bring politicized religion into all spheres. They want to police and judge and change the behavior, appearance, and comportment of other people of Muslim heritage. They tend to aim to sharply limit women's rights, though this is sometimes couched in the soothing language of protection and respect and difference. And yes, women fundamental-ists may advocate these things too, their sex making their stance no more progressive than Anita Bryant's made hers in the United States.

To be specific, then, when I use the term *Muslim fundamentalism* I am talking about a range of political movements including the transnational Muslim Brotherhood, its affiliated Freedom and Justice Party in Egypt, Hizb Ut-Tahrir, the ex-Islamic Salvation Front, the Jamaat-e-Islami, Ennahda, and an increasingly important plethora of Salafi groupings. They have all at times used or advocated violence. Their flag is also carried by or apologized for or covered up by some Muslim nongovernmental organizations based in the West, such as the Council on American Islamic Relations (CAIR), the Organisation Islamique de France, the European Council on Fatwa and Research, the Islamic Human Rights Commission, the Muslim Council of Britain, and CagePrisoners.

Sometimes, fundamentalist ideas take on a disembodied life of their own beyond the movements that advance them. Most perniciously, they are absorbed in the social gut and then spread through TV and radio, the Internet, Facebook, YouTube, sermons in mosques, word of mouth, social interaction, even graffiti, becoming what one person I interviewed referred to as "diffused fundamentalism," and what another would call "naturalized."

Invisible in their pervasiveness, these versions may be even more difficult to combat and often are the most successful in changing the ways people think they can live their daily lives. Rather like American Christian broadcasting, radio and TV talk shows in Muslim majority environments are now full of the stuff. Who is a good Muslim and who is not? Call-ins about what kinds of sex you can have with your spouse and still be a good Muslim. Pronouncements about what you can wear and still be a good Muslim. Even chat rooms filled with debate about whether Satan will enter through the mouth of a woman in niqab if she does not cover it with her hand while yawning (despite the fact that her veil's cloth does). A wonderful Arabic professor from Egypt lamented to me back in 1995, "They have taken the beautiful, aesthetic religion of my youth and transformed it into a series of bodily functions."

In addition to diffused fundamentalism and the Islamist political parties and civil society organizations referenced above, I will also discuss the more extreme Salafi jihadi armed movements such as the various permutations of Al Qaeda, the Armed Islamic Group, Ansar

Dine, and the Jemaah Islamiyah, as well as ironically named groups like the Taliban (the students) and Al Shabaab (the youth), who have regularly targeted their namesakes. All of them systematically advocate and use violence against civilians to advance their agenda. Many Salafi jihadis reject outright the four main schools of Islamic legal interpretation. Their ideology is akin to fascism and they pose the absolute worst threats to human rights. But to say that is not meant to render the others in this big tent palatable.

An unfortunate dynamic has developed. Some of the fundamentalist groups that do not profess to use violence, or at least not against Westerners, are today cast as "moderate" in relation to these Salafi jihadi groups. It is apparently "moderate" to believe in ruling with religion and that women do not really need equality. This label hides the ways such groups gravely undermine freedom of religion, the rights of women and minorities, and the vital separation of mosque and state, and thus make the ground fertile for their more extreme brethren to plough.

Such whitewashing is aided by some of these allegedly "moderate" fundamentalists' very skilled use of what is called "the double discourse," saying one thing in English or French for international consumption, and saying—and, more importantly, doing—something rather different closer to home. For example, Yusuf al-Qaradawi, the spiritual leader of the Muslim Brotherhood, tells a British TV station in a July 2004 interview that Islam does "not require a war against . . . homosexuals," while on Al Jazeera Arabic he refers to gays as "sexual perverts" who should face criminal sanction ranging from stoning to " 'being throw[n] from a high place.' "[26] After violent protest at the U.S. Embassy in Cairo over the low-budget hate video *Innocence of Muslims* in September 2012, the Muslim Brotherhood tweets on its English account @Ikwanweb that it is "relieved none of @USembassy Cairo staff was hurt," but the party's Arabic feed instead carries messages praising the demonstrations in strident terms: "Egyptians revolt for the Prophet's victory in front of U.S. Embassy."[27]

While it is only fair to distinguish between those groups openly committed to a militaristic jihad to achieve their aims, and those who say they eschew the use of force, such violence is not the only problem. The substantive agenda remains highly problematic: committed to political manipulation of religion and to various discriminations—against women, against religious and sexual minorities. In the West, there has been a strategy of treating fundamentalists not engaged in terrorism against Westerners as allies against those who are. This is disastrous for those on the ground forced to contend with both cohorts.

How some Westerners love their palatable, moderate Muslim fundamentalists! Their "moderate" Taliban, their "moderate" Muslim Brotherhood and, best of all, Ennahda. Hence, the Carnegie Endowment sponsors a public relations tour for Egyptian Muslim Brotherhood representatives to Washington, DC, in April 2012 to promote its "moderate" image and schmooze with Obama administration officials.[28] These "Islamists" look like what Muslims are supposed to look like. They say what Muslims are supposed to say, but with the roughest edges worn off. They don't ask embarrassing questions about the global economy as their secular nationalist and leftist opponents might. Instead, they talk about God and "tradition." It is all very convenient and reassuring. The world is safely stabilized in its easy-to-understand civilizational categories. A gay Arab or a secular feminist of Muslim heritage who claims to fit in the "human" category just like anyone else is nowadays too confusing, and just not "different" enough to be enticing to a certain breed of occidental multiculturalist.

In the aftermath of Tunisia's Constituent Assembly elections in which Islamist party Ennahda took more than 40 percent of the seats, the *New York Times* rushed to publish an article by a female American graduate student at Oxford who had fallen in love with the party's women.[29] From the paper's prestigious op-ed pages, three days after the October 23, 2011, elections, she cheerfully castigated the secular Tunisian women's movement as being French-inspired and basically inauthentic—at a moment of profound political challenge to that feminist movement, just when it needed the greatest solidarity. This is a very useful cover for Western governments who sometimes seem to want to do business with fundamentalists because they can supposedly keep order, just as they once did business with more secular autocrats in the same countries for the same reason. Hewing to the argument in the *Times*, there is now no reason to worry about complaints from those pesky Tunisian feminists. The joyful dialogue of civilizations can proceed without them.

HOW THE RIGHT AND THE LEFT OFTEN GET THIS ALL WRONG

Some Westerners seem to feel so good about themselves if they embrace or tolerate Muslim fundamentalism, often just calling it "Islam" or—God help us—"*the* Muslim perspective." They are then absolved of responsibility for colonialism or the Iraq War or their relative global privilege. They do not have to worry about those tricky rights questions because now these people called Muslims have culture instead.

Of course, on the other side of the debate are those, mainly on the right, who use the straw man of Muslim fundamentalism to oppose everything from the building of mosques to the confirmation of Harold Koh as U.S. State Department Legal Adviser because he once said something noncondemnatory about Muslim laws. They demonize the Arab Spring as simply an unraveling that can lead only to jihadist domination because really *someone* has to control those Muslims—be it Mubaraks or mullahs. While I have my own worries about the outcome of the revolutions of 2011, I am not in this camp either, and nothing I say should offer it anything but challenge. What I have sought is to find my own political space because I think both the Right and the Left often get this issue all wrong.

Some on the right in the United States have used the spectre of a fundamentalist ascent to justify opposition to Arab democracy—notwithstanding years of bemoaning the lack of democracy in the region as some sort of congenital defect. On the other hand, the Left has often downplayed the threat of extremism and been dazzled by the golden words of Oxford professor Tariq Ramadan in the *International Herald Tribune*, assuring them that there is no risk.[30]

Muslim fundamentalism is the kind of unifying topic that often reduces large parts of the American political spectrum to proceeding by parody. Either the right-wing hysterics are putting up billboards on I-75 south of Detroit decrying "Sharia in America," or the left-wingers who have been drinking a certain kind of multicultural Kool-Aid are there to tell us how great what they call Sharia really is, or can be if you just reinterpret it a little. One of my favorite examples of this, posted on the website of the Center for American Progress on International Women's Day 2011 and called "Setting the Record Straight on Sharia," is a glowing interview with a veiled American Muslim law professor who reassures us that Sharia is simply about "ideals of justice, fairness and the good life." She advocates its use in the United States. The piece does not say a word about what the purported application of Sharia has meant in the lives of women (and men) around the world.[31]

I am searching for other kinds of responses.

When I began the research for this book, some U.S. right-wingers were out protesting a proposed Muslim community center in lower Manhattan. If you read many of their signs and speeches, they loathed not fundamentalism but seemingly all Muslims. ("[T]he mosque is for the worship of the terrorists' monkey-god," frothed the Tea Party Express.)[32] This open embrace of hatred startles me, even after a lifetime of observing anti-Arab racism in the United States. It makes me want to build the "mosque" with my own bare hands. Except that I am convinced that we do not need more religious spaces in America right now, but rather other types of common public venues. A South Asian activist who works with the taxi drivers' union in New York City tells me that, if anyone really cares, what Muslims need in Lower Manhattan—more than 50 percent of Big Apple cabbies are now of Muslim heritage[33]—is a place where taxi drivers can stop and use the restroom.

In addition to a new mosque-hatred, another element that Muslim fundamentalism has brought out in parts of the Right in the United States is a love of torture. Of course, this was not unique to the Right, and it has been highly contagious. Since 9/11, in many of my human rights classes I often have not found a single student who will openly defend an absolute ban on torture and ill-treatment when it comes to "terror suspects." As a law professor, it has been especially horrifying to watch the involvement of prominent legal academics in this shift. Most famously, Harvard's Alan Dershowitz, in his book *Why Terrorism Works*, suggested the use of dental drills on the unanesthetized teeth of terror suspects.[34] He also recommended the use of judicial torture warrants.

Al Qaeda, a gaggle of Bush administration lawyers, and the producers of the TV show *24* colluded to make torture and ill-treatment publicly acceptable in America again. Such a cultural climate was the needed backdrop for these practices to become endemic in the "War on Terror" with near-total impunity. Former vice president Dick Cheney can now appear on television and say that he authorized torture of terror suspects and face absolutely no legal consequences.

One of the most important facilitating factors in this debate has been the unspoken assumption that we are talking about treatment to be meted out to foreign, brown-skinned Muslim men who are, after all, probably just a bunch of extremists.[35] Not only is this morally repugnant but it also makes the actual fundamentalists into victims and chips away at the little space remaining for the kind of human rights–based critique of fundamentalism I am trying to articulate.

Some on the right have justified a whole range of unpardonable crimes at least in part with claims of fighting Muslim fundamentalism—extraordinary renditions, prolonged arbitrary detention, hate crimes, and even the illegal Iraq War, which killed uncounted thousands (a subsidiary justification for which was a phony connection to Al Qaeda). The soundtrack to all of this has been a diatribe from the Far Right in the West increasingly suggesting that all Muslims are members of one big sleeper cell and that there is something inherently wrong with this religion, and this religion only. Such views contravene basic tenets of humanism and decency. They also give a powerful weapon both to actual fundamentalists and those who apologize for them by suggesting that the extremists are just fighting an oppressive, imperialist West and defending Muslim interests. Making Muslims into victims, or making them feel like they are, plays into the hands of the fundamentalists who know just how to play that card.

In fact, the two Far Rights—the Western one and the Muslim one—play off each other. As Jeanne Favret-Saada wrote in the wake of the *Innocence of Muslims* conflagration, "On one side we have cowardly networks of so-called defenders of the West who manufacture a provocation . . . and make terroristic use of freedom of expression, and on the other side Muslim fundamentalist commandoes . . . eagerly welcome this provocation. . . . [E]ach needs the other to produce the desired effect. . . . Together these militant groups cause considerable . . . damage. . . ."[36]

HUMAN RIGHTS JIHAD?

While the Western Right sometimes advocates international crimes and bigotry in response to Muslim fundamentalist violence, the Western (and global) Left often refuses to recognize the reality of that violence and the actual danger posed by its underlying ideology.[37] Both of these positions have drastic consequences on the ground for the people highlighted in this book. I must admit, however, that I am more shocked by the failings of the Left and the human rights movement because I am in their camp.

For example, my former employer Amnesty International, which has done so much good on many human rights issues, suspended and then forced out the head of its Gender Unit, Gita Sahgal, after she publicly criticized the organization for cozying up to a jihadi sympathizer and former Guantanamo detainee, a British Muslim named Moazzam Begg,[38] and his pro-jihadi organization CagePrisoners.[39] While Begg had clearly suffered at the hands of U.S. authorities, and deserved defense while detained without trial, he himself had a nasty track record of support for the Taliban, of running an extremist bookshop in the United Kingdom,[40] and of numerous visits to jihadi training camps.[41] Yet he was lauded as a human rights defender, brought in to judge a children's poetry competition, depicted on Amnesty's website reading his own poetry about "tyrants," and repeatedly given a platform by the organization.

When Gita Sahgal went public with her concerns, several of South Asia's leading women's rights defenders wrote an open letter to Amnesty that garnered two thousand signatures,[42] including those of such prominent women's rights defenders as the leading Pakistani human rights lawyer Hina Jilani, and pioneering Egyptian feminist writer Nawal El Sadaawi. In response, the acting secretary-general of Amnesty would write a letter claiming that advocacy of "jihad in self-defense" is not "antithetical to human rights,"[43] thereby actually endorsing a myth that has been used to justify fundamentalist atrocities from Iraq to Afghanistan to Algeria. Gita Sahgal was absolutely right to speak out, and she paid a high price for doing so.

A year later, I found out that the Center for Constitutional Rights (CCR), a left-wing human rights and legal advocacy group on whose board I sat, had decided to represent the interests of Anwar al-Awlaki, gratis, in a lawsuit against President Obama. Awlaki, a Yemeni American propagandist and senior figure in Al Qaeda in the Arabian Peninsula (AQAP), claimed to be a "cleric" and was at large somewhere in Yemen. He had been placed on a kill list by the Obama administration.

I certainly oppose death lists. The problem is that Awlaki had his own.

Around the time CCR took on his case, Anwar al-Awlaki had published an article in Al Qaeda's English-language magazine *Inspire* that appeared beneath a list of names and a picture of a gun.[44] That death list included Salman Rushdie, Ayaan Hirsi Ali, and a young American cartoonist named Molly Norris who had dared to produce a drawing that went viral, entitled "Everybody Draw Mohammed Day."[45] Norris did this as a satirical response to American jihadis who issued death threats to the creators of *South Park* after they tried to depict the Prophet Muhammad along with the prophets of all the world's other major religions. Awlaki railed against Norris and specifically called for her murder. Given that young jihadis around the world (including a woman who stabbed a British MP and the "underwear bomber") had claimed precisely to be "inspired" by Awlaki's "sermons," there was every reason to take his death list seriously. Molly Norris gave up her identity and went underground.

Despite my opposition, the Center for Constitutional Rights took on the representation of Anwar al-Awlaki's interests, described him simply as a "Muslim cleric," and refused to criticize any of his conduct publicly. I urged the center to find other ways to challenge an assassination policy that did not involve representing an advocate of assassinations who was at large and still threatening others. After the Awlaki lawsuit was filed, he became a sort of cause célèbre among some other lefty groups in the United States, some of which disputed his wrongdoing altogether.[46]

Finally, I felt I had no choice but to criticize the center publicly in the *Guardian* and try to set the record straight about who Awlaki was.[47] I was attacked on the left by people such as Glenn Greenwald and Begg biographer Victoria Brittain, and then praised by people such as

Andrew Sullivan. This was politically strange territory for me. I struggled to understand why the Western Left was defending the Muslim Far Right and not me or, more importantly, their victims.

The Awlaki lawsuit was eventually thrown out by the judge, as I had expected. Anwar al-Awlaki was indeed killed by the U.S. government about a year later, something I did not celebrate. Unfortunately, he never rescinded his own death list, which remains out there in cyberspace with a long half-life. The justification he proffered for killing women is also still out there and can be trotted out by armed groups from North Africa to South Asia. In 2012, CCR was again representing the Awlaki family, describing the now-late Anwar on its website in vanilla terms that suggested he could have been nothing more than a greengrocer.[48]

Finding a principled position in this political universe is not easy. Many get lost. Others just try to avoid the subject altogether. One of the characteristics of Western left-of-center responses to Muslim fundamentalism has often been to talk about something else whenever the topic comes up. The anniversary of September 11 is a time to criticize the U.S. government. An Afghan woman having her nose cut off by the Taliban becomes a platform for saying that there is violence against women everywhere.[49] I think when we talk about Muslim fundamentalism, we have to actually talk about *it*. It exists. It gravely menaces the human rights of people of Muslim heritage. It is just as deserving of critical discussion as U.S. foreign policy or the Israeli government or anti-Muslim bias. To quote one of the last articles published by left-wing Algerian educator Salah Chouaki before his assassination by the same forces he warned against, "The most dangerous and deadly illusion. . . is to underestimate fundamentalism, the mortal enemy of our people."[50]

The Algerian journalist Mohamed Sifaoui once told me that he often has to explain to European leftists and human rights advocates that "the Muslim fundamentalists are *our* extreme right." All too often, because they are (sometimes mistakenly) assumed to be the enemies of the same Western governments criticized by the Western Left, parts of that Left confuse the Muslim fundamentalists with allies. In the process, they construct a tactical alliance with the Muslim Right against the Western right wing. What else can account for Tariq Ramadan, the telegenic grandson of Muslim Brotherhood founder Hassan al-Banna, who disapproves of homosexuality, feminism, and secular Muslims, being celebrated at the World Social Forum and lionized on the influential left-wing radio show *Democracy Now?*[51] This positioning by parts of the Western Left abandons the Left on the ground to its fate. Of course, the reverse is also true, and a few radical secularists and anti-jihadists line up with the West's Far Right and its anti-immigrant, anti-Islam agenda.

The people I met while writing this book deserve for us all to rethink our positions, to neither advocate violations of human rights and discrimination against Muslims in response to the actions of Muslim fundamentalists, as some on the right do, nor tolerate the fundamentalists in response, as some on the left do. Instead, these progressive opponents of Muslim fundamentalism on the ground need our principled support.

EXPLAINING THE RETURN OF GOD

A thorough history of or explanation for the rise of Muslim fundamentalist movements is beyond the scope of this book. Briefly, Muslim fundamentalist movements have burgeoned since the late 1970s, in particular with the advent of the Iranian revolution. The Islamic Republic has consciously exported its revolution. Similarly, Saudi Arabia, a close U.S. ally and fundamentalist fiefdom where women cannot drive, has sought to spawn imitators of its Wahhabism—a rigid, anticosmopolitan version of Islam obsessed with interdictions. Based on the teachings of Mohammad Ibn 'Abd al-Wahhab, Wahhabism is described by Algerian sociologist Liess Boukra as "paving the way for ignorance and destroying the subtlety of Islamic thought. . . ."[52] Shielded by the United States, Saudi Arabia has spent vast sums of money to export even more of this ideology than it does oil.

Muslims did not get hit on the head one day, then wake up and don niqabs, grow beards, and become fundamentalists. A conscious political process fostered these developments. In some places, the failure to solve basic problems of economic justice, democracy, and human dignity, and legitimate grievances like past colonialism and current military occupation, contributed to creating fertile ground for the fundamentalist project to gain adherents. But, as I was repeatedly told along the way, this does not make the Islamists the legitimate representatives of the wretched of the earth—far from it.

Much of the fundamentalist leadership is middle or even upper class. It is with a distinct agenda that their movements sometimes offer social services where governments fail to do so. They distribute headscarves along with health care and fatwas with the food. Like the Christian fundamentalists, they offer charity, not change in the economic status quo. They usually justify the protection of private property against measures like land reform. According to an Algerian fundamentalist fatwa from the 1970s, prayer performed on nationalized land would not be accepted by God. In fact, Muslim fundamentalists often seek to defeat the movements most likely to be able to tackle social injustice—social democrats, the humanist Left, trade unions, human rights advocates, women's rights defenders. These fundamentalists spend more time talking about who gets to the next life than about who gets what in this one. "I have never heard them pronounce on structural adjustment and what Islam would say about it. Not once," Codou Bop fumes in Senegal.

American readers should especially consider the fact that many progressive antifundamentalists of Muslim heritage believe the United States supports Muslim fundamentalism in many instances. Indeed, there is no question that the United States has sometimes fostered Muslim fundamentalist groups to suit its own geopolitical agenda. During the 1980s, in the context of the Cold War, the United States poured money and military aid into the Islamizing Pakistani dictatorship of Zia ul-Haq and into Afghan mujahideen groups, no matter how extreme, as a way to counter Commumism.[53] Disaffected men from many countries joined this U.S.-sponsored jihad in Afghanistan, then went home with their training and experience.

The United States has not been alone in this blunder. Britain supported the Muslim Brotherhood in Egypt in the colonial period as a more palatable alternative to secular nationalists. As I was told by both Israelis and Palestinians I met, even Israel prefers Hamas to the secular Palestinian Authority and PLO. Fundamentalists are useful. They fulfill the stereotypes of Muslims and can be counted on to keep "their own people" in line, usually causing great suffering to their compatriots in the process.

THE WOMAN WHO MAKES PEOPLE WEEP

Making people tell awful stories has been part of what I have done for several decades as a human rights lawyer. Still, the process always forces me to ask myself some difficult questions about professional ethics. When I was in Cairo in 1997, I was invited to an elaborate Egyptian luncheon in a friend's home. I was then a legal adviser for Amnesty International in London, collecting nightmares for a living in order to combat abuse in places like Lebanon and Bangladesh. At lunch we discussed my mission to Afghanistan the year before, where I saw firsthand the devastation wrought by the warring mujahideen groups. Over plates of very green *mloukhieh*, my gracious Egyptian hostess asked me how I could justify making people relive their most painful stories. "What could you actually do for them?" she queried.

I said, earnestly, that the point was to document what had happened to these people, and to try to make sure that it did not happen to anyone else. She said that if she had had these experiences and I had come to her with that explanation, she would not have let me in the door. She might have been right to say so.

When your job is to document horror, as it was for me at times when writing this book, you try to convince yourself that it is inherently good for people to tell their stories. I am not sure that is always true. Some of the people I interviewed were desperately eager to recount their travails. An older woman at the offices of Djazairouna, the Association of Families of Victims of Islamist Terrorism in Algeria, rushed into the room and started talking at breakneck speed before I could manage to get my new digital recorder turned on. But for some it was terribly difficult. Another person I interviewed went into a depression afterward. With this research, I again became the woman who makes people weep.

Old and young, women and men, professionals and laborers, they lined up to tell me their most difficult stories. There would be no book without their collective determination to share with me even when it was painful. These witnesses knew that the best hope for politically defeating Muslim fundamentalists is that their atrocities be exposed, so they testified through their tears. Even after twenty years of such interviews, it remains hard to know the best way to react. I usually say, however uselessly, how sorry I am. It is the least that decency demands. On these trips, I developed a policy that I would not cry during the interviews, no matter what someone told me, or at least I would try not to. The people attempting to get through their awful tales with dignity deserved at the very least that I hold it together.

I remembered the words of an Algerian woman protester named Fatima at a vigil for the victims of the Amerouche Boulevard bombing carried out in Algiers by the Armed Islamic Group on January 30, 1995. Standing on newly washed pavement that she knew had been covered in human remains, Fatima said to a local newspaper: "I am having a very hard time holding back my tears but I must not cry. I refuse to give these killers the chance to think for one moment that they succeeded in terrorizing us. We will win."[54]

She was right, but I must admit that I broke Fatima's rule a few times.

EVEN I COULD BELIEVE THAT GOD IS GREAT

I spent a significant amount of time while writing this book listening to recitation of the Qur'an on an Algerian radio station that I finally figured out how to pick up on the Internet. It helped me concentrate. I also spent an equal amount of time listening to *Raï* and other temporal music from the regions. Actually, I found out by accident that I could listen to both at the same time on my computer. That is what I really want, a world where you can listen to Cheba Zahouania or the Qur'an as you wish, or even the two together.

I have a profound respect for diverse Islams, and what they and the multiple versions of Muslim culture mean in the lives of many people, believers and nonbelievers alike. Some of my father's family are very religious. My secular father himself knew more about Islamic history and teachings than anyone I know, and he proudly considered himself Muslim by culture. I too am proud of my Muslim heritage and what it means to me, which I believe it is my right to define.

The most unexpected outcome of writing this book was that, some-where along the way, I found again my own version of that heritage. Fundamentalism had pushed me away from Islam, but these antifundamentalists gave my own version of that heritage back to me in all its beauty and contradiction. When the call to prayer punctuated my interviews, I could feel myself an awestruck child again, hiding in the North African bushes near our Ben Aknoun home in shorts, looking up the valley toward the Little Atlas Mountains as the Ramadan *ithan* reverberated from countless mosques in the twilight air, and much of the country sat down to dinner at the same time—or didn't, if they chose not to, as at our house.

In Turkey during my travels, the *ithan* in Antalya rang out so sweetly as the sun sparkled on the Mediterranean that, confirmed agnostic though I am, I wrote that even I could believe that God is Great. But no one can tell me what that should or should not mean to me. As the Qur'an says, "Unto you your religion and unto me mine." There are myriad interpretations of this verse. Though I would end up in a vigorous Skype debate about the limits of this Surah with a female fundamentalist in Dagestan, personally I understand it in the widest sense, including the right to have no religion. With that freedom, "God is Great" is a glorious metaphor for me. In my life these past few years, this metaphor meant that I was given the gift of meeting the most amazing people I will ever encounter and hearing firsthand about their struggles.

My hope is that their stories will come to have meaning for you, too.

CHAPTER ONE

Creativity versus the Dark Corner:
Tales from the Muslim Culture Wars

It is a school play like none I have ever seen, not least because the girls onstage and their parents in the audience could die at any moment just for being here. At the Rafi Peer Theatre Workshop's Ninth Youth Performing Arts Festival, held in Lahore's Muamar Gaddafy Stadium on November 30, 2010, I sit in the front row with the festival's gray ponytailed organizer, Faizan Peerzada, and his pretty teenage daughter, Nur, who wears red tennis shoes and a jaunty cap. At least eight thousand people have died across Pakistan in fundamentalist terrorism, mostly at the hands of the Pakistani Taliban, in the previous three years. This violence hits Lahore hard: there were forty-four terror attacks here alone in 2010.[1] The last World Performing Arts Festival the Peerzadas held in this place was bombed, producing rain of glass.

As I look at the promoter a few seats over, I wonder how much anxiety he feels, with a chorus of kids on stage in front of him, his own child beside him. They are all here because he has convened them. He told me earlier: "It is a very stressful thing. You talk more about security these days than the creativity." I hold my breath, wondering whether they will get to the end of the show.

Faizan's father, Nur's grandfather—for whom the theatre company is named—was Rafi Peerzada, an anticolonial activist–turned–playwright who trained in England and Germany, where he mingled with Bertolt Brecht and Kurt Weill. He returned to Pakistan to revolutionize its theatre with a series of plays such as *Naqab*, about the bombing of Hiroshima. At his death in 1974, Rafi Peerzada's children took over his theatre company and renamed it in his memory. Over the years, they have staged music, dance, and puppet festivals and a wide array of plays—everything from Rafi Peerzada's own *Raz-o-Niaz* to Neil Simon's *Barefoot in the Park*—in different venues. Many of their productions are geared toward children, and all have the goal of preserving Pakistan's rich tradition of performing arts. While the end result is often dazzling, the road to get there has not been smooth.

During the preparations for their annual World Performing Arts Festival in 2008, Faizan told me he had received a letter "with a kind of a bloodstained warning underneath this very strangely done signature." A threatening call followed, complaining that, "despite the warning you are still continuing with the festival." The festival proceeded nonetheless, and it was packed. The callers, however, followed through, too.[2] "At about 9:20 p.m., I heard this first blast," Faizan recollects. "I was standing outside when the windowpane fell. There was chaos, smoke. Nine people were injured. The concert had started and all other performances had ended. There were about 18,000 people still in the venue." Luckily, many of them had already left the auditoriums and were standing outside, among them families with young children.

The theatre promoter himself went to the location of the blast to survey the damage. "Where it happened, the false ceilings had come down, lights were hanging, and glass was everywhere. If that hall had an audience, that would have been a sad thing because the impact was so big that a lot of eyes would have popped out." While he conferred with police, the second bomb detonated. "A half section of a tree fell. We were about 25 yards away." At this point in what was becoming the festival's real-life drama, Faizan Peerzada got on his walkie-talkie and quietly organized the evacuation of the entire stadium. "We asked the whole audience to leave slowly, because a stampede can kill more than the bombs. When we were evacuating, the third bomb goes off right in front of the building." Miraculously, no one was killed. But Rafi Peer audiences would know from then on that unscripted disasters could strike any of the company's shows. Thanks to the Pakistani Taliban, enjoying the arts had become a life-threatening endeavor.

The perpetrator was caught quickly on November 21, 2008, found with a map that had three targets on it—those that had already been hit. The bomber had two children with him, one a peddler of potato chips who was about twelve. "In his box, he had just a few crisps and seven explosive devices," Faizan explained. The juvenile jihadist was caught because he was dragging "this strange package" toward the main hall, full of snacks and IEDs. His attack was to be the evening's main event. "That was the idea, that they divert us first and suddenly this kid goes in." If the little boy bomber had been able to carry out his mission, the Rafi Peer audience would have been decimated by his potato-chip bombs.

Faizan was shaken but undeterred. "If you give up in front of these small mullahs, then nothing like the festival will ever happen." As he put it to the BBC once in a quote that had stuck with me even before I met him, "If we bow down to the Islamists, then everything is going to be rolled back and they will always have their way, and then there will be nothing.

"We'll just be sitting in a dark corner."[3]

Rather than shutting down for safety, Peerzada explains, he and the other directors of the World Performing Arts Festival decided that same night back in 2008 that, quite literally, the show must go on. "By one in the morning we made a strong statement that, ladies and gentlemen, this ain't going to work. This festival is going to take place. There is nothing against Islam in this." The next day throngs of people came out to show their support for the continuing event. Faizan Peerzada was simultaneously delighted and apprehensive. As he told me, "There was a young lady coming with two children. I walked up to her and said, 'Do you know there was a bomb here, and today there is a threat?' She said, 'Yes, but I was here with my mother just like these two. And those images are still in my mind.'" The risk was worth taking to make sure her children could have memories of puppets and music. In contemporary Pakistan, such resolve is the sine qua non for maintaining cultural life. "All power to the [Rafi Peer Theatre Workshop] for sticking to their guns . . . and not caving in," blogged Pakistani journalist Sonya Rehman. "My heart swelled with pride. It seemed art and culture in Lahore was not yet ready to give in."[4]

It was Faizan's second experience of such an attack that year. Some seven months earlier, in April 2008, the restaurant at Rafi Peer's main offices was blown up, after their International Mystic Music Sufi Festival. The Peerzadas did not surrender then, either: "The next day we had a performance." This persistence elicited more threats. "They said, 'You still haven't learned your lesson.' I said, 'Well, I think lessons have to be learned by you.'" Nor did the audience give up. "Did people come? Yeah. The restaurant was filled. Outside we had barbecue." Sadly, despite the resolve of audiences and festival organizers alike, the following year's 2009 World Performing Arts Festival was canceled due to lack of sponsors and the inability of the government to guarantee the event's security.[5]

The repeated armed incursions against Pakistani arts festivals are not incidental. Artistic expression poses an inherent challenge to fundamentalists because it offers the ultimate manifestation of the temporal and the heterodox. It embodies freedom of thought. Art suggests that mere human beings may also be Creators. As a result, in Muslim majority contexts many artists have faced profound risks for the content of their work, or simply for producing art whatever its content, but they have continued nonetheless.

Despite the fraught climate, the Rafi Peer company has tried to promote intercultural exchange and the celebration of diverse local art forms. From 1992 to 2008, they brought twenty-four thousand artists from eighty-six countries to perform for Pakistani audiences. This was no easy task. Even when their events are not in the bull's-eye, they have also been drastically affected by other terror attacks. After the September 20, 2008, bombing of the Islamabad Marriott Hotel, eight hundred delegates fled the company's Silver Jubilee festival. Nonetheless, the indefatigable promoter and his family simply will not give up.[6]

IF THIS CARTOON WAS SEEN BY THE PROPHET, HE WOULD HAVE HAD A LAUGH

Faizan Peerzada seems to derive some of the strength to function in this security environment from his spirituality, which is suffused with mystical Muslim traditions. He is inspired by a peaceful interpretation of "the concept of Jihad from Prophet Muhammad's very important speech out of Mecca, when Mecca was won. There were men and women together receiving the Prophet." This coed welcome was not the only thing today's Islamists might not approve of. According to Faizan, it was accompanied by music and dance. "And then in celebration the body movement, and in celebration you're able to clap. In celebration you're able to play the *duff*, you can play *nay*," he says, referencing respectively the percussion instrument and the reed flute played for centuries across a wide swath of South Asia and the Middle East.

When I Google the names of these instruments, I find that a range of self-proclaimed cyber-imams have condemned them. Muhajabah.com instructs readers that "learning to give up listening to music is very difficult. It is truly a jihad. You may not be able to go 'cold turkey.' "[7] Moreover, the singing that often goes along with the duff is only *halal*—the Muslim version of kosher—"if it is done in a halal setting." People should not listen to these instruments, or sing or dance along with them, in mixed gatherings. There should be no alcohol or other *haram* behavior. (*Haram* means sinful, a notion wielded by fundamentalists everywhere.) Except for the alcohol, which is banned in Pakistan, Rafi Peer events defy all these pseudodiktats. What is life without a little *haram* behavior?

Meanwhile, a few weeks before I meet Faizan Peerzada in Lahore, the Muslim Salvation Organization posts the even-harder-line view of a Mufti Ebrahim Desai from www.ask-imam.com's fatwa department who claims that "[t]he use of the drum as a musical instrument is expressly forbidden. . . ."[8] Apparently percussion is not permissible but an online fatwa department is.

In any case, the kitschy prohibitions decreed by these Internet imams have nothing to do with how Faizan interprets or lives his Islam. Dancing right in his chair, and playing air duff and nay to illustrate his story, he recounts: "All these things were present at the fall of Mecca, when Prophet comes down from the camel." From that moment in Islamic history, Faizan sketches a tolerant, humanist Islam. "The first thing the Prophet Muhammad says is, 'The smaller jihad is over today. Now begins the biggest Jihad.' To fight with yourself to be a good human being. Your neighbor on the right and left must eat before you, as simple as that."

As I have heard so many others do, Faizan laments the way things have changed in Pakistan. "Today we are burning our own buildings, killing our own people over an issue of somebody who makes a caricature sitting in a cold country called Denmark."[9] Citing a Hadith in which the Prophet had been kind to a woman who regularly accosted him, Faizan claims that "if this cartoon was seen by Muhammad, he would have had a laugh. As simple as that." I think about Faizan's words again in the fall of 2012, when seventeen people are killed in Pakistan, mostly by riot police, during protests over the *Innocence of Muslims*.[10]

In December 2010, despite quite a few institutions—including Faizan Peerzada's daughter's own school—backing out of the event, the Ninth Youth Performing Arts Festival I attend in Lahore includes music, films, open-air theatre, college bands, and even dance. On the schedule is the University of Management and Technology Drama Club performing *aur kitne Jalianwala Bagh* . . . a play about the 1919 Amritsar Massacre when, on the order of a certain General Dyer, British troops gunned down about a thousand people assembled for a Punjabi cultural festival. "General Dyer is present in every era in different roles in our society," the program explains. From LUMS (Lahore University of Management Sciences) comes a performance called "*Raks e Bismil*: *The story of Samad.*" The synopsis appeals to audiences to "come join Samad as he will sing for the morally wounded of our society and offer sanity to malignant fundamentalism." There will even be music by a youth band gloriously known as the "Preaching Hypocrites." All of this is completely free and open to the public, making the festival a truly democratic expression of culture—but also a security nightmare.

Unquestionably, safety remains the preeminent concern. Despite his mysticism and Sufi vibe, Faizan is harried. "This youth festival has been a very big test. Nobody wanted to go back with the Rafi Peer name to this place." But the festival director is pleased with the measures that have been taken. "I think the police have done a wonderful job. They have provided three-layered security with seven brigades for seven days." In 2010, that is what it takes for Pakistani children to perform a school play.

THE GIRLS' SCHOOL PLAY IN MUAMAR GADDAFY STADIUM

That night, I go first to see *Naang Wal* or (The Knot), a musical in Punjabi. According to the program, the play's subtitle is "Don't tie your tail to a coward's." The junior school annual show features the girls of Lahore Grammar School, who play the male and female roles and even tread the boards as mice and water buffalo. A very small actress smiles at me from the wings. All I can think is, "How did she ever become a target?"

In a country where the Taliban have burned and bombed hundreds of girls' schools since 2007, these schoolgirls dance and sing onstage with heads uncovered.[11] The pupil with the lead role, whose braids hang down her back, ought to be a Bollywood star in ten years. Her movements are precise and free of the mannerisms of amateur theatre. Even with the drama surrounding the drama, she holds everyone's attention. Each minute that passes without incident in the venue, every line recited, every note sung is a little victory. Leaning far forward in his seat, as if he could leap onto the stage at any moment should the need arise, Faizan Peerzada watches with a mix of animation, pride, and tension visible on his face.

When the music finally stops, the audience exhales. For tonight, children's theatre is still possible. The girls themselves bask in a much-deserved curtain call. One has quickly covered her hair for the occasion. The mothers in shalwar kameezes and shawls, and a scattering of fathers, fill the two-tiered auditorium with the peaceful boom of their applause. Some weep. Though the bombers made headlines here two years ago, this night and these people are just as important a story.

Faizan, his gray hair freed from its ponytail, now comes up to congratulate the troupe in Urdu. "I would like to thank all the parents in Lahore who trusted us in these difficult times." He tells them he will soon be bringing back his World Performing Arts Festival. Then he shakes hands with every one of the girls. This ordinary gesture quietly rebuffs those who seek absolute physical separation between men and women.

After the performance, Faizan invites me for tea with Nur. As we sit around a picnic table drinking from tiny plastic cups, he explains that the play is about "good over evil. The two animals being tied together by their tails makes the strong one who joins weaker." Tonight, I realize, the tails have been untied. The strong are here, perched in the exact spot where a bomb went off two years ago. Little girls with ponytails and flashing-light sneakers eat cakes and, of course, potato chips. Faizan tells me that there used to be many tables set out, but he points out that people do not want to hang out "somewhere where something like this happened." Undaunted, Nur tells me that she wants to act and direct like her dad.

We move to the venue's outdoor amphitheater for a youth music show that is part of the same festival. The table of the event's sponsor, *The News*, features a sign that says, "Fun and games to keep your spirits high and let the gloom die." Security is tight here, too. On the way in, even Faizan is meticulously searched. The first band plays rock in Urdu. Their finale, the most resonant version of Neil Young's "Keep on Rockin' in the Free World" I have ever heard, reverberates in the Lahore night.

The whole audience—made up of mutually curious clumps of teenage boys and teenage girls—dances, chants, jumps. Thank God for the mixing of the sexes! A few mothers are in attendance to watch over them. The audience gives its biggest cheer to a woman who comes out to sing in an updated Hindustani style, with a very high, thin voice. She is not great, but she has guts. Everyone looks as though they need this evening like oxygen. When I leave, I come across an open drawing space covered with graffiti. Someone has scrawled two words:

NO FEAR.

WE ALL LIVE IN A BURQAVAGANZA

As my stay in Pakistan continues, I find that Faizan Peerzada is not alone in running this art/security gauntlet. On my last morning in Lahore, on the way to the airport for my flight to Karachi, I stop to meet Madeeha Gauhar, director of Ajoka Theatre Company. The walls of her chilly office display posters for Ajoka's shows, interspersed with a large collection of drums and masks from across South Asia. Madeeha herself wears a blue shalwar kameez, earrings, and a floral shawl. It is only eight in the morning, and even though she looks fatigued from a recent journey, she offers me tea and talks animatedly about her work.

For years, the director and her colleagues have been regularly performing plays that challenge fundamentalism head-on. While Rafi Peer laudably continues its events in the face of attack, it tends to avoid deliberately controversial subject matter. Ajoka, on the other hand, goes for the political jugular. It is a consciously provocative enterprise, what Madeeha calls "a theatre of resistance," that originally took aim at the dictatorship of Zia ul-Haq in the 1980s but now challenges nongovernmental fundamentalisms as well.

Their 2007 musical, *Burqavaganza*, written by Ajoka's playwright Shahid Nadeem (also Madeeha's husband), caused a sensation. She proudly tells me its subtitle: "A love story in the time of jihad." I like her summary: "It's about a young couple who want to meet and do things which young people want to do and they are prevented by a horde of burqa-wearing individuals, whether just representing society or the police or the moral brigade." In fact, most of the cast members—male and female—appear in burqas throughout the performance, including during musical numbers. At the end, all these coverings are removed to reveal another set of masks. Despite then-President Pervez Musharraf's policy of "enlightened moderation," the play was almost immediately banned by the government due to complaints from women members of the Jamaat-e-Islami, a fundamentalist political party. (The Pakistani satirist Omer Alvie labeled the response "Fanativaganza."[12])

A bold, multidirectional work of art, *Burqavaganza* is critical at the same time of mullahs, social conservatism, terrorism, Al Qaeda, *and* of the policies of successive U.S. administrations toward Pakistan. There is even a nasty, four-handed character named Burqa bin Batin, leader of something called the Burqaida Organization. The list of characters describes him as a "larger-than-life dreaded leader of a terrorist outfit." Presaging the real-world events of May 2011, bin Batin will be killed under mysterious circumstances in Scene 22.

Yet, somehow, the play still manages to be both touching and funny in places. In Scene 3, a caller to a religious TV program confesses he finds it difficult to control himself "at the sight of naked ankles." The young couple, Khoobroo and Haseena, sit side by side in Burqa Park but must resort to texting their affection. Nevertheless, *Burqavaganza* concludes on a somber note with the execution of the couple, both of whom wear colorful burqas. They are condemned for loving each other under cover of these garments, charged "[w]ith being in love. With being beautiful. With being joyful." They are lashed, stoned, then hanged onstage.

Still, on the early December morning in Lahore when I meet her, Madeeha keeps telling me that the play is "fun." After all, it is a musical. Even when Khoobroo and Haseena have been killed in their burqas, there is still time for an upbeat coda, one last song performed by all the now-unveiled characters, who include George Bush, Tony Blair, and Musharraf. Its lyrics simultaneously lampoon and mourn the whole state of affairs: "We all live in a burqavaganza / Hidden under the burqa is a whole world // . . . Lift the veil and see the faces // . . . Your minds have been covered by these veils / You should be ashamed of your actions / Burqa can't hide your shame // . . . We all live in a burqavaganza."

At this point, the now-unveiled politicians tear off another layer of masks, revealing "a panel with faces of beautiful women, children, flowers. In the background the hanged coloured burqas remain in the spotlight. Curtain." Ajoka debuted this play onstage in Pakistan in 2007, as political violence was on the rise and the Pakistani Taliban were emergent. About a month before the play's premiere, Zil-e Huma Usman, the thirty-six-year-old Punjab minister for social welfare and an advocate of women's rights, was shot in the head while speaking to women activists. She died on the operating table at Lahore General Hospital.[13] Her murderer said the mother of two was not sufficiently covered up in her shalwar kameez. The real "Burqavaganza" was right there, just outside the theatre door.

Madeeha Gauhar dates its birth not only to Zia ul-Haq's time as U.S.-backed resident dictator from 1977 to 1988, but all the way back to the very founding of the state in 1947. As she stresses between sips of her tea, "I very strongly believe—and we have questioned that in some of our productions—that if you create a state in the name of religion then these things are bound to come about sooner or later and it came about very soon in our case."

Ajoka has also produced work whose political message, perhaps surprisingly, proved less controversial than that of *Burqavaganza*. One example is *Bulha*, first performed in spring 2001. A historical drama in the Punjabi language, this play tells the tale of Bulha Shah, the renowned Sufi mystic poet who struggled against the mullahs of the early eighteenth century and was declared a heretic. In the script, he sings,

> *Who am I, does anyone know?*
> *In a mosque no worshipper*
> *Nor a temple-frequenter. I am not pure, nor impure. . . .*
> *What is good, what badness?*
> *What is mirth, what sadness?*[14]

As Gauhar says, gazing at me intently, "Some of Bulha's verses are actually blasphemous if you look at it in today's context, where he questions the Sharia, where he not only questions but he openly rejects it." These views spring from his Sufi mystic beliefs, which Madeeha summarizes: "Everything is between man and God. Bulha and all mystics believe that God is within you. So, it is the individual and your own consciousness."

The play takes on current events in Pakistan, mirrored in Bulha Shah's own freethinking life. Audiences watch him exiled for blasphemy. Mullahs beat his followers for eating carrots during Ramadan. A group of zealots assault them for singing a *qawwali*, a form of Sufi devotional music that "is against Islam," according to the decree of a religious teacher in the play. Sona, a young disciple of Bulha Shah's who had been singing until the beatings began, rebuffs the zealots.

"Your fatwas do not apply here."[15]

Madeeha revels in the fact that even with this topical plot, *Bulha* is still one of Ajoka's most popular works, proving that the spirit of freedom is alive and well among a significant constituency in Pakistan. Somehow, this play was not subject to the uproar that greeted the blistering *Burqavaganza*. Writing about the first production in the *Friday Times* in 2003, journalist Rina Saeed Khan exclaimed: "Bulha's message is still powerful and even more relevant today—and his compassionate vision of Islam is exactly the kind that we should all be propagating in these troubled times. . . . I'll say, give me Bulha over Bin Laden any day."[16]

In the play, a character who is being led away to face a death sentence asks, "Why aren't there more like you, Bulha? If there are, why don't they speak up and if they do, why can't we hear them?"[17] I realize I am meeting the Bulhas of today on this trip. Madeeha Gauhar is herself just such a figure, though she seems far too down-to-earth ever to make that claim. The Ajoka director tells me about yet another outspoken production, the teleplay called *Mujahid*.[18] Despite its taboo subject matter, it was broadcast on P-TV, a government-owned channel with a vast viewership. *Mujahid* tells of a young boy who comes back to Pakistan from Afghanistan after the "jihad" in 2001 and shows how difficult it is for him to reintegrate into society. In the end, he blows himself up. The Ajoka Theatre Company seeks to explain, according to its website, the "extremist causes" and the "lack of hope for our youth" that make such unthinkable acts possible.

It took years to get the graphic *Mujahid* shown to the public. Even once it had been broadcast, the company's travails were not over. "After that we got a lot of hate mail and SMS messages and banners put up on the road that were against us. The banners had my name and said, 'You are a *kafir* and you are doing things against Islam.'" Madeeha knows all too well that being called a *kafir*, an unbeliever, can have dire consequences.

Given Ajoka's rebellious repertoire, it is no surprise that their performances have also received bomb threats. So far, they have not been physically attacked, as happened to the Rafi Peer Theatre Workshop, but they face ongoing harassment and verbal assaults. Smiling, Madeeha tells me that stones are regularly thrown at the gate of their rehearsal space, because "there are bad activities going on and women coming in and there is music." Notwithstanding the threats, the company refuses to cancel, or mute its message, because "that is what the fundamentalists want. They want this sort of thing to come to an end."

When I ask why she personally continues, Madeeha replies, "It is basically a commitment to an idea and to a certain vision one has of the way one wants this country to be, which is that the only way we can really survive is if we bring in a sort of secular understanding of things. That is what makes us go on." She is not alone. There are sec-ular Pakistan Listservs, secular Pakistan Facebook pages, days, move-ments, institutes. Alongside them, Madeeha Gauhar battles for a better, freer future for her country, using only her talent and her theatre com-pany. She fully understands that, as dancer Sheema Kirmani affirms in Karachi, "Now art is the only way we can fight fundamentalism." In an era when so many successful performers in the West are busy hawking perfume, modeling designer frocks, or dancing with the stars, this is an entirely different vision of what it can mean to be an artist. But it is not a vision that is easy to realize.

Ajoka does not have its own theatre, and the troupe struggles to find the funding and space for its work. When I ask Madeeha what could be done to support people like her, she says, "Obviously financial sup-port," and she waxes hopeful about the possibility of constructing even a humble performance venue. The company does not sell tickets, and its shows are open to the public. This means the audiences are "sur-prisingly all sorts of people, from all classes. You have intellectuals, you have students, you have working-class people because we invite trade union organizations—a cross section of Pakistani society."

Before I leave, she takes me out to see the yard where they rehearse and fills my arms with programs, scripts, and DVDs. My favorite is the poster from *Burqavaganza*, which features figures in burqas cut from diverse fabrics—from cloth of deep blue lapis lazuli and sultry crimson, from Pakistani and American flags. Even the Statue of Liberty wears a burqa, which covers her face but not her torch.

ALGER NOOORMAL

Pakistan was not the only place where I met artists like Madeeha Gauhar and Faizan Peerzada battling jihadism. I met them all along the way, including in Algeria and in the Algerian diaspora. In 2008, when I went to interview Samia Benkherroubi and Aziz Smati in Paris, I was speechless at first, like the smitten young fan I once was. I had to restrain myself from asking for their autographs. Samia and Aziz were, respectively, the presenter and producer of my favorite Algerian TV show of all time, the marvelous *Bled Musique*. *Bled* is the Algerian version of the Arabic word *balad*—literally "country," but its colloquial adaptation means "village" or "homeland." As the title suggests, this show, born in 1989, was a kind of North African MTV. It carried Algerian youth music to a wide audience on the national station, ENTV. Everyone loved *Bled Musique*. The program used Algerian dialect, not the wooden, formal Arabic of ENTV. So this little show simultaneously revolutionized the music and lyrics considered ready for prime time.

I used to watch it in the living room in Dad's old apartment in Algiers before he had to move out. I would check the TV program in *Algérie Actualité* to see when it would be on and then would refuse to make other plans that evening. Samia Benkherroubi was beautiful back when she graced the screen as a VJ. She still is when I meet her, with her wavy brown hair and angled face, wearing jeans and a striped shirt. But, as I get to know her, she turns out to be so much more than a pretty face. Today Samia is a committed feminist activist with a complex analysis of fundamentalism.

Aziz Smati is still a rock star, in a black vest and white poet's shirt, and he graciously tells me what fundamentalism has meant in his work, and in his life, though he is clearly uncomfortable doing so. Samia explains later that he almost never tells his story. She first met Aziz when she auditioned for his show as an unknown college student and was surprised when she got the job without *piston*—what Algerians call connections. Today, she and Aziz finish each other's sentences.

During the show's heyday, which began in a late-eighties moment of political opening in Algeria, just as there was suddenly a plethora of new political parties and newspapers, there was also an explosion of local singers. Aziz tells me that, in addition to the well-known Algerian style of Raï music, a sort of North African hybrid hip-hop, "There was also rock in Arabic, rap in Arabic, house music in Arabic, all styles in Arabic, but on TV they only showed Middle Eastern-style music."

Samia explains pervasive attitudes reflected in official TV restrictions at the time, and how they were challenged by the *chanteurs* of the day. "They sang love in a language that people understood. If you sing about love in classical Arabic—like Fairouz, Abdel Haleem, Warda. If you say, '*ouhabak*,' I love you, it was fine. But, in colloquial, '*enhabak, enmoutalak*,' I love you, I die for you, that was considered vulgar." It certainly was deemed too raw for TV. *Bled Musique* challenged these barriers by playing the first Raï clips shown on ENTV.

The show's creators and cast were inundated with fan mail. There was no *Billboard* chart in Algeria, so Samia asked the viewers to write in with their preferences, and they used those to rank the songs. It was a huge job. She would return to her dorm room with sacks of letters, getting her roommates to help her sort it all.

When I ask what their preferred tunes were, Samia instantly picks my all-time favorite: Hamid Baroudi's haunting "Caravan to Baghdad," a funky Algerian anti–Gulf War song from 1991. As she said, "We were enraged about what was happening in Iraq, and he expressed our anger. He stayed number one for a long time." In those days, when Baroudi pleased the fans, I found being in Algeria a refreshing break from the anti-Arab racism I sometimes encountered in the United States. It was a relief to be somewhere where everyone was against that first Gulf War. In 2008, Samia and I try to remember the words of Baroudi's hit, and she ends up singing a few bars. "Their cause has filled my eyes with tears. Nothing lasts, my God. . . ."[19]

If you had told me in my early twenties while I was watching *Bled Musique* that I would someday be in the star's living room, that she would sing "Caravan to Baghdad" just for me, I would not have believed it possible.

THE HORROR

That is not the only outcome I would not have believed possible at the beginning of the nineties. As the decade unfolded, as *Bled Musique* continued and was succeeded in 1993 by another Aziz-and-Samia music show called *Rockrocky*, things were taking a turn for the worse in Algeria. The post–October 1988 democratic opening had bene-fited Algerian fundamentalists, who prevailed in the 1990 munici-pal elections and began to implement their policies at the local level. No mixing of the sexes in public gatherings. No public dancing. No music at wedding ceremonies in public places.[20]

So it was unsurprising that Aziz and Samia started receiving insult-ing letters. "Stop this show. You are against the Qur'an. Music is forbidden." Samia especially remembered an obscene call that came to the studio attacking a Casbah-born woman singer named Hassiba Amrouche, a call she repeated with oral ellipses. "Why are you showing this 'beep'? You'll see what happens to you."

Aziz situates *Bled Musique* in its era. "You can't forget that this show came at the same time as the rise of fundamentalism. It was the time of the FIS—*Front Islamique du Salut*—who said music is forbidden, a sin, *haram*. Despite this, we continued." The show's crew were steadfast. They would not give in to the Islamic Salvation Front—the FIS. Samia recalls: "We were in the same mindset. The way to stay in Algeria and to continue fighting was to keep working. We didn't listen to what they said."

Ominously huge fundamentalist marches flooded the streets of Algiers at the time. Aziz described the participants: cohorts of bearded men in camouflage fatigues, including the so-called Afghans— Algerians who had returned from fighting in the U.S.-sponsored jihad against the Soviet Union in Afghanistan. "It was impressive to see them with their beards. They put on makeup even, black around their eyes, to make you afraid. It was at this time that we were doing this show talking about music while the fundamentalists were against music." Because they offered young people different ways of being, those associated with the show became lightning rods for the fundamentalists, who insisted there was only one way. "They said, 'One day your turn will come,'" Aziz remembers. "There were lists of people they would assassinate when they took power."

I asked Samia and Aziz whether there was something inherently antifundamentalist about creating their programs in such an environment. "For us, making a show about music was completely normal," Aziz answered. "There is nothing *haram* or illicit. Music has always existed in Algeria. Even our parents never said it was *haram*. Just because extraterrestrials come and tell you it is forbidden, I will not believe them. And I continued to do what I was doing."

Meanwhile, it looked as though the FIS might prevail in the flawed 1991–92 parliamentary elections. Much of Algerian civil society called for those elections to be stopped, to prevent the rise to power of this totalitarian movement. On January 11, 1992, the military-backed government intervened to do just that. The fundamentalists, who had already been engaging in acts of violence, now escalated their jihad. "Then," as Samia says, "it was an open war."

The daily toll weighed heavily on her. "Every day we bought the papers and we saw who had been killed. Victims who were well known got them lots of media coverage. Then they attacked Mr. and Mrs. Everyone. Women for sure, if they had no veil. At first, they tried to justify—he's a communist, he's this, he's that. Then they killed anyone, and anyone could be killed."

She and Aziz tell me about the artists who came under fire from the fundamentalist armed groups. For them, these are not just the legendary names I recognize, but departed friends and colleagues. Rachid Baba Ahmed, the superstar producer from Tlemcen near the Moroccan border, had recorded many contemporary Algerian musicians, had released the Raï Rebels compilation albums that brought the music to an international audience, and had even worked with Bob Marley's producer. He was gunned down on February 15, 1995.[21] Aziz remembers, "He was full of life. They wanted to kill life, all that is beautiful, everything that represents life."

I inquire about Cheb Hasni, the young working-class Raï singer who was assassinated on September 29, 1994. "He sang especially about love," Aziz reflects. "He was loved by the youth. It was to make people afraid. 'Everything you love we will kill.'" These killings were not incidental. This was part of an all-out jihad against music. "They came and gave a letter to all the music producers to say that now music is forbidden and you cannot sell it. They threatened the merchants who sold cassettes."

Samia described the mechanics of the killings by the fundamentalist armed groups in her hometown, Blida, heart of the so-called Triangle of Death, the hardest hit zone of Algeria. "When I went home at the weekends, young people who were our neighbors suddenly had weapons. It gave them power. They didn't have work or social status. Suddenly, one day they had beards and were respected because people respected religion. People didn't know what it would bring. These young men could suddenly decide who would be killed." There was one incident she would never leave behind her. "We had a neighbor who was assassinated at the end of 1993. Everyone heard him screaming when they came to get him, but no one went out. The next day they found his body, but not his head. They searched for his head for days and days. It was worse than you can imagine." "Even American horror films couldn't do things like this," Aziz interjects. Talking over him, Samia assents: "It was horror, horror, horror."

For all of Algeria, including Aziz and Samia, 1994 would turn out to be a life-changing year. The situation spiraled out of control in a crescendo of fundamentalist violence. In its often late and insufficient attempts to protect the population, the state responded with arbitrary arrests, torture, and disappearances. "It was hell," according to Aziz.

Neither the TV producer nor his presenter had the means to take special security precautions. On Valentine's Day 1994, a young man approached Aziz, then forty, on the street near his home as he waited for an early morning taxi to work. "Are you Aziz?" the boy asked. Assuming the kid to be a fan of his show, since he was regularly approached by teen viewers, Aziz said yes. But this young man was no fan.

He shot Aziz Smati four times, took the producer's backpack, and ran, leaving him for dead.

I was in Algeria at the time and wept as I watched the evening news. So beloved was *Bled Musique* that even a young doctor at the Beni Messous Hospital, where Aziz was taken, wept outside the operating room.[22] I cut Aziz's photo out of the papers the next morning, still fearing that the producer would die. But, like Algeria itself, Aziz would not let the fundamentalists kill him. After a twelve-hour operation, he came back. As the newspaper *Le Matin* said on its front page in one of my old clippings, "Today, Samia and the Rockrocky team are not in mourning. Although the perpetrators of this attack and the supporters of fundamentalist terrorism might not like it, Aziz remains with us. To produce other shows, to strive for another culture."[23] But he would never walk again.

In 2008, when I ask him about what happened, Aziz speaks with characteristic humility: "I am just part of the 100,000 dead and I don't know how many wounded." I try to gently coax him to tell me more. "I received death letters. And they executed them," he simply said. But then he continued: "So, I was the victim of an attack, which is why I am in a wheelchair. I was leaving my home. They wait for you. They know when you go out. They follow you and then when they are sure, they come to execute you."

"How did you survive?"

Aziz repeats my question, thinking about it. "I don't know. When I came to, the doctor said, 'You helped us a lot because you were clinging to life.'" The producer explains why he fought so hard. "I still have things to say. It is too beautiful to leave. As long as they don't touch my brain, I am still living." He would spend one month in an Algerian hospital, then six months in a French hospital. As he thinks back on this time, a flash of darkness in Aziz's eyes says it all. Then, shrugging, he smiles. "What do you want me to say? It could have been worse."

Bled Musique's creator has beaten those who sought to silence him. "Yes, I am not going to stay in a wheelchair doing nothing," he asserts. "Otherwise, you have to throw yourself under a train. If I fought for life, it is not to do nothing afterward. It is to continue doing what I was doing." He still directs videos, like the stylish and moving clip he made for a campaign against Algeria's discriminatory family law by the women's rights group *20 Ans Barakat* (Twenty Years Is Enough!).[24] Remaining defiant, Aziz Smati shows the women singers of *"Ouech dek yal Qadi"* (What's gotten into you, Judge?) bare-armed in his video as they sing their denunciation of the law. Bareheaded women protesters sit in on the streets of Algiers, and Hassiba Boulmerka, Algeria's gold-medal-winning runner, appears in the shorts that earned her death threats from the same fundamentalists who had taken aim at the video's director.

In recent years, Smati collaborated on a multimedia book project about Algiers called *Alger Nooormal*, with Mohamed Ali Allalou, Samia's husband, and the writer Mustapha Benfodil, both of whom I will meet farther down the road. Aziz compiled the soundtrack that accompanies the text. As he says, it is a CD "of the noises and songs of Algiers—young people who scream, chanting in stadiums, all mixed together." I wonder how he was able to make these recordings. Algiers, with its hills and stairs, is not exactly wheelchair accessible. But he did it.

At the end of our long interview, Samia and Aziz try to explain the exact meaning in Algerian *argot* of "normal" from the book's title—or, as they pronounce it, "Noooooormal." "It is an Algerian expression. It means everything is okay." It has ironic connotations, about learning to accept the unacceptable. Samia gives me an example.

"Aziz was a victim of an attack. It's normal."

LOVE STORIES IN THE TIME OF JIHAD

Not long after Aziz was shot, Samia went home to Blida. She was forced to wear a jilbab that covered her from head to toe, the only way it seemed safe enough for the hunted TV star to go back into the Triangle of Death. She should not have gone, but after everything that had happened, she was desperate to spend the Eid holiday with her family.

These natural human longings for hearth and home got a lot of Algerian intellectuals and cultural figures killed by the fundamentalists in the nineties. Samia's account makes me think of Rachida Hammadi, a journalist I had met in 1994 at a Ramadan dinner in her safe house. A year later, Rachida, who was only thirty-two, went home to be with her family for one night in a working-class area of Algiers. As she departed at dawn on March 20, 1995, a car of armed fundamentalists waited. One opened fire with an automatic weapon. His bullets hit Rachida and her sister Meriem, who tried to protect her. Both women died in the hospital.[25]

So when Samia went home to Blida for Eid in 1994, she was risking everything. She had just arrived and was sitting in the living room eating *macroutes*, a special Algerian sweet made with semolina, dates, and honey, when her brother-in-law ran in. "You have to leave right now. They know you are here." When she reaches this part of the story, she begins to cry, the grief of 1994 still fresh. But her tears do not stop her from telling me that on that Eid 1994 she was bundled into a car, swathed in her hated jilbab, and taken to her sister's house in the town of Boufarik. Given what I have heard about Boufarik, it is hard to imagine how this could have been considered a sanctuary. In fact, Samia said she was awake all night, listening to the wind.

A week later, her mother told her to leave the country. Samia boarded a plane for Paris. "I never thought I would. Even after the attack." She came to understand that she had no choice left but departure. The only options available to her and many Algerian cultural figures then, as Mustapha Benfodil framed them in his novel *Zarta!*, seemed to be "Paris or death."[26] "I was a danger for my family, my friends," Samia says. "My mother was pushing me to leave, whereas normally a mother wants her children near her." Samia went to France because her then-fiancé Mohamed Ali was there. "I thought I would go to breathe a little. I came for a short while. 23 March 1994." She still lives there, working with a women's rights group focused on North Africa and editing the occasional video.

Like many refugees, Samia and her husband did not move back to Algeria after things improved, largely because of their children's schooling. Algeria lost thousands of its intellectuals and artists not only to death but also to exile. According to one study, 71,500 university graduates fled the fundamentalist onslaught between 1992 and 1996 alone, costing the developing country $40 billion just in financial terms.[27] It will take decades to recover from this brain drain.

"So we try to go back in other ways," Samia insists. "We are linked to Algeria for life."

GREETINGS FROM BOUZID

On a summery Friday afternoon in October 2010, when I have gone back to Algeria, my old friend Saliha and I go out to the Maqam El Shahid, the monument to the martyrs of the War of Independence that graces the heights of Algiers with its elegiac cement tower. Across the street, we stumble into the city's Third International Comics Festival. In the free drawing space located in one of the tents, someone has inked a hulking bearded figure with prominent teeth overshadowing the other smaller drawings. The spectres of fundamentalism left over from the dark years Samia and Aziz had described to me are everywhere here, even on this canvas. I watch two tiny boys try to find a place to draw on the paper beneath the bearded hulk's feet.

In another of the festival tents, one of Algeria's leading cartoonists, a bespectacled man known simply as Slim (pronounced *Sleem*) signs autographs. His books famously chronicle the adventures of an Algerian Everyman named Bouzid and his *haïk*-attired female companion, Zina. (The haïk is a gauzy white veil worn by many women in certain areas before and during the colonial period, and by fewer women in post-independence Algeria until the 1980s.) Shockingly, Zina and her Bouzid are unmarried because, as Zina explains in one panel, even in a Muslim country cartoon characters do not wed. As Bouzid adds, this is also because he cannot find an apartment, a common impediment to wedlock in Algeria.

Their inked adventures, wherein Bouzid battles corrupt officials, greedy businessmen, and religious fanatics for a democratic and popular Algeria worthy of the name, reflect the country's recent history in all its sometimes-palpable absurdity. Both humor and republican conviction inhabit the cartoon squares. Despite the admiring crowd at the festival, Saliha and I manage to get Slim's autograph. I am tongue-tied as I try to express how his work captures for me the Algeria I once lived in.

Saliha sneaks off and buys me one of Slim's books as a gift. It is called *Walou à l'horizon*, a bilingual version of "Nothing on the Horizon." Among other things, *Walou* tells the story of Bouzid's struggle against fundamentalists. To me, the most striking drawings are a series of three that appear under the title "Opportunism Takes Hold" and depict fundamentalism's trajectory in Algeria and so many other places. The first one, labeled "Earlier," shows seven clean-shaven men, one smoking a cigar and one wearing a fez. The next, marked "Later," shows the same men in the same positions smiling and wearing the long, full beards demanded by fundamentalists. The third, "Later still," is just an entirely black square—Faizan Peerzada's feared dark corner. It is this square that they all—the Ajoka Theatre Company, Aziz Smati, and Slim himself—fight to keep illuminated.

That sunny October day, Saliha asks Slim to sign the book she has bought for me. She tells him to write a good dedication, as I have come all the way from America. When he finishes, I open the cover page to discover how this famous North African cartoonist of Muslim heritage fulfilled her friendly orders. He has drawn the Twin Towers with the American flag on top, and a small picture of his protagonist Bouzid sitting protectively at their feet holding an Algerian flag and sending along "Bouzidienne" greetings, as Slim jots beneath. It is a gesture of friendship between my two countries, a quickly scrawled expression of solidarity in the face of fundamentalist violence.

SURVIVING THE FATWA ABOUT BEANS

As I accumulated many sad stories about surviving extremism, I was grateful to have the chance to talk to Mohamed Ali Allalou during dinner at the Paris apartment he and Samia share. With his stubble and shaggy hair, Allalou, as he is often simply called, was relaxed despite the seriousness of our subject. This was the only interview that really made me laugh—with my mouth open, clutching my stomach.

In fact, I was in hysterics for about half the time I interviewed Allalou, as was he. All this mirth is remarkable, given that the other half of our discussion—when we were most definitely not laughing— covered topics including the murders of Algerian artists and the attack that nearly killed his close friend and collaborator, Aziz Smati. But, as I learned that night, comedy is a great weapon against fundamentalism, at least in the hands of someone like Allalou.

During the 1990s, he was an Algerian radio personality who hosted a number of shows, including a particularly well-known one called *Sans Pitié* (No Holds Barred). Allalou talked about subjects that no one else would touch—sex, drugs, homosexuality, religion, his grandmother riding a Jet Ski. "We made fun of former guerillas from the war of independence, of the state, of the bearded ones, the Islamists, the opposition."

I asked him what the Islamic Salvation Front (FIS) represented in Algeria. His answer was unique: "It was a fashion. Something we had never seen. For me, at the beginning I wondered, why am I not with them? Because when you hear the FIS spokesman Ali Belhadj, you think he says true things—the government *is* shit. We need to get rid of them. They *are* thieves." But on closer scrutiny, Allalou found he had nothing in common with the fundamentalists. "Why do they wear those clothes? Why do they impose on women? I don't agree with them about many things." He returns again to my question. "What did they represent? They represented the loss of friends who had sex for the first time in my apartment. I lived alone, and it was all wine, women, drugs, and rock-

and-roll. So, the ones who were virgins had sex at my place. The next day, the same guy would suddenly come and give you a sermon."

Despite the late-eighties party at his place, Allalou could see the fundamentalist violence coming early. In 1990, covering a demonstration for *Sans Pitié*, he heard a group of young men talking about how many virgins you get when you die during jihad and go to paradise. So he held up his microphone and asked them what a girl gets if she dies in jihad. "Does she become a lesbian, or are there guys for her?" Somehow he finds humor in the fact that he was thrown to the sidewalk, punched, and kicked, his microphone flying through the air. "They couldn't stand that you would say this or even think it."

Even as the situation deteriorated, Allalou stayed on the radio until 1993. I asked him whether he had been threatened and was quite startled when he immediately laughed again. "No. *Putain!* Damn it! In the cafés, there were always people who didn't do anything and got threats. And people asked me if I got them. Finally, I received threats, and I was saved." He issues a loud guffaw at that. "We did *you-yous* on the radio." (*You-yous* are what Algerians call ululation, a high-pitched glottal chanting, usually emitted by women in celebration. There is a chorus of them at the end of *The Battle of Algiers*.) The threats that elicited Allalou's *you-yous* came from—and actually bore the official stamp of—a Bab el Oued mosque that had been a FIS bastion. Yet, rather than cower, Allalou lampooned its senders on air.

He stops laughing when he tells me about the generalized assault on artists in Algeria as the nineties marched on. "They killed people, they killed artists because they sing about love, wine, friendship. They assassinate, they cut throats, they cut throats, *ooh la la*." His voice gets very low, remembering lost comrades of culture. "Fundamentalism abhors singing," he says. "They say it is the devil who makes music."

His pensive interlude does not last long. Humor overtakes him again, but he is not inventing these punch lines. Algeria's fundamentalists had offered "visions of Islamism that are ridiculous. It is forbidden to give your pants to the dry cleaners. Your pants—you who are pure, clean and holy—will be mixed with those of an atheist." Who knew the trousers of an atheist could be so dangerous? Capitalizing on real grievances, Algeria's fundamentalists manufactured their own Islam, alien to the way Algerians actually lived. "They invented the religion for themselves. And they mixed it with the hatred they felt from seeing their fathers who fought France and went to prison during the war of independence mistreated by this rotten state, having no rights." Allalou felt there was a lack of awareness about the content of religious texts in Algeria. "So they made their own interpretation, made their Qur'an."

As a result, the Algerian fundamentalists could say that almost anything was forbidden by religion (*la yajouz*), no matter how ridiculous, and find a constituency that would believe them. Samia and Aziz had told me this too. Apparently some fundamentalist leader had decreed that drinking water while standing up was impermissible. They had no idea why. The pressure cooker was also *verboten* because it makes noise. That interdiction was apparently based on the notion that the pot's squeal conjures up demons.[28]

Among these nonsensical edicts, Allalou identifies the most absurd of all. Algeria's self-declared mullahs said, "It is forbidden to eat beans." I lose the battle not to laugh as Mohamed Ali tries to make the serious observation that beans are "the dish of the poor." "*Waalesh*— why are beans forbidden?" I manage to ask. "Because you fart," he replies, "and then you have to wash yourself again. There are 100,000 inventions like this."

Allalou says that consequently the 1990s were years when jokes flourished in Algeria. I have thought of the decade in many ways, but never like that. It turns out that black comedy was a form of irreverent resistance, a way of fighting the absurdity and the fear. He then tells me a "*faux barrage*" joke. A *faux barrage* (fake checkpoint), sometimes made to look like it was manned by official security agents, was a device regularly used by the fundamentalist armed groups to stop and slaughter passersby. There was nothing funny about it, or so it would seem.

"A group of fundamentalists stop a bus full of ordinary people at a fake checkpoint, looking for someone," Allalou begins. "The terrorists ask the first guy on the bus, 'What is your name?' He says, 'Omar.'" Allalou makes the sound of a gunshot. Omar dies. "They ask the next guy his name. When he replies, they take him away and cut his throat." Another awful sound effect illustrates that. "The next person they question is a woman. When asked, she says her name is Malika. The terrorist says 'Malika is my mother's name,' and even though he has his knife at the woman's throat, he can't kill her. Instead, he lets her go. The last man on the bus, who is also called Omar, is then asked, 'What is your name?'

"Without hesitating, he says, 'Malika.'"

I hear myself emit a kind of strangled laugh. "That is a sad joke," I tell him. "There are only sad jokes from that time," he replies.

Mohamed Ali was in Berlin promoting a film when he heard the news of the attack on his friend Aziz Smati. His mother and sister plotted to keep him from returning to Algeria by having his sister confiscate his papers when he arrived at her home in France. Allalou's family also begged him not to speak on French TV about what was happening. "I played the main character in the film so I was invited to be on TV a lot. I did one show. My mother called." Imitating his mother in a high voice, and sounding like he was back on the radio, he croaks, "Don't do any more TV. You are there and they will kill us here."

Unmistakably serious, he sums up: "So I had to be here in France clandestinely *and* shut my mouth. I refused to be on TV anymore, because if I appear I can't shut my mouth. When they invited me to promote the film on European TV, I didn't talk about the film, I didn't give a shit about the film." That thought makes him laugh again, but then he turns grave: "They had killed Mekbel," he says, referring to the fundamentalist murder of one of Algeria's leading columnists, Saïd Mekbel.[29] "Thousands were dying. You are sick, or what? I am not going to talk about the film." Like all comedians, Allalou is poignant when he stops laughing.

Pushed into exile and condemned to radio silence, he found an artistic avenue to fight back. With Aziz, Samia, and others, he started Bled Connexion in 1998, "to have fun and joy," and to support all the Algerian artists who were being driven into a Gallic exodus by the fundamentalists. The crowning achievement of Bled Connexion was a benefit concert featuring the stars of Algerian pop music, such as Cheb Khaled. The event raised enough money to buy a wheelchair-accessible car with hand controls for Aziz Smati, by then a paraplegic and living in Paris, where he was unable to get around by Metro.

Twelve years later, Allalou is an avid Facebooker with a large following, and today he organizes Algerian cultural events at the Parisian Cabaret Sauvage, sometimes with Aziz. Though in exile, like his wheelchair-bound partner-in-crime, he remains undefeated and uncensored. Their work in the nineties has not been forgotten two decades later. One blogger posts that his crazy dreams for a new Algeria still include seeing Mohamed Ali Allalou appointed minister of culture.[30] For now, that too remains a punch line.

WHEN THE ART DIED

While Madeeha Gauhar has directed plays, Aziz Smati has produced TV shows, and Mohamed Ali Allalou has transformed local radio, Professor Said Salah Ahmed has done all these things in his native Somalia. Like the others, he stood up to fundamentalism in doing so, though in a quieter way, and, like the Algerian artists I had met, involuntary exile would be his reward. I found this artistic refugee of Muslim heritage in the spring of 2011 on a trip to Minneapolis, in the heart of the American Midwest.

Today Said Salah Ahmed is a cultural dean of the large Somali exile community in a state that is home to an estimated seventy thousand of his compatriots. We sit together for several hours at Mapps Café near "The Towers," the tall, multicolored apartment buildings that are the heart of that community. At the next table, two young Somali American women with their heads covered work on laptops. Professor Ahmed has a thinning silver scrub of hair and a wizened face topped with glasses. When I ask how old he is, his smile illuminates his dark eyes. "I tell my students and my children, 'Oh, in the civil war I lost my birth certificate, so how can I know?' " He then confesses to being born in 1945. As we talk, the professor laughs periodically as though trying to mitigate the pain of what he tells me. His laughter is sadder than Allalou's.

A kind of Somali Renaissance man, Said Salah Ahmed is a poet/songwriter/filmmaker/playwright/music promoter/educator. In the 1970s, he was the director of cultural programs for the Somali Ministry of Education. Given the level of literacy in Somalia then (reportedly just 5 percent[31]), "mass education was necessary." So Ahmed "applied art as a means of educating the masses." An actual classroom was too small for the scale of teaching needed in his country, one of the world's poorest, so he improvised. "I made a bigger classroom of the theatre. I had a complete musical band, a theatre group, and music teachers." But even this was not enough to reach a mass audience, so Ahmed developed programs for radio and TV, and made films. He also wrote songs and poems.

Said Salah Ahmed created a musical ensemble for the Ministry of Education called Iftin (light), and then he formed a theatre company in 1975. In the time of President Mohamed Siad Barre, whose 1969–1991 rule "started as socialist experiment and degenerated into dictatorship" according to the *Independent*,[32] many of those Professor Ahmed worked with in the company went to jail. A number of his own plays were banned. Meanwhile, the Horn of Africa, including Somalia, was buffeted by the shifting winds of the Cold War.[33]

For its many problems, Ahmed tells me the period of military rule in Somalia also witnessed a flourishing of the arts, and the inclusion of the disenfranchised (including girls) in these domains. During this time, he made a number of movies; one focused on the Dervish, the late-nineteenth-century Somali nationalist resistance movement, and another showed the ways people celebrated the Somali New Year. Every weekend, he traveled from Mogadishu, the capital, to rural areas in a truck with musicians to document the landmark Somali literacy campaign of the mid-1970s, which drastically increased the number of his compatriots who could read.[34]

Like many other Somalis, the professor and his family fled shortly after the onset of the civil war in 1991, when President Siad Barre was ousted and a power struggle erupted among rival clan warlords.[35] Ahmed wound up in the Utanga refugee camp in Kenya, where he continued his cultural work. He started a school for two thousand refugee children, including his own. While in the camp, he also managed to write a radio play for broadcast by the BBC called *War jiraaba Cakaaruu Iman*. (The title comes from a Somali saying that means "All existing information will come into the ear.") The piece told the story of a mythical town named Akara, where there was no violence. "It was safe from all evils of the civil war," he said. Apparently the play inspired Somalis to rename several real towns Akara, claiming the pacific zone Said Salah Ahmed envisaged for their own locales. The play's Akara even became a nickname sometimes given to peaceful individuals.

But the play's use of Islamic texts to promote peace also brought attacks on its author from people "claiming to be religious leaders, who are furious and saying I am playing with the Qur'an." As he tells it, chuckling again, this in turn both required and facilitated his resettlement to the United States. Meanwhile, the situation in Somalia continued to degenerate. The religious extremists grew more powerful, "banning one thing after another in art." Ahmed laughs again at this, as if to try to make the undoing of his life's work bearable. "My Iftin band were still intact. Some people tried to keep them together so that they can earn something. Then that was banned. No groups of that nature should continue working on this art."

During Professor Ahmed's career, as Somalia had plunged deeper into what became a kind of permanent state of civil war, attitudes toward the arts changed. In the early 1990s, a group of "religious youth" (as he calls them) tried to blow up Mogadishu's National Theatre, which was not far from a church they had also destroyed. "To them, this theatre was just like the church." They would tolerate neither. Luckily, the would-be theatre bombers were stopped by people in the area back then, and at least its walls continued to stand throughout the war, a reminder of the cultural life in which Said Salah Ahmed had been such a productive force, and that he remained unwilling to give up on.

Since coming to Minneapolis in 1995, Professor Ahmed has taught in the local public schools, as well as offering Somali language courses at an area college. His Somali Language and Literary Study Circle not only teaches Somali language but also organizes exhibitions in the Minneapolis area. The group celebrates International Mother Language Day every year on February 21. In fact, one of the young veiled women working at the next table in Mapps Café, Zuhur Ahmed, is a member of the Study Circle. When she stops to greet us, she tells me that here in Minneapolis they are transcribing the professor's work and writing down his life story so that neither is lost.

Still, even life in the American Midwest has not immunized Ahmed from the effects of the political climate back home. In 2010, when Al Shabaab—the Somali militant group that at the time held Mogadishu itself—forbade the broadcast of music, he was devastated. Many residents of Mogadishu felt the same way. One was quoted in the *New York*

Times saying that Al Shabaab had "punished our life with bullets, and today they are punishing us with a ban on all types of music."[36] That same day in Minneapolis, Professor Said Salah Ahmed wrote a short poem: "When the Art died." "The last bit of the art died," he tells me, "when they prohibited music."

> *What crime did it commit to be banned and what legal*
> * article did it break?*
> *Instead of banning the music, why don't they ban the act*
> * of killing?*
> *The lute is so innocent*
> *Why don't they ban the cannon and the rifle that erase*
> * human life?*
> *Alas! For the day the music died. I am mourning for it.*[37]

Soon the new cultural politics would hit even closer to home. In 2010, Professor Ahmed assigned a colleague in the Literary Study Circle to write about the importance of promoting the Somali language. "The next day, there was in a website a comment that said, 'You are there in Minneapolis far away. If you are around here with the Shabaab you wouldn't have said such words.'" Like Muslim fundamentalists in a number of contexts, Al Shabaab favors Arabic, the language of the Qur'an, even though it is not the predominant language actually spoken by locals.

For Professor Ahmed, this jihad against languages and melody is all a big misunderstanding. With flowing hand gestures, he explains that art has roots in religious teaching. As a practicing Muslim, he uses his craft to teach religion. "I write Islamic poems. I believe I have to use and empower my faith with poetry. Others don't understand that. They misbelieve that it is a sin."

In the current security environment, the professor no longer feels comfortable writing a play to be produced for his own Somali community in Minneapolis. He fears being labeled as someone who promotes "sin," and losing his standing in his own community at the age of sixty-six. Given the rise in fundamentalism even among some Somalis in the diaspora, it is as though he had been freer to continue his playwriting in a Kenyan refugee camp in the early nineties than he is now in Minneapolis.

His fears on this score date back to 1996, when he tried to attend a Somali concert in the Twin Cities. "There were people surrounding the theatre saying, 'Don't enter. You are paying your money with sin.' As an elderly person, I didn't want that brand of 'sinful person' who is leading the community to the bad thing. Because I believe in my religion."

If Professor Ahmed feels so censored in Minneapolis, one can only imagine the desperate situation of artists back in Somalia. "They cannot all leave," he reminds me. But the conditions for those who remain grew increasingly dire in areas Al Shabaab controlled, unable as they were to earn money as artists there. So the Somali artists in the diaspora tried to organize financial support. "Every day from one website or another we find a list of people. 'So-and-so is about to die, or is so sick. Hurry up and contribute.'"

Somalia is a society largely organized along clan lines. The professor refers to the family of Somali cultural figures inside and outside of the country as "a complete clan called the Artists." Wistfully, he tells me in 2011 that there are almost no performing artists still able to function in the southern part of the country, almost entirely Al Shabaab-dominated when I met him. "That was the trade they knew, the fame and the self-esteem they had," he says of his fellow artists back home. "That was all ruined." The dark corner came to Somalia.

What would it mean to future generations of Somalis to have this clan of artists dwindle? The international community barely notices, because Somalis often are thought of mainly as famine victims, Al Shabaab suicide bombers, or pirates—not as the poets, playwrights, musicians, and teachers whom Professor Ahmed represents. The slowly emerging Somali government expressed a renewed determination to protect artists in March 2012 when it reopened the partially reconstructed National Theatre. Several weeks later, a young female suicide bomber working for Al Shabaab— which has now affiliated with Al Qaeda—detonated herself inside the theatre, killing ten.[38] The theatre had to be reconstructed yet again, which was done by November 2012. Culture is resilient, but the road ahead will not be easy.

The arts used to be a core part of how Somalis lived. Said Salah Ahmed's career illustrates this. He tells me that, "in Somali culture, there is no celebration unless it is marked with poetry and songs, and, in more recent times, plays." Even the nineteenth-century British explorer Richard Burton noted that "the country teems with poets."[39] Another visitor once referred to Somalia, Professor Ahmed tells me, as "a nation of bards."[40] Banning music on the radio and bombing the National Theatre are grave crimes everywhere, but nowhere more so than in such a country.

As our time together ends in 2011 Minnesota, Said Salah Ahmed explains that he longs to resurrect this cultural past to save his home country's future. He wants to bring together a group of Somali artists from the diasporas to do a peace tour inside Somalia, in places where that is possible. "I tell you, the most effective contribution for peace in the Somali Civil War could be achieved." And he still dreams of moving back home. "Who can give us a release from this war one day? Just to remain and live in that motherland for the rest of the few days that are left."

In 2012, Somalia's Constituent Assembly adopted a new constitution, and a new parliament was sworn in, paving a different road ahead for the country, at least if African Union troops stay long enough to complete the job and the international community does not lose interest again. Conditions on the ground seem to be improving as Al Shabaab increasingly loses control over territory (though there are also worrying reports that it now plans to infiltrate Somalia's security forces[41]). The new hope is fragile and repeatedly called into question by Al Shabaab suicide blasts and threats to "hurt the invaders," but it is real nonetheless.

Professor Said Salah Ahmed travels back home and is able to visit places where he has not been in decades. He is delighted to tell me that the situation of artists is improving as the Al Shabaab presence recedes, and that they are again able to perform in many places. So now I dream of the day Said Salah Ahmed can produce his plays in Minneapolis and can see his works performed in a rebuilt (and safe) National Theatre in Mogadishu. Maybe he will even be able to recite "When the Art Died" in public as a reminder of the fundamentalist threat to artists—or perhaps he will no longer need to.

CHAPTER TWO

Karachi Open Mic:
Guardians of Cultural Space

Before my PIA flight to Karachi takes off from Lahore, I am startled by the sudden emergence of what sounds like the deep voice of God from the PA system. After years of traveling to Muslim majority countries, this is the first time I have heard prayers on a plane. *Bismillah ir-rahman ir-raheem* blares forth to send us on our way southward. "In the name of God, the compassionate, the merciful." As we fly on with Allah's blessing, I remember that Karachi has been a hot zone recently; militants have carried out regular attacks since a December 2009 suicide bombing on a Shi'a Ashura procession killed forty. The city also suffers regular bouts of factional fighting.[1] A month before I arrive, fifty-two died in just four days.[2]

On the Lahore–Karachi flight, the word *Inshallah* (God willing) peppers official announcements. *Inshallah* we will arrive at 4:20 p.m., and *Inshallah* the flight conditions will be smooth. I say "*Inshallah*" a lot myself by force of habit, and when we go into a sharp descent on landing I understand the sentiment of airborne *Inshallah* very well. Nevertheless, on an airplane headed for 2010 Karachi, I long for the illusion of greater certainty.

Situated in the city's well-guarded Red Zone, my hotel has an impressive security system, the most rigorous in my travels. To enter the Karachi Marriott, you first drive into a lane that parallels the building, some distance away. The car is thoroughly scanned before it is allowed to turn back toward the hotel. Passengers descend into a little outbuilding, go through a metal detector and baggage screening, and only then are allowed to walk across to the actual residence. This makes all my coming and going laborious, but as one Karachi resident said to me, "Hotel security—you hate it, but you have to have it."

I am impressed by the calm, scrappy security guards who man the entrance. There is the potential for an explosion each time they open a car hood. They are the anonymous local people who usually make up the majority of the dead at any such target, whose names or photos or crying relatives are almost never shown in international press coverage. My concern for them is not hypothetical. A truck bomb had hit 200 meters away from the hotel two weeks earlier. Twenty died; one hundred were injured.[3] A former student's parents who are from Karachi had tried to book me into a club they thought safer, but the club does not admit women traveling alone.

Precisely because I am on the road by myself, this travel can be lonely at times. So I am grateful for the people and places that adopt me along the way. Women's rights activist Nuzhat Kidvai did just that in Karachi. When I arrive, she explains that times are tough ("we are in pain"), but she assures me that "the media picks up what will make news. The more scary something looks, they portray that. On the other hand, there is also peace going on, there's activism, fun, dialogue."

To prove her point, Nuzhat invites me to T2F, a café/meeting place/cultural space/peace organization that would become my home away from home. Just off a street actually called Sunset Boulevard runs an ordinary lane crammed with apartments and shops where T2F sits in a red-brick building across from a Utility Store, a chain grocery store. You enter through the ground-floor performance space, complete with a book shop selling South Asian poetry and CDs from the All Pakistan Music Conference, Karachi Chapter. (The proceeds from sales go to fund T2F literary programming.) On the second floor—hence the name T2F—posters of Che Guevara and John Lennon decorate the café walls. A small balcony overlooks the ordinary neighborhood below. Together, Nuzhat and I attend T2F's Take Back the Tech, a bilingual event held downstairs in the performance space to discuss using Facebook, SMS, and Twitter to combat violence against women and other human rights problems, such as blasphemy laws.

During the free-discussion portion of Take Back the Tech, an older male activist ardently opposed to the blasphemy laws says he was recently involved in a healthy Facebook debate about the subject, with many viewpoints being expressed, until someone from the powerful fundamentalist political party Jamaat-e-Islami (JI) intervened. The JI member called the male activist a "nutcase" and said he should not be living in Pakistan. Here at T2F, the audience is sympathetic to the activist. Many have faced similar reactions.

Encouraged by their interest, the activist continued, saying he replied to the JI denizen in cyberspace: "You have rights and I have rights. Why do you want me to leave the country? I didn't ask you to leave the country." The JI man could find no rebuttal for that. Despite the vitriol, the antiblasphemy activist thinks this kind of engagement is fruitful, though he knows it is also risky. "This is Karachi. People are scared." The crowd at T2F seems generally to agree. A younger woman regrets that "the fundamentalists are the only ones who are visible. The JI who are killing people are visible. We have not made ourselves visible."

"Let's start a T2F movement!" someone suggests.

Several days later, thanks to Nuzhat's introduction, I interview Sabeen Mahmud, the shorthaired, thirty-six-year-old driving force behind both T2F and Peace Niche, the NGO that runs it. Today she wears jeans and an oxford shirt, though when she addressed the crowd at Take Back the Tech, she wore a shalwar kameez. While I ate a tomato-filled "Pakistani omelet" ("It has more pepper," Sabeen explains), she told me that in 2007 she had gotten tired of her work in the technology arena with "morally dubious corporations." So she launched her own project. "I thought, how about a space that would be able to host all kinds of events, would be a platform for emerging artists, graphic designers, singers, poets, people who don't have a platform?"

Open from noon until 10 p.m. daily, T2F offers patrons a classic café that promotes conversation and mingling. Students work on laptops, friends chat endlessly in Urdu and English, and women activists gather. You can order a tea and sit all day studying. In the evening, you can head downstairs for poetry and politics—or for tabla drumming classes, discussions like "Working with Sharks: A Conversation on Sexual Harassment with Fouzia Saeed," or performances by the Nusrat Fateh Ali Khan Girls Choir. Rather like Humphrey Bogart at Rick's café, Sabeen is usually there.

"In Pakistan we don't have bars. How are people supposed to meet new people?" Sabeen asks. She targets privileged youth who would be in a position to make a difference if they were educated about social issues. But Sabeen is decidedly class-conscious in the best way, and she tells them to invite their drivers to come in with them, have some food, and hear the Urdu poetry. Another concern of hers is that the café's workers should be able to attend as many of the cultural events as possible. She even hopes to start producing artwork to be displayed outside for the people in the neighborhood.

Wanting her café to be in harmony with its human environment, Sabeen has been especially concerned with good community relations. As she says, "We were very uncomfortable when we saw this space because there is dance going on and theatre that happens here while upstairs there are people who have long beards and pray five times a day." But she is proud to say they have never had any problems with the neighbors living in the apartments above. Her only local complaint has been about the arms market up the street.

Finances have posed a bigger difficulty. As buzzing as T2F is, this enterprise cannot even pay Sabeen. To keep the place afloat, she has had to take out loans, beg, borrow, and "I stopped just short of stealing," she quips. "My mother said, 'What are you doing?' I have developed gamblers' nerves." Somehow, even with her long days here, she consults in the tech field at night to bring in some money. Sabeen could have been a complacent member of the local privilegentsia, but she was raised by a mother who was committed to social justice, "rebellious from the day she was born." So, being a second-generation Karachi boat-rocker, Sabeen is determined that T2F lend itself to liberalizing Pakistani society by affording a venue. "Changing minds doesn't happen in a week. What may be obvious to you and me is anathema to that person. You need that time and that engagement to hear out the other person as well as to present your viewpoint."

Borrowing an expression from the Nobel Prize–winning Indian economist Amartya Sen, Sabeen Mahmud's commitment is to "intellectual and cultural poverty alleviation" here in Karachi. To this end, T2F has hosted more than 250 events. One of her favorites was an evening featuring well-known Indian and Pakistani singers performing together via Skype, using technology and music to break down borders between enemy nations.

Even in today's turbulent Karachi, T2F does not shy away from the most controversial topics. Sabeen explains: "We did this thing recently on the blasphemy laws. The people who were sending us the speakers said, 'You might not say blasphemy in the title.' I said, 'All our lives we have been fighting against this. We've marched on the streets for it. It is important to talk about this.' Those kind of risks, we need to take them. More people need to stand up." Siting here on the balcony of her café, she says openly: "The blasphemy law is something I really want to see gone in my lifetime. That is something that really needs more people to rise up and take a stand." She does so, at widely advertised public events.

Like so many, Sabeen feels particularly galvanized by the case of Asia Bibi. When I arrive in Pakistan, the forty-five-year-old Christian mother of five has just been sentenced to death, based on allegations by women in her village that she insulted the Prophet Muhammad. Rather like a scene from a Muslim version of *The Crucible*, this unfolded after an argument among the women about something else—sharing water. I ask Sabeen if she is optimistic about this case. "There are certainly suddenly a lot more people talking about blasphemy than there were before," she says. "It is on Facebook and Twitter." Sabeen was already an avid promoter of using social media for change back in 2010, before they came to prominence in the Tunisian and Egyptian revolutions.

Some months later, when I transcribe this part of her interview, I am struck by some of Sabeen's words that did not resound at the time: "I am hopeful. People like Salman Taseer, who is the Punjab governor, is on Twitter talking about it." Just one month after I talked to the café proprietor, Taseer would be assassinated for this very reason, shot twenty-six times with a submachine gun four days after tweeting, "I was under huge pressure sure 2 cow down b4 rightest pressure on blasphemy. Refused. Even if I'm the last man standing."

Some Pakistani lawyers would actually take to the streets to show support for Taseer's killer, Malik Qadri.[4] Qadri reportedly said that the governor was a blasphemer and this was the punishment for that crime. In August 2011, Taseer's son Shahbaz was abducted by the Pakistani Taliban for having been outspoken about his father's case. As of December 2012, he remained in captivity.

None of this has made Sabeen and T2F back away from volatile topics. For example, in May 2012, T2F hosts a discussion on "Civil Society, Extremism and Democracy" with antifundamentalism campaigner (and ex-fundamentalist) Maajid Nawaz. Just as Taseer's work touched the T2F proprietor, Sabeen's work stirs many others. The day I met her in Karachi, we had to wind up the interview when someone downstairs at open mic night wanted to dedicate a song to her. "We can go together," she says. One level down, a striking young woman with long dark hair is singing, "Let It Be." When she warbles, "There will be an answer," I am momentarily convinced she is right. Later, a prematurely bald guy with thick glasses sings Pakistani pop in falsetto along with a synthesizer and has the T2F crowd chanting for an encore. Another group of amateur musicians takes the stage, first singing the words of Faiz Ahmed Faiz, a national poet of Pakistan who was forced into exile during Zia ul-Haq's time, followed rather improbably by Leonard Cohen's "Hallelujah."

You have not heard Leonard Cohen until you hear him at Karachi Open Mic Night.

I am reminded that it is a human right to mix and to cross cultural boundaries, something fundamentalists oppose, given their taste for monolith. Tonight, for the teenagers and twenty-somethings, boys and girls sitting together in the Karachi dusk eating cheese toast and listening to their friends sing any song they choose, T2F is a safe space to mix and border-cross and just have fun.

Still, like many of those who are doing something incredibly important, Sabeen Mahmud is modest in her claims about what her work means. "There are certain buzzwords, 'combatting fundamentalism through fashion,' that get attention, publicity, donor money. We try to quietly go about our business. By its very nature, T2F is doing all those things. But you don't have to shove the message down people's throats all the time. Or give press releases to that effect, saying, 'We have had twenty musicians so we have changed everything.' We have changed nothing. We gave twenty people an opportunity to breathe for two hours. Maybe they were never able to do that and I am very happy we were able to do that for them. And I hope they can find ways to do that for other people."

A NATION STAYS ALIVE WHEN ITS CULTURE STAYS ALIVE

Seven months after I left Karachi, I met Omara Khan Masoudi, who, like Sabeen Mahmud, was trying to cultivate a space to showcase the culture of his people in the face of extremism. Based in Kabul, he had an even tougher environment.

I met Masoudi by accident. Alem, a guide from my guesthouse with seriously perfect English, took me on a tour of Kabul one Friday morning. This is not within the parameters of the security protocol I have established for myself, but in sixteen years of coming here, I have never really seen the city. Alem and the driver take me through streets full of butcher shops with sheep carcasses hanging on hooks, and past countless stalls featuring huge piles of the legendary local watermelons, and then through the large campus of Kabul University, part of which has walls topped with barbed wire. My affable guide had tried to study there during the Taliban time and had to wear a turban and grow his beard. Both he and the driver had to give up their studies for financial reasons.

Next, Alem takes me to the outskirts of Kabul to tour the reputedly still mined Gothic remains of the European-style Royal Palace of Darulaman. Built in 1923 by the reformist King Amanullah Khan, it was nearly destroyed by the mujahideen in the 1990s. Across the street stands the two-story Kabul National Museum, with barred windows and straggling flower bushes. It has been here since 1922, a silent witness to the rises and falls of Afghanistan. Out front, a rusty locomotive brought back from Germany by King Amanullah stands on a short piece of track leading nowhere. Back in the twenties, it carried commuters; today there is almost no rail service in the country.

A two-story beige block, the museum looks like a public library. Its simple exterior belies the value of its contents. Since it is Friday, we get in for free. Just inside the entrance, Alem shows me scarred Buddha heads. Then he shepherds me upstairs to see the traditional costumes from the northeastern province of Nuristan. There are no burqas, but rather bright wool dresses with contrasting leggings, heavy jewelry, and uncomfortable-looking high-heeled shoes.

The general director of the museum, Omara Khan Masoudi, a wiry man with thin gray hair, wearing a loose-fitting blue pantsuit known here as a perahan tunban, agrees to see me even though the museum has just closed and—as I later discover—he is expecting guests for Friday lunch. Lighting a cigarette, Mr. Masoudi tells me he has been with the museum since 1978. When the Soviet Union left Afghanistan, civil war came to Kabul. In 1989, as mujahideen rockets began to fall on the city, the staff moved significant pieces to safe locations in the center of town, which they assumed would be protected. The removal saved many priceless objects, including the splendid fourth-century BC Bactrian Gold, excavated from a Greek tomb in northern Afghanistan. Mr. Masoudi and four others held the only keys to the vault in which it was locked, a part of the story he did not tell me.[5] He does not seem like someone who wishes to paint himself a hero. Each key-holder risked everything to protect national treasures first from the mujahideen and then from the Taliban.

With the fall of Najibullah's Democratic Republic of Afghanistan in 1992, the fundamentalist mujahideen groups that had once fought the Soviet Union with U.S. support now fought each other. They also fought the new government, itself an unhappy coalition of mujahideen groups that came to formally rule what had become the Islamic State of Afghanistan. Since the Soviet-backed regime was gone, the United States was uninterested.

The opposition "Muj," as they were sometimes disparagingly called, occupied the western part of the city, putting the museum on the frontlines. Its director, formally a government employee, was unable to return for three terrible years. Rockets fell like a persistent rain, pulverizing entire neighborhoods. I had visited Kabul just after this period, and I saw the lingering effects of that internecine warfare among fundamentalists in an area near the museum. Virtually no cars or people were visible anywhere. On block after block of what had been residential streets, every single building had been flattened.

On May 12, 1993, the upper floor of the museum took direct rocket fire. The twentieth-century munitions instantly destroyed a fifth-century wall painting and buried a collection of pottery and bronzes beneath a mountain of debris.[6] Omara Masoudi only learned about this from a BBC broadcast. "A bad news for all people," he tells me, "especially museum people." In the chaos that was Kabul then, opposition Muj groups also looted the wounded museum.

No matter how needed he was, the director could not get back inside his facility until November 1994, when Sotirios Mousouris, the UN Secretary-General's special representative, visited, bringing journalists and the International Committee of the Red Cross.[7] Mr. Masoudi and his deputy director went along. They found the building gutted. "No roof. No windows. No doors. All broken by effects of war and also by these people," he tells me pointedly of the opposition mujahideen. A few months later, the mujahideen government of Burhanuddin Rabbani took control of the museum. Masoudi's staff tried to pick up the pieces.

Being a museum director is always a demanding job. However, Mr. Masoudi was responsible not just for displaying the nation's cultural heritage but also for saving it. This was no ordinary uphill battle, but rather one whose difficulty matches the steep foothills of the Hindu Kush that surround the city. When they did an inventory later, the museum staff found that 70 percent of the original collection of 100,000 artifacts had been looted during the civil war.[8] According to archaeologists, the missing items included the largest Greek coins ever discovered, carved ivories in classic Indian style, and the famous metalwork of the Ghaznavids, who ruled in the eleventh and twelfth centuries.[9] Even so, the museum's troubles were still far from over.

The Taliban occupied Kabul in November 1996. Initially, they allowed the staff to continue working, but these most extreme fundamentalists reversed course in March 2001 when a fatwa from their leader Mullah Omar ordered all pre-Islamic art destroyed.[10] "The real God is only Allah and all other false gods should be removed."[11] Pursuant to this dismal fatwa, the Talibs then carried out a lesser-known act of cultural pillage that was as devastating as the simultaneous desecration of the Bamyan Buddhas.[12] Members of a movement called "The Students" came to their home country's national museum and began to destroy all the human figures. One after another. On March 1, 2001, this heritage demolition was enthusiastically announced to the international press by the living, breathing oxymoron known as the Taliban minister of information and culture, a Mr. Quadratullah Jamal.[13] They had decided that "the keeping of statues is against Islam," Omara Masoudi recalls.

Exhaling smoke along with his words, the museum director told me: "In my opinion it is not true because all Islamic countries have museums and no regime ever destroyed their artifacts." Not so the Taliban. They entered the museum, pried open all the carefully organized storage facilities, and, using hammers, shattered more than 2,750 pieces. According to *Los Angeles Times* reporter Paul Watson, an Afghan archaeologist followed the Taliban through the museum, "pleading for mercy as if begging for the lives of [his] own children."[14] Such pleas were meaningless to those who felt their axes swung with God's weight behind them. "It is a decree by . . . [clerics] and the government can't stop its implementation," the Taliban ambassador to Pakistan explained.[15] After three days in the museum, the shards of Afghan history lay in a pile at their feet.

Though Omara Masoudi seems a relatively reserved man, there is no hiding his anguish when I ask him what this attack on Afghanistan's past meant. "This is a part of our history, of our heart, from before Islam came to Afghanistan." Finished with his cigarette, he handles a strand of worry beads and tells me of the rich, pre-Islamic religious heritage of his country. "No one worships these statues but they are a part of our culture. We have to preserve that."

The museum staff did what they could, according to their director, who was not present because he had taken a temporary leave. "They tried to keep some artifacts from the Taliban and they did preserve some pieces. They hid them under cotton, and paper." These Afghan curators and custodians were willing to risk death to keep history alive.

Only after the fall of the Taliban, in 2002, could Mr. Masoudi and his team begin the reconstruction. "We started our activities from zero." The initial process took two years. With limited fanfare in a country where everything was being rebuilt, they managed to restore thousands of works. Countless statues destroyed by "the Talibs" were painstakingly glued together again. "We are very proud about our ancient civilization," he says, explaining his staff's dedication. Usually, when managers recite their institutional slogans, the delivery seems canned. However, when Mr. Masoudi quotes the museum's motto, which is inscribed in the lobby, he means it:

"A nation stays alive when its culture stays alive."

In the director's office, with a fading red carpet and a large globe in the corner, as we talk through Friday lunchtime, he tells me about the ongoing labors of his staff to resuscitate Afghan heritage. "We look and it doesn't seem like a museum, but it is." He smiles even as he says, "It is too difficult for us. But we know we have to do it." They still store some of their artifacts in the center of the city for safekeeping. Now they are also digitizing their collection as a backup. Mr. Masoudi is very aware of the responsibility of transmission. He wants young people to know about the Afghanistan that existed before the war and about the rise of extremism. "We must transfer this to the next generation."

With all that he has withstood, the Kabul Museum director has hope for the works under his care, and just as Madeeha Gauhar back in Lahore longs for a new theatre space, he imagines a new building—one with security, humidity control, and a heating system. He dreams of recovering all the looted pieces and even of obtaining new ones. Apparently the current Afghan Ministry of Culture has big plans for the museum, and the U.S. government has announced a donation of $5 million toward a new building.[16] What kind of Afghanistan the United States will leave behind for the building to stand in remains less clear. American officials tried in 2012 (and will perhaps continue trying) to negotiate with the same Taliban who trashed the museum back in 2001. What would happen were they ever to control Kabul again? How many times can a sixteen-hundred-year-old statue be glued back together?

For his part, in July 2011, Mr. Masoudi tells me he is optimistic about the future not only of his museum but also of his country. "Having hope is essential for life," he explained in an online interview for the multimedia project *Kabul: A City at Work*.[17] "The sacred religion of Islam always promotes hope."[18] Given the national reality of the last thirty years, there is nothing more heartening than an optimistic Afghan. "This is what I and all Afghan people wish for—that peace may come to Afghanistan. We are praying for that. We saw the result of war. We looted and destroyed each part of our life."

Though his wife phones to remind him he is now terribly late for Friday lunch, he lingers to tell me about artifacts the museum obtained from Surkh Kotal, in northeastern Afghanistan, dating from the second century AD. They include a statue of Kanishka, the greatest Kushan ruler, a piece that was walloped by the Taliban but remade by the staff, and one of the famous Surkh Kotal tablets inscribed in Greek. Apparently the Surkh Kotal artifacts were all made by different religious groups living together peacefully in the same region.

"There was no fight."

THIS QUESTION IN MY HEART TO ASK

From Kabul I fly to Herat, the city at the center of Afghan cultural life, in a small Kam Air plane. This flight also begins with prayers. As I set off alone to the far west of Afghanistan near the Iranian border, the week after control of the city has been handed back to the Afghan authorities, even I feel a bit in need of prayers.

When I finally locate the car that has come to pick me up, we drive off toward "Heart." That is what my notes say, because Microsoft Word always autocorrects Herat to Heart, which I will come to believe by the end of my stay is not accidental. The city's famous pines line the road, light green and feathery. Men with long white beards and loose sandals speed by on motorscooters. Women stride by in the ubiquitous local style—long cloaks in a variety of black-and-white prints that cover everything but the face and hands, a step forward since Taliban days when the burqa was de rigueur. I am captivated by the miniature three-wheeled rickshaws, motorized and made of wood. A riot of hearts and Dari calligraphy, one rickshaw proclaims in large yellow letters, I LOVE YOU.

Herat is less dusty and intense than Kabul. Many of the buildings are decorated with ornate windows that look like the symmetric patterns cut in a paper snowflake. Past a park full of more pines, we come to the Nazary Hotel, set behind reassuring blast doors. The security protocol is not as rigorous here as at the Karachi Marriott, but the armed guards search the bottom of the car every time we go in. The inner door to the hotel, protected by more guards, displays a NO WEAPONS sign.

A smiling young clerk named Jawad takes me up to my room. Like Alem back in Kabul, he speaks very good English. Wearing jeans and a short-sleeved shirt, he tells me halfway up that he dreams of studying abroad. The hotel elevator is unforgettable; it plays the love theme from *Titanic.*

My room features an electric-green prayer rug, a picture of the Kaaba to indicate which way to pray, and Internet access. Barely two minutes after I stow my belongings, Hassina Neekzad arrives, wearing a Herati cloak, which I learn is called *chador namaz.* She quickly removes the garment and hangs it on the coatrack, revealing a long blue-plaid skirt and black blouse. Hassina sports large, rectangular glasses that give her a bookish air.

Within minutes, she convinces me that Herat's literary and cultural reputation is entirely deserved. Not only is Hassina Neekzad a rights advocate who works with the Afghan Women's Network, but she is also a former literature professor and Fulbright scholar. With all her accomplishments, Hassina makes my day by telling me repeatedly how happy she is that I have come and thanking me for interviewing her. I know it is what Afghan hospitality demands, but it is nice to hear nonetheless. We sit and talk in my air-conditioned room in front of a large window overlooking Cinema Square (which is actually a traffic circle).

I think I am there to interview her about her own work, but she begins by telling me about her father. It turns out the adage attributed to the sixteenth-century Mughal emperor Babur by my Lonely Planet guidebook—that you only have to stretch your leg in Herat to kick a poet—is true.[19] It is my very first meeting in Herat, and in the very first minutes I find that the interviewee's father was indeed a poet, a man named Gholam Rasul Neekzad Herati.

Speaking over the sound of honking horns in the street below, Hassina recites a few stanzas of her father's poems from the Herat of half a century ago. She says his words first in an English slowed by translating on the spot, then in lyrical Dari. One verse, "God Made this Question in My Heart to Ask," is a plea for the acceptance of human desires. "If I want something from God, I believe it is God's desire," she summarizes for me. "So I ask God not to punish me, because He created the desire in my heart. If there is something wrong in what I want, please forgive me." She copies a few lines in Dari into my notebook. I ask her what else he wrote about, and she says, "About how we should help others and about God."

But Gholam Rasul Neekzad Herati was not just a poet. He is the reason the traffic circle below is called Cinema Square. In the early sixties, he proposed to the governor to build a movie theatre there for the people of Herat, and he donated the land for it when the governor agreed. Hassina says the Herat Cinema was always full. Women and men sat side by side in the dark. No one questioned this.

In the Herat of the sixties and seventies, Gholam Rasul Neekzad Herati's movie house broadened the horizons of young Afghans. "We could watch many movies from all over the world. There was no exception." For a while at least, Hassina and her sister spent all their time there. I ask which films were her favorites. She recalls a 1968 Iranian piece called *Soltan-e-Ghalbha* (King of Hearts), starring wrestler-turned-movie-star Mohammad Ali Fardin, and a 1972 Indian musical called *Pakeezah*, about a courtesan who tries to redeem herself through love. Nowadays, it would be unthinkable to project such works here. Hassina tells me about the theatre scene that also thrived in Herat during the heyday of the cinema. "The ladies were dancing. But now, we don't have that." Her voice trails off as she looks out my window. The Herat Cinema that once stood there was destroyed.

When that happened, Hassina was in Iran, having fled the fighting as many other Afghans had, so she does not know which group of fundamentalists knocked down her father's theatre, the mujahideen or the Taliban. Human rights activist Horia Mosadiq, originally from Herat, would later explain in detail that the cinema that her parents used to frequent for the films of Alain Delon and Elizabeth Taylor was burned by the Taliban, then completely flattened by fundamentalist warlord-turned-governor Ismail Khan in 2002. This "was a big shock to many Heratis like me and my mother," she tells me via e-mail. The cinema "was the only symbol of the golden years in the country." Nothing is left but the name, "Cinema Square," still applied to a circle without one.

THE PUPPET SHOW IN EL QODS EL SHARIF

If Omara Khan Masoudi and Professor Said Salah Ahmed were right that culture can promote peace, and if the Karachi dancer Sheema Kirmani was right that art is one of the best ways to fight fundamentalism, what will be the consequences of cutting children off from arts and culture in places where fundamentalism is increasing, where conflict is rife? I wonder about this in many contexts, but nowhere more so than in Palestine.

In December 2010, I arrive in East Jerusalem to interview Palestinians about their own rising tide of fundamentalism. Here the pollster Jamil Rabah tells me how worried he is about the trend in favor of "Islamic dominance" among Palestinians, the majority of whom he believes now want an "Islamic government." Fundamentalism is on the rise due to the alchemy of poverty, corruption, closure, internal violence, and occupation, Gazan researcher Hadeel Qazzaz tells me. "The only escape for these people is God. They can only hope for a second life, a better life." Hadeel thinks that eventually the Islamist movement Hamas will take over the West Bank. "It will get much worse before getting better."

Indeed, the culture wars have already begun. Palestinian American literature professor Rima Najjar was accused of insulting Islam and reportedly driven out of her post at the Arab-American University of Jenin due to student outrage that she taught the Iranian memoir *Persepolis*, which some claimed—probably without reading the book—was an attack on Islam.[20] In Gaza, Hadeel Qazzaz recounts, a youth group in which her nephew participates was harassed by Hamas for organizing an event to commemorate the Palestinian national poet Mahmoud Darwish. "They took some of his poetry, and said that he's a *kafir* because he used sometimes some kind of images which they consider against Islam."

Human rights advocate Randa Siniora tells me what a big reversal this is from the much more progressive seventies and eighties. The about-face is partly due to the pro-fundamentalist propaganda that fills the only media to which young Palestinians have access. "Imagine," Jamil Rabah suggests, "when you're not allowed to see the other side, to hear about the other side, to understand the other side."

It was in this environment that my old friend Terry Boullata founded the New Generation School in the West Bank town where she used to live. Part of what she tries to do at this elementary school is to give poor West Bank kids a wider view of the world. Every year, she faces the drama of organizing the school field trip amid the logistical mess that is the Arab-Israeli conflict. The kids say, "Please, Miss, we don't want to go to Jericho again." Jericho is a nice place to take a bicycle ride and see the ruins of the ten-thousand-year-old "City of the Moon." But if you are a child, and if you have been to Jericho many times because no permit from the Israeli authorities is required to get there, you might want to go somewhere else next time.

So this year Terry has decided she will attempt to take the kids to East Jerusalem, where most have never been, to see a play at the Hakawati, the Palestinian National Theatre. *Attempt* is the operative word. She has been told by Israeli military officials that she will need a permit for each child to cross the Wall, even though legally, because they are under sixteen, this is not required. Terry says that on the ground the law does not matter.

She spends days on the phone—to Israeli officials, to Israeli peace activists, to Israeli journalists—trying to organize a children's outing. As instructed, she sends all of the kids' ID-card numbers to the Israeli civil administration. A student body is reduced to a list of digits. On the eve of the field trip, with no sign of the permits, my friend is a nervous wreck. Should she attempt the checkpoint anyway, without the permits?

I listen to her on the phone pleading with a prominent Israeli journalist, Amira Hass, saying she has to give the children some hope. These are ghetto kids and they need something to smile about. Terry says she worries about the increasing tensions in the classroom brought on by the stresses the children live with in the ongoing conflict. Amira

Hass goes to bat for the kids, threatening the relevant Israeli officials that she will write about it if they are denied entry. But still nothing is certain, and Terry is trying to imagine how she will handle so much youthful disappointment at a checkpoint.

The night before the outing, she and I go to a wedding party near Bethlehem. In between a few bouts of dancing, she spends the evening on her cellphone, stressed and smoking. No school field trip has ever been so difficult to organize. The final call of the night informs her that there will be no permission given for any kids with mixed West Bank and Jerusalem parents.

The next morning, New Generation School is in an uproar. Terry has a lengthy conference with the teachers about permits and IDs and who can go and who can't. Oblivious to the obstacles, the kids are wound up with delight at the impending adventure. Meanwhile, the teachers count and sort the *hawiyas*, the identity cards. The husband of one of these teachers is upset that they would even try to take the kids across the Wall just to go to the theatre. It is too risky. We pile the students, dressed in their school uniforms, onto three big buses. I will ride alone with one load of children because the teachers, all adults with West Bank IDs, must travel separately from them. They have to walk across at the place ominously called "The Terminal," while their pupils will, theoretically, cross on their buses.

As we set off, the adults are nervous but the children are jubilant. What is this mythical Jerusalem that they have never seen, though it is just a few miles away? What exactly is a theatre? They are out of their seats and dancing in the aisle, shouting and cheering. I try in vain to get them to sit down. The road to Jerusalem winds in places, causing the bus to jolt occasionally. No one cares too much. The party ends abruptly when we approach the Israeli roadblock. One boy shouts out, "*Mahsum*." They all know exactly what this means. Checkpoint. Without any instruction from me, they sit immediately, suddenly still and quiet as ruins. Terry's "ghetto kids" remain frozen. Will there be a field trip today, or not?

Then, unexpectedly, we are waved through. Amira Hass's threat to write in *Haaretz* about the attempt to prevent children from attending a puppet show seems to have worked. Cheers erupt on the bus. The driver puts on Arabic music and everyone—boys and girls—claps and dances. We emerge from a tunnel into blinding sunlight and Jerusalem comes into view on the left, shimmering as only it does. Shouts of "El Qods," the city's Arabic name, fill the bus. It is a carnival now, and I reflect on the importance of what Terry, with Amira's help, has done. Palestinian researcher Mahdi Abdul Hadi had stressed to me that to promote tolerance and combat extremism you have to reach the youth above all else. If only for this moment, the children are in the light.

When we arrive at the theatre, the kids sit in the courtyard out front, eating snacks produced from their backpacks and reveling in the particular electricity of the moments before a play begins. For once, they do not have to think about soldiers or checkpoints or Islamic prohibitions or the difficulties of life in today's West Bank. They have an afternoon far away from the dark corner. For many of these kids, this will be the only time in their lives they go to the theatre. When Terry asks who has never been to this part of Jerusalem before, nearly all the hands go up.

Still the activist I met twenty years ago, she gets on stage with a bullhorn and introduces the play. Terry tells the kids she hopes Jerusalem will be open for them someday. The puppet show begins with the appearance of a magician, a worm, a monster, and an enchanted book whose pages display first in color and then suddenly in black and white. Again, the kids cannot stay in their seats. When the play is over, the puppeteers come out and explain all the secrets. Later, the actors say they fought tears onstage, looking out at this enthralled audience that had managed to come from behind the Wall. Women's rights advocate Naila Ayesh told me she thinks social attitudes will begin to change when people have "access to move freely." Isolating the more conservative West Bank from the historically more open and cultured city of Jerusalem, where many Palestinian cultural institutions have long been based, can only make things worse.

I wonder what new horizons this day might have opened for the kids, a day that had to be fought for by an unrelenting Palestinian school founder and a stubborn Israeli journalist, a day that most of their fellow West Bank children will never have. It is a tiny but important victory in the war against extremisms. The puppet show in El Qods El

Sharif reminds me of a drama that the veteran women's rights activist Akila Ouared once staged with children in Algeria. The main character decides not to become a suicide bomber because he gets the lead role in a play. He has something beautiful to live for. Because art means he does not face what the cartoonist Slim called *Walou à l'horizon*: Nothing on the horizon.

CHAPTER THREE

The Imam's Liberated Daughter and Other Stories: Women Battling Beyond Stereotypes

"Sexism is at the heart of this totalitarian project," Iranian sociologist Chahla Chafiq says of what she calls Islamism. Subordinating women—in the family, in the street, in the bedroom—is central to most fundamentalist visions for society around the world. Muslim fundamentalists aim to control the womb, the unmentionable areas of the body—what the Qur'an calls "the unseen parts." Sometimes those are even said to include the faces of women. Fundamentalists also seek to restrict women's movement, space, being. As Nighat Khan, dean of Lahore's Institute of Women's Studies, told me, if women try to create their own spaces like her institution, "They're considered threatening." ("We don't know what they do behind closed doors," say their detractors.) On the other hand, when women try to mix with men in shared public space, "They can be threatened." Women's rights activists then live a spatial conundrum. Ultimately, Khan says, in the face of fundamentalism and conservatism, "You can be nowhere."

This Islamist obsession with all things female means women of Muslim heritage are in many places the first to walk the gauntlet of rising fundamentalism, whether they are simply appearing in public, practicing professions that are off-limits, or, most of all, championing women's rights. Whether they wear burqas or bikinis, they live at Ground Zero. "It feels as if we are seated on a bomb," a young woman from Niger tells me. "We are at the frontline in this country," explains Mary Akrami, who runs Kabul's first shelter for battered women.

Women's human rights defenders, a category that includes some men, are then everywhere one of the most important forces contesting fundamentalism. "Every step forward for women's rights," Nigerien sociologist Zeinabou Hadari argues, "is a piece of the struggle against fundamentalism." To quote the writer Katha Pollitt, "The opposite of fundamentalism is feminism."[1] This is as true among people of Muslim heritage as anywhere else.

No matter how many challenges feminists have faced on this terrain, they have had important victories when they have stood together. Zaynab Elsawi, who coordinates Sudanese Women Empowerment for Peace (SuWEP), told me how she and others protested in front of a Khartoum courthouse in 2009 against the sentence of flogging meted out to female journalist Lubna Hussein for the crime of wearing trousers in public.[2] One of the protesters was an older, heavy-set woman from a generation that had known life before such restrictions. Young soldiers came to drag the protesters away and threw them one after another into a truck. When they got to the older woman, they could not lift her, so they told her to go home. Outraged, she hired a taxi to follow the other arrested women to jail.

In prison, they all faced "a very much stimulating investigation," Zaynab laughs. "They asked us to write that I am not going to do these kinds of things again. And we said 'No, we are going to do it again and again and again.'" From jail, the arrested women sent messages around the world. Many others came out to demand their freedom, as they had demanded Lubna Hussein's rights. "The reaction was much more than what the government expected," Zaynab thinks, "so they decided to release us." Lubna Hussein's sentence was commuted. Across the regions, across the miles, this defiance of fundamentalism echoes in the lives of countless other women activists of Muslim heritage.

REJECTING PUNISHMENTS "IMPOSED BY GOD"

Aïssatou Cissé is a human rights activist, a novelist, and, since the 2012 elections, a special adviser to the president of Senegal. Unable to walk since birth, she is permanently in a wheelchair. Nevertheless, she is unstoppable. When I am invited to give a lecture on women and revolution in North Africa at Cheikh Anta Diop University in Dakar in the summer of 2011, Aïssatou attends, even though there is no elevator and she has to be carried up several flights of stairs. She lives in an inaccessible world but makes it her own.

Among Aïssatou's many causes—including the Global Campaign to Stop Stoning and Killing Women, and her work against early marriages—the one that is closest to her heart is the fight for the rights of disabled women and girls. Some interpretations of religion, she tells me, consider "handicaps" to be "a punishment imposed by God." Though some conservative religious associations give charity to the handicapped, they also teach that the Qur'an says they should not go to school. As a result, Aïssatou comments, many disabled Senegalese children are torn from the classroom and kept away from other children. "Their biggest fear . . .," she has written, "is to be considered supernatural incarnations: the children of *jinns* [genies], that according to some beliefs can either bring great wealth or a great deal of unhappiness."[3]

To combat such notions, Aïssatou produced a comic book, *The Stories of Nafi and Khadija*, about the (mis)adventures of a wheelchair-bound eleven-year-old named Nafi, and of Khadija, a young albino girl in love. Nafi, sent to beg on the streets of Dakar, survives sexual assault by a stranger, and, with the support of NGO activists, overcomes this ordeal and is able to return to school. Meanwhile, Khadija's romance with her *bien-aimé* Demba is threatened by the objections of his conservative family to a *pounée*, the Wolof word for albino. Demba's mother travels to consult a *marabout*, a religious leader, hoping to gain support for breaking up the couple. Just when you think the story will end badly, Aïssatou's marabout espouses a tolerant Senegalese Islam, devoid of prejudice. His counsel about Demba's love for an albino? "These beings are like you and me. . . *Domou Adama leñu!*" They are human beings.

As this happy ending suggests, Senegal has a tradition of relatively liberal Islam that leaves space for tolerant interpretations of culture and women's advancement. Aïssatou's own family's ferocious support of her freedom is one example; the election of a historic 43 percent of women to the Parliament in July 2012 is another.[4] However, Aïssatou worries that such attitudes are under pressure from rising fundamentalism, a trend she knows can undermine her work. She tells me she is afraid. This is a word I have never heard her use. Her fear is provoked by such developments as funding pouring in from the Gulf to finance Qur'anic schools in Senegal.[5] She is likewise concerned about an influx of foreign Qur'anic teachers who "try to shape you, change your mentality, going as far as to teach the child that her mother and father are bad parents because they allow her to do certain things which are forbidden by religion."

Misinformed children grow up to become misinformed adults. She tells me a story that captures the cost of this trajectory. A woman of Wolof ethnicity in the north of Senegal married a man from another ethnic group. As a Wolof, she had not been excised. (Unlike many of the 140 million women and girls of different faiths worldwide living with the consequences of female genital mutilation, or FGM,[6] this woman still had both her clitoris and her labia minora intact.) Though FGM is illegal in Senegal, and only an estimated 28 percent of women here have suffered this practice,[7] the Wolof woman's in-laws refused to eat food she cooked because she had not been excised. (I cannot help wondering just how they think food is prepared.) No one would speak to this woman. So harassed was she, Aïssatou continues, that finally she submitted to FGM as an adult. "Now, they say she is pure, and only now can she join the family, because religion rejects the impure." Cultural conservatism uses the faux alibi of religion to justify pre-Islamic practices like FGM. Aïssatou is irate.

"It is not religion that says it!"

Incensed by such stories, Aïssatou headed to the north of Senegal in her wheelchair to lead a seminar on FGM. A man in attendance grew increasingly angry with her, accusing her of making things up. He asked if she was Muslim, if her father was Muslim. Aïssatou retorted, "You have the right to question me, but I would like it if someone can show me where it is written in the Qur'an, in which Surah, that you must be excised." The women in the workshop had never heard that this "rule" was not written in the Qur'an. Enraged, the man left.

Muslim women must be proactive, Aïssatou urges. They cannot

simply listen to what male leaders say about religion. Internationally, groups like Malaysia's renowned Sisters in Islam (SIS) do offer alternate feminist interpretations of the religion's teachings. "There are conflicting interpretations available," SIS cofounder Zainah Anwar reminds me. "There is nothing divine about the choice you make." However, not enough women in Senegal have embraced the understanding that diverse interpretations of Islam are available to them, Aïssatou thinks.

If they do not learn the Qur'an, Aïssatou warns, they are left with men interpreting it for them. "Personally, I refuse that." While her body is differently abled, her spirit is utterly ungovernable. "It is not for anyone to tell me how to act in terms of religion or my everyday life. One must refuse indoctrination. When someone wants to impose something, they say that religion says so." I ask if she is afraid to say such things openly. "No, on the contrary, I am relieved to say them," she responds.

Aïssatou Cissé is uncompromising, a quality whose value in the fight against fundamentalism is inestimable. She is known for her dress sense and plunging necklines. Aïssatou rejects shame. To say that someone knows no shame is usually meant as an insult, but it is actually a sign of liberation for many women. The wheelchair-bound activist proudly tells the disabled women she works with that they have a right to a sex life.

I AM YOUR PROFESSOR

Dr. Fatou Sow is the international coordinator of the network of Women Living Under Muslim Laws (WLUML). A sociologist, she was my supervisor when I taught at CODESRIA, the Council for the Development of Social Science Research in Africa, in a summer Gender Institute on "Gender, Culture, Politics and Fundamentalisms in Africa." The title of our course is long because, as Fatou regularly reminds me, "One must avoid the trap of thinking everything goes back to Islam. All customs and all conservatisms are not in fact 'Muslim,' even though Islam is used to rubber stamp them." Gambian activist Amie Joof underscores Fatou's concern when she tells me, while I am in Dakar, "You see a lot of confusion between religion and culture." For Fatou

Sow, this means feminists must take on both what she calls religious fundamentalism and cultural fundamentalism.

Dr. Fatou, as our students call her, has taught at universities in Senegal, France, and the United States, but she is spending her "retirement" back home by the seaside in Dakar. She is one of the least-retired people I know—still writing, editing, lecturing, traveling, and wrangling the coalition of activists around the world who make up the brilliant, vital, and sometimes unwieldy WLUML. WLUML's particular contribution, Fatou suggests, has been to popularize a women's discourse based in the camp of secularists of Muslim heritage.

At seventy, she is coediting a book about sexualities in Senegal with a group of activists. At the university, she taught courses, including one about reproductive health, to predominantly male students. After menopause, she was amused when her students in their twenties and thirties would tell her, "Madame, post-menopausal women, it is well known, do not have sexual needs." Fatou nearly swears at this ("espèce de . . ."). "These young people who have never had sexual relations with a post-menopausal woman, who have never dared think about the sexuality of their mothers, decide that once a woman is not producing children, she has no more sexual needs." These assumptions are ironic, because for many of them, if a man takes up with a woman the age of his daughter, "it's normal because men have sexual needs until they die." Fatou does not let the question rest. "So, I said to them, have you asked your mothers this question?" "Of course not," they reply.

"But if you haven't asked the question, how do you know the answer?"

All this reticence about sexuality is new, according to Fatou, and increasingly the result of fundamentalist pressure on education and society, which she dates back to the rise of Ayatollah Khomeini in Iran. There are popular traditions of erotic song and dance in Senegal that she says make Beyoncé look tame. Fatou Sow, like most Senegalese of her age, grew up with them. As Dr. Fatou's collaborator, Codou Bop, aged sixty, recalls it, they and other Senegalese of their generation grew up dancing. "At the end of Ramadan in everyone's house, we danced. We danced all year." Men and women together.

At age twenty, Fatou says, she would shake hands with any man. But, for the last fifteen years, she often avoids holding out her hand to young men. "If he doesn't shake my hand, I will give him a smack. I can't stand it." She has had male students come to meet her in her office but decline to shake her hand. Their excuse? "It is in the Qur'an." Fatou insists this has nothing to do with the Qur'an but rather with certain Arab cultural practices alien to Wolof culture. She is well aware of the insult implied, just as clear as if a student had refused to shake her hand because of her race. "As a woman, I am to be respected. I am not your mother. I am not your mistress. I am your professor and you must respect me by shaking my hand."

Today Fatou is pessimistic when she sees the reports that pour in to the WLUML network. On July 11, 2012, twenty-three-year-old Ms. L.I.E. was condemned to death by stoning for adultery in Khartoum.[8] The information was circulated through the WLUML network by a Malian colleague. On September 4, 2012, a sixteen-year-old girl was sentenced to public flogging in the Maldives under what is called Sharia law after confessing to premarital sex.[9] This news is shared with us by a Nigerian networker. "I despair for Muslims," Fatou tells me. "Every day there is a case of a woman being attacked for what she wears, or what she does. I find this very depressing."

Fatou stresses that she does not resist Islam but rather an Islamic discourse that is "aggressive and offensive." More than that, she says, "It crystallizes around the rights of women." What worries Fatou most is that secular discourse seems to be fading.

Is secular or religious discourse on women's rights more useful? I ask.

This is the great debate among women's rights activists of Muslim descent. It is chic nowadays in the West to focus solely on those who reinterpret Islam to make women's rights arguments, rather than those who, like Fatou Sow, fight for women's rights from a broader perspective without recourse to religion. For Fatou, the best approach depends on the context. In certain places it may be appropriate to make what are sometimes called "Islamic feminist arguments" within a religious paradigm. "But as a Senegalese," she insists, "I refuse to reinterpret the Qur'an to change the family law. I am not going to enter into the religious debate. I do not want to close myself off." Above all, she argues

that the strategy for combating fundamentalisms must be a political one
that takes the debate off of "the religious terrain where they wish to trap
us. Nowadays, all questions take you back to the Qur'an. You try to
discuss AIDS and they reply, 'Ah, yes, the Qur'an says that you should
not have homosexual sex.'"

LIVING UNDER MUSLIM LAWS

I first read the work of iconic Algerian feminist sociologist Marieme
Hélie-Lucas, now seventy-two, when I was a graduate student in the
early 1990s. She wrote some of the earliest articles critiquing the status of women postindependence, and specifically the Algerian Family
Code, which reduced them to virtual minors. Fundamentalism did not
just fight the Algerian government from without. It had also crept into
the law itself through this dreadful code justified in the name of religion
and opposed for decades by Algerian feminists because of the discriminatory nature of its provisions on marriage, divorce, and inheritance.[10]
I will never forget my own failed attempts to resolve my father's estate
in Algeria. When I questioned the gender-discriminatory distribution
of assets that was supposed to occur pursuant to the Islamic inheritance provisions incorporated in the Family Code, the legal official I
was dealing with pointed his finger upward.

"Madam, you cannot argue with God."

Marieme addressed all this in a 1987 classic, "Bound and Gagged
by the Family Law,"[11] in which she also detailed how fundamentalists threatened to throw acid on the faces of women attending the first
postindependence feminist gathering in Algiers in 1981. Steeped in the
politics of Algeria's independence movement, Hélie-Lucas chose not to
end her quest for freedom when the French army departed. She saw the
rise of fundamentalism coming early in the new country. "It developed
because the Algerian state did not keep its promises." Being such a Cas-
sandra was lonely. By the time fundamentalism had become obvious
enough for her friends on the Algerian left to join her in speaking out
against it, it was too late to avoid disaster.

In the 1980s, Marieme founded the network of Women Living
Under Muslim Laws (WLUML), which Fatou Sow now coordinates.

It started as a kind of solidarity action committee that became increasingly formalized. The network originated in 1984, when three women were arrested in Algeria for protesting the Family Code. Marieme encountered a group of feminists from all over the world while in The Hague and asked if they would help support the incarcerated Algerians. They in turn wrote to other women to ask them to do the same. As a result, protest letters from around the world flooded the office of Algeria's president. The women were freed.

Initially, Marieme did not consider taking action about issues beyond her home country. But she saw that the international coalition worked. This first lobbying effort was one of the biggest successes of her political life, she tells me. Subsequently, she received letters from Indian women who had helped in the campaign, asking the Algerian women on whose behalf they had mobilized to join them in efforts for women under threat elsewhere. Those involved realized how groundbreaking it could be to mobilize women from within Muslim majority countries and communities transnationally.

Before long, WLUML was an international powerhouse, a network of women's rights activists from seventy countries, "from South Africa to Uzbekistan, from Senegal to Indonesia with an international headquarters in France and bureaus in Pakistan and Dakar."[12] One of the group's focal points is "exposing fundamentalisms." To that end, despite a shoestring budget, WLUML is involved in a wide range of projects—from condemning specific cases of fundamentalist violation of women's rights (like the murder of Pakistani women's rights advocate Farida Afridi in July 2012) to producing and promoting indispensable new resources that can help save others from such a fate (including a book entitled *Mapping Stoning in Muslim Contexts*, authored by a coalition called Justice for Iran). Part safety net, part group therapy, part advocacy organization and part Open University, WLUML blossomed amazingly from one woman's attempt to free three others.

While many people in the world know something about the oppression of women of Muslim heritage, they may know much less about the organized resistance of those same women. In "Heart and Soul," a WLUML action document that has become a kind of informal history, Marieme pleads: "Know that women also struggle in Muslim countries because that is where we draw inspiration and strength from."[13] The efforts of WLUML networkers are analogous to those by feminists everywhere challenging sexism. What is distinct, Hélie-Lucas argues, is the particular role of religion and especially its fundamentalist variants: "In our societies we are told that the circumstances under which we live cannot be changed because God said it should be like this. . . . This is also what brings us together." In the face of such religiously justified discrimination, WLUML seeks to "build bridges among ourselves," to break the isolation faced by some women fighting fundamentalism.

This model differs entirely from "aid," which, as Marieme notes, goes only in one direction: from the haves to the have-nots. WLUML instead offers a reciprocal exchange, and a celebration of the diversities and unities of women of Muslim heritage living in a wide variety of contexts. Women from Nigeria sign petitions on behalf of those in Pakistan, trial observers are sent from Malaysia to Fiji, and so on.

WLUML brings together women who work from a secular perspective (who predominated in the group at first) with those who seek to progressively interpret within religion (whose ranks increased after the 1990s, when the organization's international office moved to London). Marieme, an avowed atheist, argues that those who use feminist reinterpretation of Islam to promote women's rights and those who advocate from a secular human rights standpoint should be allies, given the power of the shared enemy they face. Their work can be complementary.

However, there are also dangerous traps to consider when acting inside religion, she avers. "If God and the Prophet said there will be slaves, there are slaves." Pakistani human rights lawyer and former UN expert Hina Jilani was also skeptical when I spoke to her in Lahore about what is called "Islamic feminism." "This has not gotten us anywhere. In a country where you have seventy-two different sects of Islam, and seventy-two different interpretations, a seventy-third will not matter." In her view, such reinterpretation of religion is "of secondary importance as far as human rights activism is concerned. I don't think that the mullahs are very much bothered about that. What excites them are people who say, 'We have to go forward, this is the reality and this is the modern world.'" Iranian women's rights activist Mahnaz Afkhami agrees, telling me, "If you're in the army, the general is always going to win. In the religious context, there is a hierarchy. If you're a woman, the guy who is the general in the religious army is not going to even pay the slightest attention to what your view of the text is." Still, notwithstanding this ongoing debate, there are many women who advocate each of these approaches (or sometimes both) in the WLUML network (just as there are in this book), battling together against common foes: patriarchs, militarists, racists, and fundamentalists.

After a long career of resisting fundamentalism, Marieme Hélie-Lucas remains deeply frustrated by its continuing strength and our relative weakness. She knows that in many Muslim contexts, secularism has been "rubbed out" by "terrorizing dissenters."[14] And she knows only too well how little global support is offered to these dissenters. "[I]t seems presumed," she types out in angry letters after the Pakistani Taliban attempt to kill schoolgirl Malala Yousafzai in the Swat Valley, that "Muslims do not deserve equal access to . . . freedom of thought and freedom of conscience. Presumed Muslims are under cultural arrest; they are bound by customs and religion and should remain so, while the rest of humanity enjoys universal rights."[15]

In defiance of such mistaken assumptions, Hélie-Lucas will stay up until 4 a.m. to translate someone's solidarity statement and push the rest of us to keep going. In her spare time, she runs a website called Secularism is a Women's Issue (SIAWI) to showcase even more of these outsider views. Like Fatou Sow, sometimes she despairs, but she still works harder than many activists half her age. Ultimately, perhaps because of the unlikely success of that very first letter-writing campaign that sparked WLUML, Marieme still believes it is worth trying to be heard against the odds. As she wrote to me during the Anwar al-Awlaki controversy, "Breaking the silence is a great thing for us all."

DECONSTRUCTING SHARIA IN NIGERIA

"The baobab connotes spiritual strength . . . and fortitude . . . in distressing times."[16]

Ayesha Imam and the women she worked with for years in the Nigerian organization BAOBAB for Women's Human Rights possess those very traits. The group, founded in 1996, fights to protect women's rights in the maze of the Nigerian legal system, with its overlapping religious, secular, and customary laws and courts. Ayesha tells me they use tools from whichever system can "recuperate rights," believing it is often possible to arrive at similar conclusions by working through Muslim discourses or international human rights. "My issue," she underscores, "is not where you come from, but where you arrive at."

With her colleagues, she tried to "deconstruct what is Sharia. How does it get to be Sharia? Is it divine or is it merely religious?" In the eighties and early nineties, some of the Sharia courts in Nigeria had come up with "what we may call progressive" interpretations, "as opposed to following somebody's idea of how it should have worked in thirteenth-century Arabia." Ayesha Imam's efforts to support women living under these Muslim laws brought her, inevitably, to work on fundamentalism. "Fundamentalism hit us in Nigeria so it was absolutely necessary, because otherwise fundamentalism was going to close us all down, close all the dreams down, close all the hope down."

The backdrop for this, a resurgence of communalism, was sparked in part by the harsh impact of structural adjustment and ensuing battles for resources. Structural adjustment—economic reforms imposed on Nigeria by international financial institutions—also meant there were many unemployed, uneducated young men looking for something to do. For them, "this was an opportunity to have power and assert themselves," as Ayesha sees it. "They told women in taxis and buses that they had to sit in the back seats." There was "general intimidation."

This in turn led to greater emphasis on Sharia law in Muslim majority segments of the population in the late nineties in the north of Nigeria, and then to enactment of new legislation in the early 2000s.[17] "The reaction among the Muslim community was really mixed. Human rights workers and those who identify strongly as democrats argued that we need secular law. The laws being brought in under the guise of Muslim laws are conservative, and detract from human rights." Even some religious conservatives opposed Sharianization, Imam recalls, on the grounds that you could not have Sharia law before you have economic development so that people can actually live good lives.

"You can't cut off people's hands for theft if they have no other means of gaining a livelihood."

Any such opponents, however, became targets of "vigilante responses." Death threats, beatings, threats of being burned. In one state where the governor delayed enacting a Sharia Act and set up a committee to study the matter, there were even threats to his family. Ayesha recalls attending a meeting in Abuja with the governor who started Sharianization. Young men throughout the hall were telling women where they could and could not sit. "Every time a woman got up to speak, they were yelling and drowning her out. It didn't matter if you were wearing a hijab or not." This was new, Ayesha underlines. When she was a younger feminist, "You didn't get shouted down. You were not in fear of being physically attacked, or being burned or harassed. You'd go to public meetings and people would get up and argue with you and they might laugh."

As fundamentalism began to transform Nigerian lives, Ayesha and BAOBAB became involved in the cases of women who were facing sentences of stoning. One of the first, that of Fatima Usman, ensued when the woman's father took the man who fathered her baby to court to get child support. "He had no idea he was going to set up his own daughter for the possibility of being stoned to death." (Today Usman remains technically out on bail, as the case has never been finally resolved. Nor, thankfully, has the sentence been carried out.)[18] Most such cases began with vigilante groups forcing the police to prosecute and ended in "lots of people convicted of *Zina* [unlawful sexual relations] and whipped because they were not married." If people do not appeal, they are taken out and whipped right away, Ayesha laments. "It was really important to establish the principle that you can appeal. It's your right.

"It's not anti-God to appeal."

However, it was difficult to rally victims of such prosecutions to fight back. "They thought, as Muslims, if they were charged under Muslim laws, they could not defend themselves. It would be tantamount to arguing with God." I had heard those words before. While working on the case of a thirteen-year-old mentally disabled girl, Bariya Magazu, who had been charged with Zina and faced public whipping, Ayesha's team had to spend a week in the girl's village "arguing with her father, her family head and the village head that it was not impious to file an appeal under Sharia law." This is what law as sacrament does to people.

Though Ayesha succeeded in convincing Bariya's family members, while the appeal was being filed the nonliterate teenage villager who had just given birth was whipped publicly for the sex she had been coerced to have. "Afterwards," Ayesha wrote in an outraged statement for BAOBAB, "humiliated, bruised, crying and in pain, she was left to make her way home alone."[19] Ayesha points out to me: "The dominant ideology is that good women are secluded, so to be whipped in public view is a really horrible disgrace."

Ayesha was also involved in efforts to defend Amina Lawal, a Nigerian woman famously sentenced to stoning for adultery in 2002 (and later acquitted). Imam was critical of parts of the Western response to the case, which ignored women's rights advocates on the ground. Some Western advocates asked for a pardon, which was neither possible nor politically feasible. Local activists instead chose legal appeals that would immediately stay execution. "If you don't have an appeal, they can take action and you might win the principle, but it's a little late for the person involved." Another reason the local women's rights defenders opposed pardons is that, "technically, you are saying, 'Yes, we did wrong, but please forgive us anyway.' The point we wanted to make was that there hadn't been any wrongdoing."

The women of BAOBAB also raised money to support defendants who were unable to earn a living while being prosecuted: "Having to hop off to court all the time, they can't work in the fields, they can't go sell their stuff." Worse still, "the stress of it is horrendous." So the activists try to offer the psychological support needed to overcome the defendants' feelings that they are challenging their own religion. BAOBAB's contribution was "to make it known that you could fight and you could win. The more we did that, the more people were willing to fight against it and the less people felt like, 'I am a Muslim, I cannot criticize.'"

Every one of the Sharianization stoning sentences has been successfully appealed with the support of women's human rights defenders, resulting in acquittals (or nonperformance of sentence, as in Usman's case), and there have reportedly been no new cases since Amina Lawal's acquittal, though the laws remain on the books. In the battle between stone and tree, it is the BAOBAB that has prevailed.

Above all else, BAOBAB tried to make it known that debate and discussion were still possible, that multiple understandings have been employed by Muslims. "Therefore, it is not anti-Muslim to say, 'Well we can abolish the death penalty, for example.'" BAOBAB pointed out that in the Qur'an, the Bible, and the Torah, slavery was recognized, but "today, in the Muslim world, nobody—by and large—thinks that slavery is a good thing and should be justified by reference to Islam."

For Ayesha, space for debate and maintaining the flow of knowledge are absolutely critical. This is the only way people can work through on their own, "to something you and I would recognize as rights." Rights must be part of a process, not a mere proclamation. "People can't be told my version of rights any more than I am willing to be told some conservative right-wing version of rights. People have to allow other people the same level of tolerance." But Ayesha knows this is by no means easy. If Nigerians are preoccupied eking out a living, "it's very hard to take the time to discuss." Most of all, she thinks it vital "to recognize that there is a possibility of fighting for change within our communities." This thought brings me back to BAOBAB's slogan, which encircles the eponymous African tree on the organization's logo.

"You can't change the past, but you can try to change the future."

THE IMAM'S LIBERATED DAUGHTER

Thirty and unmarried, Aminatou Daouda Hainikoye is originally from the west of Niger. Daughter of a liberal imam, she has a degree in law and specializes in women's rights. I first met her in Dakar at the WLUML-sponsored Feminist Leadership Institute. When she comes to see me alone in the evening at my hotel in the Nigerien capital, Niamey, she wears a fabulous red and blue boubou with a black scarf around her neck and dangling earrings.

Aminatou's home country, one of the poorest in the world despite its uranium reserves, is not the easiest place to be a woman, even less a women's rights activist. Though half the Nigerien population is female, 73 percent of those who live in extreme poverty are women.[20] Only 38 percent of girls go to school, and one in three marries before her fifteenth birthday.[21] Still, Niger is formally a secular state and the mainstream of Islam here has traditionally been tolerant.

Fundamentalism hit the country in the 1990s, Nigerien women's rights advocate Zeinabou Hadari assesses, due to a mix of factors: the rise of extremism in neighboring Algeria and Nigeria, economic pressure created by debt restructuring, the impact of Nigerien students returning from studying abroad (where they were influenced by the ideas of the Muslim Brotherhood), and a new democratization that fundamentalists exploited. Programs that defended women's rights were dismantled as fundamentalists blocked efforts to limit the early marriages of girls and spied on women's group meetings.

So today in Niger, Aminatou explains, "Fundamentalism is a real check on the promotion of women's rights." It is based on what she sees as bad interpretations of the Qur'an, as well as the cacophony of diverse misinterpretations with which various marabouts fill the airwaves. Aminatou underscores the financial causes of the rise of fundamentalism in her country. She points particularly to poverty and the devaluation of the West African franc. The fundamentalists use this fragile economic environment all too well. "In the beginning, they offer you money to adhere to their version of religion, to wear the burqa, the hijab, the niqab. They give out money, food, bags of rice, cooking oil. Even if you are not convinced in your heart, you accept so as not to die of hunger."

An activist in Islamic associations, a primarily middle-class milieu, she says she knows many fundamentalists personally—those who are "open to debate" and those "who will not even look at you." The imam's daughter laughs at the about-faces made by some young newly minted fundamentalists who used to go to nightclubs or to "change women like shirts."

As a believer, she strongly supports the secularism of the Nigerien state as a foil to extremists. "People are afraid of these guys. They have political ambitions. It is a way of checking them." In her view, the state has been justifiably vigilant about the rise of political Islam and has played a significant role in blocking it. As long as the political will is there, and the state fulfills its responsibilities, she does not fear the future. This optimistic view stands in sharp contrast to what I hear from Nigerien woman magistrate Moussa Satou, who says, "I worry that in ten years we will become a fundamentalist state." I hope it is the imam's daughter who is correct in her prognosis, but the regional dynamics prevailing now across the Sahel are not promising.

Based as it is in her faith, Aminatou Daouda's critique of Nigerien fundamentalists is especially blistering. "They want to take Niger back to the era of the Prophet, Peace Be Upon Him. They do not think that religion can adapt to different contexts. You must be a little clueless to think this." She sees her religion rather differently. "Islam can adapt to all epochs. Islam is not a closed religion, it is open." Very secure in her beliefs and identity, she has no fear for Islam, which she deems robust, organic, and something that "must evolve as the world evolves." "That is what really shocks me with them," she says of fundamentalists. "They think Islam must remain frozen."

At university, Aminatou wrote her thesis about the UN Convention on the Elimination of All Forms of Discrimination against Women (CEDAW). The fundamentalists had used marches and fatwas to try to block Niger's CEDAW ratification altogether, and then to impose limiting reservations that would hamper its application when those first efforts failed. The Nigerien reservations, or legal limitations on the treaty, seek to allow continued discrimination against women in the family even while ratifying a convention entirely designed to end gender bias, and Aminatou believes they do not hold up "from an Islamic point of view."

Apparently, a "very cool" woman marabout called Zeinab, who preached on national TV, had worked with the Nigerien Ministry of Foreign Affairs to promote CEDAW ratification, issuing fatwas in its favor. But Zeinab was killed in a car accident on a trip to promote the convention in rural Niger. The fundamentalists said she died because of her fatwa in favor of CEDAW. " 'All those who speak against Islam will end up like her,' they say."

In contrast to such claims, Aminatou Daouda's father the imam supports her work for women's rights (though her going out in the evening took some getting used to, as did the frequent work-related visits to the house by male civil-society colleagues). "Thank God, he understood. He lets me travel to meetings and workshops. I cannot thank him enough because he really helped me."

Inspired by the atmosphere in her family, she thinks the best way to fight fundamentalism in Niger is to promote a tolerant Islam. "Fundamentalism means going above and beyond the limits of religion itself." In that, she sees an arrogance. "We did not create religion. We must not think that we will protect it. No!" She quotes a Qur'anic verse in which God says that He created the religion and that He is the Guardian of His religion. Extrapolating from this verse, Aminatou Daouda gives me her take on the American would-be Qur'an burner, Christian fundamentalist Terry Jones. "On Facebook, I wrote that he does not bother me, because I know that God is in charge of His religion. It is up to God to react."

In her universe, a Muslim should not trouble others or make demands on them. She has no problem with atheists. "It is their choice and I respect it." Coexistence is Islamic for Aminatou Daouda: "Islam told me this: a Muslim must be tolerant, must support the other, in whatever context." I walk with her out into the dark October night in her many-colored boubou. In front of the Hotel Gaweye, she grabs a cab home alone.

OUR DAUGHTERS WILL BE ABLE TO WALK IN THIS COUNTRY

"Street harassment is against Islam." "Disrespect to any woman is disrespect to humanity." "I have the right to walk freely in my city."

Fifty women and a few male supporters filed through the dusty streets of Kabul carrying these banners on July 14, 2011, the week before I arrived in Afghanistan.[22] A new organization called Young Women for Change had called the march from Kabul University to the offices of the Afghan Independent Human Rights Commission. They did so after their organization's pilot research project indicated that eighteen out of twenty women in the capital city who go out in public are harassed—"assaulted, pinched, grabbed, groped, even slapped"— on a daily basis.

The college student who founded Young Women for Change, Noor Jahan Akbar, comes to see me wearing the most minimal of scarves around her young face, and she dispenses with it entirely as soon as she enters the guesthouse lounge. The daughter of educators, Noor Jahan says she learned the value of gender equality while growing up.

On July 14, 2011, she and the other young women distributed fliers and talked to bystanders on the street. Their public presence followed a "night letter" (unsigned missive) they distributed among university students, stating that street harassment is un-Islamic because the Prophet Muhammad said nobody but those who are inferior in character will disrespect women. Young Women for Change also argued in human rights terms that women are equal with men and deserve the same dignity. After the night letter, they published a "call to action" on street harassment, even delivering it to the Ulema Council, comprising the country's leading clerics. Only then did they take to the streets.

The day of the march, some watchers along the route supported them, Noor Jahan recalls. Others took a dimmer view. "One of the religious TVs in Afghanistan dedicated its Friday preaching to insulting us, saying we were not dressed appropriately, and therefore deserved to be harassed." Noor Jahan says that even one participant in full hijab was told she was dressed inappropriately.[23] "It's threatening to men to see women being empowered. They feel like the lifestyle that has preserved for them the right to dominate women is going to change. This fear causes a lot of anger." Religious "extremism" is also to blame, as what she terms "wrong interpretations" of the Qur'an and the Hadith dictate that women are to stay at home.

The young Afghan activist, who bears the name of a legendary seventeenth-century Mughal empress, is proud to tell me that, after asking for official permission for their event, her group received good police protection. Not only did fifteen Afghan policemen come along, but "they walked with us, and handed out our fliers." It seems to have been an educational experience for the police, who were so upset by those harassing the women protesters that some of the cops shouted at the shocked hecklers: "In Afghanistan, we are all Muslims and in our culture mothers are to be respected. Every one of you has mothers and sisters and wives. Would you feel okay if your mother was harassed like this?"

Like the resilient wild tulips that grow in parts of their country, these Young Women for Change are no shrinking violets and did not simply rely on the police. They photographed the catcallers, which sometimes caused them to stop. Most important, they did not give up, no matter what anyone said. "The women who came with us, stayed with us the whole time."

As part of their campaign to turn out supporters, the route they would take had been publicly announced two weeks in advance. They then received threats via e-mail and Facebook and over the phone. After giving interviews on Afghan TV, Noor Jahan was told she would be found and punished. "But none of this means we are afraid because even an angry approach shows they are thinking and questioning their beliefs." For safety's sake, the Young Women for Change revised their route two days before the event, but, despite denunciations and real risk, they hit the streets nonetheless.

Noor Jahan expected much worse than the reactions they got. "Before going, my stomach was like turning around the whole morning because I was so nervous that something would happen security-wise. I would feel awful for arranging this event and putting so many men and women in danger, but we were all safe." Additionally, the media broadcast their message. Her face shines when describing this first political success.

At nineteen, this young Afghan is already thinking about her own intergenerational responsibility. The night before the march, she sent a motivational message to the participants: "Because of your fights our children will be treated better." Though she fears a civil war when international troops leave Afghanistan, she is positive about her country's future in the very long term. "I will probably not be alive to see that day, but I think dreaming is important, and nourishing the dream in other women around me is the first step toward achieving it.

"Our daughters will be able to walk in this country."

The criticism she receives, she takes on the chin. "More than once I've been called someone who promotes Western ideas, a non-Muslim." For Noor Jahan, this charge says more about those who utter it than about her. "According to Islam, it is a sin to call a Muslim a non-Muslim." Nor is she shy about replying: "Usually, I say, since when is safety and respect of women an idea that is Western? If you say we don't have this, you're really disrespecting our culture." Young Women for Change actively promote this safety and respect of women, not only through demonstrations and educational events but also in the most contemporary ways. When I meet her, Noor Jahan Akbar is busy planning a safe Internet café for women in Kabul's Karte Char neighborhood.

Her views on women's rights have been nourished by her academic research on traditional women's music in Afghanistan. Women have been singing at house parties, weddings, and birthday gatherings for years. While they are unpublicized, these "couplets and quatrains that women sing are actually feminist ideas, that have been silenced." The lyrics Noor Jahan has gathered discuss early marriage, "the thirst to go to school," complaints about fathers and against violence. Quintessentially Afghan, she wants to use this folkloric music to "advocate for women's rights as an Afghan idea." Whatever people might think about her country, whatever the Taliban might have tried to ban, she knows her history.

"My ancestors have been singing for many centuries."

BELOW THE RADAR IN PAKISTAN

In a grad-studenty Lahore apartment full of books, I meet Sarah Suheil and Kyla Pasha, the editors of a very bold online publication on sex and sexuality in Pakistan called *Chay Magazine*. Though they look the age of my own students, they are junior professors. Sarah and Kyla think sex and sexuality are critical areas for discussion in their country. Whether gay or straight, "nobody talks about it, and it's shrouded with religion and shame," according to Sarah, who teaches business law. "We don't talk about sexual relations between a husband and a wife that are perfectly 'legitimate,'" adds Kyla Pasha. Paradoxically, alternative sexualities are "almost easier to discuss openly because you can say them out loud in order to condemn them," she tells me. Transgender women are very visible in some Pakistani weddings and funerals, Kyla explains, "and their prayer is supposed to be especially efficacious."

Sarah, who says she prefers the term *conservative* or *orthodox* over *fundamentalist*, explains that with all the urgent issues in today's Pakistan, they struggle to find enough time to run *Chay*. She also works on land rights and has been involved in protests against both Talibanization and militarized responses to it. In spite of their numerous commitments, Kyla, a poet who teaches cultural studies, had originally wanted to start a café, perhaps like T2F in Karachi, a literal space for discussion of sexuality. "But, my contention was that we may get blown up or shut down, or both." Instead, they shifted to the idea of a magazine for readers across the sexual spectrum. Their call for submissions to *Chay* describes a hope that "sex and sexuality should enter the public discourse," as a way of combatting "unhappiness in our daily lives" as well as "violence, shame, depression, ill health and general social malaise."[24] Among other topics, they seek contributions on "sex-positivity, virginity and enjoyment."

While simultaneously working on her computer, Kyla tells me that though it is open to straight and gay views, she feels that *Chay Magazine* has "opened up a lot of space in which a lot of queer people voice their feelings and frustrations. It's broken one boundary that way." Recent posts have discussed topics as diverse as reconciling sexual identity and faith, and police brutality against eunuchs. Despite the stigma associated with homosexuality in Pakistan, Suheil and Pasha have found it easier to get writers to express themselves openly about gay themes. In an issue dedicated to religion and sexuality, Junaid Jahangir reminds us that some liberal Muslim leaders such as Imam Daayiee (the first openly gay imam in the United States) have even approved Muslim same-sex unions. "Based on the evolution of Muslim thought," he wonders, ". . . would it be too much to ask . . . thoughtful and rational members of the Muslim clergy to review the case of gays and lesbians based on the principles of compassion and fairness?"[25]

Some of *Chay*'s gay writers argue that they must look beyond faith when it is interpreted to exclude them. Writes MH Tarrar, in a tract equally appropriate to some versions of Christianity, "For my part, I refuse to believe that if I, as a good person, make a concerted effort to treat people fairly . . . and generally live my life with a sense of caring. . . . Well, any religion that would . . . condemn me for trying to find love with someone of my own biological gender, is a faith I'm better off without."[26]

The name of the magazine that allows such voices to be heard— *Chay*—is itself taken from the Urdu letter that stands for a curse related to the female anatomy, a word Sarah and Kyla are trying to reclaim. While the publication is for now online and in English, they are seeking ways to produce a print edition, and an Urdu-language version, but have to carefully consider security and resource implications. "We've had a lot of negative feedback in a spam kind of way," says Kyla.

Reading the comments under their mission statement on *Chay*'s website, one finds a mix of responses. Some are resoundingly support-ive and grateful. "Best of luck. . . . We need more liberal thinking in this country." "Thank you for doing this." Others sermonize and vilify: "You should all follow teachings of Islam and not the path of Shaitan. He will take you to Jahanum." Satan and Hell are common responses of many different kinds of fundamentalists to open expression of sex-uality. "Why don't you people open a brothel. Read Quran . . . then you will know what wrong thing you are doing. Jerks." Another irate commenter replied to that last cyber-pundit: "Why don't you do us all a favour and screw your secret hijabi girlfriend?"

I think about the difficulty of navigating these sorts of tensions when I meet two women in Pakistan whom I will call Shirin and Aafia. Queer Pakistani sexual rights activists, their work is as challenging as their identities might suggest. "That's why we're very below the radar," Aafia explains. They have a "social support group" for what we in the United States would call LGBT people, but it is all "very hush, hush, hush." Most members of their support group are closeted; homosexual sex is technically illegal here as "against the order of nature" and punishable by up to life imprisonment under the Penal Code.[27] Fundamentalists make everything infinitely more dangerous, but they are not alone in their virulent homophobia. In fact, "the hardest thing for people to negotiate is their families," Aafia reminds me. Sitting across from me with her chin-length hair and jeans, Aafia considers herself "completely out." Her family knows. People at her workplace know. However, she thinks about sexual identity in a complex way, and the label *lesbian* sits uneasily with her.

From these two women I learn to be careful of superimposing my understanding of sexuality categories on the context here. The entire question of whether or not LGBT orientation is an *identity* is a signifi-cant one for some queer people in Pakistan, "because they're comfort-able in the little space they've created, where a few people may know and then they can go about the rest of their life pretending to be straight,"

Aafia briefs me. In the current environment, queer Pakistanis with such views fear the consequences of going any further. "They're like, 'Let it stay under wraps. You bring it to people's attention, that will cause backlash.'" Aafia herself does not agree with this view and wants to make sexual identity something she can discuss openly, regardless of the times.

Hence, creating their support group had deep meaning for Aafia, and it allowed her to make critical connections. Looking at Shirin, she says, "Before we started this group, I actually didn't know any queer people at all. The first or second lesbian I met, was it you?"

"I'm not a lesbian," Shirin corrects.

"Whatever, bisexual person," Aafia continues. As is true for people with minority sexual identities in many places, whether small-town USA or Lahore, this solitude had a high cost. "There was a time of absolute depression and isolation. I didn't know anybody so I thought there must not be anybody. Then I met people and I thought we have to get together so nobody feels that isolation."

Does the current security environment in Pakistan make their work harder? "Well it was already hard anyway," avers Aafia. Still, like anyone here, they now live with heightened security risks due to an upswing in jihadist terrorism. "We go about doing whatever, protesting, but anything could happen. You sort of have to close your mind to that risk at some point." Shirin is convinced their work is tougher now. A friend of theirs who started a Pakistan Queer Liberation group on Facebook ("a closed-ish ecosystem") received comments that Islam prohibits such activities. When some of the participants said they were secular, "the responses became violent and vehement," Shirin recounts. "If it got on anybody's radar and they decided they needed to do a jihad of some sort, it wouldn't take much."

In the current environment, Shirin worries not only about the Taliban but also about fundamentalist lone wolves, "some righteously indignant observant-in-his-own-head, very faithful Muslim person who says, 'Who are these bad women?' That's all it would take." Extremism has magnified the risk of such responses, she suggests, by putting forward "the legitimacy of violence as an honorable thing." In light of that putatively "honorable" violence, almost no one faces more risk from fundamentalists than LGBT/queer people of Muslim heritage, which is why several I meet request anonymity. For her part, Shirin regrets having to ask me not to use her real name. Still, she remains optimistic.

"Someday, I will not need to ask people to do this—*Inshallah*."

THE LAST STRONGHOLD OF MEN OVER WOMEN

Thoraya Obaid was the first Saudi to head a UN agency. In 2001, she became executive director of the UN Population Fund, also known as the UNFPA, remaining in this job until 2010. UNFPA is not just any agency, but one that has become a lightning rod because it works on family planning and reproductive health. In 2001, the United States, under the Christian fundamentalist–influenced leadership of George W. Bush, began withholding money from the organization, falsely accusing it of promoting forced abortion in China.[28] Thoraya has dealt with all kinds of extremism.

Her home country of Saudi Arabia is one of the most closed societies in the world—my words, not hers. Women still cannot drive, though in recent protests they have gone out and done so anyway. Apparently confused as to what century we are in, the *Mutaween* (religious police) harass women in public for wearing nail polish or being insufficiently covered, though in May 2012 one brave woman challenged such a medieval posse at the Hayat Mall in Riyadh, tweeting footage of their harassment to the world.[29] Ten years earlier, when girls in Mecca tried to escape their burning school, the *Mutaween* blocked their exit because they were not properly covered.[30] Fifteen died. The situation of foreign workers—often from the Philippines or Sri Lanka—is similarly terrible. One case that has really stayed with me from my time at Amnesty International was the flogging of a group of Filipino migrant workers who had been arrested at a party and accused of "homosexual behavior."[31] They were given fifty lashes a week for four weeks, then deported.

This is among the worst conceivable interpretations of Islam, yet the United States government has long unfathomably referred to its close ally Saudi Arabia as "moderate." All along my journey, progressive women of Muslim heritage have complained bitterly about the role of the kingdom and also about the way the United States has shielded and supported it. In Pakistan, Nighat Khan underscored the irony of the right-wing battle against Sharia in the United States while the U.S. government buttresses its Saudi counterpart. "They're the supporters of the biggest Sharia State in the world." Iranian Chahla Chafiq thinks Saudi Arabia represents an "Islam of the rich," and she reflects that "Western powers do not speak about Saudi Arabia even if they stone people." In fact, when Saudi Arabia was hauled before the UN Commission on Human Rights in 1998, after Amnesty International filed a complaint against it for practices like amputation and flogging, the United States said nothing. As the legal adviser who had worked on the complaint, I was horrified when it was reportedly disposed of in an hour behind closed doors.[32]

As a Saudi of a certain age, Thoraya Obaid sees herself as holding moderate views. However, taken in her own context, her stance is positively progressive. I speak with her in Jeddah via Skype. At sixty-seven, she feels she was spared the worst of fundamentalism personally, growing up "during that period in the Middle East when it was liberal." King Faisal reigned then in Saudi Arabia, and though he was a staunchly conservative anti-Communist who promoted pan-Islamism, even he supported the education of women, thanks to the influence of his fourth wife. Thoraya became the test case for this policy. The first Saudi woman given a government scholarship, she went to study at Mills College in Oakland, California, in 1966. "I was the only one because there was this feeling that if Saudi women went to America, they will marry Americans and 'get corrupted.'" It was not easy. She found herself in the heart of the American sixties when "as a 17-year-old girl I had all that pressure of paving the way for Saudi girls to come to America." Her first day at Mills, she took the bus to downtown Oakland and rambled until her feet hurt. It was the first time she had ever walked outside alone. This trailblazer would go on to earn a doctorate from Wayne State University.

When she graduated, her father attended the ceremony, standing out in the crowd in his long white gown and traditional headdress. On their trip home, he became preoccupied, finally telling her he was not sure how they should emerge from the plane when landing in Jeddah. When the plane parked, a huge delegation of men, including Thoraya's brothers, waited for her on the tarmac. Her father held her hand. As Thoraya herself remembered in a 2002 speech,

> we walked down the stairs, my face uncovered for the very first time—an act against the traditions of that time; my father held my hand firmly in his left hand, and the Mills Bachelor's diploma in his right—and waved it high up in the air. I never covered my face again; because my father sent a clear and loud message to the society—education was my honour as well as his. [33]

That was possible in Saudi Arabia then. Thoraya thinks that things began to change with the Iranian revolution. Afterward, Saudi fundamentalists multiplied. They became "part of the government system, mainstream in a sense." They had "their own funding, weapons, prisons, interrogation places." After the 1991 Gulf War, the Wahhabist trend "took over the country." Her own father, a religious man educated in Medina under Sheikh Sharabi, "one of the progressive Sheikhs at that time," did not recognize this new Islam. At eighty, he used to return from praying at the mosque and say that they had been told to spread their legs when standing so they touched the worshipper next to them, to prevent the *shaitan* (devil) from coming in between them, something that had never been done before. He would ask Thoraya, "Were we not Muslims before?

"Is this the new Islam that I don't belong to?"

Everywhere I went, from Algeria to the Somali diaspora, people had pointed the finger at Saudi Arabia and at Saudi funding as a key factor in the rise of fundamentalism and Wahhabism throughout the Middle East, North Africa, and beyond.[34] Thoraya acknowledged that money had been widely disbursed "quote unquote for development." The building of health centers abroad with Saudi money had been accompanied by "messaging and proselytizing. It is amazing to see the amount of money invested." The precise amount is difficult to quantify, though it is in the billions of dollars.[35] She also recognizes with concern the large numbers of Saudi youth who have joined "fundamentalist violent groups," what they call "the Saudi Afghans."

In her home country, the fundamentalist message is also spread by public institutions. Thoraya recounts a visit with a group of young women in Al Qassim Province, the country's most conservative, "where the Wahhabis come from." The girls told her that they have "to learn how to live double"—learn one thing at school and live something else at home with friends. At school they are told, "It's *haram* to wear jeans, *haram* to dance, *haram* to hear music, *haram* to go out, *haram* to do all kinds of things." At home, their mothers let them wear jeans, dance with their friends, listen to music, and go out to coffee shops. One girl asks of Thoraya politely, "Now tell me, Auntie, who's lying to me? My mom, or my school?"

Thoraya Obaid looks to a range of factors to explain the rise of fundamentalism fueling the prohibitions that confused the young residents of Al Qassim. "Wars, the position of America, the Palestine/Israeli conflict, the Iranian revolution, the rapid changes that are taking place, the young generation who want quick change Western style, taking only the superficialities of the West. It just makes people feel that they are lost and the only thing that remains for them is religion."

Known for an approach characterized by "cultural sensitivity" in the United Nations, Thoraya advocates supporting "moderate voices of Islam," and reinterpretation of a "feminist Islam." At the helm of UNFPA, she was known for being a centrist in her views. She says she seeks "words that would allow people coming together rather than fighting each other." However, she also struggled behind the scenes for women's rights, finally losing her temper with the Egyptian ambassador, she remembers, when his country and others were pushing back on issues of reproductive rights. "It's called the Cairo Plan," she reminded this diplomat, referencing the program adopted by the UN International Conference on Population and Development held in the Egyptian capital in 1994 and agreed to by his government at the time. The document guarantees women the right to control their own fertility. "What is the story?" she demanded of the diplomat. "Were you immoral in 1994 and now you're becoming more religious?" In the face of such regression, the former UNFPA chief remains convinced that "at the centre of human progress is the quest for human dignity. . . ."[36]

Thoraya Obaid—Saudi, PhD holder, mother, Muslim, retired UN director—notes that fundamentalisms across the spectrum are always "related to women," especially to women's reproductive rights and sexuality. "This is where they feel their power. Women went out to work, they couldn't control it. It is the last stronghold of men over women."

MY FATHER WAS A FEMINIST

When I ask Shirin Ebadi if she thinks it important for women human rights defenders from different Muslim majority countries to work together against fundamentalism, she says, "Of course." Then she quickly turns my query back on me.

"Why do you only ask about women? Men can help as well."

Many men in Muslim majority populations are involved in the subjugation of women and girls, in violence against women, and in propagating the fundamentalist notion that these things are divinely sanctioned. However, many other men in the same countries are also significant contributors to the battle for women's equality and are against fundamentalist gender codes. They must not be forgotten. For example, a Nigerien journalist I met in 2010, Albert Chaibou, who runs a civil society advocacy and media group called Alternative, had just organized a congress of women from across his country to discuss promoting women's rights through new laws. Writing about this in his organization's newspaper, he asks, "Can Niger construct a real democracy and sustainable development while marginalizing half of its population? Certainly not."[37]

My own father's final book, published in Algiers at the end of the dark decade, was a historical and anthropological study called *Algerian Women: Victims of a Neopatriarchal Society*.[38] The front cover features the Arabic calligraphy rendering of a quote from Rumi, the renowned thirteenth-century (male) Sufi poet.

"Woman is a ray of divine light."

Some of Mahfoud Bennoune's male friends would infuriate him by telling him, "I bought your book for my wife." My father would reply, "I didn't write the book for your wife—I wrote it for you." He believed that women's human rights should also be a vital cause for men.

In 1999, my father dedicated his last book to his older sister Zohra, who seems to have died at the hands of someone in her husband's family under circumstances that were never clear, and for which there was never any accounting. I do not think my father ever got over this, especially because it was shrouded in secrecy. In one of his last revolutionary acts, Mahfoud Bennoune spelled out on the title page that his book was for "my sister Zohra, victim of Berber-Arab-Islamic traditions." When I am in Sidi Moussa, Algeria, in 2010, a young psychologist working with female survivors of fundamentalist violence tells me she has read the book and has not forgotten those words.

The reality of male misogyny in Muslim majority contexts cannot be denied. Given the depth of women's subordination, Mona Eltahawy was right to ask of Arab men and Arab societies, "Why do they hate us?"[39] Fundamentalism has enflamed that hatred and formed it into a creed. But generalizations are also not the end of the story. I will never forget an Egyptian taxi driver who picked me up in Tahrir Square in spring 2011. He was celebrating riotously over the news he had just received on his cellphone that his wife had given birth to a daughter. He was so happy about it that he would not let me pay my fare.

Though he struggled with the baggage of patriarchy, my father over the years became a feminist. Nothing was more important to him than my education and my freedom. He told me that during his years in French prison during the War of Independence, he first began to think critically about the situation of women in Algeria, because his deprivation of liberty came to resemble theirs.

Many of the women's rights advocates I met also talked about the significant role played in their lives by a progressive father. Maternal contributions have been crucial as well, but perhaps the positive influence of a paterfamilias is less expected. These men are the opposite of the fundamentalists. Thoraya Obaid tells me she wants to publish an entire book about the way in which women in countries like hers were influenced by liberal patriarchs. "Had it not been for their fathers in a strict patriarchal society, they would never have had the opportunities they had." In her own case, her Saudi father dreamed about her having opportunities equal to those of her brothers. As "a devout Muslim, [he] interpreted the command in the first surah of the Koran as instructions to all Muslims—men and women." That first revealed word is *read*.[40]

Haja Salamatou Traoré, a devout feminist midwife who fights in

Niger for decent treatment of women with obstetric fistula, told me, "My father was a real Muslim and built many mosques, but he let his daughters go to school and choose their own husbands. This is real belief."

When I ask Dr. Fatou Sow how she became a feminist, her answer is startling yet familiar. "I had a father who was in a certain way a feminist." This accounted in part for who she has become. "My father always said, 'I want you to go far in your studies because I want you to have a good job, and to be able to take care of yourself.'"

"The first time I heard that a woman should be independent was from my father."

Codou Bop, cofounder with Fatou of GREFELS—the Research Group on Women and the Law in Senegal—tells me she too became a feminist "because of my father." He defied gendered roles. "He took care of us. He said, 'I am raising children who are autonomous.'" Codou Bop's Muslim father died as he lived, making no distinctions among his children. "When he died, he left equal shares to his daughters and his sons. And my father learned the entire Qur'an before going to European school." Part of why fundamentalism is so shocking to these women's rights defenders is that it represents a rejection of the open Islams of their fathers. While some other Muslim patriarchs restrict and abuse their daughters, these progressive fathers, who nurture and defend, who stand against fundamentalism at home, must not be forgotten.

THE LIBERAL MULLAH OF HERAT

In his tight turban and long white beard, Syed Ahmad Hosaini does not look anything like what some might think a women's rights advocate should look like. I meet him in Herat at a market full of women artisans that has been built by the Italian Provincial Reconstruction Team. He has just concluded a women's rights workshop for a hundred participants that was part of an Afghan government campaign. As I arrive, the stately mullah descends the stairs surrounded by women asking him questions. After I introduce myself, we go back up to the meeting room to talk about his work. Despite the weight of our subject matter, the scene is comical, for there is a violent hot wind blowing through the window, and as I sit with the mullah, it nearly carries away the head-scarf I have to wear here time and again, leaving chunks of my curls blowing in the breeze. Syed Hosaini looks as though he could care less.

He tells me how happy he was to take part in the workshop, and to tell women that "Islam did not say that your rights should be violated." If their husbands and brothers "break their rights," they are not respecting Islam. During the workshop, he stresses the importance of women's consent to marriage. "If she doesn't want to marry a man, she should say, 'I don't want to marry him.' If she wants him, she should say, 'I like him.' " The women asked him to come back for a second day, but he could not, for his work continues elsewhere.

He is an unlikely women's rights advocate, a former mujahid whose idea of women's equality, admittedly, might not be exactly the same as mine. However, Syed Hosaini's experience working with Afghan refugee families in Iran brought him to rights advocacy "because he found out how many problems people are facing." Bearing the honorific title *Syed*, which refers to descendants of the Prophet Muhammad, he is ready to dive in to the most charged debates in Afghan society. "We cannot leave the fundamentalists alone to do their work." This soft-spoken, bearded man thinks it is important to invite them, talk to them, even try to raise their awareness through meetings, teaching them about "moderate Islam."

Syed Hosaini undertakes such endeavors daily. He has given trainings about women's rights and human rights to mullahs across the fifteen districts of Herat Province. Very specific about the topics he covers—which include "gender-based violence," "gender inequality," "child rights"—he says without ambiguity: "Women's rights and men's rights are equal in Islam." The liberal mullah has also taught this in meetings and roundtables, on TV and radio. He is well known in the region for this work—too well known. "If I go outside the city, my security is not assured." He has received numerous "warnings." Undeterred, he says, "If I am not here to raise the awareness of people, who will do that?"

He faces a very difficult security environment as a "women's rights activist," a title Syed Hosaini proudly applies to himself. When I offer him a ride, since he has stayed on to talk to me and evening is coming, he thinks of my safety first and has the driver take me back to the hotel—which is out of the way—before taking him home.

In the Nazary Hotel car, he tells me about an old spoonmaker he once visited. Syed Ahmad Hosaini told the spoonmaker he appreciated his work, which served society. Mr. Hosaini says he himself has been working for forty years and nobody has appreciated his work or told him that it was good. He is glad that I have come to talk to him, as he did with the spoonmaker. In the Herati dusk, I think about how many people like the liberal mullah—men and women—are out there doing the quiet, unappreciated work against extremism and for women's equality. I wish I could talk to them all.

TALKING ABOUT GAZA OPENS MANY WOUNDS

Naila Ayesh was tortured in Israel's notorious Moscobiya Detention Center in East Jerusalem during the first Palestinian Uprising, and she miscarried as a result. When I meet her in 2010, she has not settled for an easier life but is still an activist. With short, dark hair and wearing a pink sweater, she smokes and drinks tea and tells me about her current work running the Gaza Women's Affairs Center. Though she originally came from the West Bank, and now lives there, she travels back and forth to Gaza, where she previously resided, for her work with the center. "Every time I go to Gaza, I still feel how warm and giving people are despite the problems they face." Still, living conditions are beyond terrible, such that even "talking about Gaza, it opens many wounds." Those wounds are reopened by Israel's November 2012 assault on Gaza that misses the offices of the Women's Affairs Center but reportedly kills 103 civilians and wounds a thousand.[41]

Even when I am in the Middle East in 2010, Gazans, who live in a tiny strip of land between the Mediterranean and Israel, are already caught between the devil of Israel's siege and the deep blue sea of Muslim fundamentalism. I had been to the Gaza Strip in 1987 and had seen the misery even then in hot, overcrowded refugee camps. I want to return to Gaza but do not have the media credentials necessary to circumvent the Israeli military siege. However, my memories from 1987—no substitute for a return visit—are still vivid. In Jabalia Refugee Camp, now with a population of 110,000 and regularly bombed over the years by Israeli forces, I remember a lake of sewage that stood open for children to walk or fall in. I can only imagine what it must be like now, after being hit repeatedly by Israeli military attacks—including one that killed ten members of a single family.

Young people, who make up 60 percent of the Gaza population, continue to live in misery. "There are no resources for youth to live their youthfulness," says Naila in 2010. No jobs, no fun activities. "The only thing available for them as kids is the mosque. That's where the brainwashing starts." In that hothouse environment, "religion becomes linked in their minds with resistance." Espousing fundamentalist Islam becomes synonymous with opposing the policies of the Israeli government toward Gaza, when instead it simply contributes to the misery of other Gazans. This can only become worse after each Israeli bombardment.

In such a climate, the work of the Gaza Women's Affairs Center is arduous. It carries out research and advocacy on local women's issues and documents them through videography. Sitting in the Ramallah sunshine in December 2010, Naila tells me of their most recent inquiry into women and inheritance, on the basis of which they are producing a manual that explains to women how to claim their due. The center also has a small job-training program that serves fifty women a year. "But, we cannot of course create jobs in the thousands like Hamas is doing."

Publishing the only Gazan women's magazine, called *Al Ghaida*, has gotten the center into some trouble, especially when it pictured a bareheaded woman journalist who had authored one of the articles. Hamas confiscated many copies of that issue. The center is regularly "accused of bringing Western ideas and culture into the community," and its staff have even come under attack from Hamas's Ministry for Women's Affairs. Nevertheless, they manage to maintain a good reputation among local people, Naila feels, because they aim to meet women's needs and avoid imposing their views.

What can it possibly be like to do this work between the hammer and the anvil? "You see the depression, you see the sadness. But we cannot leave it that way." Naila and her colleagues are determined to continue their work as long as Hamas does not attempt to take over the center's board. Still, when she looks ahead, Naila is filled with trepidation: "We see the darkness of the future. It will take long years before we see light at the end of the tunnel." While previous generations had been shaped by Israeli occupation, now there are other problems as well. "It's very dangerous, this coming generation," because it is "growing up under another layer of repression from Hamas."

The situation of women is "really going backward." In recent years, it is as if Gazan women's rights advocates have had to start their work over again from the beginning. "That's the tiring part." Polygamy is on the rise and fundamentalists have brought group weddings to Gaza—a hundred grooms marrying a hundred wives all at once with the Hamas government's support.[42] Hamas's announcement that it would give money—anywhere from $200 to $3,000—to any man who married a war widow from Israel's 2008 attack on Gaza has become an impetus for both polygamy and potentially abusive relationships. "They don't consider the problems that erupt the day after the marriage if she has children, or he has a previous wife," Naila points out. "Basically, the widows are left with a room in a family house."

This is all part of the Hamas social agenda. The group's violent acts against Israelis have gained it the most press; its coercion of Palestinians is much less discussed. Islamic clothing is required of girls in public schools, even for the dwindling numbers of Christian pupils. This is accomplished, Naila recounts, not through written Hamas orders but rather through rumors and fearmongering. While the organization might "deny that it had given such an order, it is enough that Hamas would give a small indication here or there. Families would be afraid. The school administration would be afraid. The order is implemented accordingly." These fundamentalist tactics are repeated in many places.

Women cannot have their hair cut by a male hairdresser, or smoke an *argeela* (a water pipe) in public in Gaza. In fact, restaurants have been closed because women smoked them there. A UN-sponsored summer camp, where boys and girls participated in gender-segregated activities like swimming and singing, was torched.[43] Women and couples are harassed, beaten, and interrogated on the beach—the only place to go in much of Gaza. "They didn't allow them to defend themselves while they were sitting there," Naila reports. "Or to love. Even to love." Not many victims of this social persecution will speak out. "There are tons of cases that people are afraid to talk about."

Then there is Asma Al-Ghoul, who is entirely unafraid to talk, Naila tells me. Al-Ghoul is a secular feminist and journalist from the Gaza border town of Rafah who became famous after she stopped wearing a headscarf in 2006.[44] While Al-Ghoul's immediate family supported her choice, she had two very public run-ins with the Hamas police. Back in 2009, she had taken a stroll on a beach with a group of men and women to visit another friend at his home. Asma Al-Ghoul and the others were stopped and questioned by Hamas's "moral police," who tried, according to press reports, to force them to sign a form saying they would not repeat such "inappropriate interactions." In 2010, while fasting during Ramadan, Al-Ghoul cycled up the Gaza coastline to challenge the Hamas ban on women riding bikes. She has even confessed in print to smuggling a copy of Salman Rushdie's *Midnight's Children* into Gaza.

In Naila Ayesh's opinion, if more people like Asma spoke out, change could come. She also thinks an overall improvement in Gaza's miserable living conditions could make a significant difference in attitudes, "because basically nowadays people cannot even get their basic needs met." Her plea to readers in the United States is "that America will one time take a decision in favor of the Palestinians who have a just cause." A real political settlement is essential, she knows, to moving forward on her issues.

Naila was hopeful that Hamas's popularity in Gaza was waning in 2010.[45] "Many supporters of Hamas nowadays after they have practiced Hamas on the ground, they don't trust them anymore." Unfortunately, some of them simply move further to the right and now support Salafist groups. Naila thinks that many who voted for Hamas thought it was a way to oppose Israel's policy toward Gaza, but they have found instead that Hamas is simply consolidating its own power. She witnessed a December 11, 2010, demonstration in Gaza City organized by the Popular Front for the Liberation of Palestine, which brought together an array of anti-Hamas, leftist, and secular forces.[46] As many as 100,000 attended. "It was an opportunity to express that people are not with Hamas." However, reports suggest Hamas's popularity to be on the rise again after Israel's "Operation Pillar of Defense" in November 2012.

In fact, "Hamas has been the perfect police for the Israelis in Gaza," Gaza-born researcher Hadeel Qazzaz tells me. Terry Boullata gave me a concrete example of this policing function as she recalled that when women like her demonstrated during the first Palestinian Uprising against Israeli occupation back in 1988, Hamas supporters would sometimes attack them, even before Israeli soldiers got there. "They thought that we are infidel ladies," Terry explains, "who are in a vulgar way exposing ourselves, so that was a shame on us. We better put on veils before we go to demonstrate."

Such a bleak political landscape leaves women like Naila Ayesh with very little space in which to work. She and her family had to leave the Gaza Strip in 2008. Since then, when she is in Gaza, she always takes a taxi and no longer walks from place to place. But there is one thing she swears she will never do: cover her head. If forced to do so, Naila Ayesh will stop going to Gaza altogether.

BURN YOUR BURQA!

In Sudan, women can receive forty lashes for not wearing what officials call Islamic dress, Fahima Hashim, who works with the Salmmah Women's Resource Center in Khartoum, tells me via Skype. "Islamic dress has to be defined by the individual security person who catches you." Women cannot make legal arguments against it, or advance their own opinion about appropriate covering. "That has been left to people who had never seen a woman in a trouser, or a woman in a skirt that is just beneath the knee." In younger days, at university, Fahima and her colleague Zaynab Elsawi could wear what they wanted to. She wonders why, in a country like Sudan, where "we have a lot of problems with education, health, poverty," the government now wastes time on this issue. "There are many more important things that the government should be doing than who is wearing what." Still, many thousands of women have been lashed for this offense, Zaynab says.

These Sudanese women have developed systems for dealing with a situation in which allegedly religious garb is reduced to a sign of acquiescence to state coercion. "I remember in the mid-1990s when we used to have our scarves in our bag. We called it 'just in case.'" She narrates an experience that explains why. "I was caught because I wasn't covering my head. This guy took me to the court. By the time we reached there, I took out my scarf and I put it on my head. He wanted to scream at me in front of the security guard, saying, 'She's not covering her head.' Then, he turned and found me covering my head. I said, 'Well, I always wear it. You didn't see?'"

"It's not me," she concedes, "but you have to do it."

In one of the few pictures I have of my Algerian grandmother, a peasant woman, she wears a tiny scarf that barely covers a handful of her hair, a knee-length skirt, and short sleeves. This was back in the 1970s. The trajectory of the twentieth century had been away from veiling. A Lebanese friend who attended Cairo University tells me that in the fifties and sixties there wasn't a single veiled woman there. When I arrive at Cairo University in March 2011, a significant majority have their heads covered, and much else as well.

The single most important fact in the debate about veiling is that *no specific garment for women is required by Islam.*[47] To argue otherwise is to make one's own human, nondivine interpretation. A bra and panties can cover what the Qur'an calls your "unseen parts." As the journalist Leila Boucli wrote in a special issue on the veil in the review published by the Algiers-based Center for Information on the Rights of Children and Women, "The Islamists try to say this is a settled question by posing the veil as a commandment of Islam, like praying or fasting [during Ramadan]."[48] It is not. As Soheib Bencheikh, the former mufti of Marseille, reminded me, "The veil is *not* one of the five pillars of Islam." However, the fundamentalists try to block such arguments, Boucli notes, in the very way they frame the topic. "All debate . . . becomes apostasy."

There is a spectrum of so-called modest garments—simple headscarves, hijabs that provide more coverage of the neck and shoulders (and sometimes of the chest and outer rim of the face), jilbabs that cover the whole body in a loose robe sometimes accompanied by gloves and even boots, niqabs that cover everything but the eyes, and finally the burqa—a sort of ghost costume that hides even these. Various reasons are cited for wearing this gear, including everything from coercion to religious pride in diasporas. But covering nowadays ultimately means putting women in a uniform advanced by Muslim fundamentalists. That uniform is often imposed by threats, violence, indoctrination, stigma, or even blaming insufficiently covered women for natural disasters, which is an increasingly popular tactic from Aceh to Algeria. Sometimes demands for modesty escalate from the headscarf to the jilbab and so on. What will women do when even the burqa is not deemed modest enough? That is where stoning and other literal methods of erasure come in, when garments are not enough to make you disappear.

Sometimes women say they choose such attire. Everyone assumes that is the end of the story. Nevertheless, that does not change the meaning of covering, and such "choices" increasingly happen in contexts infused with fundamentalist teachings about purity and the shamefulness of women's bodies. Muslim women did not wake up one morning and say, "I live in a hot climate, let me shroud myself as much as possible." While Leila Boucli recognizes that there may be a variety of individual motivations for a woman to wear a veil, at the end of the day, the practice "is doubly discriminatory: it separates women from men, and it separates 'honest' women from the rest." Boucli's concern is entirely borne out by a fatwa from the all-male European Council on Fatwa and Research. (This Muslim Brotherhood–linked foundation, based in Dublin and headed by Yusuf al-Qaradawi, seeks to unify Muslim jurisprudence in Europe.) The council's fatwa calls on all Muslim women in Europe to veil: "Thus by her dress, she presents herself as a serious and honest woman who is neither a seductress nor a temptress."[49] In a single fatwa, the rest of us have become unveiled whores.

In parts of the world there is an onward march to cover women's bodies and elsewhere to uncover them—with all this often justified in the name of women making a choice. To me, this justification of "choice" misses the point about the overwhelming politics of the presentation of the female form. If one is given a menu with two options—say, covering up and being a good Muslim or not covering and being a loose woman or a bad Muslim—and one chooses to be good rather than bad, certainly that is a "choice." But is it actually a reflection of personal preference? The real question is, How did we end up with the limited menu?

In every single place I visited or heard about, from Fiji to France, from Toronto to Tunis, I was told of steadily increasing pressure on women in recent decades to cover more of themselves. This has been a process of radical change, not of the preservation of tradition. The assumption made too often in the debate in the West about this is that protecting the veil is protecting some sort of cultural status quo, when in most contexts the veil itself, and the new more restrictive veils in particular, are themselves an assault on the preexisting cultural status quo.

Many of the garments in the veil category are not at all indigenous to the locales where they are being imposed or "chosen." For example, women in Niger traditionally wear boubous in a stunning Crayola array of colors, with accompanying headdresses that have nothing to do with niqabs or hijabs advocated by fundamentalists. Madame Fatimata Mounkaïla, a professor of literature and NGO activist I meet in Niamey, resplendent in her pink boubou, exclaims: "We are not Saudi and we do not want to dress like them." Some women do now wear hijabs in Niamey, an entirely foreign mode of dress here. And Mme. Mounkaïla's retort?

"You do not have to wear the burqa or question the rights of others to be a Muslim."

This drive toward covering is not simply a product of individual women reading the Qur'an and interpreting the text to mean they must cover their bodies to be good Muslims. It is happening, at least in significant part, because of right-wing political movements telling them that this is what Muslim women do. This idea increasingly infuses popular culture and media—whether in the form of Al Jazeera Arabic pressuring its much-watched women anchors to cover up,[50] or the new, terrifying all-niqabi TV station set to broadcast from Cairo,[51] or the multibillion-dollar "Islamic" apparel industry and its "modest" fashion shows.[52]

I remember a flyer I saw posted on a Palestinian bus in East Jerusalem in December 2010. It demonstrated how to cover yourself appropriately if you happened to be female. The "public service announcement" showed a picture of a curvaceous young woman in jeans and hijab, another wearing a skirt and simple headscarf. "This is not hijab," the text in Arabic beneath their photos explained reproachfully. Next to the drawing of a woman wearing a full jilbab and a long scarf hanging over her head and chest all the way down to her elbows, was a green checkmark. This was supposedly the right way to dress. This was not the Palestine I had known since I started traveling there in 1987. From the bus window I saw numerous young women still refusing these dictates, bareheaded or wearing fitted jeans and knee-high boots along with their small headscarves.

Strangely, while many feminists of Muslim heritage have been fighting against the impulse to obscure their female compatriots,[53] some Western feminists have fallen in love with the veil. One of my most surreal academic experiences was sharing a podium with distinguished American historian Joan Scott at Yale Law School. Scott claims the veil is a celebration of female sexuality and that feminists from Muslim majority countries who decry it are hysterical.[54] Algerian feminist lawyer Wassila Tamzali, in an open letter to the French feminist movement, laments views like Scott's and says the veil has had yet another "victory," by dividing feminists and confusing feminist discourse.[55] For example, when a young British blogger named Adele Wilde-Blavatsky dared to write in 2012 that the hijab was discriminatory and rooted in men's desire to control women's sexuality, noting that "Muslim feminists" have spoken out against such garments, she was bizarrely vilified and accused of asserting white privilege in an open letter signed by seventy-seven North America–based feminists.[56] (I wonder whether similar tributes await me.) Today, Fatou Sow, who says that before age fifty she had never seen a veiled woman in her native Senegal, finds herself exasperated by feminists in the West who now defend veiling to her, using the language of rights.

"I say, 'What is this, the freedom to be oppressed?' "

Sadly, "the veiled woman" has now become the trope for all women of Muslim heritage in the West. As Wassila Tamzali raged in her brilliant book *An Angry Woman*, with regard to the disappearance of unveiled feminists from "the countries called Arabo-Islamic" in Western imagery: "We are today . . . invisible to your eyes. We are condemned to solitude."[57] Similarly, Sudanese feminist Zaynab Elsawi, who fights against the veiling imposed in her country, asked me urgently via Skype from Khartoum to make sure that Americans "know that people like us do live, and do work and do exist. We use the minimum space we have to continue our struggle."

I have no problem with individual veiled women whom I know themselves sometimes face discrimination in the West. However, I do find some of the more restrictive garments truly distressing, the obvious negation of the women who wear them, and by extension the negation of other women in the same environment. Not-being-veiled is a condition that is only possible in the presence of veiling.[58] And not-being-veiled has been a life-threatening condition in many circumstances. So I also have no problem with other women (and men) *choosing* to make a harsh critique of the meaning of veiling. This is deemed offensive by some in the liberal/left/human rights camp in the West. Yet, thinking critically about what it means for women to need to conceal themselves seems to me the only way to support women on the ground battling the ever-encroaching fabric erasure of women's bodies.

Here are just some of the critical views I heard along the way.

Tarek Fatah told me in Toronto that the burqa is "the flag of fascism." The Pakistani Canadian founder of the Muslim Canadian Congress argues that his fellow Canadians, steeped in a multiculturalism gone awry, should grasp that "there is no rational argument for anyone with any sense to take up the case that women have the right to mask their faces." For him, this practice is a nonsensical attempt "to get closer to God by hiding."

As a dancer of Shi'a heritage, Karachi native Sheema Kirmani is inherently concerned with physicality. She complains that the hijab is an "unaesthetic thing I don't want to see, a pain to my eyes and emotionally oppressive. The human body is something beautiful, and shouldn't be hidden."

Yanar Mohammed was photographed burning a hijab, in post-Saddam Iraq no less, for a magazine cover seen around the world. Why would she risk doing that when she already faced death threats for her women's rights advocacy? "Hijab to me is something that is forced on my head and it is shameful. It is shameful on the society that forces it on a woman's head." Her mother's generation had fought hard to unveil themselves, now younger generations were, to her dismay, being re-veiled. After writing that Islamists seem to believe that women's skin has radioactive material in it and so must be covered, she was sued for injuring religious feelings.

Nor is Yanar the only person rejecting such forced robing of Iraqi women. An Iraqi trade unionist in a village outside of Baghdad had complained to her that Al Qaeda had come to his town and was distributing the burqa. "The burqa in Iraq is a thing we have not seen before," she clarifies. "It is so weird." The trade unionist was well respected in his village, so people asked him what they should do about this. He replied, "We will not submit. We'll stand against them." They did, and they were able to protect the village for a time. Five months later, however, Al Qaeda killed the trade unionist who opposed the burqa. "Now all the women in that village wear it," Yanar mourns.

She tells me that the Iraqi government had distributed black plastic bags to be used for trash at one point during the Saddam years. The new garments now pushed on Iraqi women resemble Saddam's refuse receptacles. "We didn't know that in 15 years, they are going to be putting us, the women, in those black garbage bags. They don't even leave you space to breathe."

When I go to the Pacific island nation of Fiji, where there has been a Muslim population of South Asian descent since the late nineteenth century, human rights lawyer Imrana Jalal tells me that, concomitant with the rise of fundamentalism, there are increasing numbers of hijabs, niqabs, and burqas even here. In the middle of the Pacific Ocean. This is not at all the tradition of Fijians of South Asian descent, who used to wear shalwar kameezes and saris and cover their heads only to go to mosque. Now, I am told by another Fijian Muslim woman that there are even some efforts to keep women out of some mosques altogether. Fifty-year-old Imrana Jalal concludes that things have changed a lot since she was growing up. Her own father opposed veiling; now, the Muslim schools here require it.

Back in South Asia, in Pakistan, retired Justice Magida Rizvi tells me the niqab shocks her. "I don't recognize it." It came only slowly, a "very subtle shift in dress gradually, until our eyes were open." More and more women put on scarves. Now, the niqab is "everywhere you look." There is a frog-in-hot-water aspect to this. When the heat is turned up slowly, you do not notice until it starts to boil. UN independent expert on culture Farida Shaheed described this with regard to reactions to fundamentalism generally: "Every day there is a little something, every day over a period of a year. Then you realize that your acceptance, your threshold has gone up. You just accept this as a part of life." That is precisely what has happened with covering.

Pakistani feminist academic Nighat Khan says she is "totally ambivalent" about the hijab. Many of her feminist friends think it is a choice. On the other hand, she thinks "it's dreadful, whether in France or in Pakistan." Nighat does not understand why Muslim men do not cover their heads. "If Muslims need to cover their heads, and God is for both, then both should."

Commenting on the Iranian chador, a garment that has traveled far in the years since the Ayatollah replaced the Shah, Iranian women's rights activist Mahnaz Afkhami asserts that it "was a way of saving the purity of the woman, on whose behavior depended the honor of the male members of the family. This was not an approach to gender relations that is in any way conducive to equality." She concedes that the Qur'an asks "modesty" of women, but her interpretation is that *modesty* does not require any particular garment. In her view, if women really choose to be heavily covered, so be it. However, "you certainly can't work in a factory. You can't drive a bus."

In 1970s Iran, the chador was disfavored (though no longer banned, as under the last Shah's father), and women could be seen in short sleeves and short skirts. As of the 1980s, women were uniformed by the Islamic Republic in mandatory chadors or hijabs. During the Iranian revolution, Mahnaz remembers, the Islamists produced children's books depicting chickens without feathers. "They said the woman who doesn't veil is like a naked chicken with no feathers."

As thought-provoking as my exchanges about covering were throughout my travels, the single most memorable discussion I had on the subject of veiling was with Heba Hafiz, a divorcée and women's rights advocate in Egypt. Her father, who was otherwise not strict, had imposed the veil on her. She found herself "living a life, *yani*, full of misery and I always do what others want and not what I want." When her father died, she decided to remove her veil. "My connection with God is my connection with God. I can do better without a veil." Off it came. "I had, of course, a civil war."

Her mother and even her unveiled sister opposed her decision, fearing how she would be judged. It is bad enough not to wear the veil. It is another thing altogether to make the conscious choice to remove it. Heba argued with her mom, "It's my rights. It's not your hair." She said that wearing the veil made her "always sad. I didn't smile at all." Now she is herself again. "It is me, Heba, nowadays." When I met her at Beano's Café in Cairo, she had shiny locks and an irrepressible grin.

"I enjoy being me," she said.

I was taken to see Heba by her friend Doaa Kassem, a young woman who insists that she covers her head by choice. She does so with boldly colored scarves that always match her ensemble. Heba and Doaa seem quite happy together, neither judging the appearance of the other—an ideal example of the potential coalition between covered and uncovered women who "would like to free our identities from political competition," as Yakın Ertürk, the Turkish former UN special rapporteur on violence against women, described it to me. Fundamentalism is a major obstacle. I wonder what will happen to Heba and Doaa in the new Egypt, where, after the election of Muslim Brotherhood President Mohamed Morsi, squads of veiled women enforcers have reportedly taken to the streets to harass their unveiled sisters.[59] Heba's bare head will be unacceptable, as will Doaa's bright scarves.

Will either of these two women be able to enjoy being herself?

CHAPTER FOUR

To Speak Out and Die: Journalists Writing for Their Lives

Algerian newspaper publisher Omar Belhouchet went to the town of Blida on February 11, 1996, to attend the funeral of a reporter who had been assassinated by fundamentalists. Given the danger, he was the only journalist there to mourn with the family. Afterward, as Belhouchet drove back to Tahar Djaout Press House in Algiers, he could see smoke rising near the offices of his paper, *El Watan* (The Nation). The second fundamentalist bomb to hit the headquarters of Algerian journalism in the 1990s had just detonated. Its force manifested the countless fatwas against the press. The scene was apocalyptic.

Belhouchet decided right then that, in honor of those who had died at their desks, he and his surviving colleagues would get the next day's editions out, no matter what. Though it had killed eighteen and wounded fifty-two of their colleagues and neighbors, a booby-trapped Peugeot J5 van could not stop the journalists of Algeria. "Tomorrow," the publisher told his haggard staff, "the newspapers must appear."

As *El Watan* journalist Ghania Oukazi would write, "The shredded bodies of our colleagues and of passersby in Hassiba Street will not allow us to give up."[1] Algerian journalists faced not only fundamentalist terrorism but also intense pressure from the state not to expose its scale. They bucked them both. Omar Belhouchet explained to me: "Some weeks we buried a journalist and then found out another had been imprisoned by the authorities or a newspaper suspended." He himself faced thirty prosecutions between 1993 and 1997 for his paper's reporting about national security matters.[2] On February 11, 1996, the journalists at Press House would defy government and terrorists by getting out the news of the latest fundamentalist attack on their own offices in devastating detail.

It was Ramadan, near dusk. The smoke had barely dissipated over the rubble. Their dead colleagues' families were just learning of the losses. Belhouchet told his journalists to go break their fasts if they were not eating, and to come back as soon as possible if they chose to.

Returning to Tahar Djaout Press House after dark under these conditions was no easy decision, and telling the story almost fifteen years later remains visibly painful for Omar. When he recalls that eighteen of the twenty journalists who returned that night were women, I am again the woman who makes people weep. We sit in silence for a few minutes. Just as Omar would not be defeated by events on that day in 1996, so too he would persist in recounting the story, however many spectres it still conjures up. He tells me that somehow they did get the papers out that night.

Under the banner of *El Watan*, they published a page for each of the other dailies based at Press House, including those whose offices had been utterly destroyed. At the time of the bombing, Belhouchet had already survived a 1993 attempt on his life while driving his children to school, an attack he told me was claimed by an Islamic Salvation Front newspaper in London. He lived in what he had described back then as "semi-clandestinity."[3] Nevertheless, on February 12, 1996, he signed his name to an editorial on the front page of his paper, describing the scene at Press House after the blast. "We had the impression we had survived either an earthquake or an aerial bombardment. . . . The place we had baptized with the name of the first martyr of press freedom in Algeria, Tahar Djaout, is now nothing more than debris. The offices of *Le Soir d'Algérie*, the paper that was hardest hit by this unimaginable aggression, are completely destroyed."[4] *Le Soir* had lost three of its writers. In the special compilation for February 12, 1996, the page devoted to this paper simply bore its name and an eloquent hand-drawn diagonal line across the page.

A journalist at *Le Soir* then, Mohamed Sifaoui left his desk next to the window a few minutes before the attack to walk outside with his editor-in-chief, who wanted to tell him a joke. "A joke saved me," says the man who now documents fundamentalist violence full-time. *Le Soir* columnist Mohamed Dorbane, returning with groceries for his family's Ramadan supper, saw Mohamed Sifaoui leave. "I'll take your place," he said. Dorbane went to work in Sifaoui's spot. A few moments later, Sifaoui recollects, he and his editor heard the explosion, "or I should say, we felt it." They raced back. Sifaoui found Dorbane dead at his desk by the window, hit in the head by shattering glass.

"The one who took my place had taken my place."

The newspaper's surviving team went to the hospital with the wounded and to the morgue to identify the dead. Because he was one of the few staff uninjured, a shell-shocked Sifaoui was dispatched to inform Dorbane's family about his death before they heard the news on television. When he knocked on their door, the writer's eleven-year-old son answered. "I would not wish that moment on anyone," Mohamed Sifaoui says.

It was on such a night that the skeleton crew at Press House fought to get out the papers, no matter what. Though they had been hit hard, the surviving journalists were not cowed. They chronicled the loss of their colleagues. One article told how reporters desperately tried to help rescue workers detect a sign of poetry-loving culture editor Allaoua Aït Mebarek, whom they believed to be buried in the debris. Given its terrible condition, his body—which was already at the morgue—could only be identified hours later. "The news of his death was confirmed for us late in the evening . . .," the article records. "Our souls were battered, but we swallowed our tears so as not to seem defeated."[5]

Being both victims and witnesses that day, the journalists also itemized the destruction in the surrounding working-class neighborhood of Belouizdad: " 'I was preparing *f'tour* when suddenly the ceiling of the kitchen fell on my head,' explains an old woman."[6] As night fell and it began to rain, *El Watan*'s A. L. Chabane observed bewildered residents trying to hang sheets against the cold wind that blew in through shattered windows and punctured walls.

The opinion pieces written in the ruins of Press House that night were defiant; some signed with full names, others with the initials or pseudonyms many were forced to use to protect their families. S.B., oozing sarcasm, insisted that the "'heroism' of the armed groups so touted by the 'moujahidin,' as well as their understanding of 'jihad' and of sacrifice has been verified yet again. . . . These 'defenders of justice' of a bygone era were born and trained not to die in the service of God as they proclaim, but to spread death and to kill life."[7]

That morning, *Le Matin*'s Naïm B had been typing an article entitled "A people facing fundamentalist barbarism," about nine car bombs that had just been set off in the poor Algiers neighborhood of Bab el Oued, when that barbarism struck again near where he sat. Later, he returned to his keyboard and finished the piece, proclaiming on his paper's page in the special issue that, "with every inch of terrain abandoned to fundamentalism and its murderous ideology, fundamentalist terrorism redoubles its ferocity so as to impose its will on society."[8] On that day, the journalists refused to give in to that ideology or its violence. As Omar Belhouchet explained to me, "We were never intimidated by these people. I said, 'We must not be afraid. We will continue our work. They have to kill us all to stop that.'" Even the Armed Islamic Group, which claimed responsibility for the attack, could not kill that many, that fast.[9]

In October 2010, an *El Watan* staffer helps me dig up that legendary edition of February 12, 1996. It was produced as an act of will by journalists who had survived the conflagration, had been trapped under office furniture, had wrenched the bodies of their friends from the rubble, and then (some) had broken their fasts and gotten back to work. It is a testament in black and white to the fact that in Muslim majority countries journalists have long been on the frontlines of documenting the impact of fundamentalist groups, and many have refused to relent, regardless of the peril this brings. "Pen against Kalashnikov. Is there a more unequal struggle?"[10] Ghania Oukazi had asked on that night of "rubble, dust and tears"[11] back in 1996.

"What is certain is that the pen will not stop. . . ."[12]

THE *ANARTISTES* OF PRESS HOUSE

Tahar Djaout, one of the first Algerian intellectuals cut down by assassination in 1993, had expressed the reporter's predicament perfectly: "If you speak out, they will kill you. If you keep silent, they will kill you. So speak out, and die." And he did. The nineties violence made Algeria, according to a 2012 UN report, one of the five deadliest locations for reporters in the last twenty years.[13] A total of a hundred press workers, including sixty journalists, were killed by the fundamentalist armed groups between 1993 and 1997, a terrible history chronicled by *El Watan* scribe Ahmed Ancer in a book appropriately titled *Encre Rouge* (Red Ink).[14]

Algerian journalists themselves, Ancer recounts, came up with the grim term *media corpse* to describe their own dead. This expression captured the motivation of the fundamentalist armed groups who targeted the press in part because it *got* press. But this violence was also, as the UN special rapporteur on extrajudicial executions described the murder of journalists, "the most extreme form of censorship. . . ."[15] The journalists' counter-attack was to survive, to keep writing no matter what. After columnist Saïd Mekbel was killed, the newspaper for which he wrote, *Le Matin*, reprinted his articles over many days "to spite the killers."[16]

I had been to Press House once during the dark decade, back in November 1994, to interview reporters who had to leave their homes under death threat from the fundamentalists and at the same time had their newspaper closed down by the Algerian government. From that day to this, I am always slightly in awe of Algerian journalists—the risks they ran, the truths they tried to tell. They transmitted the news of assassinated women,[17] of popular protest against terrorism,[18] and of government malfeasance.[19]

My first return visit to Press House since those dark days came in October 2010, when I arrived in search of Omar Belhouchet. The offices of his paper remain Spartan, even though *El Watan* is one of Algeria's best Francophone dailies—a sort of North African *New York Times*. Resolutely antifundamentalist, it has also stood up to the government and has been shut down by the authorities five separate times. In the 1990s, it carried reports about Algeria by international human rights groups in full—even if its staff did not always agree entirely with the way these organizations characterized the situation—and ran critical responses to them as well.[20]

El Watan published many of my father's topical writings from the 1990s—many that could have gotten him killed, such as his two-part missive to the Algerian fundamentalist leader who had fled to the United States: "Open letter to Mr. Anouar Haddam (spokesperson of the ex-FIS and the terrorist groups in the United States)," which appeared in September 1995,[21] or the three-part "How Fundamentalism Created a Terrorism Without Precedent," from November 1994.[22]

Given the history, both personal and political, I arrive back at Press House with a sense of nostalgia. In the absence of Omar Belhouchet, who is traveling during my first visit, I am lucky to meet one of his current star writers, Mustapha Benfodil. Despite his slightly graying hair and years of journalistic experience, Benfodil looks like a student. A newsman since 1993, he has written for a number of Algeria's other major French-language dailies, including *Le Soir d'Algérie* and *Liberté*. Back in the 1990s, he became a "war reporter without training" when Algeria and its independent press (only five years old at that point) faced an Islamist onslaught.

Ahmed Ancer had told me about working conditions then: "We couldn't report in the countryside. Within thirty minutes, it could be known that we were there and we could be killed." So journalists often had to rely on using the phone, relaying information from the official press agency, or, as Mustapha Benfodil himself characterized it, "being embedded" with the security forces. With limited possibility for thorough investigations, the young Algerian press had made some mistakes, Benfodil assesses, but also had played a vital role, providing a needed voice against violence when civil society was so limited, and keeping up the national morale. "I am not afraid of the word *engagé*," he affirms.

In 1994, Mustapha was captured and tortured in Boufarik, where he then lived, by people who said they were from the Armed Islamic Group. Preoccupied with what he was reading on the train home from work that night, he was taken by surprise when he arrived at the nearly empty station. He was thrown into a pit and brutalized. The three men who nabbed him assumed he was a student, because he had his nose in a book and carried a backpack. As he was accosted, his press card fell out. He quickly claimed it was a student card. "Otherwise, they would have killed me." His tormentors debated at length whether or not to shoot him, but finally they simply told him not to go back to the university.

Afterward, Benfodil was forced to take refuge in the offices of a left-wing political party in Algiers for some months, and he found himself even more committed to journalism. He survived the February 1996 bombing at Press House because he had been sent on assignment to write about the celebration of Ramadan among the Tuaregs of southern Algeria. Otherwise, he would have been at his desk at *Le Soir*, the paper whose offices were gutted. The assignment editor saved his life.

Despite such experiences, or perhaps because of them, Mustapha is a sort of Algerian Renaissance man—a writer/journalist/novelist/playwright/visual artist/democracy activist. His first novel, *Zarta!*, published in 2000, a very Algerian *Catch-22*, is about a journalist pseudonymed Z.B. who is forcibly conscripted into the military, then held in secret detention by the government, ends up in a mental hospital, and yet is still relentlessly pursued by the fundamentalist terrorists he calls "*bismillahistes*," who even rape his sister. After all this, Z.B. refuses to give up because of "the thousands of people who believed in [his] words."[23]

While journalism remains Mustapha Benfodil's day job, away from his desk he maintains an indefatigable commitment to filling as much of Faizan Peerzada's "dark corner" as he can all by himself. He struggles to get his plays performed in Algeria's official cultural spaces (even while they are staged by prestigious companies in France), partly because he talks frankly about religion. As a result, he has taken to staging *lectures sauvages* (wild readings) in public places, regularly resulting in his arrest.

In October 2009, he cofounded a Facebook-based group called Bezzef ("Too much!" in Algerian dialect), a collective of artists and independent opponents of the government that carries out creative protests. One of the first consisted of an "unauthorized" public reading of the work of Algerian writer Kateb Yacine at the 2009 National Book Fair, where a number of titles had been censored.

The members of Bezzef have referred to themselves as *anartistes*, a marriage of anarchists and artists, a phrase Benfodil first coined in his exhilarating 2007 novel *Archaeology of Chaos (Amorous)*. Mustapha contrasts his *anartistes* colleagues' limited ability to act with that of the fundamentalists, who can hold programs in mosques, who have "divine legitimacy." While Bezzef was not permitted to open an office and is confined to organizing in cyberspace, the fundamentalists "can do what they want." This contradiction is repeated in many locales. Governments that are allegedly battling terrorism hamstring the very circles—journalists, artists, trade unionists—that offer the best riposte to the fundamentalists. These sectors find themselves encircled.

Still, the *anartistes* remain undeterred. A few months after I meet him, Mustapha goes on assignment to Si Mustapha, a town fifty kilometers east of Algiers, in an area infested by the resurgent forces of Al Qaeda in the Islamic Maghreb (AQIM). AQIM consists of remnants of armed groups from the nineties that took out a franchise with Bin Laden in 2006. Thanks to AQIM, there have been repeated terrorist attacks in Si Mustapha, even an assassination of the mayor, as well as intense counterinsurgency operations.

It is in this unlikely location that Mustapha finds a community group called Afak. The group, whose name means "horizons" in Arabic, offers an alternative, "modernist vision," and cultural projects for local people—a place to listen to music, storytelling for children, even chess matches.[24] Afak's president, Rabah Merchichi, tells Benfodil bluntly: "Our goal in creating this association was to block fundamentalism." Despite the importance of these efforts to human rights and security, he struggles to obtain the necessary funding.

I read Benfodil's article about the idealistic activists of Si Mustapha just as I have returned from a Pakistan in the throes of suicide bombings. So I am struck by the picture above his piece that shows a slogan written out front of Afak's vulnerable headquarters: "I love life." According to Mustapha's reporting, the group offers the town's only library, hosts theatre and music groups, and caters to young people. "There is life behind the curtain of terror," he writes.

When, inspired by Mustapha's article, I visit Afak in November 2012, the activist who brings me there insists we can only stay for thirty minutes because this is now "the most dangerous region of Algeria." Behind an unassuming gate, I find boys and girls playing basketball together outside, a gaggle of smiling, bareheaded teenage girls on the Internet inside the well-organized library, and everyone eagerly anticipating a children's play at 6 p.m. that they regret I cannot stay for. At the center, Afak's treasurer, Said Zaoui, a small, welcoming man with a gray mustache, tells me the most important tool for countering fundamentalism is courage. He and his colleagues have it in spades.

One of Afak's most innovative projects that I learn about in Mustapha Benfodil's article is to support a women's honey collective. Its members are trying to work in territory where there is a grave security risk from AQIM, yet they keep bringing in their sweet harvest nonetheless. AQIM gets at least minimal international press notice for its repeated attacks here; the stalwart female beekeepers who brave more than stings get almost none.

Benfodil describes Afak and its apiculturists as "a hive of the spreaders of hope, who embody all the energy of civil society, which is far from having given up despite the persistence of terrorism and the failures of the state. . . ." His words evoke the efforts of so many of those I have met. His words are the only reason I learn about Afak.

YOU CAN'T RIDE A CAMEL, AND DUCK

Six months after I first meet him in Algiers, Mustapha Benfodil's art installation, *Maportaliche/ Ecritures Sauvages (It has no importance/ Wild Writings)*, is censored at the Sharjah Biennial, one of the Arab world's most important art festivals, held in the United Arab Emirates.

Benfodil's installation likely disturbed the Sultan of Sharjah on many fronts, as it included sound recordings from the Arab Spring, and graffiti telling the president of Algeria to "get out," Tunisian style (*dégage*). But what really got him in trouble was the text from his play *Les Borgnes* (One-Eyes People), which appeared on a T-shirt worn by one of the installation's headless mannequins. This passage is called "The Soliloquy of Cherifa":

> *With each breath of the wind*
> *I see a hand lay on my panties and rip my hymen . . .*
> *Vaginal sacrifices for lustful gods*

My nights were haunted by the cries of all those virgins that
   they had
Scratched Molested Maimed Bitten Eaten
RAPED
KILLED
After being blessed
By the penetrating holy word of Allah
The sperm of his Prophets
And the spittle of his apostles . . .
A forest of beards all around
Barbaric Beards
Halal meat
From every bit of my skin crops up a bastard
and every religious desire becomes infamy[25]

Explaining his work, Benfodil conceded that "[S]ome . . . have crit-
icised this text as obscene and blasphemous. Indeed, it may be that [it]
. . . can be interpreted as pornographic." However, he had not made any
of this up.[26] This part of his installation was, in fact, a kind of journalism.
". . . [T]he sequence is a hallucinatory account of a young woman's rape
by fanatic Jihadists, representing the radical Islamism experienced in my
country during the Civil War in the 1990s. The words may be shocking
but that is because nothing is more shocking than rape itself. . . ."[27]

Maportaliche/Ecritures Sauvages was ordered destroyed by the
Sultan of Sharjah. This erasure captures the way in which the large
number of victims of rapes by fundamentalist armed groups in Algeria during the 1990s have been hidden from view despite the efforts of
some Algerian journalists to document them. As the festival's curator
later dissected the response, "The supposedly 'blasphemous' statement
was an excerpt from a testimony recorded, by the artist, of a woman
who had been raped by radical Islamists and was throwing their own
words back at them. . . . Lost in the fray of the 'scandal' and the accu-
sations of blasphemy was that the indignation . . . was actually against
the words of the Salafist rapist. The artist merely made them visible."[28]

Shortly after the destruction of *Maportaliche*, I corresponded with
Mustapha about publicizing what had happened to his work. As I had

done with my father many times over the years, I felt I had to say some-thing about the possible security risks he faced in light of the criticism that the work was blasphemous. He e-mailed back: "Thank you very much for worrying about my security . . . but I am not afraid of these people. I have lived in the heart of terror all my life and these Abuwhat-evers will never separate me from my country, my skin or, even less, my convictions."

Mustapha's grit recalled something Iranian photojournalist Kian Amani had said to me in October 2010, a few weeks after I met Benfo-dil. When I asked Kian why he was letting me use his name, he told me about an Iranian expression that says you can't ride a camel, and duck: "You are tall. You are riding a camel. You are visible. You can't have it both ways. If you want to do something and have an impact, you have to accept the consequences."

WHEN WE DREAMED OF A BULLET IN THE HEAD

In November 2010, after my trip to Niger, I finally manage to meet Salima Tlemcani, one of Algeria's most famous war correspondents from the 1990s, back at Press House in Algiers. I remember reading many of her front-page stories at my father's house in which she documented the litany of abuses by fundamentalist armed groups—bombings, targeted assassinations, kidnappings, rapes. I cannot imagine how many times she must have risked her life to write the story of Algeria's long night.

Forty-something and wearing jeans, she carries the history of her journey deep in her eyes. Salima, too, has just returned from Niger when I meet her. Unlike my relatively secure stint in Niamey, she undertook the more difficult task of investigating Al Qaeda in the Islamic Maghreb in the north of Niger.

When Tlemcani first joined *El Watan* in 1992, she wrote about envi-ronmental issues. As the nineties unfolded, she gave that up for the ter-rorism beat. "It was abnormal that I would write about the environment when scores of people were falling every day." Despite her shift in focus, her perspective on security issues remains shaped by her interest in the environment. She thinks in terms of systems and the bigger picture, as she tells me how she saw it all coming back in the late 1980s. "I lived a daily verbal terrorism, violent sermons about women, against women who do not wear the hijab, who work, who dare to occupy public space, who are not submissive. I saw the threat coming from far away.

"I said to myself, if these people take power maybe three-quarters of the population will die."

For Salima, the fundamentalist terrorism in Algeria in the nineties can be distilled in one awful thought: "The worst thing that can happen to a journalist is to find herself writing about violence in her own country that affects her family, her immediate environment." When this happens, the meaning of one's work transforms; the sense of one's future prospects also. "You arrive at a point where you live with the idea that you will die. Your only worry is to avoid that this death will be the most violent. You dream of dying with a bullet in the head."

When Salima said this, I had a start of recognition. From 1994 to 1997, I had repeatedly urged my father to leave Algeria for his safety, especially after he debated the ex-FIS spokesman Anouar Haddam on the radio in August 1995. When it became clear that he would not leave, I stopped praying my secular prayers to the universe that my father would not be killed. Instead, I began to ask that if he were to face death, it would be very fast—a quick shot to the head, rather than the throat-slitting or mutilation in which the fundamentalist armed groups specialized. It was a relief to hear Salima confess that she had had similar thoughts for herself. Now I understood I had simply been dreaming the dream of the Algerian journalists for my father.

Algerian jihadists justified much of the violence that gave us these terrible dreams, Salima Tlemcani tells me, by misapplying the writing of Ibn Taymiyya—a thirteenth-century Islamic scholar whose work has inspired many Muslim extremists. The awful genius of the fundamentalists was to use religion as the justification for the most sacrilegious behavior. "They always found verses to take out of context to justify what they did. They said in communiqués: 'We will protect the children we kill from growing up and living in an impious society of apostates.'"

"Sometimes," Salima admits, "when I look at old issues of the newspaper from that decade, I say it is not possible we survived such a situation."

THAT'S NOT MY DAUGHTER

At Press House in November 2010, I ask Salima Tlemcani about the widespread rapes perpetrated in the 1990s by members of the fundamentalist armed groups—the ones to which her colleague Mustapha Benfodil's censored artwork had testified. Tlemcani was among those who first broke the story of those assaults. "At the beginning of the nineties, it was not kidnappings, but fathers who 'marry' their daughters to terrorists. They call them, 'mujahideen,' holy warriors. The women are submitted to a situation of sexual slavery. They have no right to say no." This was only the beginning. "In the second phase, people didn't let their daughters marry terrorists, so they kidnapped girls. It was collective rape. When a girl gets pregnant, they kill her." Then there were also rapes at the time of massacres. "They rape on the spot and then they kill, and what awful deaths.

"You could write books and books and you would still never . . ." Tlemcani's voice trails off.

I was in Algeria in 1994 when one of her articles about these atrocities hit the front page. In "Scenes of Horror in Birtouta," she wrote about the "Emir" of a fundamentalist armed group and his men who had invaded the home of a poor family. Their goal was to take the two daughters, students aged fifteen and twenty-one, for what was called *zaouedj el moutaa* or temporary marriage, a rare Shi'a practice previously alien to Algeria. The young women were to become divinely sanctioned sex slaves.[29] Members of the family of Zoulikha and Saïda Boughedou attempted to protect them from such a fate. This enraged the Emir, who dragged Zoulikha and Saïda away by their hair. A few hours later, what remained of their decapitated and mutilated bodies was found nearby on the Algiers–Blida expressway.

Autopsies indicated the Boughedou sisters had been raped. Before they were killed in the name of God, their toenails had been removed. Salima theorized that they had "refused to serve as wives to the Emirs." To write so openly about this was as dangerous as anything a journalist could do. Still, she did not dull her pen in fear: "Their faces, serene in death, must have been twisted by intolerable pain for hours from the torture . . . of collective rape to which they were subjected by barbarians who claim to act in the name of Islam."[30]

As I transcribe Tlemcani's interview later, I think again of the censored "Soliloquy of Cherifa." Why is it that such rapes are not considered blasphemy, but documenting them is? Between 1993 and 1997, five thousand such rapes by the fundamentalist armed groups were reported, Salima Tlemcani explains.[31] In her view, the actual figure is considerably higher.[32]

An experienced journalist, Tlemcani realizes that, at a certain point, statistics are numbing. As she has done in her reporting, she boils it down to one story of rape, to one real "Cherifa," "an adolescent girl of seventeen recovered by the military in a forest, seven months pregnant." The girl was taken to the psychiatric hospital of Blida. When the hospital arranged for her father to come to see her, the daughter was brought in "frail, even half crazy." Salima narrates: "As soon as she sees him, she says, 'Papa.' The man turns his head to the army officer who rescued her, and says,

" 'No, that's not my daughter.' "

The officer was furious. Afraid the father would kill the young woman because she was pregnant, the soldiers separated them. What happened to this "Cherifa" may never be known, her soliloquy never heard. "There are girls who didn't want to go back to the house, who ended up in prostitution, others went crazy," Salima recalls. There is often no option for personal or social or familial survival after this particular kind of nightmare, no matter the will of the victim. "Even if she comes back from far away, her parents will never accept that she says she was raped because it is seen as a harm of which you must never speak." I think then I understand Mustapha Benfodil's use of capital letters in his censored text.

RAPED KILLED

Except for the efforts of a few Algerian feminists and a few journalists, no one has done the work of documenting this part of the atrocities. Not one leading international human rights organization ever produced a single major report on these rapes during the 1990s.[33] NOT ONE.

I ask Salima Tlemcani why the armed groups had used the rape of women as a method of terrorism. It seems contradictory to demand that women be "pure" and then rape them. In Tlemcani's opinion, the armed groups targeted women in this way because of their symbolic role in Algerian society: "If you touch her, you take away everything. She is the source of life, the honor of the family. A raped woman becomes the shame of the entire family, the tribe, the neighborhood." As with terrorism generally, there were concentric circles of victims—primary and secondary. "It is with this violence," Salima says, "that you push others to fit in the mold they prepared for the society."

A SUICIDE BOMBER BREAKS THE FAST IN CHERCHELL

I ask Salima Tlemcani whether the crimes of the fundamentalists in Algeria were an exception. A prominent Arab American academic once tried to tell me this was the case. Salima is irate. "No. It is an example. When I see what is happening in Iraq today. When I saw what happened with the Taliban. How is it that people are not making the parallel? The violence started here when the first Algerians came back from Afghanistan. It was a model they imported from there." She points to African analogues. "Look at what is happening in Somalia, or with Boko Haram in Nigeria. It is the same thing." Within a year of her making this assertion, Boko Haram will blow up the UN headquarters in Abuja, and Al Shabaab will blow up the Ministry of Education and the newly rebuilt National Theatre in Mogadishu.

Salima had walked a gauntlet to document many such attacks in Algeria. Moving from one relative's home to another, she lived on the run, always carrying her underwear and her toiletries case with her so she could be mobile. She traveled with no protection to the sites of massacres, interviewing those who had escaped. Sometimes she was unable even to carry a pen or a notebook, which would give away the fact that she was a journalist, the most hunted of all prey.

The war correspondent's eyes fill with tears only once during our conversation, when she tells me that some members of her family asked her to stay away from them during the nineties because it was too dangerous to be near her. It is an awful thought, that those closest to you are driven by fundamentalist terrorism to want you farther away.

Moving on quickly, she reveals that perhaps the single hardest thing was giving up her name. Salima Tlemcani is not Salima Tlemcani, but X. "In 1995, in a family meeting they obliged me to change my name or give up my profession." I ask if it is all right for me to say that Salima Tlemcani is a pseudonym. She sighs. "Everyone knows it is. Now it is stuck to me and I can't leave it behind."

Sadly, Tlemcani cannot leave the terrorism beat behind either. About nine months after I meet her, Algeria is again beset by fundamentalist violence, now called "residual terrorism." AQIM carried out thirty-two attacks in two months in 2011, killing or wounding as many as two hundred.[34] Salima pens a memorable article for *El Watan* about the worst of these, a strike on the military academy in Cherchell during Ramadan 2011 that killed eighteen, including two civilians who lived nearby.[35] "The day after a double suicide attack aimed at the officers' mess of the Cherchell Military Academy, the local population is still in shock. . . ." One soldier, she reports, was killed with the young son he had brought along to share in the celebration of *Laylat al-Qadr*, marking one of the last nights of Ramadan. In the nearby residential neighborhood, a man who "was barely 40 was struck by an iron bar that pierced his throat. He had just returned home to finish preparations for his impending marriage. He gave up the ghost in the arms of his mother. . . ."

I keep wondering what kind of déjà vu Salima must be having covering this story; she has described this terror before. Salima Tlemcani is unquestionably up to the task of documenting yet another round of Islamist atrocities, as difficult as that may be. When she investigated the activities of AQIM in Niger's northern desert in the fall of 2010, she went disguised as a Tuareg man. She is one of the most liberated and fearless women I have met anywhere. As a result, she is irritated by Western stereotypes. When Salima came to the United States in 2004 to accept a journalism award, her interpreter asked where her scarf was. Her reply was that she had just come from taking her summer vacation in Algeria on the beach in a two-piece bathing suit.

THEY WILL NOT CEASE TO KILL US

Writing about Muslim fundamentalist armed groups is dangerous everywhere, and nowhere more so than in Pakistan. At the end of

2010, the Committee to Protect Journalists named it the year's deadliest country for reporters, an "honor" that had gone to Algeria back in 1996. While Pakistan's fatal year was still ongoing, I meet the outspoken Lahore-based journalist and political analyst Khaled Ahmed at the headquarters of the South Asian Free Media Association, where bomb barriers and police stand out front. Upstairs, towers of books and papers fill Ahmed's small office.

Wearing a classic journalist's vest and sneakers, Khaled has prominent dark circles under his eyes. He is one of my most pessimistic interlocutors. Before I get very far, he tells me that fundamentalism "is the dominant subject of Pakistan." According to Ahmed, "A very Middle Eastern new understanding of Islam, which is very strict," now predominates in the country's 6,761 *madrasas* (religious schools)[36]—"the nodal institution from where the extremist worldview fans out to all corners of the world."[37] Moreover, secularists are undermined, he feels, by Pakistan's constitution, which "favors Sharia."

In this environment, Ahmed tries to continue his work as best he can. He is a consulting editor at the *Friday Times*, Pakistan's oldest independent weekly, and a contributing editor at the *Daily Times*, a secular paper that was owned by the late Salman Taseer (the Punjab governor assassinated for speaking out against blasphemy laws). In his spare time, he authors longer policy articles with such titles as "Islamic Extremism in Pakistan," which demonstrate how "Jihad and the consequent 'weaponisation' of Islam have inflicted permanent damage on civil society and state institutions."[38] He keeps writing such uncomfortable truths, and sometimes appears on television to discuss them. But it is not easy. "They send you a threat, and you know the threat is real, so you muffle yourself."

Several years earlier, Ahmed wrote an article on internal rifts within the militant group Lashkar-e-Taiba (Army of the Righteous), alleged to be close to the Pakistani military and to have been involved in the 2011 Mumbai attacks. After his article appeared, Khaled Ahmed was sued by some Lashkar-e-Taiba members, "righteous" men who had actually talked to him for the story in the first place. "They sent me a legal notice. I could go to the court and defend myself, but then I could not get any lawyers. The lawyers were too scared." Ahmed went to talk to government officials about his situation. They were scared too.

One government official told him his only recourse would be to apologize to the members of Lashkar-e-Taiba. "So I went and apologized, and it was very humiliating." Even his editor had to beg forgiveness of the militants. Later, the Lashkar-e-Taiba leader took a liking to Khaled Ahmed and told him behind closed doors that the Inter-Services Intelligence (ISI), Pakistan's CIA, had asked the militants to make him apologize. Just like so many I met in different contexts, he was caught between state and non-state thugs.

Six months after I met Ahmed, his fellow journalist Saleem Shahzad was horribly beaten to death and dumped in a canal (probably by the ISI, which had been threatening him) after writing scathing articles about jihadi infiltration of the Pakistani military.[39] When I hear this news, I immediately think of Khaled Ahmed, because he talked a lot about links among Al Qaeda, Arab jihadis, and the Pakistani military. "Many army officers are Islamists," he had told me. "They hate America, and that actually undermines their will to fight these people." With such an analysis, he faces threats from all sides.

Lashkar-e-Taiba's taking him to court is just one example of the kind of scrapes into which Ahmed's writing has gotten him. "I've had bigger trouble earlier on with Sipah-e-Sahaba, which is now atomized into many organizations linked to Al Qaeda. There was a time when it was in the coalition government in Punjab, and I was in a newspaper and we wrote something very insulting about the founder of this anti-Shi'a, sectarian organization." Sipah-e-Sahaba, the political party–cum–terrorist group in question, was not amused. "They came to my office and said, 'You come with us.' And I had to go because they would have killed me right there." Khaled was bundled off to a safe house. "People were being tortured, Shi'a youth. I could hear their shrieks. There was this young boy who was their commander, and I knew this could be the end, so I just went down and touched his feet, and said, 'I'm sorry.'" Compared to publicly apologizing to Lashkar-e-Taiba, "that was actually much worse." He made amends to stay alive. As for the juvenile jihadi: "The moment I did that, he was okay." Khaled Ahmed would live to write more articles.

Despite such humiliations, Khaled Ahmed keeps trying to write honestly and openly about fundamentalism and terrorism. Imtiaz Alam, director of the South Asian Free Media Association, described how tough this can be: "It's a very painful struggle. There's an effect on your life and your family." Forty Pakistani journalists have been killed since 9/11.[40] Salima Tlemcani's dreams of avoiding the most violent kind of death are sadly relevant here, too.

Like their Algerian colleagues, Pakistani journalists also have to battle government censorship, especially in Urdu. As a result, they publish mainly in English, were there is more freedom of expression. "So you will find a lot of independence of opinions in terms of reporting on religion in English," Khaled Ahmed clarifies, "but very little in Urdu, which means that most of the people will not know what is happening to Pakistan." This creates a disconnect between some of the best reporters and the broader public.

While I have focused on media as a site of struggle against fundamentalism, Khaled sees this depiction as applying only to a minority of the press. "Media is the source of fundamentalism." Having just completed a review of the Urdu press coverage of Asia Bibi's death sentence for blasphemy, he says, "Every newspaper wants her dead, and not pardoned." Some journalists may disagree, but they "just don't provoke these guys." Many journalists will avoid at all costs crossing their profession's red lines by violating what he dubs "the rule on religion."

According to Ahmed, the dominant Urdu-language narrative accepts the fundamentalist groups and terrorism, and claims "they have become bad because of America. Therefore terrorism is somewhat justified. If you delink yourselves from the Americans, their claim is this terrorism will go down." One hears this in the Western press also, and from Western peace movements.[41] Ahmed dismisses such views. The terrorists already control certain areas of Pakistan, he notes. "They will actually not be interested in rolling back once we delink ourselves from the Americans. I can predict very easily that they will not cease to kill us."

ACCORDING TO RELIGIOUS PRACTICES, YOU SHOULD NOT LIVE ON THIS EARTH

It has been four days since Muqtida Mansoor received his latest e-mail death threat.

Despite his thin, boyish face, Mansoor is perhaps in his fifties. He has a tidy mustache and wears a nonmatching striped shirt and jacket. A columnist for the Urdu-language *Daily Express*, he is also a professor of global economy. The writer/professor describes his newspaper as liberal, Ismaili-owned, and balanced. (Ismailis are a minority group within the Shi'a of Pakistan.) Mansoor positions himself within his paper: "I am writing on the liberal side. Then there is writing on the religious side."

His latest trouble stems from his article entitled "The Fragile State," which gave examples of how religious and political dissidents elsewhere have remained relatively safe. Bertrand Russell freely authored "Why I Am Not a Christian." Noam Chomsky criticizes U.S. foreign policy without being arrested for it. Sartre was "supporting the Algerian movement for liberation." Finally, in the the last paragraph, Muqtida Mansoor made the mistake of mentioning blasphemy, shortly after the conviction of Asia Bibi for this "offense." "I wrote about an illiterate woman who is not aware of blasphemy—how can we think she has done this act knowingly?" He deplored the way "religious parties have stood like an iron wall against any change in . . . the controversial law of General Zia," referring to the law on blasphemy under which Bibi had been charged. Mansoor was equally critical of the way these parties had opposed any mercy for Bibi. "If this attitude continues," he concluded, "then religious minorities in Pakistan will feel insecure, which is not acceptable in a democratic society."[42]

His article came out first thing in the morning on November 29, 2010. By 9:30 a.m., the death warrant had reached his in-box. "I was sitting in my office and when I opened my e-mail, a message having the title of my article as the subject came. It was abusive and filthy and threatening." Though he's a little embarrassed to quote the exact language, he does anyway. "You are a son of a bitch. These people are *Kafiroon*, non-Muslims, and you are supporting such a woman.

"You have no love for your life."

Despite this ominous missive, Mansoor has no misgivings about what he writes. "What I am doing is according to my conscience. I don't have bad feelings about the e-mails and those calls. I believe I will be to my death a secular, liberal person who truly believes in democracy."

His work appears in the Urdu-language press, whose freedom Khaled

Ahmed had indicated to me was greatly circumscribed. Unquestionably, the columnist is frustrated by the limitations. "The major problem is we cannot criticize any religious group. Being a writer, I want to write according to my mind." But he knows where the boundaries are nowadays. "I can criticize the President of the country with abusive language, but I can't criticize any of the religious groups and their heads. Not for their behavior or beliefs." This confirms what Khaled Ahmed called "the rule on religion."

While Muqtida Mansoor has clearly broken this rule, the Karachi columnist does not seem unhinged by the latest threat, even though his city at the time is no easy environment for being accused of supporting the "*Kafiroon*," a slur for non-Muslims. He has lots of relevant experience. Mansoor and many of his like-minded friends have received such threats before, via e-mail and SMS. "I wrote an article on fundamentalism just after 9/11. I criticized the role of the religious groups. My point of view was that maybe America is wrong, but they are also wrong." His piece also discussed the funding of terror groups. "So, I received a call from a religious scholar who said that according to the religious practices and customs, you should not live on this earth."

Terrified, Muqtida Mansoor's wife tried to convince him to stop expounding on such topics in print. "I said, 'No, someone has to come out and face the situation because without that we are not going to change our society.'" He stresses that he avoids insulting language, or engaging in personal attacks. Like columnists everywhere, he simply states his opinion, and he has the temerity to expect his right to his own views be respected. Instead, the rise of fundamentalist madrasas that spew hatred against people like him and ideas like his, "are producing a large number of blind-minded fundamentalist people who think that any person who is contrarian is to be killed. We are at the stake. Anytime we can be killed."

Regardless of the contents of his in-box, Muqtida Mansoor remains optimistic. If the Pakistani government "stops patronizing these groups, they don't have roots in the public." Ordinary Pakistanis do not live fundamentalist lives. "They enjoy visiting the cinema halls. They are religious, they go to the mosque, but they also go to the music programs." As an example, he describes his daughter's father-in-law.

An educated and religious person, he apparently "offers five prayers a day, but sits in front of the TV watching dance shows." Such mingling of pleasure and practice is in stark contrast to the strictures of the fundamentalists. "God be praised, who warned me against the television, it will never enter my house," recited Ali Belhadj, the number-two man in Algeria's Islamic Salvation Front.[43] He feared all the illicit things he might have seen. The ordinary Pakistanis whom Muqtida Mansoor describes have no such qualms, but he thinks "a group of near 5 to 10 percent are politicizing the religion for gaining power."

This writer's determination to pen his columns as his conscience dictates is an important contribution to a gentle struggle against jihadism. When he and Khaled Ahmed and others continue their work despite extremist bullies, those writers of Muslim heritage who have fallen to the fundamentalists, like Tahar Djaout and Saïd Mekbel, like those killed at Press House in February 1996, live on.

ISLAM HELPED ME SURVIVE

After the pleasant warmth of the Karachi winter, the Russian December is biting. But, in the Moscow office of Said Bitsoev, deputy editor of *Novye Izvestia*—an independent newspaper with a history of outspokenness—the hospitality is very warm. Said takes an electric kettle out of a desk drawer to make me tea, and cuts up a cake.

Unlike in Pakistan, where Muslims are the majority and their heritage defines the state, it is much harder to get Muslims to talk openly about fundamentalism in Russia, where they are a sometimes-disfavored minority. During my stay, I get caught in a crush of Russian nationalist youth rioting in the streets, chanting, "Russia for Russians" and denouncing "Caucasians." Here, the term *Caucasians* refers to the predominantly Muslim residents of turbulent republics such as Chechnya, Dagestan, and Ingushetia.

Russian journalist Nadia Azhgikhina warns me that, while "fundamentalism is the worst enemy of any democratic development," I must also understand its particularities in the former Soviet Union. I am determined to try to grasp the specificities of these contexts, rather than fitting them into the paradigms I know from North Africa and South Asia.

Luckily, when I meet Said Bitsoev, who is originally from Chechnya, he is very open to discussing the topic of Muslim fundamentalism, which he says is "very close" to him. Pale and wearing a striped shirt and dark trousers, he looks no different than any Russian on the street. Born in Grozny, a city he says is "difficult to mention" because of the suffering it has known, he studied journalism at Moscow State University. After obtaining his degree, he returned home. There he became first a correspondent, then editor-in-chief of a major newspaper, *Respublica*, from 1982 to 1992, the last decade before the 1991 breakup of the Soviet Union and the tumultuous year afterward as Chechen separatism blossomed.

Around the same time things began to fall apart in Algeria, they deteriorated calamitously in Chechnya. Chechen journalists found themselves caught between the atrocities of the Russian state and the increasingly radical Muslim separatists who battled them. Bitsoev's colleagues were killed and attacked. In 1992, the year Chechnya declared its independence over Russian opposition, Bitsoev fled to Moscow after receiving death threats for writing an article criticizing separatist Chechen leader General Dzhokhar Dudayev. There he began what he calls his "second life," at the age of thirty-five.

"All this time, Islam helped me to survive, to save myself and my family. It was not an obstacle, it was something that really helped me."

Flight did not mean this Muslim journalist stopped writing about what was happening back home. As a war correspondent, he continued to return, despite the protracted fighting between Russian troops sent in to quash independence and Chechen rebels trying to secure it at any cost. This strife would ultimately claim as many as two hundred thousand lives, according to Said, with Russian bombardment flattening Grozny.[44] Nowadays, the wars are technically over, and he is able to go back for more tranquil visits, even vacationing in Chechnya for a month shortly before I meet him in December 2010. Compared to the 1990s, the situation has greatly improved, but life remains hard there. There is "a climate of fear," as Russian journalist and human rights activist Gregory Shvedov describes it. "You expect that a door might open any moment, and Russian soldiers or local enforcement officers will enter your house and do anything they want with you and your family."

I ask Said Bitsoev what he thinks about such reports of the human rights situation in his native province, which is infamous for its 1990s atrocities by Russian soldiers, local authorities, and the armed groups they battled. (One expert suggested in 2005 that "over half of the Chechen population has been affected by death, injury or displacement.")[45] Said gives me an answer reminiscent of Algeria. "Human rights have been violated, but not in the way it is covered in the human rights reports. The truth is somewhere in the middle because there were a lot of radical people who are really bad for Chechnya." There was a fight against those forces. When the radicals were arrested and prosecuted, "They declared it as a violation of human rights."

As in Algeria, even though a formal peace has returned, the "radical movements," as Said calls them, persist. "These groups deny civil education. They deny personal freedom." As in Afghanistan, the extremists tend to have grown up during the wars, and the Islam they claim to purvey is a radical departure from local religious practices. Before the wars, most Chechen Muslims had followed an esoteric, spiritual Sufi Islam in which saints were venerated, in sharp contrast to the harsh dogma of the radicals. In fact, Caucasus expert Svante Cornell argues that the Wahhabi groups were "widely despised by ordinary Chechens."[46] Said tells me the fundamentalists who emerged in the nineties tried to impose new modes of dress—"mostly they demanded women wear Islamist clothes"—and new patterns of violence. "Suicide is a very grave sin in Islam," he says caustically, "but these radicals brought in this idea that you can blow yourself up to celebrate Islam."

The Chechen fundamentalists not only killed and "self-bombed," as my interpreter put it, but also tried to remake the position of women. "Using this flag of Islam they were able to kidnap women." They even tried to impose polygamy. "Progressive women did not want it at all." Much of this continues today. According to a harrowing 2011 Human Rights Watch report, current Chechen president Ramzan Kadyrov's "virtue campaign" has led to a "dramatically deteriorating situation for women's rights."[47] Tellingly, every single witness interviewed for that report was so frightened about reprisals that not a single real name appears.

Kadyrov has argued against female use of cellphones, spoken

repeatedly about the need for Chechen women to cover their hair, and required female civil servants, university professors, and students to veil. "My dream," he told *Newsweek*, "is that all Chechen women should wear headscarves."[48] President Kadyrov has also claimed the inferiority of women and labeled them men's property.[49] Russian authorities have acquiesced to all of this under the system known as "Chechenization."[50] As long as Kadyrov opposes independence, he can do what he likes at home. To consolidate this power, and undercut even more radical Chechen insurgent groups, Kadyrov has campaigned intensively against women's freedom.

In the main, the nontraditional practices Kadyrov promotes first came to Chechnya with the arrival of fundamentalist foreign fighters near the end of the first war in 1995.[51] "Pakistani people appeared in Chechnya declaring they were fighting for jihad," Bitsoev says. As many as several thousand foreign jihadis poured in. Idealists of their own twisted kind, "these people came here thinking they came to protect Islam." Instead, they killed Muslims, undermined local Islams, and gave the Russian authorities an excuse for *zachistki*, vicious "mopping up" operations in Chechen villages. Svante Cornell argues that extremism was "a distinctively alien phenomenon grafted upon the Chechen struggle as a result of the war."[52] The influx of non-Chechen jihadis resulted in what he called "the Afghanisation of Chechnya" and "the spread of Kalashnikov culture." An "Islamic State" was declared in the republic in 1996.

Paradoxically, the war that brought the province to that state started at what Said Bitsoev considered "the best moment for Islam in Chechnya." In the 1990s initially, he said, "There was a lot of freedom." This was a new post-Soviet reality in a region whose population had been deported en masse by Stalin in 1944. Mosques were built and it became possible to write about religion. Ordinary Islam evolves over time, Said believes. "But the radicals are looking back, and they want to put the country back in the dark ages—pray five times a day, wear long clothes, your appearance should be Islamic." This risks holding Chechen Muslims, he thinks, "back from real life."

The friendly Chechen journalist clearly loathed the outside jihadis who magnified this risk, and he deplored what they had done to his homeland. "The foreign fighters brought a lot of fear. I was not able to sleep without a gun under my pillow. There is an assumption in Islam that if your neighbor is afraid of you, you do not have a pass to Paradise. Everybody in Chechnya was afraid of these fighters. That is why I cannot count them as real Muslims."

The foreign fighters are mostly gone now, he tells me, killed by federal troops or Chechens, or "just escaped." But they have left behind a new breed of Chechen "radical-thinking Islamists." These Islamists are, in his view, partially motivated by their dislike of the government and buoyed by copious funding from Arab countries, especially Saudi Arabia, and Islamist networks. After Said's recent vacation in Chechnya, he stayed on for a month "to write about the new life." Social life is entirely altered, for better and for worse. Grozny is being rebuilt, but the radicals have taken advantage of the recent suffering of the population, offering some material support and preying on the uneducated. "This is a real threat." Their point of view to him suggests "a Muslim person is not born for life. He or she is born for death on the way to Paradise."

Especially upset by the fundamentalists' attacks on liberal Muslims, Bitsoev stresses that "the worst thing was they were hunting for those Muslims who were representatives of tolerant Islam, and killed these people. So, now we do not have many progressive Muslim leaders." He gives me the example of Umar Idrissov, an eighty-year-old mufti from Urus-Martan, southwest of Grozny, who was assassinated in June 2000 by a Wahhabi group called Wolves of Islam.[53] Idrissov, he reports, was cut down by the Chechen fundamentalists because "radical people wanted to replace him, to put radical leaders in his place."

Just two days after Said tells me this, Anas Pshikhachev, the mufti of Kabardino-Balkaria, a Russian republic west of Chechnya, is murdered. The mufti was a deeply principled man, according to Gregory Shvedov's media group *Caucasian Knot*, and one who stood up to both the fundamentalists and the authorities. "Wahhabism can bring great harm," the mufti had warned in a local paper.[54] Before his death, he repeatedly received threats, even some made right to his face. "We've decided to kill you. What do you think of it?"[55] He told the authorities that all muftis in the North Caucasus needed protection, a point made terribly clear on December 15, 2010, when Mufti Pshikhachev himself was shot at his front door by two young men.

Such elder statesmen of tolerance in the Caucasus were both respected by their people and ardently opposed to the extremists' agenda, and they paid a price for both. Nevertheless, Said himself attempts to work against the fundamentalists through his writing, and by speaking publicly when he is back in Chechnya.

On the ground, however, things remain difficult for those who do not surrender to the fundamentalist agenda. In 2010, *Caucasian Knot* first broke the story about unveiled women being shot with paintball guns on the streets of Grozny, allegedly by local security personnel.[56] One woman lost her eye. President Ramzan Kadyrov said he did not know who was doing this, but that if he did, he would give them an award. One witness estimated that as many as sixty women had been shot with the paint bullets.[57] Leaflets appeared saying that if women still did not cover, more "persuasive" means would be employed. After that, most women complied.

Living far away from the frontline reality of this new Chechnya, which still concerns him, Said Bitsoev says he does not experience any daily discrimination in Moscow. However, he thinks the state does demonstrate ignorance about Muslims. For the two million people of Muslim heritage who live and work in this city, there are only four mosques. "There is no place to pray." Thousands worship outside on the pavement. The Muslim population has no representatives in the government, "so the government is not sensitive to their problems." Trying to improve the image of his coreligionists here, he writes in *Novye Izvestia* on each Muslim holiday, explaining its meaning to Russians.

The amiable, liberal deputy editor-in-chief who once had to sleep with a gun under his pillow is a very proud Muslim. Hence, he is horrified by what the fundamentalists have done to the image of Islam internationally. He wants to tell Americans that "Islam is a religion of good will, of tolerance." However, he is not sure how best to do that. "Nobody would believe that because there are a lot of angry Muslims with guns and beards. They are more visible." He realizes that people like him are relatively inconspicuous. "Radicals are interesting for the public because they are loud. They are a kind of entertainment.

"We normal people are boring."

As an example of this ignored normality, Said tells me that after his sister's husband died, leaving her a widow with a four-year-old daughter, he brought them to live with him. "I take care of her and I feel I have to. There are a lot of positive values of Islam." He is not decreeing what others should do, only setting standards for himself. "When you do something good in honor of Allah and your heart is full of beauty and satisfaction, you know there is a God above you, and you follow how He shows you."

Feeling isolated at times, Said Bitsoev says we should work together on the subject of fundamentalism in the future. I hope we will. I am moved by his Islam that offers no fatwas against anyone, that reflects humanism, that only rarely appears on TV screens in the West.

L'CHAIM TATARS

Radik Amirov, who is president of Russia's League of Muslim Journalists when I meet him in 2010, buys me the best bowl of borscht I will ever eat.

I arrive at the café near the wire service where he works by way of Moscow's Park Kultury metro stop, hit just eight months earlier by a seventeen-year-old Muslim fundamentalist suicide bomber from the Caucasus. She killed fourteen. That dark history is the first thing Radik tells me about, pointing out that "there were Muslims who were killed and injured. Bombing does not choose whether you are Christian or Muslim." He condemns the attack, reminding me also how much ordinary peaceful Muslims are suffering from ongoing repression in the North Caucasus.

Born in an autonomous region of the Russian Federation called Tatarstan, Amirov arrives wearing a red Russian team jacket commemorating the 2010 Olympics. He has short dark hair, a little stubble on his face, and delicate hands. Originally from a small Tatar village in the South Urals, a region where there has been a significant Muslim population since the tenth century, he finished his schooling and then served in the army, "as usual for Soviet men." His grandfather Abdullah had died fighting the Nazis while in the Red Army.

Like Said Bitsoev, Radik studied at Moscow State University's Faculty of Journalism, in his case at the end of the 1990s. During those years, he realized he wanted to work on "religious issues," in keeping with his "Tatar roots." So he became press secretary to Moscow mufti Ravil Gainutdin, also a Tatar. In that capacity, he observed the problems facing Russian Muslims up close. He says they have to be less passive. "Unfortunately, most of us are sitting and waiting for Allah to help us." The mainstream Muslim population has lost a lot of time in the last fifteen years in the battle against fundamentalism, according to Amirov. "We could have organized good madrasas or a good Muslim university." Instead, the Muslim leadership here was bogged down by infighting.

The lack of moderate Muslim schools at home in Russia saw young people leave to get their "Muslim education" in Pakistan or Saudi Arabia. He does not have a high opinion of what some of these students learned. "They came back completely different people. They said you should not greet Christians, that you should hate Jews." A friend of his returned and tried "to teach me how to live." They found themselves "on different sides of the barricades."

In his day job at the time when I meet him, Radik Amirov heads a press club called The East, which offers media resources related to what he terms "the internal and external Muslim world," both in Russia and beyond. This is part of what he thinks Muslims must do—more work to offer their own self-representation on the Internet, radio, and TV. Part of the story that needs to be told, Radik thinks, is the long, proud history of Muslims living in peace with Christians and Jews in Russia, and fighting together against Napoleon and the Nazis. "There were no religious wars throughout this time."

Amirov sees himself as representative of the mainstream Muslim population here. "We are normal," he laughs, again echoing Said Bitsoev. "Most Muslims are like me. There are lots of journalists and politicians and people of culture and postmen among Muslims." Asserting that he represents the majority with his open views on religion and coexistence, he still argues that, as a population, "We must work on ourselves and avoid the fundamentalist mentality." It is wonderful to hear someone both speaking positively about his community and also accepting its responsibility.

He recently edited *L'chaim Tatars*, a book of true stories about what he argues are historically congenial relations between Muslims and Jews in his native Tatarstan and in other parts of the former Soviet Union. The cover of the small, hardback volume he gifts me is decorated with a crescent and a Star of David. "We have the same Prophets, the same values, rules and traditions," Amirov insists. One contribution, from a Tatar Olympic medal–winning gymnast named Yana Batirshina, explains, "I am glad that I am Muslim and I have Jewish blood." Yet another chapter memorializes good things Jews and Muslims have done for one another. It tells the story of a Jewish doctor who cured a Muslim boy, and then his parents saved Jewish boys during World War II. The Muslim boy in question, Abu-Bekir Shabanovich, grew up to become mufti of Belarus. For Radik, this history stands in stark contrast to today's "war of civilizations." When I ask how we can work to stop the mutual prejudice lately increasing between Muslims and Jews, Radik says, "I don't know. I'm looking for the answer all my life."

Unfortunately, the League of Muslim Journalists ceased operations after I met Radik Amirov due to registration difficulties, a perennial problem for NGOs in Russia. So Radik continues to seek out ways to promote understanding. In 2012, he became the editor-in-chief of an Internet news portal appropriately called *Russia for All*.

Some of the journalists I met confront fundamentalism head-on. Others document it, analyze it, challenge it, and survive it. Radik Amirov personifies an alternative to it. He transcends narrow categories, being Tatar and Russian, tolerant and interested in tradition, a citizen and a believer, a Muslim and a modern journalist.

CHAPTER FIVE

Growing Roses in the Triangle of Death

"Oh my God, oh my God," the wizened Muslim woman in front of me says, looking skyward.

"*Ya rabi, ya rabi.*"

During Algeria's dark decade, Fatma Bisikri's husband, an Arabic teacher, went to do the grocery shopping in Ben Achour, the poorest area of Blida where they lived. He was stabbed and then shot to death by two masked terrorists. I think Fatma, now seventy-one, is finished with her story when she tells of running through the streets without her shoes to find her husband. But this is only the first chapter.

Two years later, someone pounded on her door at night. She did not want her daughter to open the door, but her daughter did. Three or four armed men in the recognizable "uniform" of the fundamentalist armed groups—baggy *seroual* under a long *qamis*—pushed their way in.

"I do not want to talk about this," Fatma tells me in her small, strained voice. Then she keeps talking. I am grateful for the presence of my friend Lalia. There is too much grief to absorb alone here at the office of Djazairouna, the Association of Families of Victims of Islamist Terrorism. When Fatma Bisikri continues telling us her history, Lalia begins to cry. "*Smhana, smhana.*" "Forgive us, forgive us."

Fatma says the armed men dragged six of her nine children, aged thirteen to thirty, from the house. She held onto the legs of one fighter, sliding along, until he kicked her to the ground. Then she ran out after them, screaming: "Give me back my children."

The fundamentalists put a knife to her throat. "What are you looking for?" one barked. Even her maternal instincts could not overcome the fear they knew how to provoke. She retreated into the house. Not a single neighbor came out to help. There had recently been eleven killings in a home nearby. Terror had become mundane.

At first light, in a torrential rain, Fatma Bisikri went to look for her six children. All too soon, she found them. The fundamentalists had cut their throats and dumped their bodies in a *oued*, a nearby riverbed. The smallest details are what make a crime against humanity all too personal. They are what finally make Fatma Bisikri sob. Not long before that macabre night, one of her young sons had been crying that they had lost their father and did not have new clothes for the Eid holiday, as other children did. His older sister, a teacher, managed to buy him new pants. He was wearing them when he was murdered.

Why did this happen? Later, someone suggested to Fatma that it was because her daughter refused to stop teaching despite being ordered to do so by the local fundamentalists in their crusade against education. Or it could have been because people in the area had previously given succor to the terrorists, thinking they were fighting for religion, but then stopped helping them due to the jihadists' local atrocities. None of these theories can answer the big *why*, or ease this mother's continuing agony.

After the murders, Fatma applied for a new place to live to get away from the mouth of hell her home now seemed to be. However, she has never been given other housing. So Fatma Bisikri remains alone in the same location with the view of the *oued* where she found her children's bodies. She wants to sleep in a different place, but she has nothing. "*Andi walou.*"

Still, this woman with her shrunken face and battered heart gives us her galette, a flat bread, when she learns we have not eaten all day and Lalia is diabetic. We try to refuse it, but the people of the Triangle of Death have kept their hospitality, and she will not let us turn it away. Lalia observes that the generosity of those who have nothing is amazing.

By the end of our meeting, Fatma is nearly chanting in her grief. "*Irhab, irhab, irhab,*" "Terrorism, terrorism, terrorism." "*Sadak allah,*" "God has spoken the truth." Though I feel I have reopened her children's tombs this late afternoon, she somehow thanks me on the way out in bilingual Algerian style. *"Merci, mademoiselle."*

"Rabi isatrik." "God protect you."

BECOMING AFGHANISTAN

The road that brought Algeria to the 1990s apocalypse Fatma described was long, and strewn with many victims. The country was liberated from 130 years of brutal French colonialism by a War of Independence from 1954 to 1962, when as many as a million Algerians died. Among the fallen was my grandfather, a peasant leader named Lakhdar Bennoune. His son Mahfoud Bennoune, my father, was a liaison officer in the National Liberation Front and spent four years in French prison, surviving torture for which there was no redress.

Independence was followed by several decades of ostensibly socialist single-party rule in which considerable progress was made building the young country, but human rights were sometimes harshly repressed by an authoritarian regime. Socialism waned when I was in the eighth grade in Algiers and Chadli Benjedid became president. He attempted to use the fundamentalists to scare his critics on the left, a misguided game that got out of control.[1] In the early eighties, Benjedid turned to *infitah* Algerian style, a model of unregulated privatization that generated a starkly visible gap between the haves and the have-nots. This provoked a youth-led revolt in October 1988; the army killed five hundred in a week.[2] Afterward, the government placated the public by launching an electoral process and legalizing opposition parties, including the Islamic Salvation Front (FIS), whose agenda violated Algeria's constitutional ban on parties based on religion. This moment of democratization was exploited by the FIS, whose precursors had long been militating in mosques and had a significant organizational head start.

The FIS participated in the electoral process even while its leaders were saying they did not believe in democracy except as a means to come to power, and its associates were already engaging in violence against women and young conscripts.[3] Most of this was overlooked by outsiders too busy celebrating the advent of a multiparty system. There is one summary version of Algeria's 1990s trajectory that is told in the

West—the fundamentalists were participating in the elections, their victory was stolen, and that was when trouble started. This is a gross oversimplification.

Openly declaring that they would abolish democratic institutions, the FIS leaders proclaimed that they would rule through a *majlis al-shura*, a cabal of clergy. Some Algerians joked that the party's slogan should be: "One man. One vote. One time." The FIS campaigned under the banner: "No Charter, No Constitution, Said God, Said the Prophet." They described the mixing of the sexes (*mixité*) as a "cancer" and besieged women's college dorms to impose their own curfew and assault women who tried to leave. Their prescription was simple: "Islam is the solution."

They wrote the word *Allah* in the sky over one of their rallies with a laser, and some said it was a miracle.

Their words and deeds terrified liberal Algerians. The FIS second-in-command, firebrand Ali Belhadj, asked, "If we have the law of God, why should we need the law of the people?"[4] About nonfundamentalist Algerians, he raved, "One should kill these unbelievers."[5]

In the opening days of 1992, when it looked like the FIS would win, and never relinquish power, hundreds of thousands demonstrated on the streets of Algiers, calling on the government to halt the electoral process midway.[6] The military-backed government did so on January 11, 1992, and it later banned the FIS. As terrible as the situation became afterward, many argue it would have been worse had Algeria's murderous fundamentalists been allowed to dismantle the republic from the inside. As one intellectual told me, "We would have become Afghanistan." Democracy is not just about a process called elections. It is also about the substance, about making decent choices available that afford dignity and equality. The FIS was not such a choice.

In any case, the cancellation of the second round of the 1991–92 parliamentary elections was no panacea either. A decade of conflict ensued, with the military-backed government on one side and fundamentalist armed groups, some linked to the FIS, on the other. This was not a classic civil war between armed opponents. Most of the bloodletting was directed by the armed groups against civilians, a violence known simply as "*le terrorisme.*"[7] "The whole civilian population was taken hostage," a professor would tell me. Meanwhile, the forces of the state used arbitrary detention, extrajudicial executions, and grisly torture, and carried out something like eight thousand forced disappearances. The army, while partly successful in defeating the armed fundamentalists militarily then, has remained a major force behind the scenes to this day, with troubling consequences for democracy and the rule of law.

I recently found a drawing by Ali Dilem, one of Algeria's leading political cartoonists, that I had cut out of the paper while visiting in December 1994. The caption reads: "Suicide attempt at Orly Airport." Beneath it, Dilem drew a nervous little man asking for a one-way ticket to Algiers.

I flew to Algeria five times during the nineties. During the last of these visits, in 1996, my father asked me not to return. One of the only times we went out, we had lunch in a restaurant. On our return, he said he spent the meal imagining a bomb exploding, and trying to think what he would say to my mother. It would be nearly a decade before I would go back.

NO GRAVE TO MOURN AT

By October 2010, when I am in Algeria to begin work on this book, the country has changed a lot. It is now decidedly capitalist, with ads everywhere for cellphones and foreign cars. There is also relative security, and it is wonderful to see the Didouche Mourad, the main street of Algiers, filled with people—eating ice cream, texting, flirting. But there are also headscarves everywhere, a huge change from my childhood, and one even occasionally sees niqabs that cover everything but the eyes.

I walk across Algiers to find Maître Adnane Bouchaïb in his law office on the third floor of a building with no working elevator. In the unusual October heat, Adnane wears a short-sleeved shirt and tie. He is thin, and solemn even when he smiles. I have come to see him because he is vice president of a group called Soumoud, its name meaning "steadfastness." Founded in December 1996, Soumoud is a collective of families of those who disappeared at the hands of the fundamentalist armed groups. Adnane Bouchaïb tells me that about ten thousand people met this fate.

Some victims were picked up at fake checkpoints. Others failed to respect the "orders" of the armed groups or went to school or worked as professionals—all considered punishable "crimes" by the fundamentalists. Still others were simply caught up in an ever-expanding net of reproach. "The terrorists," as many Algerians simply called them, "declared the Algerian people in its totality to be non-Muslims," Adnane remembers. This happened when the armed groups lost *any* popular support and so decided that "the people are against Islam." Such *takfiri* practice, in which one declares one's fellow Muslims unbelievers, rendered everyone an acceptable target.

In his 1994 series in *El Watan* entitled "How Fundamentalism Produced a Terrorism Without Precedent,"[8] my father would write that Muslim fundamentalists deemed Algerian Muslims to have been misled by the modern secular nation-state and thus in need of "re-Islamiz[ing]." This required "that 'real Muslims' and fundamentalists . . . declare holy war against Muslim society itself." Those claiming Islam as their politics hated ordinary Muslims and acted upon that hatred, a pattern that would be repeated from Somalia to Pakistan. Adnane Bouchaïb argues, "Political use of Islam can only lead to violence. If you apply law from fourteen centuries ago, there will be violence."

His association has had to contend with that violence and assist its victims. Simultaneously, it has had to confront the state as well. Soumoud's members repeatedly encountered *la hogra*, the arrogance with which officials often treat ordinary people, even victims of terrorism. But they did not give up. They took legal initiatives to get families of the disappeared recognized as victims, and to obtain the papers needed when someone's body has never been found.

Mr. Bouchaïb is the first of many I hear denouncing the country's 2005 Charter for Peace and National Reconciliation.[9] This law codified nearly blanket impunity for many state and non-state perpetrators of the dark decade. "The two parties decided to amnesty each other. The victims were never allowed to say a word about this." The charter even criminalizes some forms of public debate about the conflict. This has given the country a bizarre official amnesia, when no one older than fifteen has forgotten what happened. The paradox is most acute for victims' families: "Now we find ourselves with former terrorists, in little villages where everyone knows everyone."

Against this Kafkaesque backdrop, Soumoud has straightforward demands. According to Adnane, there are mass graves containing corpses from the nineties that have been pointed out by repentant terrorists but never touched. His group wants them opened. "The state has the means to remove the bodies, identify them, bury them, and give the families a place to mourn." Soumoud's members continue to call for these measures, as "they have no grave to mourn at." This includes Adnane himself, who has never been able to bury his own father.

Like his son, Maître Mokhtar Bouchaïb was a lawyer. On his way home to Médéa, 100 kilometers from Algiers, after a court appearance in the capital, he was kidnapped on December 16, 1995. That "terrible year," Adnane recalls, the region was declared "liberated" by the terrorists as the forces of the state receded and "hid in their bases while the population was left to die." As Mokhtar Bouchaïb returned home to the Triangle of Death, he was taken at a *faux barrage*, a fake checkpoint, with three others. Six months later, his car was found, completely destroyed.

The unknown leaves your imagination the perpetual captive of a million possibilities, each more awful than the last. While other victims could speak the unspeakable thing that had befallen them or a loved one, Adnane could not. When we got to the most critical plot point, he could only tell me what he did not know.

The day after his father's disappearance, twenty-year-old Adnane went to the gendarmerie. The officers would not open the door for him. He sat outside and cried. Late in the afternoon, they finally let him in and he filed a report. Intimating that his father—the president of the local bar association—might have gone to fight with the terrorists, the gendarmes demanded witnesses to his abduction. The frantic son managed to find others who had been stopped at the same place and took them to the police station. The survivors identified those running the checkpoint as members of the Islamic Salvation Front before its dissolution. Still, there was no news of Mokhtar Bouchaïb.

Struggling to deal with his loss, and the bureaucratic nightmare that ensued, Adnane met Ali Merabet, whose two brothers had been abducted in the town of Sidi Moussa. "We had the same problems. We wanted the recognition of our kind of victims." So they founded Soumoud. Because they were victims of non-state armed groups rather than the Algerian security forces, they were overlooked by rights groups, according to Adnane Bouchaïb, especially the International Federation of Human Rights and Amnesty International. "They never wanted to talk to us," he said. "I went to a meeting of the UN Commission on Human Rights and was ignored."

Being sidelined by international organizations was devastating. "It was a fatal blow because all was closed here. The only way to talk about our suffering was at the international level." They needed global rights groups to "write about what we lived, what we suffered." Instead, for many victims of the armed groups, like Adnane, it seemed the international human rights organizations defended the fundamentalists: they "closed their ears and talked about rapists as political opponents who defended a just cause.

"We were treated badly by everyone: international NGOs, the state, the terrorists themselves."

So the Algerian victims of fundamentalist terrorism searched for other allies. Unexpectedly, they found the families of those disappeared at the hands of the state, represented by a group called SOS Disparus (SOS Disappeared), and they have worked in a complicated coalition to secure some kind of justice since 2005. It was not easy at first, but, "we realized that what we demand and what they demand are the same." Together, they have drafted proposals for a truth commission. I now understand all too well why it is necessary. The lack of formal investigations, precise documentation, and trials for the crimes of the nineties has made my own research on Algeria particularly difficult.

In late 2010, I ask Adnane whether he worries about the return of fundamentalism. Unquestionably. "Fundamentalism is back because the state wed the fundamentalists. The state learned a lesson from the power the FIS had from using religion."

Sitting in Adnane's small office under his father's picture, with the late afternoon heat streaming in, I can feel the grief the lawyer still lives, though he never complains. I ask if he had been concerned about how dangerous it was to found a group for victims of fundamentalist terrorism while the terrorism was still going on. "I lost my father at twenty," he said. "Sometimes I wished to be kidnapped and killed just like him so it would have been over already. No, I did not consider the danger."

JOURNEY TO THE TRIANGLE OF DEATH

The next day I head into the region where Maître Bouchaïb's father vanished. A cordial older cab driver takes me to Blida on the expressway. Mountains appear on the horizon announcing we are on our way to the Mitidja, a hilly plain extending southwest from Algiers, containing some of the country's best agricultural land.

The driver tells me life is not like it once was. The only time things are familiar is during Ramadan, when families eat together in the evening. It is nice to think about Ramadan this way. As a kid, I always enjoyed the ritual of the Holy Month, the extended *ithan*, the visiting, and the special sweets like *qalb el louz*, made with semolina and orange flower water. But in 1994 I began to dread this month, because that was when the fundamentalists killed the most. Nowadays, Ramadan seems to be oppressive to many as grocery prices skyrocket, and those who choose not to fast have to pretend all day or risk arrest for illegal eating.[10] This is a change. In the seventies during Ramadan, a journalist tells me, they served food and wine at lunchtime in the cafeteria of the ruling party's newspaper for those who wanted it.

In fall 2010, on the road to Blida—my road back to 1994—as the driver and I discuss all the changes since then, we pass the military airport. Soldiers stand at attention inside what look like armored phone booths, aiming machine guns. (Al Qaeda of the so-called Islamic Maghreb still kills policemen and military personnel regularly in Algeria.) There is no mistaking that we are now in the Triangle of Death.

Though this name sounds like a reference to the Bermuda Triangle, it is instead the label given in the 1990s to this zone of Algeria hardest hit by fundamentalist pogroms—North Africa's very own Ground Zero. With the help of the documentation department at *El Watan*, I found the four-part series my father wrote in 1999: "Outline of a social history of the triangle 'of death.' "[11] He explained that the area roughly covers the Mitidja plain, about 100 kilometers long. In the 1990s, even its earth was threatened—by desertification due in part to the exodus from rural districts provoked by terrorism and the counterterror tactic of destroying forests to deprive armed groups of a hiding place. As my father wrote, "The Mitidja of yore, which was a source of life, has been transformed into a place where life is sacrificed in the name of Islam!"[12]

Mahfoud Bennoune placed some responsibility for this on the history of extreme French repression in the region, which had been home to notorious colonial torture centers. But he also blamed the postcolonial leaders, especially for the way they mismanaged the struggle for control of the area's precious agricultural land. "In the 'triangle of death' as everywhere in the country . . . injustice, . . . nepotism, . . . greed, corruption, and violations of rights . . . by those in charge of state institutions from top to bottom ended up making the bed of fundamentalism."[13] Ultimately, this gave rise to "a terrorized Mitidja."

In October 2010, as the taxi driver and I continue on toward Blida, the capital of this former zone of destruction, we are greeted by an unexpected road sign:

"Blida, capital of roses, wishes you welcome."

When we drive into town this Saturday afternoon, shops and pizzerias are cheerfully crowded. A policewoman directs traffic. Large groups of men sit by the side of the road, watching cars go by. My friend Lalia Ducos, an Algerian activist visiting from Paris, and her cousin Fayza, who lives here in Blida, wait for me in the street. Lalia's family treats me like family. I find myself in an old house with high ceilings and floral-motif moldings. They even have a few rose bushes out front, but the flowers are not in bloom. Improbably, I am among friends and smiling in the Triangle of Death.

We eat a dinner of *chorba frik*, a hearty soup full of coriander, green wheat, and lamb. Lalia insists I should feel free to excuse myself and go work, which I do. Then, she and Fayza come to my room anyway, but I am glad they do. Fayza tells us about life here during the dark decade. About beheadings in the neighborhood. About her father reporting one day that men had come to the door and ordered him not to let the women out with their heads uncovered. Fayza's father begged her to stay inside for fear she would be harmed. "Father, I would do this for you. But, I will not do it when strangers come to the door to ask."

Fayza refused to cover her head throughout the 1990s and still does not; she says she knows how to make herself respected without a hijab. Then she tells of a family friend, a teacher, who was killed in front of her students for appearing bareheaded in the classroom back in the decade. I make a vow to avoid covering my hair during the travel for this book. If these Blideans did not submit, who am I to?

It is a vow I am mostly able to keep.

ALLAH GHALEB

The next day, I'm able to find the house of Malika Rouabah only because a member of the victims' group Djazairouna takes time off from her job at the *souk el felah* (farmers' market) to guide me through the labyrinthine neighborhood where Malika lives. Here, addresses are irrelevant.

Malika Rouabah put in thirty-five years as a nurse in the local hospital, named for Frantz Fanon who used to work there. Her passport photo shows a pretty, self-assured woman with stylish short hair and hoop earrings. In the last year before she was to retire, on the evening of October 3, 1997, at 7 p.m., she was leaving for work with her thirteen-year-old son. As she locked the door, a *heb-heb*, or rocket of the kind often fired by fundamentalists from the mountains onto Blida, fell behind her.

"It was Kabul here in Algeria."

Her son was spared, but Malika's back took the force of the blow. "I fell just outside my door." In an instant, she was paralyzed. After ten days in a coma and months in the hospital, after three failed operations, she was told to go home. "We can't do anything for you," the doctors concluded. She has been lying here in bed in her darkened living room ever since. For thirteen years. Pale and graying, looking as if the physical person she once was is lost inside of her somewhere, Nurse Malika cannot sit up and has no medical bed to aid her, so she lies flat all the time. "And here is my reward for thirty-five years of service," she says.

Her son was a victim too. "He was in shock. He failed out of school because he came to the hospital and brought me milk and food." Nurse Malika's one happiness is that this son, unemployed for years and now in his late twenties, recently passed an entrance exam to train as a fire-fighter. "This is my recompense. *Hamdulilah*," "Thanks be to God." She tells me candidly she would have strangled herself long ago if not for her son.

When she describes life in Blida in the nineties, I respond, "*Quelle horreur.*" For once I stand corrected on this paltry word. "It is worse than a horror," Malika says. At the hospital, "they brought us heads without bodies. Or bodies without heads." The paralyzed nurse distinguishes between the fundamentalism that wrought all this and ordinary, lived Islams. "I am a Muslim. I know my religion. But why do they impose? I live my life and no one can tell me what I have to do."

From the vantage point of her sickbed, Malika remains ambivalent about the national reconciliation. "It is good because there would have been more massacres otherwise. But, it is not good because they were pardoned." It is the silence about grave crimes and the criminals who perpetrated them that she finds most galling: "Now, you can't touch the terrorists, you can't talk about them. They say, 'Don't say, "You were a terrorist." ' I will say to a terrorist that he is a terrorist. If they want to cut my throat, let them come. Is this a life that I have?"

Malika's final injury came a year after the rocket attack, when her husband left her and married a second wife. "*Allah ghaleb*," she sighs. This Algerian expression of resignation literally signifies that "God is all powerful," but it also means "alas." "*Allah ghaleb.* I have no husband now. He comes to visit only once in a long while."

Anytime I have to listen to anyone say that the Muslim fundamentalists are the representatives of the downtrodden, or that they embody the liberation struggle of the Muslim people (and I have heard such comments in the West), anytime I hear anyone describe anything to do with them as a "holy" war, I will think of Nurse Malika flat on her back in the dark for thirteen years after a lifetime of healing others.

DJAZAIROUNA

Because of my family background, I often thought about the intellectuals targeted by fundamentalists in the 1990s. However, fundamentalists also killed countless ordinary people, in working-class urban areas and poor rural districts, in places like Blida. Djazairouna, the Association of Families of Victims of Islamist Terrorism, headquartered here, represents many of them. Its name means "Our Algeria."

At Dar el Houria (House of Liberty), Djazairouna's headquarters, the first two women who come in to talk with me are insistent that I should tape them. They begin speaking before I can even get my new digital recorder switched on. Goussem Hamdani, in her white scarf patterned with blue flowers, talks in long, rushing sentences. Yet, to indicate how her husband, Abdelkader, was killed, she simply draws her forefinger across her throat. The fundamentalist terrorists thought her husband, a carpenter who worked at the University of Blida, had stolen a stash of their weapons hidden on campus.

Almost nine months pregnant at the time, Goussem was assaulted by the armed men who took Abdelkader away. After they hit her in the stomach, she nearly went into labor. They told her she was "impious" and broke her teeth. Her ten-year-old daughter's head was smashed into the wall, and she remains brain-injured. Goussem Hamdani tells me that she herself "suffered the worst humiliations and torture." This likely means she was sexually assaulted, but I cannot stop her long enough to ask. And I know that a euphemism may be all that can be spoken here.

When the armed men finally went away, she took her kids, aged three, six, and seven, plus the wounded ten-year-old, and ran. On foot. At night. She was right to go. The men returned the next day, telling her neighbors again that she was impious and must be killed. Goussem went to the gendarmerie to report what had happened. They suggested her husband had joined the terrorists. "If we don't find him, we will decimate your family," the gendarmes menaced.

Abdelkader was eventually found with his neck slit open by the fundamentalists. There should be a word in English for *égorger* (to cut the throat). It is the word for the 1990s in Algeria. Fayza, my hostess in Blida, tells me that some peasants in the unprotected rural zones here would sleep with grease on their necks, trying to deflect any blade applied to them in the night.

Why did the fundamentalists do such terrible things? I ask the widow Hamdani. "*Choufi, Madame*, look Mrs. We are Muslims, and they said it was jihad. But the people realized what they were doing. So they wanted to make people afraid."

A thirty-seven-year-old woman in a pink headscarf, immaculate eye makeup, and long robe comes into the room of Dar el Houria where I am conducting interviews. Still frightened, she does not want me to use her name. She is a hairdresser, and her husband was killed by terrorists in 1998 while she was pregnant with their second child. At the time of his murder, the hairdresser had come to stay with her parents down in Blida, which was relatively safer, and her husband had remained at their home in the mountains.

After her husband died, people came to her parents' home to express their condolences, assuming she had been killed with him. That was how she found out he was gone. Then, she says, "I became crazy." So she went to see a marabout, a local saint believed to be capable of healing. Consulting such figures is very popular here, but it is deemed heretical by fundamentalists. The hairdresser opines at length about the extremists who took the father of her children. "These people hide behind religion.

"Even in the time of the Prophet, they did not do what they do now in jihad."

As Algerian counterterrorism expert Liess Boukra has written, "Jihadism is not jihad,"[14] the modern practice being far from the historical doctrine its practitioners try to use to justify their actions. These contradictions infuriate the young widowed hairdresser from Blida. "They say adultery is *haram*, then they kidnap girls and they are raped by fifty men. How can you talk about religion after this?" I ask her how one can fight fundamentalist violence. She insists she does not want her words used to justify military intervention in Algeria, as occurred in Iraq. Terrorism is an Algerian problem that has to be resisted by Algerians, she says. The widowed hairdresser believes that everything comes from the people. In Algeria, people turned against terrorism: "They became aware."

She is still in shock, but her life is better now. "In the decade, we didn't go out. Now we laugh. We go to weddings. We come back from the beach at 1 a.m." I am glad to hear it.

I wish I could share every one of the stories I heard in Blida. If anyone is confused about what Muslim fundamentalism can mean in the lives of Muslims, the members of Djazairouna, many of whom are deeply religious themselves, can set them straight with stories of their Algeria.

Some commentators in Algeria and abroad have insinuated that the authors of these crimes were unknown. However, every single one of the women I met that day in Blida was sure their family members had been killed by the fundamentalist armed groups active in the area. The one most mentioned was the Armed Islamic Group (GIA). I asked again and again about the identities of the perpetrators; to the local victims I interviewed, the answer was clear. They could see the way these men were dressed, or they knew them, or the men made threats that made obvious their affiliation with the fundamentalists—such as calling the victims "impious." Many of the victims were also mistreated by the forces of the state when they attempted to report what had happened, and they found themselves lost in the middle like Adnane Bouchaïb. "Terrorism in Algeria was not beaten by the army, but by the people," Adnane argues. Others expressed gratitude for the protection of the army, without which, as one woman said, "everyone would have been killed."

I thought I knew what happened in Algeria in the 1990s, but nothing quite prepared me for these stories. "It is a bottomless well of suffering," Lalia says. Muslim fundamentalism has shown these Muslims of the Mitidja no mercy.

Leaving Dar el Houria, Lalia, Fayza, and I drive back through the streets of Blida, different people from those who had set out that morning. That evening the rain falls in great noisy cascades until the streets run with water. It is as if the skies are trying to wipe away all that has happened here, all we have heard, and bring back the fabled roses of Blida.

THE DUTY OF TRUTH

Cherifa Kheddar, Djazairouna's president, is one of Algeria's most important human rights advocates. When I meet her, she wears a gray suit and black pumps. Her hair is chin length and jet-black and she looks tired, having worked a long day before our grueling discussion begins. I receive her in the salon that Fayza's family has given over to me. It is furnished with backless couches, and low tables with lace covers. In this serene environment, we relive some of Cherifa's most difficult moments.

"My mother went to Mecca on pilgrimage in 1996. She went with a group of Algerians to see the imam of the Grand Mosque and asked for a fatwa against what was happening in Algeria. The imam replied: 'No, that is politics and we are not involved in politics.'" Why can't you get a fatwa when you actually need one? Forty days later, armed thugs came to the Kheddar house in Blida and shot Cherifa's mother and niece (who survived) and her sister Leila (who did not), and tortured her brother Mohamed Redha to death.

Three months later, on October 17, 1996, Cherifa Kheddar founded Djazairouna, along with other survivors. "People were burying their families alone. Others would not go to the funerals because you would end up on a death list. It was as though the victim was deemed guilty." Cherifa knew all too well what a difference this support made. Thousands attended the funeral of her sister and brother. "There were so many people the road was blocked." This extraordinary solidarity, likely due to the high profiles of Leila, a lawyer active in the local bar association, and Mohamed Redha, a businessman, eased their family's pain. "My mother said even in our sadness, we were lucky. I thought, 'No victim should be buried in anonymity.'" So she started Djazairouna to stand with suffering families across the terrorized Mitidja in their worst moments. Attending a burial became a political act. "In Algeria, women do not go to the cemetery for funerals. But we went in large numbers, women and men. From then on, the families of victims said, 'Our dear ones are not guilty, they are only victims. And should be buried and respected as such.'"

Though the nineties are over, Djazairouna's work is not. At the bottom of every e-mail Cherifa sends me is the group's slogan: "For the duty of memory. For the duty of truth. For the duty of justice." Today, its members persist in their work to fulfill those duties by taking care of victims and fighting to preserve their history.

To Cherifa's dismay, and that of her fellow advocates, there has never been a thorough inventory of the crimes of the 1990s in Algeria. Here in the Triangle of Death, where everyone can tell stories of slaughter, it is easy to see how the international press arrived at a figure of two hundred thousand dead in the conflict.[15] But no one really knows how exact it is. I ask Cherifa about this statistic. "It is just a supposition because until now the Algerian state did not give real numbers." She ponders for a moment. "I think that number is about right. I think about two hundred thousand people were killed by the Islamist armed groups." But, Cherifa, like Adnane Bouchaïb, is a universalist, so she does not stop the accounting there. "On the other side, there were thousands who were arrested by the security forces, who were afterward tortured and assassinated. And there were also some thousands that until today their families do not know what happened to them."

During the 1990s, some commentators put forth a thesis known as "*qui-tue-qui*" (who kills whom). They suggested that no one knows who authored the terrorism in Algeria in the 1990s, and that perhaps some or all of it was carried out by the state (or through its manipulation) to make the fundamentalists look bad. Depending on whom you ask, this argument was first made by Algerian Trotskyites, or other left-wing political parties, who loathed their government above all else, or by certain Islamist spokesmen addressing the international community. The local version of 9/11 conspiracy theories, this notion was unfortunately adopted by some on the left in the West and even fed by human rights groups.[16] My employer at the time, Amnesty International, which has done so much good elsewhere, repeatedly described the atmosphere in Algeria as one in which there was simply "confusion as to who commits what crimes." Such notions are parroted all too often in Western academic gatherings even today. As Mustapha Benfodil analyzed it for me, "The truth was one of the victims of violence."

All this has terribly undermined victims' attempts to get their history recognized and perpetrators held accountable. I am not naïve about the reality that in many countries intelligence agencies infiltrate armed groups, but, having listened to so many victims, I think it is clear that Algeria's fundamentalist armed groups were indeed culpable for their very own atrocities.

Many of the jihadists themselves made little effort to hide their crimes.[17] "When you hear about killings and throat-slittings in a village or town," GIA commander Abou el Moundhir explained in his group's international newspaper, "you should know . . . it is the application of GIA communiqués ordering [us] to do good and combat evil."[18] He assured readers his men only killed "those who deserved to die." There is no question that the state also had blood on its hands, but its armed opponents' atrocities were far greater, were widespread and systematic, to use the terms of international criminal law, were unimaginable.

On this topic, Cherifa is indignant and very precise. For her, legal responsibility on the one hand and factual or moral attribution on the other are two distinct questions. "The state is responsible for all whose security it failed to guarantee. But, for the advocates of the *qui-tue-qui*, those people have no proof." Cherifa and other Djazairouna members did extensive work on the ground during the darkest years of the dark decade. "The day after the massacres, we went to the places where they happened and people not only described the terrorists, but they knew who was a member of the Islamic Salvation Front. They recognized the terrorist of the neighborhood who was there killing."

Without hesitation, she calls out those who do not have her firsthand experience. "Now if people who were not there want to testify in our place, that is something else. If they meet the affected families, the one whose son was killed by the Islamists will tell you he was taken by the Islamists." In the small villages where abuses often happened, everyone knows everyone else's business. She recounts what local people would tell her on the ground in the Triangle of Death after any given atrocity in the 1990s. "When we go to a village and talk to a woman, and ask, 'How do you know it was the Islamists?' she will say, 'The cousin of my husband was with them and the cousin of my husband was a terrorist.' When, for example, I had friends whose children were taken by the security services, they say, 'I knew my son was taken by the security forces.' There is no confusion in the minds of these citizens."

Why is there so much denial elsewhere that fundamentalists killed here? I will again encounter this denial about Islamist killings in a month's time in Pakistan. In Algeria, Djazairouna's president says it is difficult to comprehend because it flies in the face of the evidence. "The Islamists here never said, 'It was not us.' They took responsibility publicly. There were lists posted in the mosques."

YOUR TWO EYES ARE GONE

When Cherifa Kheddar speaks directly about the killing of her family members, the only indication of how hard it is to tell this story is that her already rapid-fire speaking style gets steadily faster, and her voice sinks lower. "It was the twenty-fourth of June 1996. I was lying down in my room. Someone said, 'Quick, come, something is happening.' I got up running, my sister too and my mother." So the family's collective nightmare began. "We opened the door and my brother was standing there." Five men surrounded him, pointing weapons at his head. "We had to let them in."

This was no random wartime violence, but rather the implementation of the armed men's ideology. As Cherifa relates: "They started with their fundamentalist preaching. 'You shouldn't have done this. Why do you have a TV? Why cigarettes?' For a long time, they gave us an Islamist sermon." Then the situation deteriorated. "We lived in adjoining houses, ours and our brother's." First the armed men took Cherifa's brother, Mohamed Redha, to his house. Then they came back for her sister Leila. "My mother said, 'I will not let my daughter leave with men.' But my sister said, 'No, I want to see my brother. Let me go.' "

At this point, Cherifa decided she had to do something before it was too late. Profiting from the general confusion, she fled through her room and out into the garden. From there, she went to get the security forces. But it was already too late for Leila and Mohamed Redha.

"When I came back, I found my brother on a red velour carpet. But he didn't have a red carpet. He had a white carpet. It was his blood that had dried. They tortured him for a long time in the bathroom. Then they cut his throat." Cherifa does not falter for a second as she describes what she found, but her voice is now very low. "My mother was washing my sister because she was bleeding from both sides. When they saw I had fled, the armed men said, 'Quick, the girl is gone.' So they shot my mother, my sister, and my niece. And they departed." The scene was bleak. "My mother they left for dead. But she was only wounded. My sister was wounded, but at the hospital they couldn't save her. She had three bullets in her brain."

Cherifa seems especially haunted by something that happened at the very beginning. "When the terrorists entered I said to my brother, 'They will kill me.' He said, 'No. They will not touch a hair on your head as long as I am alive.'" She thinks the terrorist chief was paying close attention to her brother's words. "As long as he is alive we can't be touched, so they started with him."

I cannot understand how this woman, one of the sanest people I have ever met, is able to relate this story without falling to pieces. How is it possible to transcend such a night? So I ask, "How did you survive this experience?"

"Survive?" she asks. "I don't know if I survived."

"A part of you leaves with them. My brother was older than I. My sister was younger. It is your two eyes, or your two legs that are gone. I was not whole for years. It was a pain I would not wish on anyone."

Most of those involved in the attack on the Kheddar family were later killed by the security forces. Cherifa knows this because after the murders of her brother and sister, she would visit the local morgue every time terrorists were killed. "I tried to identify the terrorists who killed my family until the day when I found them."

In the face of much of the politically correct Western rhetoric in recent years, Cherifa insists that, "instead of just battling terrorism, you must fight fundamentalism. Fundamentalism makes the bed of terrorism." This is not just an ideological point, but a very practical one. "They will not lack recruits, these groups, as long as there are young people indoctrinated in the universities, in their communities." She challenges the indoctrination that makes people fundamentalists, and the impunity for the crimes they then commit.

Hence, Djazairouna opposed the amnesty that was given to state and non-state perpetrators alike. It was all intolerable. You lost your family to the fundamentalists, then your loss was erased. The only way to respond was with a metaphor. "The day of the referendum, we decided to go to the cemeteries and to bury the Charter of National Reconciliation and our voting cards with our loved ones."

As a result of her opposition to the "reconciliation," Cherifa nearly lost her civil service job, and she did lose her public housing, which she had to go to court to recover. She still takes care of her mother and an autistic brother. Despite everything, she has regained some joie de vivre. But she overworks herself and, given the stress of contending with both the fundamentalists and the state, battles high blood pressure.

We stop talking only when called to dinner by my host family, who have been waiting over an hour to eat. Cherifa stays to dine with us on *bourek*, dumplings filled with meat. Throughout this friendly meal, I think about how she has described contemporary Algeria, where fundamentalist social attitudes are on the rise again. "Women will attack you and say, 'How do you not wear the scarf? Didn't God show you the good law?'" Cherifa Kheddar remains defiant. "I say to them, 'Did you spend the night with God so you know what God wants?'"

THE SEWING CLUB OF SIDI MOUSSA

Sidi Moussa is a depressing town sixty kilometers due south of Algiers on the edge of the Triangle of Death, surrounded by villages and scattered houses. Like Blida, this place was battered by the 1990s and remains full of ghosts. Even Algeria's leading sign-language specialist, Nacer Ouari, who appeared on a TV program for the deaf each week, was shot down in the street here in 1995.[19]

In November 2010, I join veteran feminist activist Akila Ouared for a visit to a center run by her Association for the Defense and Promotion of the Rights of Women. We are expecting to observe sewing and pastry-making classes for young women, but it turns out the students will not be present today, so we talk to the teachers. Lamia wears a lace hijab over a purple jacket and trousers. Another teacher is quite young, and her plucked eyebrows stand out under her hijab. The third woman is a little older and sports a purple leopard-print scarf.

The center where they work is named after Amel Zenoune-Zouani, once a twenty-two-year-old law student with the same dreams of a legal career that I had in the nineties. She was killed at a *faux barrage* outside the town in January 1997 because she refused to abandon her studies. I try to find her family in Sidi Moussa in 2010 but am unable to locate them.

I think of Amel Zenoune dead in the street when I look at the covered heads of every one of the teachers today in Sidi Moussa. Her death was meant to make them all obey. But Amel lives on in every small act of female resistance here, like going out to sew when going out to sew is forbidden. It is no accident that Amel's name means "hope." Her eponymous center now offers precisely that to other young women. Hope is still needed in Sidi Moussa. Though Amel's mother, Houria, cut the ribbon when the facility opened, it was too dangerous to put up a plaque outside with her name on it. This place that bears her name cannot bear her name for now. Hope remains unspoken.

The fundamentalist campaign against education, so similar to Taliban assaults on schools in Afghanistan and Pakistan, was at its apogee in Sidi Moussa. As one teacher explained, "We found 'leave school or we will kill you' written on the chalkboard." There was a bomb in the same school. After that, kids did not go to class for days. Another teacher says, "I went to school and they came to tell us if you go out, you will come home in a coffin."

This assault on the educational system limited the horizons of its former students. "I couldn't have the *bac* because of terrorism." (The *bac* is shorthand for the baccalaureate exam, success on which is required for university entrance.) This rite of passage was greatly complicated by the dark decade. "We couldn't really study. You learn all the time that friends or family have been killed and you do not have the head for this." Another woman said she had not even made it that far. "Because of terrorism, my parents would not let me go to high school." In this terrible environment, women were often forced to stay home for their "protection." One teacher tells me that as many as four hundred women from this area were kidnapped and raped. "We never saw them again." This terrorized the entire population. "We stayed awake all night. You heard them screaming, 'We will assassinate you.'"

I ask what they hope for now that Sidi Moussa has arisen from the worst of its nightmares. Like true educators, they focus on their pupils' prospects. "The girl at her father's house, if she doesn't marry, no one will help her and she will be alone." Given the stumbling blocks, their students' commitment moves the sewing instructors. "There are girls who come from surrounding villages, who come through the forests. Some of their fathers or brothers refuse that they come, but they come anyway." Some of those women then use the money they save by doing the family's sewing to buy food to take home to those same male relatives. The sewing classes meet from 8 a.m. to 4:30 p.m. But the teachers understand their pupils' constraints. "Some girls come when their brothers go out and go home before they do."

I ask the teachers of the Sidi Moussa sewing club whether their work makes them happy. Encircled by her brown lace hijab, the light in Lamia's eyes switches to bright. "I love to sew and I want everyone else to love it. As I have benefited, I want other women in need to benefit." However, sewing is only one part of what occurs at the school. "Here is a place we can talk. We close the door, we take off our veils and show our haircuts. There are no men who come in." In this space, the women weave together a new way of living. "During terrorism we could not talk because we were afraid of each other, but slowly now the girls express themselves. They wait impatiently for this hour to come."

When the interviews are done, the teachers show us the embroidery their students have produced on decrepit sewing machines. They serve us cakes in a cold room while we warm our hands on glasses of tea. As they come outside to say good-bye, a woman in full niqab walks by in the street, entirely shrouded in dark cloth save for the smallest of holes for her eyes.

How do women's souls survive, I wonder, in the somber places of the world like this? The sewing teachers of Sidi Moussa have taught me the answers. By embroidering even when you must do so in secret, by choosing purple leopard print for your headscarf when you have no choice but to wear it, by gathering with other women when the men are not paying attention to whisper dark secrets from the time of terrorism and reborn hopes from the time after, by quietly fighting the fundamentalism that chokes women's lives, stitch by stitch.

DYING FOR KNOWLEDGE

Amel Zenoune-Zouani's watch stopped at 5:17.

That is the moment she fell in the street on January 26, 1997, an instant after a member of the Armed Islamic Group cut her throat on the outskirts of Sidi Moussa.

In November 2012, when I am finally able to locate them in a *quart-*

ier populaire east of Algiers, I spend several hours talking with Amel's mother, Houria, and her surviving daughters. Sitting on the couch in front of her TV, Khalti Houria (Auntie Houria) as everyone calls her, wears a long blue dress and glasses that hang around her neck. Both stalwart and shattered, she shows me Amel's watch, which was returned by the gendarmes. Its white face features small green flower buds just under the spot where the glass is broken. The second hand still aims optimistically upward, frozen fifty-seven seconds after 5:17, approaching a 5:18 that will not come.

Twenty-two years old and a third-year law student at the University of Algiers, Amel lived in the dorm. She wanted to visit her family on that seventeenth day of Ramadan, a day known as *Ghazwat Badr* in commemoration of a historic Muslim victory. So she boarded the bus for Sidi Moussa, and would never finish law school.

Amel's mother tells me everything she had heard about what happened on the bus. Just outside the town, the vehicle was stopped at a *faux barrage*. Amel occupied a seat behind the driver, who was a neighbor, and held her schoolbag. Though she did not cover her head in Algiers, and wore makeup, she had a friend's shawl wrapped around her hair when the men from the Armed Islamic Group climbed aboard. One came to Amel, hit her on the shoulder, and said, *"Ahl al houkouma"* (partisans of the government). "Get up. Kill her." They grabbed the law student by the arm. Still, she dared to say, "Don't touch me." According to Khalti Houria, Amel then "turned and looked at everyone." Even now the mother appeals to her daughter's fellow passengers as she weeps: "Amel did not speak but begged you with her eyes and asked you to save her." No one could. "When they got out of the bus, one armed man had a knife and was rubbing it on the pavement, preparing to kill her."

There are two versions of what happened next. Some said Amel was kicked as she was getting out of the bus and fell to the ground; others remembered that she had her throat cut while still standing. Her death was an atrocity. It was also meant as a warning. In the moment after Amel's watch stopped, the GIA men told all the other passengers: "If you go to school, if you go to the university, the day will come when we will kill all of you like this."

The terrorists had posted placards all over Sidi Moussa saying that young people must stop studying and stay home. As a law professor, I want to understand why a young woman with her whole life ahead of her would continue her legal education when she could be murdered as a result. Apparently, Amel had said to her father, "I will study law and you will always have your head high. I am a girl, and you will always be proud of me. I will do the work of a man." Mrs. Zenoune, herself a housewife, had long dreamed of her children studying. All six did. Amel's sister Amena explains: "Our mother inculcated in us the idea that studying means you are a free woman. Mom said, 'I am ready to lose all four of them. I will sacrifice them for knowledge.' When people remember 'Amel Zenoune who was assassinated by the terrorists,' they say, 'The girl who was killed for studying law.' People say, 'She was the example for us.'"

While still cherishing the values Amel died for, her death was an agony for her family. And so was the way they found out about it. Sidi Moussa, as the sewing teachers had recalled, was then a wasteland of terror. Its people had no running water, no electricity after the terrorists attacked the power station, and no telephone service. So the family was never sure when to expect Amel or their other daughters home.

Finally, twenty policemen showed up at the door, but, faced with the mother and her younger children, the policemen found themselves unable to deliver the news they had come to give. One asked Houria how many of her daughters studied in Algiers, then told her enigmatically that she and her husband had been ordered to meet the prosecutor in Blida the next day. Their work undone, the cops drove off and left the family wondering in the dark. Khalti Houria had a bad feeling. Any of her college-student daughters, or all three, could have been headed home that night.

When the police left, a group of neighbors came to the apartment, including the bus driver's wife. Everyone assumed that the family now knew the news. Khalti Houria begged the driver's wife, "Fatiha, tell me." So the driver's wife shared as much as she could: "They cut your daughter's throat." This answer only left terrible questions for Khalti Houria. "I said, 'Which one?' One neighbor said, 'The one who wore glasses.'" No one seemed to know the precise facts.

With no one able to give her a definite answer, and no working phone, Khalti Houria ignored the evening curfew and took off with her young son, running through the perilous streets of Sidi Moussa until she got to the gendarmerie. When she finally found herself face-to-face with a gendarme, Khalti Houria remembers saying, " 'My son, tell me how many of my daughters.' He said, 'Madame, one only. The one who was at the law school. She was wearing jeans and a coat.' " The bereaved mother insisted: "Swear to me." He swore. So, in the most awful moment of her life, she actually felt gratitude. "I prayed and I sat and kissed the earth and I said, 'God give me strength.' They were all three at the university. It was a little less painful that it was one rather than two, or three." Even as she found out she had not lost three daughters, the reality that one was gone, and how, sank in.

But Khalti Houria's agony gave way to rage. "I sat on the ground and said everything that came into my mind. That hour my struggle began." Her daughter Amena describes the mother's long walk home through the desolation of Sidi Moussa. "The commissariat was far from where we lived. All along the road, Mama insulted the terrorists. She didn't stop. The police said, 'If we had ten mothers who had lost their child who did what Mme. Zenoune did, the terrorists would never have won in Sidi Moussa. Never.' There are many who died before Amel, God have mercy on her soul. No one had done what Mom did. It was enormous to make that journey. Not to have fear. For her, it might have been in her head, 'Who cares anymore?' " In the dark streets of the martyred town, Mrs. Zenoune taunted those who had taken her child. "You killed Amel. Come and kill me."

Eye-to-eye with the terror she had felt over the previous terrible years, that night she defied it. When she got home, she threw open her door that was always bolted shut. "Let them enter." Khalti Houria continued denouncing the murderers on the balcony of the family home well into the early morning hours when the neighbors got up for Zuhour, or Ramadan breakfast. "*Ya haggar.*" (You who are unjust.) "You killed her because she was studying. She was beautiful. She was better than you. Amel, Amel, Amel." After her jeremiad, the gendarmes came and told her husband that the rest of the family should leave Sidi Moussa immediately.

They buried Amel and left their lives behind them.

One of Amel's younger sisters, Lamia, later overcame her own despair and went to law school in Amel's memory, practicing today in Algiers, as her older sister hoped to. "Fundamentalism will not win, even if they say, '*Allahu Akbar*' all day long," Khalti Houria swears.

Lamia the lawyer takes me into the small, neat living room to see Amel's framed portrait, which hangs on the wall. The law student had pitch-black hair that fell just below her shoulders, and luminous dark eyes that are now the centerpiece of this room. She was not smiling when the picture was taken, but her determined expression displays what her classmate Adnane Bouchaïb had told me about her: that she had both the eloquence and the lively personality needed to be a successful lawyer. "She had a big future in front of her," Adnane recollected.

Somehow, in the portrait on the living-room wall, Amel looks both serene and entirely aware of what her future might actually hold. Her face captures perfectly something she said to her mother not long before her murder. "Mom, please put this in your head. Nothing will happen to us, *Inshallah*. But if something happens to us, you and Dad, you must know that we are dead for knowledge. You and Father must keep your heads high."

Amel's watch stopped at 5:17, but she lives on in Algeria and everywhere else women and men continue to fight fundamentalism, by striving for knowledge, and by keeping their heads held high.

RAFD MEANS REFUSE

In March 1993, the prominent academic Djilali Liabes was gunned down by fundamentalists, most likely from the Armed Islamic Group, while leaving his apartment in a suburb of Algiers. After his funeral, a few women met at the headquarters of a left-wing political party to decide how to respond. "We said, we cannot go to funerals and not do anything," Kheira Dekkali, a retired social worker, recollects. "We were always crying—over the dead, over the intellectuals who were leaving. Crying doesn't change anything. We must do something. We had a responsibility."

So Kheira and others created RAFD. The name of their organization was both the Arabic verb meaning "refuse" and the French acronym for *Le Rassemblement Algérien des Femmes Démocrates* (Algerian Rally of Democratic Women). As Kheira told me, in their case RAFD meant "refusal of fundamentalists, refusal of intolerance, refusal of terrorism." Among its adherents the group counted left-wing activists, students, and housewives. According to their official self-description, they "shared the categorical refusal of the Islamist project for society which is the negation of women's rights." They believed that "fundamentalism represented the death of our country."

Four months after the menacing knock at my father's door that first set me on the journey to writing this book, when intellectuals and activists (then "the Bosnians of Algeria"[20]) were being cut down regularly, a small group of RAFD women stood protesting outside the president's office in Algiers wearing bull's eyes made of cloth to symbolize that they faced bullets that were all too real. The group's spokesperson, Zazi Sadou, was one of those who bore a target that October 1993 day. When I first met her in 1994, she had been in the crosshairs of every fundamentalist thug in the country for a year and a half, moving constantly from place to place to survive, away from her home and child. "If I lower my vigilance, if I create one habit, I am dead," she told me. "It's not a situation where we can peacefully return to our kitchens. Sometimes I'd like to." Zazi has a rich speaking voice and an enviable ability to express complexity with crystal clarity. Standing on the public square with a bullhorn, she denounced terrorism despite the fact that terrorists could have taken her out at any moment.

It is a miracle she is alive.

Former RAFD member and journalist Malika Zouba apologizes that she cannot acquaint me with the whole RAFD story, that others will have to fill in the gaps. "Because in 1994 I left Algeria. I had to leave because . . ." She hesitates. "I was afraid to die. *Voilà.* To be assassinated." It is the first time someone says this to me openly. Another RAFD member, Saleha Larab, would reveal to me how alarmed she became over her own inappropriate lack of fear. "Ten years of terror . . . had ended up killing in us a sentiment as human as fear," wrote Mustapha Benfodil.[21] Nevertheless, Malika Zouba had maintained enough equilibrium to feel frightened.

Zouba began receiving threats on the phone as early as December 1992. A voice said he knew she worked for the newspaper *Alger Républicain*, a left-wing daily with a prestigious pedigree in Algeria's independence movement. Callers cursed at her in Arabic. Then her journalist colleagues started to be killed, to disappear, giving potency to those threats.

Next RAFD's leadership roster became a formal fundamentalist death list. "The police told us our names were on a list found on a terrorist who was killed or arrested. It contained our names, professions and addresses." Malika had a visa for France and thought she could just leave for a few months. "And then I would go back. After I had been forgotten." It did not work out like that in practice. "Afterward it was a spiral of violence, so I stayed in France. *Voilà*."

I ask what it was like for her as a person of Muslim heritage to receive death threats from groups claiming to act in the name of Islam. From someone so measured, her answer is blistering. "I do not recognize them. For me, they are people who seize religion simply to take power. They have nothing to do with Islam. It is impossible to say of a religion like Islam that it is the death of ideas, physical death, the death of progress. No religion can be reduced to this.

"I deny them the title of Muslim."

Unlike the Islamic Salvation Front they opposed, the women of RAFD received little international sympathy. Kheira Dekkali disdained the Western response: "*C'était le blackout* [There was a real silence]. The Western position was that the Islamists were democrats. We were called militarists. I said to Europeans, 'Wouldn't you want your army to defend you if you were attacked?'" Kheira adds: "We were radical and we were criticized for this. We could not resist the fundamentalists if we were not radical." After a bombing on a crowded street near a police station that killed as many as a hundred, RAFD organized a demonstration right in front of the bomb crater itself. The police told them it was too dangerous, but the activists gathered anyway and filled the crater with flowers.

Especially appalling to Kheira was the international use of the term *eradicators* to describe people like her. Cambridge professor George Joffé defined eradicators as "those who rejected all compromise with political Islam, through violence if need be."[22] There are two faulty presumptions here: (1) that it was possible to compromise with Algeria's "political Islam," and (2) that the violence was chosen by the "eradicators." As H.Z. wrote of the epithet "eradicators" in the Algerian newspaper *Le Matin* in 1994: "This term designates those who peacefully oppose the fundamentalist social program. . . . Thus, supporting democracy, political pluralism and modernity means you are an eradicator! Being against the instrumentalization of Islam for political ends means you are an eradicator! Yet . . . it is fundamentalism that eradicates."[23]

"We are eradicated, killed, had our throats cut, and they call *us* eradicators," says Kheira, echoing H.Z.

During my years as a legal adviser at Amnesty International in the nineties, I saw up close the point of view she described. I shared AI's concerns about state torture and disappearances in Algeria, but I could not understand the organization's paltry response to much more widespread violence by the fundamentalist groups. Moreover, AI seemed oblivious to what the fundamentalist agenda itself meant for human rights.

In May 1996, an Amnesty expert recently returned from Algeria briefed our colleagues, clearly alluding to RAFD: "There are some women's associations: the most visible (though very small) is the one linked to a left-wing political party and which focus (*sic*) its activities on 'eradication' of Islamism and openly supports the militias." That was the only thing the expert had to say about RAFD or popular opposition to fundamentalism. As for the phenomenon the women of RAFD were battling, the only time the report used the word *Islamist* was in relation to "Islamist victims of HR violations." The brief contains just one short paragraph about "abuses by armed groups," most of which is devoted to saying that victims of terrorism failed to provide Amnesty with information to substantiate claims of such abuses. Regrettably, this characterized the organization's attitude toward Algeria at the time.

Even without the support of international rights groups, RAFD soldiered on. When high school student Katia Bengana was dragged out of class and murdered by terrorists on February 28, 1994, for refusing to wear the hijab, RAFD held a protest in front of Ibn Khaldun Hall, the prominent public auditorium where in happier times I had attended concerts of Andalus, North African classical music. "Frankly, I thought there would just be scores of us," Malika Zouba admits. "At the beginning, there were not very many. But then we saw women coming from everywhere, almost a thousand."

They came for Katia, for all the other Katias. They came before Facebook and Twitter and cellphones. They came because a friend had telephoned to tell them, or they saw a notice someone had risked her life to post. Indeed, when the women of RAFD convened public events, they found that many others were simply waiting to be mobilized. Some participated out of ideological resistance to an Islamic state. "Others just wanted their kids to be able to swim, go to school and live in a normal country," Kheira Dekkali noted. RAFD gave women something useful to do with their anguish. Yet again, as they had during the struggle for independence, the women of Algeria came onto the country's streets to fight for its soul. They came for themselves with their heads uncovered, knowing they could be the next victims. They came to be counted among the living, rather than among the dead.

"Never will I forget the first woman who arrived," Malika says. "She carried the picture of Katia Bengana, and she had her two daughters with her." Like the Pakistani woman who took her children to the continuation of the Rafi Peer World Performing Arts Festival after it had been targeted for attack in 2008 Lahore, this Algerian mother knew that her kids had to fight for their futures. Together they would take a stand, come what may.

RAFD members were not the only ones refusing. Resistance had become etched into the way Algerians lived. When the fundamentalists said no one should go to school, all the kids attended and their mothers waited outside for them. When the fundamentalists prohibited visits to the Turkish bath (*hammam*), women went anyway. For Kheira, as for so many I met, Algerian women did more to counter fundamentalism than men. During one demonstration, someone said to the women of RAFD:

"You are the men of this country."

On March 8, 1995, International Women's Day, RAFD organized a mock trial of the Islamic Salvation Front and its leaders in Ibn Khaldun Hall. Feminist leader Nabila Djahnine had been killed three weeks earlier, as had music producer Rachid Baba Ahmed. You could feel the fear in the capital city. People avoided moving around unnecessarily. Yet the trial went ahead, complete with testimony from witnesses who were actual victims of the fundamentalist armed groups. Omar Belhouchet, the director of *El Watan*, would bear witness for the journalists. A woman whose daughter had been kidnapped and raped would also speak.

Openly. Publicly. In Algiers.

"We did not invent anything," Zazi Sadou says. "We just took their public statements, the FIS platform. It was not theatre. These were not actors, they were people who had suffered." Still, Zazi recalled an article in the international press disparaging "these westernized women who speak French and organized a *mise-en-scene* to condemn Muslims." The left-leaning French newsmagazine *Le Nouvel Observateur* put sarcastic quotation marks around the words "testimony of the dead" in describing the accounts of fundamentalist killings offered at the 1995 tribunal, lampooned the event's "theatrical" tone, and even criticized the presence of police outside to protect the participants, notwithstanding the terrible threat to them.[24] So much for international solidarity.

The decision to attend the RAFD mock trial of the FIS leaders, like the choice to go to the Rafi Peer Arts Festival in Lahore after jihadi bombs, was not an easy one. Zazi remembers, "There were flyers put up around Algiers in which the armed groups threatened the women who came with death. They distributed communiqués in mosques. In Sidi Moussa, in Boufarik. But women came in massive numbers." Zazi estimates that "there were 900 people, mostly women, who came from everywhere." The hall was so full that many sat in the aisles, and others could not even enter.

It is hard to imagine how RAFD pulled off this standing-room-only event. It was almost as if someone had tried to put fascism on trial in 1938 Germany. But these women were desperate to send a message to the world, whatever the risk. According to Zazi, "This tribunal was a way of sending a large SOS. Look this way. The victims exist. Those who are dead did not kill themselves. They were 'executed.'" As punishment for those crimes, the mock tribunal symbolically condemned the FIS leaders to death, rather like the verdicts at Nuremberg. Personally, I oppose the death penalty under any circumstances, yet even the most cutting-edge global human rights law allows it "in time of war pursuant to a conviction for a most serious crime of a military nature."[25] The sentences were intended to draw attention to that very "seriousness."

The tribunal made a difference, as did all of RAFD's acts of overt defiance. Slowly, they began to be heard, to be interviewed on foreign TV, to be able to give a voice to the "*other* Algeria," as Zazi Sadou called it. The price for such resistance was high and paid in extreme risk, stress, and trauma. Many of the members have suffered serious physical and mental health consequences since then. Still, looking back sixteen years later, Zazi has no regrets. "We made up this shock troop that chose life over death, liberty over abdication, resistance over oppression, at risk of our lives. When I see the state of the country now . . .

"But, I would do it all over again."

THE LEGACY OF MOHAMED OF BLIDA

In Algeria, and beyond, I see that the people of Muslim heritage who oppose Muslim fundamentalism do so in myriad ways. They document fundamentalist violence while facing it themselves. They wear metaphoric targets while in the sights of the most vicious killers imaginable. They refuse to kowtow. They grow roses in the Triangle of Death. Back in Blida, I first came to know what that means.

After a bewildering day of interviewing victims of terrorism at Dar el Houria, we drive home. Souhila Aissa, the blue-eyed forty-three-year-old with a dark hijab who has organized our meetings and kept the office open for us while the North African shadows lengthened, now rides along in the late afternoon sun. She too is a victim, she informs us matter-of-factly as we try to move through the traffic, thwarted by rush hour and trapped in the car with the lingering grief of all those we have met. Her husband was killed, she says. Now, she focuses on raising her two sons and on her work with Djazairouna. She manages to smile. I am too numb from this day to take in what she says.

The next day, Souhila tells us more. Her husband, Mohamed, a violinist, was a devotee of music and sports. Throughout the early nineties, he was threatened by the terrorists who said music and sports were sinful and forbidden by the Qur'an. He was ordered to give up both.

Mohamed refused.

Then he was told to close his music store—a place where children could study piano, guitar, violin, or saxophone. Otherwise, the terrorists said, they would take all the kids out and kill them. He said, "Kill me, but not the children." His father urged him to go along with what the terrorists ordered, but Mohamed said, "I cannot let them impose their dictates on me." The pressure mounted. He finally closed the music school but still refused to give up sports, continuing to coach a local basketball team. "Kill me if you want. I will keep doing sports." One day he received a call to meet friends at a café frequented by athletes. He assumed this concerned a tournament he was organizing. When he arrived at the café, a bomb exploded out front, killing him and fifteen others. Souhila believes her husband was the intended target. "He was eliminated."

Mohamed of Blida was murdered by Muslim fundamentalists at the age of thirty-eight.

"I live with this always in my head," Souhila says. "If I forget, it is a treason." With a wistful smile, she shows me a photo of her late husband. He wears a red tie, has prominent eyebrows and a large mustache, and stares intently at the camera. Like so many portraits of murdered Algerian intellectuals I have seen that were taken in the 1990s before their deaths, like the portrait of Amel Zenoune-Zouani, something deep in his eyes seems to know what is coming. But even though the premonition I read on his face has come true, and Mohamed has been cut down for his determination not to give up music and sports, hope prevails. His two sons, Fethi and Amine, are nineteen and fourteen now.

One wants to be a guitarist and the other an athlete.

CHAPTER SIX

Reading Spinoza in Tehran

On April 18, 1991, what I had feared for years actually happened to Roya Boroumand. "My father was killed in Paris at our apartment," she tells me. "He was stabbed multiple times and my younger brother found him in the hallway." The slain Abdorrahman Boroumand had been a founder of the first pro-democracy opposition to Iran's theocratic government, and had also been jailed under the Shah's authoritarian rule.

"Then Bakhtiar was killed," Roya continues her story. Shapour Bakhtiar, a longtime dissident and then Iran's transitional prime minister, had dissolved the notorious secret police known as SAVAK and then had gone on to head the National Front opposition group in exile. A close friend and associate of Roya's father who also lived on the outskirts of Paris, Bakhtiar was attacked at his home on August 6, 1991. His throat was slit. "And a hundred plus people were killed all over the world." Roya puts her own loss in this litany of victims of what the *Washington Post* called "the systematic extermination of Iran's political foes."[1] These killings were carried out by "meticulously organized death squads directly linked to . . . Iranian President Hashemi Rafsanjani."[2] With the integrity of someone who has worked on the cases of many victims of Iran's theocrats, Roya explains her own family's misfortune in relation to those of others; her loss is neither more nor less important, just closer to her.

Around the time of Abdorrahman Boroumand's murder, Algerians were being told by some academics at home and abroad that their country had to go through a "fertile regression,"[3] by allowing the fundamentalists to take power. This would purge the society of Islamism by giving its proponents room to discredit themselves, thus leading to democracy. Malika Zouba had described to me what Algerian fundamentalists pledged this would actually look like. "The Islamists promised they would change everything. Women would go back home. There would be no constitution. Just the Sharia." In October 2010, journalist Saleha Larab declared in Algiers, "Those who say the fundamentalists should have come to power make me laugh."

I think about this again when I read the *Washington Post*'s analysis of the assassinations of Iranian opposition figures, including Abdorrahman Boroumand. "Behind all these crimes stands *a sovereign state with all of its logistical capabilities.*"[4] That is precisely what the Islamists get when they take power in places like the Islamic Republic, and what they would have gotten if they had taken power in Algeria. In fact, many Algerians replied to calls for a fundamentalist "fertile regression" in their country with a single word:

"Iran."

Now more than thirty years old, Iran's theocratic regression shows no signs of ending or of proving fertile (except perhaps in giving many young people an allergy to the religious politics with which they are stuck). Instead, it has led to the mass slaughter of Iranians such as Roya's father, an exodus of intellectuals and opponents of the regime like Roya herself, and a prolonged sociocultural deterioration that will be difficult to undo.

I wanted to go to Iran for this book but was warned not to do so, as my topic could endanger anyone I interviewed. (The situation in that country is such that when I am in Herat, an Afghan journalist tells me his Iranian colleagues like to visit because they find more freedom in Western Afghanistan.) Since ordinary fieldwork was impossible, I was lucky to meet Roya Boroumand, a historian by training who runs an Iranian human rights organization based in Washington, DC. This short-haired den mother to a band of young exiles looks perpetually tired and works constantly, but she still carves out substantial time to introduce me to recently arrived Iranian rights advocates, and even to translate. By the time I leave her office, I almost feel I have made a very brief visit to Tehran.

Roya first wants to situate herself for me. "I was born in a Muslim family." There had been a certain trajectory in her family. "I was born in a conservative town in Isfahan. My grandmother had a chador, and my mother didn't. My grandmother spent her life praying, and my mother didn't. And she wasn't considered a bad Muslim." Different ways of being were deemed acceptable then. Her grandmother's religiosity had not translated into support for the Islamic Republic when it was declared in April 1979. "My grandmother thought these clerics had gone nuts, that clerics should not rule."

In prerevolutionary Iran, Roya's father was a lawyer and activist who supported the National Front, an organization associated with democratically elected Prime Minister Mohamed Mossadegh. (Elected in 1951, Mossadegh was overthrown by a CIA-engineered coup d'état in 1953 after he ordered the nationalization of oil interests.) The National Front worked against the Shah and was banned. During the revolutionary period, Mr. Boroumand became the National Front's emissary to Ayatollah Khomeini in Paris before his February 1979 return to Iran.

Roya's father could see a totalitarian state coming early on, because the Ayatollah told him openly that he would not recognize *any* political parties. Once Khomeini came to power, the summary executions began swiftly. So, Abdorrahman Boroumand, his friend Bakhtiar, and some of their colleagues, fearing the rise of an Islamist government and committed to nonviolence, opposed the Ayatollah and fled with their families. From France, they began documenting the first abuses in postrevolutionary Iran.

"No one was interested," Roya says acerbically. "The Iranians weren't interested, the French weren't." She became disillusioned and focused on her studies, earning a doctorate from the Sorbonne.

Then when her father fell to the death squads of the Islamic Republic, Roya Boroumand became one with the victims whom he and she had both been working to support. "You prioritize the victims, and then you experience what you've been theorizing." Her bereavement was shaped by the indifference she encountered. "You feel very helpless. You get maybe a news flash, and that's it. No one cares who he was. He was probably a bad guy. He was in exile. Probably a supporter of the Shah. But, generally you're lost. Somehow you feel you have lost your country, lost a loved one, and all this is just a passing news item."

Like Cherifa Kheddar, like Adnane Bouchaïb, Roya walked on after the cataclysm. She left France and came to the United States. She worked for other victims, consulting for Human Rights Watch's Women's Rights Program about, among other things, Algeria. This put her in contact with Kheddar, who by then was living her own nightmare in Algeria. Roya recognized the anguish in Cherifa's voice on the telephone from Blida; she still remembered it vividly when we met. "I was concerned by the generally limited interest the mainstream international human rights groups showed for these victims of Algeria's armed groups, including the women victims I was assigned to cover." Roya Boroumand knew well what such indifference meant.

When Roya's consultancy at HRW ended, her sister Ladan moved to the United States. It was the optimistic nineties. The Internet boomed. Inside Iran a new generation, raised in theocracy, began to make its voices heard. On April 18, 2001, the tenth anniversary of their father's murder, Roya and Ladan struck back.

They incorporated what Roya terms a "victim-oriented research and education group" called the Abdorrahman Boroumand Foundation. "We named the foundation after him not because we liked the long name that makes it impossible on a card," she says dryly, "but because we thought we have to send a message to those who killed that physically eliminating people doesn't eliminate their ideas.

"This name is going to come and haunt you."

This was a decision made by many who lost loved ones to the fundamentalists—to remember by going forward. Leila and Mohamed Redha Kheddar were similarly evoked in Djazairouna, Maître Bouchaïb and the brothers Merabet in Soumoud. In the work and witness of those organizations, the names of those lost would haunt all who sought to hide the crimes of the fundamentalists.

Roya and Ladan began to systematically document the abuses of the Islamic Republic, to show all the ways in which this regression would never be fertile. Starting a human rights group to document human rights violations in Iran, when your father was killed in exile in part for doing just that, takes particular fortitude. "If the regime kills us," Ladan told a reporter nonchalantly in 2006, "we hope someone else will take up the task."[5]

The timing of their foundation's 2001 launch proved tricky. Five months later, the Twin Towers fell. "Seeing these people die was terrible, and it's somehow our fault too. We're all Muslims and we're not fighting these people." That is what some people in the West believe. The reality, as Roya knew, was altogether different. "We did try, and we got killed. People got killed. Clerics got killed. The bulk of the victims of the early years were people who were fighting fundamentalism." She desperately wants non-Iranians to understand this.

"I don't pray or fast anymore, but I used to. Can you blame me for not being interested in practicing a religion that is used to justify the kind of violence we are witnessing in the Islamic Republic? But most of the victims of politically motivated executions, who were charged with 'waging war against God' and executed in the thousands, were practicing Muslims. They prayed and fasted." Though being labeled a "bad" Muslim might be a death sentence, being a "good" Muslim was still no guarantee of safety. "So, it's not that they didn't try to fight. They were revolutionary. They were anti-Shah. They thought the religion is more progressive than what Khomeini was offering. And they got killed."

Roya and I share a deep frustration that all of these efforts are barely given a footnote in official histories. She recalls June 1981 demonstrations called by the National Front to oppose a new penal code based on *qisas*, a set of harsh "eye-for-an-eye" criminal punishments. In response to the demonstrations, Khomeini said, "This is a protest against Qur'an. . . . The National Front is from today convicted of apostasy."[6] Given the number of people killed for apostasy, this was tantamount to calling for their deaths. Still, Iranian progressives went out onto the streets to defy the Islamic state. "But they had no support outside the country," Roya observes. Even without that backing, many did not submit. "In the early months after the revolution, if they saw someone was going to be flogged for having alcohol, they would gather and prevent the Revolutionary Guards from beating them. They would try to protect people from being killed."

It was that history of defiance that Roya and Ladan sought to preserve with a tiny budget and an office located in both bedrooms of
Roya's house. "We couldn't hire just anyone because it was my house.
And I had no life and I have no life." But the people who attempted to
stanch the tide of fundamentalism deserve to be remembered, so the
sisters Boroumand do not give up, whatever the cost in long days.

PERSONAL RESPONSIBILITY UNDER DICTATORSHIP

The people killed were lawyers long held in prison, doctors stripped
of their worldly goods, nurses who spoke to the press, women in love,
salesmen deemed apostates. All cut down in the name of "God's Republic." *Omid*, which means "hope" in Persian, is the centerpiece of the
Boroumand Foundation's work—an Internet database of the victims of
the Islamic Republic, killed with or without a death sentence, "regardless of their politics, or the alleged crimes they were killed for." Visiting
http://www.iranrights.org/english/memorial.php is like returning to
the Triangle of Death.

The case that makes me crumple at my computer is that of "A young
girl in Tehran in 1981." Originally reported by a journalist, it is not just
a tribute, but a warning. "Arrested for swimming in her home pool in a
bathing suit, she was found guilty of causing 'a state of sexual arousal'
in a neighbor from whose house she could be seen. She was sentenced
to sixty lashes in April 1981 but died after the thirtieth lash."

I ask Roya Boroumand to give me an estimate of those killed since
the revolution. She does not know but tells me they have documented
more than fifteen thousand cases in *Omid* and are not yet done with the
1980s. Their database is not simply a roster, because "lists become very
anonymous." When possible, they interview families. Besides information from relatives, they go through all the Iranian newspapers day by
day, culling reports on executions. Daughters of a lawyer, they also are
historians. Committed to accuracy and detail, they note what was written on a warrant, who signed it. It is painstaking work.

In addition to defending truth and memory, Roya says they do this
work as a way "to promote a culture of human rights." The sisters and
their organization provide "food for thought," by translating classic

writings on rights into Persian. For example, Ladan selected Hannah Arendt's "Personal Responsibility Under Dictatorship" and Spinoza's "Freedom of Thought and Freedom of Expression Under a Free Government." The words of these two European Jewish philosophers born three hundred years apart could not be more relevant to the quest for liberty in the Islamic Republic of Iran. Arendt fled the Nazis, Spinoza's parents the Inquisition. Notably, Spinoza was also excommunicated at twenty-four, "with the consent of God," by the Dutch-Jewish leadership for nonconformism.[7]

It is no accident that the Farsi versions of Spinoza and Arendt resonate in Tehran. A recently arrived refugee told the Boroumands he read the translated "Personal Responsibility Under Dictatorship" over the phone to a friend locked up in Tehran's notorious Evin Prison. It must have been eerily familiar. Arendt's work grapples with the moral and political culpability of those who lived in the Third Reich and claims there is "no such thing as obedience in political or moral matters."[8] However, the philosopher adds a caveat: "The only domain where the word could possibly apply to adults who are not slaves is the domain of religion, in which people say . . . they obey the word or the command of God because the relationship between God and man can rightly be seen in terms similar to the relation between adult and child."[9]

A lawyer visiting from inside Iran whom I will call Soraya tells me: "The leadership of theologians—we don't want it." It is no wonder. The *vali-e faqih*, Iran's very own Guardian of the Umma, a position held by Ayatollah Ali Khamenei since 1989, has more power than any mere human being should have, because of course he is not a mere human being. "He owns the people," the lawyer notes, "that leader who is like a father and who makes decisions for his children." In other words, recalling Arendt, the father is God in the family, the *vali-e faqih* or Supreme Leader is God in the family of Iran. To question Him is to blaspheme. I ask the lawyer from Tehran what it can possibly be like to do her work under such a system. She says when she goes to court she has difficulty breathing. But claiming exactly the personal responsibility of which Arendt wrote, the lawyer not-named-Soraya goes anyway, even though "it is hard for my heart to beat."

In the equally apropos Spinoza chapter on freedom of thought, the Amsterdam-born Jewish freethinker issues a rejoinder appropriate to fundamentalists everywhere: "[T]he object of government is . . . to enable [men] . . . to employ their reason unshackled."[10] A system like Iran's, where, in Soraya's words, "laws are religion-based and unchangeable," clearly fails that test.

As I peruse the Spinoza chapter the Abdorrahman Boroumand Foundation had translated, I gasp. Again and again, though written in 1670, his words sound like he is talking about contemporary Iran. "What," the philosopher asks, "can be more hurtful than that men who have committed no crime or wickedness should, simply because they are enlightened, be treated as enemies and put to death . . . ?" In their introduction to the chapter on their foundation's website, the Boroumands posted a quote from a young Kurdish Iranian prisoner who had just been executed. The doomed man's message sounds as though he had studied Spinoza. "Can we fear our destiny and our end," Ehsan Fattahian asked, " 'we' who have been sent to death by 'them' because we were hoping to find an opening to a better world?"[11] Just as the Dutch Jewish philosopher had described it, "[H]e that knows himself to be upright does not fear the death of a criminal and shrinks from no punishment."

As Roya and Ladan's literature selection makes clear, they are true universalists. "We should consider ourselves as human beings," Ladan says. "We should get beyond the cleavage between the West and the non-West." Fashionable Western cultural relativists who sometimes justify veiling, FGM, and rule by *majlis al-shura* as authentic and unassailable "cultural practices" are seen by many in Lahore, Niamey, and Tehran, and by Ladan herself, as simply purveying another kind of racism. Iranian women's rights activist Mahnaz Afkhami has a name for this new relativism reserved for Muslims today: "Islamic exceptionalism."

Meanwhile, on the ground, lawyers in the Islamic Republic like Soraya pursue their Sisyphean task of claiming human status for their clients who are shackled by religious laws. In this context, advocates for human rights employ creative strategies, she tells me. "They use the sayings of Ali to say these religious rulings have to be appropriate to the times, and have to evolve with the society." Even though Ali was believed by the Shi'a to be the rightful successor to the Prophet Muhammad, citing him is to no avail.

So advocates like Soraya also use human rights arguments, but then they are met with cultural-relativist rebuttals and, worse still, with "Islamic human rights." Voices like hers invoke equality but are told it is a Western notion. "We say these are natural rights. We are born equal," the lawyer retorts.

To support voices like hers, the Boroumands try to promote universal human rights norms in the Islamic Republic. For example, their foundation translated into Farsi the 2007 Yogyakarta Principles on the application of international human rights law to sexual orientation, aiming to raise awareness in a country whose president publicly swears it has no gay citizens. "Tolerance," Ladan says, "becomes the normal reaction to intolerance."

She and her sister have organized the translation of numerous UN human rights instruments on the administration of justice and sent them to all of the Iranian authorities for whom they could find e-mail addresses. As a result, their website is filtered in Iran and can be accessed only by those who know how to overcome the device. Ladan says with a hint of pride, that she has heard anecdotally, "Sometimes when they arrest activists they ask: 'Are you in touch with the Abdorrahman Boroumand Foundation?'"

The name does haunt the authorities.

THE SMARTEST TOTALITARIAN STATE

As a historian, Roya Boroumand had studied totalitarian ideologies, and she thinks about the nature of Iranian state fundamentalism within that framework. "It wants to be a theocracy but it is a totalitarian ideology that has been smart enough to take the cover of religion so it couldn't be attacked. It's the smartest totalitarian ideology." This is not meant as a compliment. "There is a central office for the Friday sermon," Roya offers as an example. "What does that tell you?" In the piece translated by the Boroumand Foundation, Hannah Arendt wrote

that "[t]otalitarian society is monolithic," and "all public manifestations . . . are 'coordinated.'"[12]

Beyond this internal coordination, Muslim fundamentalist ideologies and the movements that advance them are also connected across
borders, whatever their own particularities. In their scholarly writing,
Roya and Ladan Boroumand have described "Islamism" as "a self-
consciously pan-Muslim phenomenon."[13] They are painfully aware
of the transnational impact of the Islamic Republic. Though Iran is a
predominantly Shi'a country, it has contributed to the radicalization
of Sunni religious authorities as well through international institutions
such as the World Congress of Friday Imams and Prayer Leaders,
which tried to shape Friday sermons around the world to match the
message of the Islamic Republic.

Mahnaz Afkhami stressed to me the significance of this cross-bor-
der impact. "I'm certain that had Iran not fallen to the fundamentalist
theocrats, this would have been a different region. That was a tragedy
for both Iran and also for the whole region." Like U.S. ally Saudi Arabia (and now increasingly Qatar), Iran has exported fundamentalism,
its own virulent strain of political Islam metastasizing not by a natural
process but through its active promotion and by spending lots of its people's money. So, transforming the Gulf region is critical to the whole
problem. "I think that if Iran changes course," Roya avers, "it would
undermine people like the rulers of Iran in other countries. It would
undermine their appeal, as the fascists lost their appeal when they lost
the war." Moreover, getting out the news of what kind of lives people
actually lead in the Islamic Republic is critical. "When the reality comes
out, the human costs of this, people will think twice. Most of them have
no idea what's happening inside Iran—people who support it."

Roya had been working all day to convey to me the depth of the
religious repression they are fighting. She is tired, but she is on a roll,
asserting the right of Muslims to be just as individual as anyone else.
After the revolution, "the people who took power represented a part of
Iran, but they were not a majority. If they were, they wouldn't need vig-
ilantes in the streets." The minute you need morality police with sticks
like they have in Iran or Saudi Arabia, then you are imposing an inor-

ganic "morality" that has to be imposed because it is not lived. "If they were representative, they didn't need thirty years down the road to still flog people so they covered their damned heads. One of the things that Khomeini said about the Revolutionary Guards," Roya recalls, "was that their function is to familiarize people with the traditions.

"What kind of traditions are these that the people are not familiar with?"

PHOTOGRAPHING THE REPRESENTATIVE OF GOD

On Halloween night in 2010, Roya says I should come to her house. All the "kids" are there. Around the table these young refugees eat pasta, laugh at each other's jokes, and speak Farsi and English all at once. Yet it is no ordinary Halloween party. Everyone here has a real-life horror story to tell.

On one side of the table sits thirty-year-old, curly-haired Kian Amani. He first taught me the expression "You can't ride a camel, and duck." He has lived those words. Back home, he used to be a documentary filmmaker and photojournalist for Iranian news agencies. "We were the eyes of the people." For that, Kian was arrested and beaten multiple times.

He explained to me some of the tribulations of working in a theocratic context. "If you take pictures of a government official, it is like you are taking photos of a representative of God. You cannot take pictures that do not look good." Journalists face repression in many places, but "in Iran what is difficult is that they have the hat of religion and they apply rules that are hundreds of years old. They have their own interpretation of those things. It is hard to fight." On the nights before he was scheduled to go to the Supreme Leader's office to take pictures, Kian would have supreme anxiety.

It was never easy to be an independent-minded photojournalist in the Islamic Republic. But in June 2009, when mass demonstrations broke out after allegations that President Mahmoud Ahmadinejad's supporters had rigged the vote to defeat reform-oriented candidates, the situation became much worse. Kian covered in depth what were called the Green Movement protests, in support of reform candidates.

He watched young people being shot dead in the streets. (As many as seventy-two men and women reportedly would be cut down in three months.)[14] While the initial rallying cry was "Where is my vote?" the slogans broadened. "This is a government that says it takes legitimacy from God, and is now shooting the people." In his quiet, unassuming way, Amani described the demonstrations as having been "against 30 years of oppression. People chanted for a republic of Iran, rather than an Islamic republic." *Istiqlal, azade, jumhuria irani.*

Proud of the peaceful nature of the 2009 demonstrations in Iran, even though they failed to change the government, Kian asserts that "the Iranian people showed they had learned democracy. There were three million people out. They preferred to walk in silence and not use violence against anyone. The violence came from the state." How different this was from the choice made by Algeria's fundamentalists to sharply escalate their jihad when their electoral hopes were dashed back in 1992.

Iran's government also made the choice to use force to suppress the Green Movement. In their response to the demonstrators, "you can see fundamentalism in action," Kian affirms. Apparently the Revolutionary Guards chanted religious expressions or the names of prophets when attacking. On June 16, 2009, Kian himself was thrown to the ground, beaten, and kicked by seven Basij militia men while photographing a pro-democracy demonstration. The notorious Basiji are volunteer paramilitaries who serve as the popular auxiliary of Iran's Revolutionary Guards. One of these Basiji stabbed Kian in the back, calling out, *"Ya Hussein,"* referring to Hussein ibn Ali, martyred grandson of the Prophet Muhammad, a legitimate contender to be caliph in the seventh century, according to Shi'a tradition.[15] Bleeding on the pavement, with Hussein's name echoing in his ears, Kian feared the worst: "I saw death for a minute."

Using a ballpoint pen, he re-creates the stabbing for me. When I ask whether he went to the hospital, he laughs sheepishly. After he was knifed under the sacred invocation of "the leader of the martyrs," a friend rushed Kian to an emergency room on a motorcycle. The security forces were waiting, so they could not even enter. Later, another friend delivered him to a different hospital that they thought was secure. The doctor took him into an examining room and closed the door. "What are you doing here, idiot? This is a Ministry of Intelligence hospital."

"What should I do?" Kian asked. The doctor replied, "I will bandage you and give you a tetanus shot. Then go quickly. Tomorrow, see if you can find a hospital to give you stitches." The still-bleeding photojournalist staggered out. But he was stopped by a guard outside who ordered him to wait for the police and file a complaint. Kian gave a fake name and address and hurried off, while the guard wrote down his friend's license-plate number.

Even that incident did not make Kian Amani leave Iran. He decamped later in 2010 because he was making a documentary film about gay Iranians he was then calling *Human and Human*, which he knew "the government would not like at all." To make his film, he spent time living with members of Iran's gay population. "Some of them go to religious events, and are believers, and they are miserable. At the same time they are just hanging out. There are cafés." Just before I met Kian, I had interviewed a gay Kurdish Iranian from a border region; he did not even want to tell me his name and he whispered part of his interview. It took a long time "to know myself," he said. Four times, he attempted suicide for his "family's honor." Roya Boroumand reminded me, as she translated, that according to Section 141 of the Iran penal code you can be executed for "sodomy."[16]

I think of Kian's film and the frightened Kurdish man again in September 2012, when I hear President Ahmadinejad tell CNN's Piers Morgan that "homosexuality is a very ugly behavior." According to Kian, the sources of the difficulties for Iran's gays are found both in the fact that "Iranians traditionally have a problem with homosexuality" and also in what he called "the official religion," the version the president's comment reflects. Homophobic tradition and totalitarian Islamic politics "reinforce each other."

Kian's film pictures one gay man stabbed by his own father, another one shot during the Green Movement protests just like any other demonstrator. He shows me footage from his movie that had been smuggled out of the country by a trusted friend. Kian told the friend that if stopped at the airport with this "offensive" material, he should immediately denounce Kian and save himself. "It belongs to him. Here is his address. Go and get him." Between his daring movie and the controversial pictures he continued to take, Kian found he was always scared about being caught. "There is no way you could sleep comfortably or live in that environment." After the Green Revolution was stamped out, leaving Ahmadinejad securely in power and able to continue terrorizing those Kian had filmed and photographed, "you had a society that had lost hope." His own photography website was repeatedly blocked. All this finally made him pack his bags.

Nevertheless, in the fall of 2010, Kian was personally still optimistic, and he believed that "we will soon see results." He opposed a military attack on Iran but argued that sanctions should be tightened and tied to human rights, "like the sanctions on apartheid South Africa." Most of all, he emphasized solidarity with those he had left behind, "who are trying to bring change." As we sat at Roya's table that peaceful Halloween evening, I was glad to see Kian Amani relaxing with the others. He had not had much to laugh about in recent years. That morning, he had told me that the situation back home was so bad that in the June 2009 protests he heard Iranian demonstrators say of their Islamic rulers: "They don't have the atomic bomb, and look what they do to their own people. What would they do to the world if they got the atom bomb?"

THE STUDENT PRISONER

Kourosh Sehati arrives late for dinner at Roya's. Looking a little like the lead singer of Creed, he has eyes older than the rest of his face. His hair is shoulder length and he wears a green armband that says IRAN. Expelled from university for peaceful political activity with the United Students Front during years of widespread student protest against the Islamic Republic, I dub him "the student prisoner" in my notes. Only thirty-two, he has already been jailed six times, beginning at age twenty-two. The last time, he faced a six-year sentence for opposing the government as a member of an illegal organization, but it was ultimately reduced by the Supreme Court when the group turned out to be perfectly legal.

His worst detention was under the Revolutionary Guards intelligence branch, which kept him in solitary confinement for months in a five-by-six-foot cell, beat him until his ribs broke, and interrogated him blindfolded night after night. "They wanted me to confess against others in the student movement on TV." His family did not know where he was. He had eye problems and scabies, became ill, endured hunger strikes. A nineteen-year-old fellow prisoner suffered a heart attack. During his last detention, Kourosh was kept with ordinary prisoners— his cellmates murderers and drug traffickers. "Seventy or eighty percent of the prisoners . . . had gone crazy because of the severe torture. . . ." Some would "wander around the rest of us naked and urinate."[17]

When he was in Evin Prison in 2000, Kourosh Sehati spent months in the "extremely filthy" quarantine ward with two restrooms for a thousand prisoners.[18] He broke his leg during the daily exercise period but was denied medical treatment. Evin is infamous for torture of political dissidents; ending up there "is every Iranian's nightmare," wrote an expatriate Iranian journalist who spent two weeks in the prison.[19] But Kourosh says he actually preferred being held in Evin because at least his whereabouts were known. When he had been detained in an intelligence services facility, a Revolutionary Court judge had told him, "We will take you where no one can find you."[20]

During this entire odyssey, the student prisoner could not maintain legal representation. "The first time I had a lawyer, but the lawyer was not authorized to read the file." The second lawyer who volunteered to represent him, seventy-year-old Mohammad Ali Safari, was himself detained and interrogated. "So then," Kourosh sighs, "I didn't get a lawyer anymore."

With steel in his spirit, every time the student prisoner was released from Evin or another of the black holes in which he'd been kept, he went right back to openly opposing the theocrats—organizing a public gathering in memory of Mossadegh, commemorating political assassinations, speaking to the international media. In 2004, he was summoned before the Revolutionary Courts following a protest in support of political prisoners in front of the Tehran UN office. "The Revolutionary Courts are illegal,"[21] he told those who summoned him on the telephone, and refused to appear. But this time Kourosh faced a fifteen-year term. So, in June 2004, he crossed illegally into Turkey.

Very religious himself, he was willing to go to jail repeatedly, and ultimately to become a refugee, to defend secularism. I ask Kourosh why as a person of faith he would reject theocracy. "Religion is a very personal thing," he answers. "It's about your relationship with God. When there's religion in government, it's very bad." In such an environment, if you are accused of transgressions against the authorities, "then everyone will say, well, this is against religion." Western multiculturalists sometimes argue that separation of mosque and state is an inherently different issue for Muslims than separation of church and state is for Christians in the West. But like many secularists of Muslim heritage, Sehati, an Iranian believer, has staked his life on the view that "religion and politics should be separate." He is scathing in his condemnation of his government's claims to act in the name of God. Echoing Malika Zouba in Algeria, he says, "Islam is only a tool to further their goals. They are not true Muslims."

For Kourosh, there are diverse strategies for confronting theocracy, using both religious and human rights arguments. "We have some groups in Iran, Ayatollahs, that are against the government because they say this is not real Islam." Meanwhile, theocracy is "turning the current generation in Iran against religion." According to the student prisoner, "They say, well, if this is Islam, if this is Muhammad, then we don't want that kind of Islam." As to his own approach, he resolutely defends universal human rights.

Kourosh Sehati does not mourn his days in prison or his lost youth, nor does he seek to dramatize his own experience. In fact, he smiles in an almost embarrassed way as he tells me, without embroidery, about the dreadful things that have happened to him. I only find out the worst details later from a witness statement he gave to the Iran Human Rights Documentation Center.

I ask how it changed his life to be imprisoned when so young. At thirty-two, he said, "I'm old." But "there is a saying in Iran that bad things lead to good things, and for me gaining this experience will allow me to be stronger in other parts of my life," Kourosh reasons. "This is a value for me, to have paid a price for my ideas." He was willing to make the sacrifices because of all that was at stake in fighting religious repression. "No country in the world has arrived at democracy freely." Now, being far away from home, as he is, has its own cost. "I can't see my family. My father was summoned to the Ministry of Intelligence because of what I'm doing here, but compared to the people in jail, this is not much pressure." A year after I met him, Kourosh's father died. Neither he nor his brother, also a political refugee, could bid him good-bye.

THE ANTITHESIS OF FUNDAMENTALISM

Mahnaz Afkhami was the first (and only) minister for women's affairs in Iranian history.

Assuming her post in 1975, she served at the very end of the Shah's era. "It was politically an autocratic regime," she recognizes. At the same time, "there was a substantial amount of cultural liberty." All these years later, she still thinks that most Muslim majority countries have not matched the "variety of lifestyles, variety of personal expression that was not only permissible, but accepted in Iran" at that time. In fact, back in 1975, Mahnaz was one of only two ministers for women's affairs in the entire world. At first she was reluctant, "[c]onscious that joining the government might adversely affect [her] role as a spokesperson for women."[22] However, observing the "encouraging results" achieved by the only other women's affairs minister (in France) at the time, Afkhami agreed to join the cabinet of Prime Minister Amir Abbas Hoveyda.

Still, she does not whitewash the regime, which was known for imprisoning and torturing political opponents under the watch of the CIA-trained SAVAK. In this patriarchal society, she had to battle the government for every step forward for women. As minister, Afkhami championed a new and improved family law, commissioned the first study of honor killing, and pressed for a new law to prohibit such killings. The Iranian women's movement mobilized to exact these concessions from the Shah's government. Many of them also supported the initial phase of the revolution. They went into the streets demanding "more freedom, more equality," Afkhami says. She herself clung to the belief that through the efforts of genuine Iranian democrats, "wonderful, brilliant, committed patriots," they could build "a moderate inclusive democracy. All this was completely obliterated in the fundamentalist effort."

While she headed the Women's Organization of Iran, and then as a government minister, Afkhami had backed the 1975 Family Protection

Law that provided for alimony and greatly restricted polygamy, even granting a wife the right to divorce if her husband married again. The first big "revolutionary" act of the Islamic Republic was to abrogate this very law. Roya Boroumand had decried the lack of an international response to this move when I discussed it with her. "Outside Iran, no one said anything. Where were the feminists? Women came out in the streets in the thousands and they were beaten, they were arrested. Where were the Muslims?"

As we talk about revolutions that have set women back, in light of the transitions of 2011 in North Africa, Mahnaz Afkhami remembers the double-talk of the fundamentalists in Iran in 1977–78. They co-opted the language of women's rights in highly sophisticated ways, which she thinks were dazzling to some Western feminists. When the mullahs railed against the use of women as sexual objects, they actually meant that "women should be veiled head to toe." This, she finds, is a lesson to be drawn from what happened in Iran—that you have to evaluate fundamentalist groups based on deeds and not just words. "People talk about democracy, but actually they're not willing to do what democracy means."

In a 1963 fatwa, Ayatollah Khomeini had said that women's political participation was tantamount to prostitution. But the fundamentalists "are very adaptable" when necessary. When Khomeini observed the presence of women in the revolution, he changed the fatwa, encouraging "the sisters" to be active in politics—meaning to support the Islamic Republic. For women involved in politics who were not Islamists, the cost would still be terribly high.

When the revolution occurred, the minister for women's affairs found herself on the list of the top twenty people to be executed—wanted dead or alive. All her family's property was confiscated—"home, pictures, belongings, everything." There was a price on her head, a bounty applicable whether she was found inside or outside of Iran. At the time she was condemned to death, Mahnaz Afkhami happened to be at the United Nations, involved in the final efforts to set up INSTRAW, the United Nations International Research and Training Institute for the Advancement of Women in Tehran. The negotiations that were supposed to take two weeks took six. Meanwhile, the revolution accelerated. She was told if she returned home, the transitional government would arrest her. Mahnaz would never go home again. "Women's activism gave me some of the most nourishing experiences of my life. It also caused me to lose my country, and then it saved my life again."

The only other woman minister in the prerevolutionary government was executed—an event that still weighs on Mahnaz Afkhami. Farrokhroo Parsa, the former minister of education, had been long retired. "They wanted to kill a woman public figure. I sometimes wonder if they would still have killed her had I been there." Parsa was a physician and teacher who, with Afkhami's encouragement, had ordered the revision of Iranian textbooks to improve the image of women. Postrevolution, Parsa told schoolgirls and women teachers that they did not have to veil inside classrooms. Teachers themselves were demanding this exemption. On May 8, 1980, Farrokhroo Parsa was hanged for "spreading vice on earth and fighting God," the same charges as those leveled against Afkhami.

Today, the sole surviving female former cabinet minister heads the Women's Learning Partnership (WLP), which coalesced at the 1995 Fourth World Conference on Women in Beijing. The participatory partnership has grown to twenty countries and twenty languages, with bases from Afghanistan to Nigeria. Fundamentalism is "the central issue" they work on, Mahnaz explains. They have their work cut out for them. In August 2012, WLP sent out an action alert trying to block Iran's plans to segregate university classrooms and bar women from up to seventy-seven majors, including engineering, accounting, and chemistry.[23]

With all her years of hard experience, Afkhami tells me she thinks "to fight fundamentalism, you need to have a vision. You cannot change anything unless you have a vision of what is the life you want to lead." The fundamentalists have a big idea. Those who oppose them must also have one. "They express those ideas clearly and are courageous about expressing them. We also have to have big ideas, and we have to be courageous."

With vivid memories of the fashionable views of revolutionary Iran held by some in the late 1970s, she deplores what she sees as the "infatuation" of some Western academics with fundamentalism.[24] "People are promoting ideas, which if applied to their life, they would find horrific, but they apologize for or even applaud these ideas in other people's lives." Some leftist academics have to accept their responsibility, she thinks, for making "Khomeini and the fundamentalists in Iran palatable to the West." She does not know how anyone can justify a regime that has put women "on par with the insane and the minor."

Mahnaz Afkhami, lifelong fighter for women's equality, who narrowly escaped a firing squad for being an "enemy of God," sums up what Iran's regime has meant in her own life. "The fundamentalist revolution not only destroyed my history and my identity and my connections and my family. Not only that, they have destroyed my country's last thirty years. There was a time that I couldn't talk about this without crying.

"If you gave me a chance, I would be crying again."

THE MAN IS THE GOD OF THAT FAMILY

Thirty-five-year-old Kurdish Iranian Aida Saadat has shoulder-length hair, dark eyes arched by waxed brows, and enviable cheekbones. While she talks, she occasionally pumps her fists, which is incongruous with her petite appearance. Aida, as I am told, "is not your Tehran Green," meaning she is no stereotypical liberal middle-class denizen of the capital.

Originally from the city of Qazvin, Aida was active with the Million Signatures Campaign that began in June 2006. For three years, she worked on its website and advocated for political prisoners. The campaign sought to change Iranian laws that discriminate against women by raising awareness among the population and collecting a million supporting signatures from people in the street.[25] Its founding petition describes some of the de jure inequality they try to undo:

> According to Iranian penal codes, a girl at nine . . . is considered . . . an adult. If she commits a crime . . . punishable by execution, the courts can sentence her to death. If a man and a woman become paralyzed as a result of an accident, the punitive

damages provided to the woman . . . equal half of those provided
to the man. . . . The law allows a father who obtains court permission to marry off his daughter . . . before the age of thirteen
. . . to a man as old as seventy.[26]

The Million Signatures Campaign engaged popular participation in
the process of reforming such laws, concentrating on face-to-face interactions. This approach avoids what founding member Noushin Khorasani called "sterile elitism" but also exposed activists to risks.[27] "The
first year it was not a hard thing to do," Aida Saadat recalls, "but little
by little, there was a security concern. We were arrested while gathering signatures." Large numbers of women campaigners were rounded
up, as many 180 over time, Aida among them.[28] "I was even arrested
once while we were trying to hold a ceremony of solidarity for women in
Iran." On that day, June 12, 2008, she became one of those who needed
that same solidarity.

"It was not a long time in prison but it was a good experience." She
guffaws as she says "good experience." In Iran, where a significant
majority of human rights activists have been jailed, it is a rite of passage.
That time, Aida was only kept a few days, but later she was pursued
repeatedly by the authorities—"sometimes by phone calls and sometimes by written summons." Charged with propaganda against national
security, she was acquitted.

The Iranian government was perpetually at odds with the Million
Signatures campaigners. While the activists tried to change laws on
marriage and divorce to benefit women, Parliament was busy loosening
legal restrictions on polygamy even further.[29] All avenues for progressive reform of such laws had been closed off. "Even our website where
we were trying to write about discriminatory laws was blocked, and
those who were working on this were arrested," Aida recounts.

When I ask about the best tactics for challenging fundamentalism in
a country called "the Islamic Republic," she is flummoxed. "I'm afraid
there's no answer for that." From exile in the United States, she worries
about her fellow activists back home. "My friends are still trying to do
something, but they cannot hold any meeting. They cannot go to the
street to talk to people. Everything is kind of at an impasse."

In December 2009, this young woman full of love for her country was prosecuted yet again, this time for participating in the uprising after the highly contested presidential elections. "We were trying to document, and talking to different people whose families were killed in the street, being involved with the Mournful Mothers [mothers of murdered 2009 protesters], doing interviews with media outside Iran." This work put her on a collision course with the authorities that would seal her fate—to become a refugee like Kourosh, Kian, and Mahnaz. Intelligence agents who knew her name followed her to her Tehran neighborhood at night, questioned her, then hit her with their batons until she bled on the sidewalk. The agents said they would be back. That same night, Aida Saadat fled.[30]

Somehow, improbably, she laughs again when telling me she ran across the frontier into neighboring Turkey at night, evading patrols. She was the only woman in the group. Right after she made it across, eleven people were arrested on the Iranian side of the border. "We were the first group which came out, and after less than five minutes, they were shooting and some were arrested. I don't know what happened to them." She tries to check tears that well in her bright eyes. "This guy died next to me."

Not only was her flight perilous, but Aida had to leave behind a young son in Iran. They would be separated for nearly three years until his arrival in the United States in 2012. Still, this activist refuses to accept the victim's mantle. Instead, she tries to make things better for others. "I'm concentrating on the work I'm doing right now with refugees." Saadat wants to go to law school. Meanwhile, she wants activists in the United States to pressure governments to raise the issue of human rights in Iran. "We are always talking about sanctions. But nobody is talking about how to support Iranian human rights defenders."

ASIEH'S EYES

Asieh Amini makes the sign of the noose around her neck.

This is a dramatic contrast to her kind, round face. She wears a green vest and long earrings and looks like a professor of literature. Possessed by a case she worked on involving a young woman hung for "crimes against chastity," she cannot stop talking about it. The noose is tied to her, too, now.

After seventeen years as a journalist with a big newspaper, Asieh became editor-in-chief of a feminist website called *Zanan-e Iran* (Women in Iran), in 2003. Having come from a liberal family, she had lived with relative freedom. Her life changed forever when she read a newspaper article about a young woman named Atefah Sahaaleh, who had been executed in public in the Iranian city of Neka in 2004. The paper claimed Atefah was twenty-one. Through her own connections, Asieh elicited information suggesting Atefah was much younger than that. The journalist found herself compelled to know the girl's real age, to discover why she had been executed. "Why? Why? Why?" To get some answers, the journalist picked up and went to the girl's desolate hometown north of Tehran. There, she met Asieh's entire family and saw her ID card, which proved she had been only sixteen at the time she was hanged.

Amini had reported on many social topics before, but never on such executions. The girl's death transfixed her. She began focusing on women's rights, investigating executions and trying to understand the legal system. Before that, she had known almost nothing about human rights. "No, I was a poet, I was a journalist, I was in my dream, my good situation. I had to understand the other life that my neighbors had, that other women had." So the woman from the liberal family with the good life jumped off the high board into dangerous waters. She started writing about what had happened to Atefah Sahaaleh.

"I wrote about her every night. I cried until morning. How did this happen?" Establishing the precise details of Atefah's case remains difficult; stories diverge and the Iranian government has made it virtually impossible to verify the facts. But Asieh discovered the girl's father was a penniless heroin addict. Her mother died in a car crash when she was a child. A lonely, rebellious, and unsupervised kid, she was abused at every turn. At the age of thirteen, Atefah seems to have been raped repeatedly by a man in her family who then gave her to his friends. She was jailed, lashed. Then, it seems, she may have been sexually abused by members of the morality police. In court, she reportedly removed her headscarf, to the horror of the man who would seal her fate, Judge Haji Rezai.

On August 15, 2004, Atefah Sahaaleh was executed for "crimes against chastity." Judge Rezai, who allegedly was also involved in Khomeini's 1983 campaign of mass executions, hanged this victim himself, hoisting Atefah, who had never harmed anyone, onto a crane in front of a crowd in her own neighborhood.[31] He left her body hanging for forty-five minutes.

In Asieh's soft-spoken words: "That was very terrible. But I published it." Once she had done so, she began to look into other cases of women who were sentenced to death, languishing in prison and awaiting execution. She began reporting on "juvenile executions, women's executions and of course stoning." She signed her name to those stories too.

Iran's penal code is so sadistic that it actually specifies that whenever a person is sentenced to multiple *hadd* punishments, "they should be executed in a sequence, so that the execution of one . . . may not destroy the possibility of the execution of another."[32] In other words, one is to be lashed within an inch of one's life (but not killed) so that one can still be stoned to death for offenses like extramarital sex.

Disturbed by all that she was uncovering, Asieh and some friends founded the Stop Stoning Forever Campaign. She tried to arrange pro bono lawyers for as many Iranian death-row inmates as possible. I read later that her campaign saved the lives of a score of people facing execution and stoning; a whole group of women were let out of prison after she publicized their stories. Not all the endings were so happy, however. An article called "Asieh's Eyes," by activist Soheila Vahdati, relates: "When the campaign's efforts could not stop the stoning of Jafar Kiani [for adultery] in [the city of] Takistan in 2007, it was Asieh who went there and took pictures of the pit where Jafar was stoned to death."[33] Asieh later said, "There were bloody stones on the ground. I touched one, and when I came home, I could not move for hours."[34]

So taxing was her work that she developed serious eye problems that, according to her doctors, were caused by "severe stress." The journalist who had tried to get others to see what she had seen nearly went blind. Simultaneously, she experienced significant memory loss. You begin to understand why when reading her description of this time in her life in a piece she penned called "The Island." "I would go town to town, following the cases, victim by victim. . . . But when I got close to them, I could not separate myself from them. . . . They have become a part of my awareness and my dreams."[35] Asieh then asks, "But who is to teach us what distance to keep from our cases and what to do when you get involved?"[36]

Eventually, there was no distance at all. In 2007, Asieh Amini was detained just like those she wrote about. Interrogated in Evin Prison, she was forced into exile after the 2009 elections. Her friends and colleagues, and even her lawyer, had been arrested one by one. When the website she worked for was denounced for influencing world public opinion against the regime, she finally bolted for Norway.

Despite what Amini has seen and documented, despite illness and exile, she has not given up. She blogs. You can find her on the Internet wisely admonishing human rights defenders "to first learn how to take care of her/himself, then the rest of the world." When I meet her, she is almost bubbly, though I can still see Atefah somewhere deep in Asieh's now-famous eyes. Mixing Farsi and English, she lingers to finish our discussion in the corridor of the conference hall where she had given a lecture about the women's movement in Iran, even as friends try to pry her away for a much-deserved Saturday-night dinner.

As she leaves, she assures me in an impassioned run-on sentence that if Iranians had a free choice, they would never again choose an Islamic system.

CHAPTER SEVEN

The Ramadan Basketball Tournament

The struggle against Muslim fundamentalism is truly global now. Yet, I am still startled to discover it in 2011 in Minnesota's Twin Cities.

Thousands of Somali refugees live in poor conditions in a massive high-rise public-housing project called "The Towers," located in a Minneapolis neighborhood sometimes known as "Little Mogadishu." That is where Burhan Hassan grew up. His uncle, Somali American activist Abdirizak Bihi, traveled to Kenya in 1996 to rescue his widowed sister and her four-year-old son and bring them back to the Midwest. After a little over a decade in the United States, a teenage Burhan—allegedly recruited through a local mosque—would become "Little Bashir," a fighter for Al Shabaab, in the home country he had never known.

Through a colleague at the University of Minnesota Law School, I connect with members of the Somali population in this unlikely host city with its notorious winters. These Somali Midwesterners, driven here by decades of war back home, have recently been retraumatized by the conflict they thought they had left behind. Al Shabaab, the fundamentalist armed group that has fought an insurgency since 2006 and that became an affiliate of Al Qaeda in 2012, had recruited a small but significant number of young men from Minneapolis, like Burhan Hassan, to wage jihad in East Africa. The recruitment dynamic was transnational; there are Somali kids who have gone missing from Canada and England as well.

But it is a Minnesotan, twenty-six-year-old Shirwa Ahmed, who became the first U.S. citizen suicide bomber when he blew himself up in Somalia on October 29, 2009, killing thirty. The FBI director claimed Ahmed was "radicalized in his hometown in Minnesota."[1] I want to understand how this could happen in Middle America, and to find out who is trying to keep it from happening again.

BURYING BURHAN

Burhan Hassan's uncle Abdirizak Bihi is a longtime community organizer and currently the director of the Somali Education and Social Advocacy Center, a no-budget outfit he founded in 2003 that relies on volunteers. I am warned he is "controversial." After I meet Bihi, I can only assume this is because he has been so outspoken and specific in his criticism of Al Shabaab, and of all those who failed to stand up to this militia. He and his family have lived the consequences of these failures at close range.

Moving to America had seemed like a great development for his nephew Burhan. "He was a very eager kid, he wanted to come here. Immediately, he picked up the whole culture and the language." The boy excelled at calculus, and got As and Bs at Roosevelt High School. When I see Burhan's picture in the YouTube film of his uncle's testimony in Congress, he is a skinny kid with glasses who resembles his uncle. On YouTube, Burhan also appears so unaware; he still has that heartbreakingly vulnerable look of nice teenage boys.

"We had a problem," his uncle continues. "This community is comprised of over 65 percent single-mom households, and they are all below the poverty line. It was difficult for them because of lack of opportunity." Such an environment was ripe for exploitation. "Then, the 'mosque phenomenon' spread," Bihi notes. Desperate to keep his nephew on the straight and narrow, Bihi paid for the young man to participate in an after-school program at the Abubakar As-Saddique Islamic Center in Minneapolis, which had a Qur'anic school for Somali American youth.

Burhan Hassan appeared to thrive there, even spending his weekends at the institution and receiving an award for learning to recite the Qur'an. Under the challenging socioeconomic circumstances in "The Towers," it seemed to his uncle a positive thing to "have your kid learning his religion, his culture, and most of all, not ending up in the back seat of the car, or stealing, or hurting other people, or doing drugs. A lot of kids turn out really good."

But then, "since 2006, this new phenomenon—Al Shabaab—started recruiting here, in one particular mosque." Al Shabaab recruiters and leaders, he explains, "knew just how to become the dad these boys never had." Before long, twenty Somali kids went missing. "On November 4, 2008, my nephew left." The night of Barack Obama's historic election, this African American teenager who dreamed of Harvard disappeared. "My sister calls me to look for him." The family found Burhan's old laptop loaded with sermons in English by none other than Anwar al-Awlaki.[2] They began to realize that the boy's disappearance was a piece of a larger puzzle. "We met other families in the police station looking for their kids. We found documents, itineraries. The next day I summoned the FBI. They had no clue. They have never seen Muslim families saying we have a problem. Usually we keep quiet."

"Now, I know why we keep quiet." Abdirizak Bihi and his sister were stunned by the abuse he faced at the hands of the religious establishment when they did speak out. "The mosque leadership were our friends, ironically. We met them five, six times." The personal connection offered no shield. "Then one day we called on the imam to meet with the families. He did not show up. Unusually. Then, we see on Somali TV: There is the imam, calling us infidels and tools of the infidels, saying, 'These families were trying to destroy the mosque.'" This was in sharp contrast to Bihi's own vision of what he was trying to do by exposing the Al Shabaab recruitment drive: "Save the religion I love from a very small number of extremists."[3]

Like so many others, his family had donated to the house of worship that now denounced them. "My sister, like any other woman, would give her gold." These well-intentioned donations, meant to support what was thought to be a legitimate religious institution, instead helped pave the road to hell. ("By the way, they are rich," Bihi claims about the mosque his nephew attended.) Yet, as in other religious communities, people give not only their much-needed funds but also their allegiance and their trust. So, as in the early years of the child sexual-abuse scandal in the Catholic Church, that trust makes it hard to demand answers when something goes wrong. "Once I questioned their practices, I had my whole family on me saying, 'Don't do this,'" Bihi remembers.

The mosque leadership, he reports, was determined to keep the affected families from going public.[4] "So, they used this network. They sent people to my sister and other mothers, saying, 'Don't talk to Bihi. Don't talk to the police.'" Seeking to maintain a code of silence, the mosque leaders offered three reasons for keeping quiet. After hearing these, I no longer wonder that more people have not spoken out. "One, the Americans are infidels. They hate Muslims. They will send you to Guantanamo. It's a narrative that has kept people quiet, even before us." Single mothers who do not speak English may, he says, have deep-seated fear of the government, making this threat especially powerful. If fear is argument one, shame is argument two. "Number two, they also use a moral obligation. By you speaking out, you will be a good tool to eradicate Islamic society here, and close the mosque." Finally, they pile on divine sanction. "Third, they say that you will end up eternally in hell for doing this."

But neither threats of Guantanamo nor threats of damnation could silence Abdirizak Bihi. The scale of his family's loss outweighed both. According to his testimony before Congress, "Burhan would periodically call his mother from Somalia. . . . The last time [he] called . . . he told my sister that he was sick." The boy was apparently vomiting so violently that he had lost his glasses over the side of a boat on which he was traveling. Then, "[o]n June 5, 2009, my sister got a phone call from another recruit who told [her] that 'Little Bashir' was shot in the head . . . and that he had helped bury Burhan." The family received reports that the son of Al Shabaab's leader had killed Little Bashir for "insubordination." However, they suspect he was actually murdered because of fears he would cooperate with American investigators, as the boy had finally promised his mother he would come home to Minneapolis.[5] Instead, Burhan Hassan was buried somewhere in Somalia at the age of seventeen.

LOYALTY TO THE TEAM RATHER THAN GOD

As a result of his family's odyssey, Abdirizak Bihi decided to testify at the polarizing March 2011 hearings held by the House Homeland Security Committee, organized by Committee Chairman Peter King, on Islamic radicalization in America. These hearings demonstrate all the failings of the debate in this country about Muslim fundamentalism.

King, a right-wing Republican congressman from New York, clearly had his own unfortunate agenda for organizing such hearings, and he had in the past decried the proliferation of mosques in America (though he later suggested he meant mosques that do not cooperate with the authorities).[6] The event was unfortunately labeled "The Extent of Radicalization in the American Muslim Community and the Community's Response." Framed as such, it risked playing into the hands of both the anti-Islam fringe of the Republican Party and Muslim fundamentalists who try to convince Muslims that Americans vilify them. On the other hand, King's liberal and Muslim American critics seemed to act as if there was no problem at all.[7] Islamic radicalization? What Islamic radicalization? Any such discussion can only be an Islamophobic plot to discredit the Muslim community. The most absurd comparison was to the McCarthy hearings of the 1950s. Such theories are a great boon to Muslim fundamentalists, who label any attempt to combat them an attack on all Muslims. The critics did not say what should be done to tackle the actual problem; they did not even admit it was real.

Representative Keith Ellison, an African American convert to Islam noted for being the first Muslim member of Congress, wept as he ended his testimony at the Islamic radicalization hearings by talking about Mohammad Salman Hamdani. A twenty-three-year-old Muslim American police cadet and first responder who died on 9/11, Hamdani was at first disparagingly suspected of links to the attack because of his religious background and Pakistani heritage (though later buried with full NYPD honors at a funeral attended by Mayor Michael Bloomberg).[8] The initial response to Hamdani's death testifies both to the depth of prejudice in the United States as well as to the awful problems jihadist groups inflict on Muslim populations in places where they kill in the name of Islam.

Crying over such a story is entirely understandable, but there are many others one could also weep for at a hearing about "radicalization." Congressman Ellison referred to the hearings as "the very heart of scapegoating." But he had almost nothing concrete to say about Muslim fundamentalism—the ideology underpinning the radicalization that the hearings were about, and what it has meant in the lives of millions of Muslims.

The congressman's tears, which received far more press coverage than the story of Burhan Hassan's death, are the only thing most people remember about the event. That is a lost opportunity on all sides to support people of Muslim heritage who oppose fundamentalism. "The victims of the bloodthirsty version of Islam were first and foremost Muslims," as Algerian journalist Malika Zouba had reminded me. Hence, those who think their role is to defend the rights of Muslims have no choice but to tackle this problem.

Bihi, who had lost his sister's teenage son to a violent death far away, did not weep during the hearing. For him, it was too important a chance to tell the nation about what happened to his family, about the destruction of their Muslim American dream by Muslim extremists, and about the American failures that facilitated it. The hearing was also an opportunity to publicly excoriate the institutions he felt had let down his family and his community. For daring to do that, he has paid a high price. He was smeared in the local press and received anonymous calls attacking him for daring to point fingers at the mosque he believed to be involved.

Still, Abdirizak Bihi persisted in trying to fight Al Shabaab, with minimal financial resources at his disposal. He was angry with some of the mainstream Muslim community organizations like the Council on American Islamic Relations (CAIR), which he feels covered up the problem of Al Shabaab recruitment. He alleges that CAIR took the side of the mosque against families like his and indicated to the U.S. government that any criticism would be a reflection of anti-Muslim discrimination. Bihi was alarmed by what he saw as the pervasive denial of the problem, including by community leaders more concerned with consolidating their own power. So he organized several local demonstrations against CAIR in Minneapolis. With just one hour's planning, fifty Somalis gathered at one such rally in June 2009, the week after Burhan was killed, to denounce what they believed were CAIR's efforts to discourage Somalis from cooperating in the investigation. "CAIR Out! Doublespeak out!"[9]

CAIR later cosigned a letter with the Abubakar As-Saddique Islamic Center to Minnesota law-enforcement agencies claiming those leading the charge against Al Shabaab recruitment here are "anti-Muslim," "fear-mongering," and "unrepresentative." "I'm not anti-Muslim," responded one of them, Omar Jamal. "I'm anti–Islamic terrorism."[10] Fighting this kind of reputational war is grueling.

Yet Abdirizak Bihi remains determined to engage, because in a climate of rising fundamentalism, "there is no alternative for kids. I hate the victim card, but it's facts that we're learning." In addition to the immediate culprits, he blames "the extreme harsh conditions of poverty. I blame those at the state level, at the US level for not doing anything for the community. I think many issues contribute." But ultimately, he still holds "the leadership of the mosque solely responsible for my nephew and all those kids that are missing."

To tackle extremism, one must first acknowledge it. Then one must also try to explain it. "Somali people don't sympathize with Al Shabaab," Bihi tells me in May 2011, "but they don't find alliances, whether it's in Somalia or here. I blame the international community's failure in engaging Somalia as a stable community. As long as that doesn't happen, Europe and America will not be safe. I said this two years ago," he recalls, referencing Somali-born teenager Mohamed Osman Mohamud's attempt to detonate dummy explosives at a Portland, Oregon, Christmas-tree lighting ceremony in November 2010.[11] While the fake explosives turned out to be part of an FBI sting operation, Mohamud allegedly said that he wanted everyone who came to the gathering to perish, and that he would not have minded if children were among the dead.[12] This means Americans now have a vested interest in what happens in East Africa, where African Union peacekeepers reclaimed Mogadishu in August 2011 and in 2012 had the group on the run.

Al Shabaab has itself faced increasing defections as local Somalis increasingly resent their use of amputations, their draconian rules banning things like musical ringtones, their attacks on the tombs of Sufi clerics (which provoked street protests), and their use of hated foreign jihadis. Even when famine spread across Somalia in 2011, Al Shabaab was more interested in blocking "infidel" aid workers from their lands than saving from starvation babies born into Muslim families.[13] One defector told the BBC: "I realized they were not about religion. They were about killing people."[14] Meanwhile, the new Somali government attempts to find its feet, offering increasing hope of a new beginning. Nevertheless, the local Al Qaeda affiliate still has a foothold in southern Somalia and remains capable of carrying out terrorist atrocities—not only inside the country but also in neighboring Kenya and Uganda. Undoing the damage they have wrought in an already devastated nation will take years.

Abdirizak Bihi continues his lonely work. "I don't know if we can survive," he confesses to me in 2011. "But my strategy was if we win the community, more people will talk to the authorities, and they will be able to indict more people. Eighteen have been indicted because of the community."[15] He tells me, pushing his glasses onto the top of his head, that working with the community is key. "The US government, or any government, has to have that strategy. They cannot rely on people like me. I'm crazy. How many crazy people will you find?"

Bihi is not alone, however. He has catalyzed elders in his community to speak out. He gives me a copy of a "Somali American Elders Press Release," dated September 1, 2010.[16] The elders—an informal collection of highly regarded men, and ever-greater numbers of women—have long tackled community social issues. Their statement stresses the positive contributions Somalis generally have made in the United States, expressing gratitude for the welcome they have received in Minnesota, along with a commitment not to let "a few evil-minded individuals . . . spoil our hard-earned reputation and our excellent achievements." The elders try to protect that reputation and defy Al Shabaab by, that very same month, holding a Ramadan Iftar dinner to which they invite local law-enforcement figures.

The September 2010 press release contains a list of nine numbered points that openly take on their home country's extremists. They do not mince words. Point 4 says, "We, Somali American community elders acknowledge the sinister and inhuman acts of Al-Shabab terrorist organization has inflicted [*sic*] on our fragile community by brainwashing and recruiting some of our Somali American youth." The statement also describes the grim reality back home at the time it was drafted in 2010. "We also acknowledge the daily carnage, human suffering and pain Al-Shabab inflicts on the Somali people in Somalia as well as the recent barbaric acts in Uganda."

The latter is a reference to 2010 Al Shabaab bombings in Kampala targeting those watching the broadcast of the soccer World Cup, killing seventy-six. While the bombing clearly was intended to punish Uganda for its participation in the African Union peacekeeping mission in Somalia, it also followed an extremist fatwa issued on the Internet in June 2010 by a member of the Sharia Council of *Minbar al Tawhid wal Jihad*, a college of radical Sunni scholars. Council member Abu al-Walid al-Maqdisi inveighed against Muslims watching the World Cup because "these matches are invented by our enemies, and through the matches they seek to distract us from jihad,"[17] for they promote "loyalty to the team, rather than God." A month later, bombs ripped through a packed Kampala restaurant and sports club three minutes before the end of the World Cup final.

Unlike those attacking soccer games, Bihi sees sport as a healthy outlet for young people, and as a way to diminish vulnerability to Al Shabaab recruitment. Many Somalis in Minneapolis share his enthusiasm for athletics. The day after I talk to him, when I visit the Sahara Restaurant at lunchtime, a group of young Somali men boisterously absorb a soccer match on TV between some Arab teams. They embody the comment posted at the bottom of a story about the June 2010 fatwa against football: "90% of Arab men believe there is soccer in paradise."

Given such popular attitudes obviously shared by many Somalis, Bihi tried to launch a sports league to promote alternatives for local youth. It was no simple undertaking. "I have to beg around in the community. I go around the businesses here with young people and collect money. So, we got the money and rented a gym." The games he had in mind were very serious. "Four hundred young men played basketball. Why? One day, Al Shabaab exploded themselves in Uganda in the World Cup. I have to come up with something here. Because they will have recruiters here. So, I went to the community and said, 'I have a gym. All the teams lined up.' Within two or three days we opened the gym up. We brought Somali engineers, doctors, elders, moderate imams—that was a big setback for Al Shabaab group.

"I call it the Ramadan Basketball Tournament."

This endeavor was an uphill battle limited by lack of funds.[18] "We never got money. We tried to keep this place open. We planned five or six teams. We ended up playing for four months. And every week we have to find a way to keep the gym open; 400 people were playing." Bihi says he was overwhelmed by demands from people to include their kids in the program. Like Mohamed of Blida, who had refused to give up sports in 1990s Algeria even in the face of jihadi pressure, he knows that giving young people something life-affirming and fun to do together here in Minneapolis can make a bigger difference than you might think. Joy is antifundamentalist.

In an insular, interconnected community, the organizer of the Ramadan Basketball Tournament often knows his opponents very well. "A couple of them called me—recruiters. We had coffee yesterday. Somalis always talk to each other. They said, 'We know you are smart, but this is not your idea. Did the FBI give you money to do this?' I said, 'I wish.' They would go around to the businesses and say that the FBI are giving us money and I'm making millions of dollars and not to give us money." In reality, when Abdirizak Bihi goes to visit other families who have lost their children to Al Shabaab, he sometimes has to borrow gas money,[19] and he is regularly battling eviction.

As he would later tell the *Washington Post*, sometimes Bihi's own wife and daughters get fed up with his thankless work and tell him, "Give up. Burhan is dead."[20] But he cannot. He still thinks of his own nephew, and of other kids he works to protect from recruitment who sometimes also call him "Uncle."[21]

In a 2012 follow-up conversation, Bihi sounds more upbeat. Things back home are improving since the London conference on Somalia held earlier in the year, and the election of a new president in September, though they are nowhere near being out of the woods. There is now, as he frames the new situation, "huge hope in a big mess." Moreover, the Somali population—and Somali Americans—have turned increasingly against Al Shabaab because of its slaughter of students and doctors in suicide attacks, and its daily cruelty. But, even on the retreat, the terror group still recruits. Bihi believes they have taken three or four more local youths since Ramadan 2012, including a twenty-year-old named Omar Farah.

To Bihi's delight, however, on October 18, 2012, a Somali American from Minnesota named Mahamud Said Omar became the first person convicted for Al Shabaab's recruitment here.[22] The verdict, he thinks, "sends a good message to the parents who lost children and shows that these guys are not untouchable." There has been a huge shift in attitudes and more people have joined him in speaking out, making his work less lonely. He is pleased that the administration of Barack Obama and the international community have engaged constructively in Somalia since our last meeting, contributing to a newly growing but vulnerable stability. Yet he still feels the U.S. government and local officials have not invested sufficiently in Somali American youth, so Minneapolis's Somali community remains in a "fragile situation." Hence, Mr. Bihi continues to try to cobble together social and recreational programs on a shoestring budget. Currently, he is attempting to set up a youth photography program with volunteer teachers.

Despite his powerful sense of purpose, Abdirizak Bihi is weary from the level of responsibility he feels. "I wish we could have more leaders. I wish the government would make it easy for those leaders who could do this, so I could go back to my life."

THE IMAM OF MINNEAPOLIS

One imam spoke out resolutely against Al Shabaab's recruitment in Minneapolis: Imam Sharif Mohamed. Imam Sharif, whose name roughly translates as "noble descendant of the Prophet," arrived in the United States in 1996. Two years later, he founded his mosque, appropriately named *Dar al-Hijra Masjid* (House of Flight), across from the

"Towers" housing project. In addition to offering spiritual guidance, Imam Sharif often provides family counseling, mediating between parents who came from Somalia and their U.S.-born children.

When I arrive at his mosque, a kids' program run by women is underway. It is almost snack time; the women unpack grocery bags. I take off my shoes and head upstairs. The imam welcomes me at the modest desk in his cramped office that features both Arabic and Somali calligraphy on the walls. Wearing an embroidered cap and simple suitcoat, he has a neat, short beard. He apologizes regularly for his English, even though it is very good. Imam Sharif says he would most like to be described simply as "a Muslim." When asked for further clarification, he says it would be accurate to specify that he is a liberal imam.

I ask how much he worries about extremism in the community he serves, given what has happened with recent Al Shabaab recruitments. According to Imam Sharif, the media has exaggerated the problem. He does the math for me. "There are maybe thirty thousand Somalis that live here, and maybe twenty went back," to fight with Al Shabaab. Press reports a few months later suggest that about twenty-five young men have been recruited from Minneapolis, and perhaps forty from the entire United States, but his point is well taken.[23] Nevertheless, the imam is stepping up to the plate, aware of his own responsibility. "We need imams like me to say that this is against our religion. We need to say it loudly."

I reflect on the protest organized in Minneapolis in 2009 after "Somalia's 9/11"—the December 3, 2009, suicide bombing carried out by a Somali from Denmark. He targeted a medical graduation ceremony in Mogadishu, killing twenty-two, including the tireless minister of health, Qamar Aden Ali, who was trying to improve hospital conditions. Disgusted, a hundred Somali demonstrators, including Ali's brother, rallied in the Minnesota slush outside the Brian Coyle Community Center, carrying signs that read, SAVE SOMALIA NOW.[24] These Somali protesters braved the elements to speak their opposition "loudly," just as Imam Sharif deems necessary. But such stories do not go national or global, and they should.

The imam himself is one of those who has stuck his neck out to address the problem of extremism, regardless of whether or not the world pays attention. When the group of local youth was discovered to have left for jihad in Somalia, "First, I condemned it," he said. "I think I may have been the only imam who condemned this publicly. I said it on the BBC. I said, 'This is wrong, this is not part of our religion, part of Islam. Anyone behind this is a criminal.'" He was unequivocal, and his condemnation was very visible.

Did it cross his mind that he was putting himself in danger? "Not here," he said of the threat he might face, "but maybe in Africa. I may be on Al Shabaab's list. Two years ago, when there was a suicide bombing in Somalia, I had a lecture and said, 'We, the Somali people, were Muslim before Al Shabaab.'" Al Shabaab representatives came to the lecture to monitor his words. "They put me on YouTube and when I went to Europe people recognized me. I received some nasty phone calls, but I don't think it's Al Shabaab, just people saying that I'm not a good Muslim."

In addition to speaking out, he has tried to do something concrete about the damage done by Al Shabaab's recruitment. "Second, we created a committee who tried to do three jobs: to talk to the media, to mediate between the mosque and the people who are finger-pointing, and to work with the parents. We created a group to deal with the authorities, to say we are ready to work with you but we do not want the community to be treated with hostility." I later discover that Imam Sharif went out of his way to meet with the female relatives of those lost to Al Shabaab recruitment, and to offer his support in their time of grief. "Oh my God, you should have seen their faces," someone who was present tells me about the women's appreciation of the imam's visit, during which he offered prayers and support. "He is an amazing person."

Beyond opposition to terrorism and the recruitment efforts of Al Shabaab, the stalwart imam also tells me he advocates equality of men and women, promotes women's rights activism, and had even suggested to Somali cab drivers in Minneapolis—who had recently refused to carry passengers from the airport if they had duty-free alcohol with them—that there was no reason they could not do so under Islam.

All of these positions are significant, and the fact that he espouses them openly even more so, for around the world the fundamentalists have sometimes managed to push many nonfundamentalist people of Muslim heritage into a state of self-censorship (either out of fear or discomfort), especially in contexts where Muslims are a minority. For example, I could find no evidence that a single Arab American or Muslim American organization spoke out in support of Saudi blogger Hamza Kashgari,[25] who faces blasphemy charges and possible execution for daring to imagine a dialogue with the Prophet Muhammad in cyberspace. I agree with Hussein Ibish, the prominent Arab American blogger and former American-Arab Anti-Discrimination Committee (ADC) communications director, that "Muslim . . . individuals have an especial, and urgent, responsibility to categorically oppose this outrage. . . . If Muslims don't want their religion to be misrepresented by such actions, they must openly and loudly repudiate them."[26]

Imam Sharif Mohamed of Minneapolis does exactly that. He has maintained his liberal convictions along with and as part of his humanist practice of Islam, and also as a component of his leadership of a Muslim congregation. Not only that, he speaks his mind about these convictions. And he does not appear defensive about them in the slightest. "A lot of times people criticize me and say, 'You are not conservative or a real Muslim.'" He replies, "I'm not what you say, but Islam is the way."

THE SUCCESS STORY AND THE SUICIDE BOMBER

Right after I meet Imam Sharif, I am introduced to Somali American community worker Abdirahman Mukhtar. Wearing a suitcoat like the imam, and a silver-colored tie, he has a light moustache, looks younger than he is, and is the poster child for immigrant success. Now thirty, he fled Somalia at seventeen because of the civil war. Due to stints in refugee camps and the war's interruption of his schooling, his education was then at the level of a nine-year-old. Nevertheless, through sheer East African grit and all-American hard work, he graduated from a Minneapolis high school with high honors and attended the University of Minnesota, where he was president of the Somali Student Union.

He is very conscious of being a role model. Like so many Americans, Muslim and otherwise, Abdirahman Mukhtar's life was affected by 9/11. "One of my dreams was to be an air traffic controller. My second day of college was 9/11, so you can imagine how that turned out." Today he has three sons, continues to live in the heart of the community, and works with immigrant youth. "I tell them you can be anything," he says. This is the American dream with a Somali twist. In the midst of a career transition, he himself has just started a new job as African Outreach Liaison with a local library.

Abdirahman is passionate about the basic needs of his community. At least 60 percent of this population lives below the poverty level.[27] "There are about 1,800 young people under age eighteen in these high-rises. And they have one gym in this neighborhood, and it's the one gym in Minneapolis that is not a wood floor. It's cement. There is one community center." This is not just a problem for Somali youth. "America is nationwide struggling with youth violence. They would rather Facebook or watch YouTube than go to the library or play soccer outside."

The response of the authorities to the Al Shabaab recruitment scandal weighed heavily on the community, continued Abdirahman. "It affected college students more than anybody else because a lot of the young people that law enforcement interviewed were college students." Many innocuous pursuits became suspicious activities. "A lot of the people who were traveling were college students who were doing study abroad. So when they came back, when they were leaving, they were questioned a lot." While I hear in Minneapolis that it is vital to stand up to Al Shabaab recruiters, I am also told how important it is not to stigmatize Somali Americans because of this issue. College students were not the only ones who felt the strain. "Parents who dealt with that pressure of having the FBI knock on your door, that was really tough— someone who cannot speak the language, does not understand."

Nor does the community, he thinks, have the sense that many in the media recognize their achievements. "They don't talk about the Somali youth who came here not knowing any English and are teachers now." Stung by this, he has many other examples. "They don't talk about single mothers running businesses. Eighty-five percent of Somali businesses are owned by women." He points out a strip of female-owned concerns across the street from where we sit: Sahara Restaurant, the A1A Travel Agency, and Milano Beauty Supply.

Given the odds many of these proprietors have themselves had to beat, Mukhtar has no sympathy whatsoever for the reasons given to explain why his former high school classmate Shirwa Ahmed became a suicide bomber. "He was not young. He's not what the media is making him. He can make his own decisions. I made a decision to attend a college and raise kids here and some of our schoolmates chose to be in the Army, but he made the choice of going—and that is who the newspapers write about."

BOTH ENDS OF THE WORLD ARE BECOMING VERY EXTREMIST

I visit the Starbucks most famously frequented by Somalis, a Minneapolis landmark and supposedly one of the most financially successful Starbucks in the country. It sits in a strip mall not far from the University of Minnesota campus. A tornado the previous day has knocked out the power. Some regulars, a large group of Somali men mostly in their thirties and forties, have brought a circle of chairs outside, where they are having a loud discussion. Explaining that the café is closed due to the storm, they offer me coffee from a dispenser set up outside. East African hospitality prevails even in a midwestern parking lot, and despite the intense political debate in which they are engaged.

As I meet my next contact, Zuhur Ahmed, she says of the Somali Starbucks, "Whenever I am grabbing my coffee, I find out what happened in Somalia that morning." Ahmed's head is covered and she wears a long dress, but there is nothing "modest" about her. The only Somali woman in the Twin Cities with her own radio show, Zuhur is ambitious and accomplished and assertive. She is pre-med; journalism is just a hobby. She is also a member of the Somali Language and Literary Study Circle initiated by Professor Said Salah Ahmed. "I am very much in love with Somali literature," she enthuses.

Zuhur's broadcasting career began when she was asked to translate into Somali the announcements made over the PA system at her Minneapolis high school. "I thought it was a cool thing to do." This led to an internship with a Somali radio show, and then to her own program on KFAI, a community station known as Radio Without Boundaries. Her show, "Somali Community Link," began airing in July 2007. "I applied for and got this slot even though there were like a zillion applicants."

Tired of the predominantly negative coverage of Somalis, she decided to do her own, and "talk about current issues in the Twin Cities"—mainly in Somali but sometimes in English. She got off to a bumpy start: "My first show was a disaster." In the beginning, her audience was small because she wanted to talk about what was happening in Minneapolis, rather than in Mogadishu. But, over time, she developed the confidence to take on tough topics: youth issues, health, STDs, obesity, single mothers, elections, "and stuff like that." Moreover, she wanted to explore such themes in depth and "not do headlines."

Then, an unfortunate coincidence brought Zuhur Ahmed to a mass audience. In October 2007, she interviewed a troubled young member of the Somali community named Zakaria Maruf, who had been in a Somali street gang called the Hot Boyz but gave that all up for Allah. He wound up working at Walmart. In early 2008, he joined Al Shabaab and went to Somalia. Maruf in turn recruited others. In the *New York Times*, he was described by an acquaintance as "the 'I'll take you to the battlefield' person."[28] Zakaria Maruf was tight with the first Somali American suicide bomber, Shirwa Ahmed, and later said he would be willing to carry out the same kind of mission. By 2009, Maruf would be dead in faraway East Africa. When the Al Shabaab recruitment story broke, Zuhur's show was rebroadcast in its entirety on National Public Radio. "These kids were crying out for attention," she remembers. What they found in extremism was "a place where they are the center of attention."

The intrepid student/reporter tried to understand what had pushed these young men through the Al Shabaab pipeline and back to a Somalia most of their parents had fled. She wanted to "dig deep, ya know." What she found were young people who saw no other way of belonging, or being heard. "Every venue for them was closed, and that was the new discovery, the new thing that welcomed them. Something that they can believe in, that opens the door for them: Religion."

These lost young men would go into a particular kind of mosque and be "found" in all the worst ways. "I don't know where they get their teachings from but they become very extremist, and I think a lot of it has to do with identity crisis. They were rejected from their Western culture and they were rejected from the Somali culture. Maybe they thought, this is something that can accept us." That, Zuhur figures, is what pushed them to the outer limits, "because they feel like they want to hold it tight," this kind of religion they had discovered. "They don't want to be rejected by it either." At first, Al Shabaab made a nationalist appeal to recruits following the 2006 Ethiopian intervention to oust the fundamentalist Union of Islamic Courts from Mogadishu. Later, however, their appeal was based in a transcendent Islamist ideology that could override even normally strong clan identification. The call to arms was romanticized and became, to a few, irresistible. "I would like to talk to my brothers . . . there in the West," one Minnesota-bred suicide bomber recited on the Internet before his death. "Brothers, come to jihad. Die like lions."[29]

I ask Zuhur if she thinks her community generally is becoming more fundamentalist. Her response is entirely unexpected. "Did you watch *Jesus Camp*?" This is a documentary film about the indoctrination of young Americans by radical Christian groups, including preparation to fight against Muslims. Just as Zuhur worries about what is happening to Somali youth, she worries that other American youth in the Midwest are becoming "very anti-Muslim.

"I believe that both ends of the world are becoming very extremist."

As some Afghans I met had said of their country, Zuhur tells me that Somalis were not especially "close to religion" until the civil war. "This whole concept of jilbab and hijab didn't exist. Women used to be half-naked in their cultural dresses." She thinks the return of religion has a lot to do with losing hope "when bad things are happening." Uncertainty pushes people to seek absolutes as a kind of anchor, but that anchor can drift, pulling them in a different direction. "As the world is changing, and people are feeling less accepted, they are returning to their religion, and then that itself shifts. Where it goes, God knows." What worries her is not the return of God but the way this return is used. "Obviously there is extremism, there are the terrorists in this world, what I call the power-hungry freaks, regardless of what religion or country they are from. They are taking advantage of those vulnerable people."

In parting, I tell Zuhur Ahmed that she may have to give up medical school to become a journalist. "That's what I've been told all over," she replies. A few days later, she will interview Attorney General Eric Holder during his visit to Minneapolis—"the only media person allowed to," she beams. But when I catch up with Zuhur again in 2012, she has given up journalism for the medical field, still haunted by the slow death of her infant brother with no doctor to help during the Somali Civil War back in the early 1990s. The former radio host is studying for her medical-school entrance exams while talking to me. She is pleased to note that, in the improving climate back in Somalia, more Somali Americans are returning home now to engage in humanitarian work. She hopes to join them but for now waits to see what she calls "real change" first.

I enjoy my visit with members of the Somali population of Minneapolis, the combination of African and midwestern cultures is one I grew up with. My host, a Somali colleague at the University of Minnesota, takes me to a Somali restaurant with plastic tablecloths and sparkly lights. The goat he so highly recommends is succulent, served with seasoned rice, a little bit of vermicelli inherited from Italian colonization, and a salad with green lemon. Though I have much to thank him for, my host will not hear of letting me pick up the check.

I leave Minneapolis with a deep appreciation for the people I have met, and for the dreams of the community in which they live. I understand how concerned they are that the Al Shabaab recruitment issue not be the only thing that is known about their community. Later that same week, when another young Somali American from Minnesota makes headlines by blowing himself up in Mogadishu to murder two African Union peacekeepers,[30] it is the quiet contributions to peace and understanding made by people like Abdirizak Bihi and Zuhur Ahmed, by Abdirahman Mukhtar and Imam Sharif Mohamed, that I want to remember.

CHAPTER EIGHT

Why I Hate Al Qaeda: Surviving and Challenging Fundamentalist Terrorism

"**W**hy don't I come with a suicide jacket?" the young voice on the phone said.

"Okay, I don't care, come with the suicide jacket," Pakistani peace activist Diep Saeeda retorted. "Bring more suicide bombers as well." Then she went on planning the rally against the blasphemy law.

Next she received an e-mail. "You are a threat to the Muslim *umma*." Diep tried to reply, but her message would not go through. The address was a decoy. To be told you are an enemy of the *umma*—the Muslim people—in a city like Lahore in 2010 is no mere insult.[1] It has been less than two months since a triple-suicide blast thought to be the work of the Pakistani Taliban killed twenty-five at a public procession in this city, "scattering bodies into the streets and sowing panic."[2]

Still, Diep's protest went ahead.

Nearly fifty people stand on the sidewalk near the chief minister's office, ironically under an official banner welcoming His Excellency the Iranian Ambassador. The protesters hold their own banners in Urdu and English that condemn the sentencing of Asia Bibi, a Pakistani Christian woman, to die for allegedly insulting the Prophet Muhammad. "A secular state to protect minorities." "No More Blasphemy Laws!" They denounce law 295c, which was used to convict Asia Bibi. "295c is not Islam." A junior academic holds my favorite sign: "Root cause religious extremism." Sohail Warraich, a human rights defender who helps organize my research in Lahore, says these are the slogans he has been chanting his entire life.

Tonight, passersby nearly fall off their motorbikes as they stop to look at those who stand against intolerance. They include young activists in jeans, a woman with her head covered, and grandes dames of the women's movement in shalwar kameezes. Here at this intersection, watching peaceful protesters challenge theocracy despite the threat of suicide attack, I first meet Diep Saeeda, the tired-looking convener who herself wears a shalwar kameez and flip-flops. On her knees on the pavement, she writes out signs. While we talk, a group of policemen arrive—responding, they say, to the warnings Diep received. "This is a security threat. Now you disperse."

The policemen want to "interview" the demonstrators. They want to know whether or not they are Muslim. "Their entire purpose was to scare the shit out of you so that you would go home," the young woman who held the sign about religious extremism tells me the next day. But she stood there nonetheless. In fact, the small phalanx of protesters found themselves with policemen in riot gear in front of them and a few angry-looking "bearded ones" (as the fundamentalists are sometimes called here) lurking behind. But they stood their ground, chanting and waving their signs.

There have been public gatherings condemning the violence in Lahore since my visit as well. At least six hundred "members of civil rights organizations, singers and students" attended a candlelight vigil at the Liberty Roundabout and a rally at the Press Club in May 2012 after militant attacks on mosques belonging to the minority Ahmadi sect killed ninety-five.[3] Everyone in the United States who watches television knows about Pakistani terrorists, but until the Taliban shooting of schoolgirl Malala Yousafzai in October 2012, most did not know about those who were standing up to the terrorists. Pakistani peace activists—that is not a stereotype, but it is a reality.

SHREDDING RAHMA

We are deeply concerned at . . . increasing militant attacks . . . and consider these . . . threats to the entire society. We show full

> solidarity with families . . . of those . . . injured and killed in . . .
> barbaric terrorist attacks. . . .[4]
>
> —*Joint Action Committee for People's Rights, Pakistan*

Many groups in Muslim majority societies regularly denounce terrorism, even when doing so is dangerous and receives minimal international publicity. In the West, it is sometimes assumed that Muslims generally condone terrorism. The Right often presumes this because it views Muslim culture as inherently violent. The Left at times imagines this because it interprets fundamentalist terrorism as simply a reflection of legitimate grievances.

In fact, many people of Muslim heritage—though not yet enough—are ardent opponents of fundamentalist violence, and for very good reason. Statistically, they are much more likely to be victims of terrorism than its perpetrators. Terrorism directed against Jews, Hindus, Christians, atheists, or anyone else is equally appalling, and Muslim fundamentalists have also killed many across these categories. But those most commonly on the receiving end in recent years have been people of Muslim heritage killed by Muslim fundamentalists. During Ramadan 2012 alone, Al Qaeda claimed responsibility for 131 attacks in Iraq, killing four hundred.[5] A 2009 study of Arabic media sources by the Combating Terrorism Center at West Point found that only 15 percent of Al Qaeda's casualties between 2004 and 2008 were Westerners.[6] Between 2006 and 2008, fully 98 percent of Al Qaeda's victims were of Muslim heritage.[7]

I think of the celebrated Arab American filmmaker Moustapha Akkad, who made films about Libya's independence struggle and the life of the Prophet Muhammad (as well as the moneymaking *Halloween* movies). He perished at a wedding along with his daughter and fifty-five others, including relatives of the bride and groom, during a 2005 bombing by Al Qaeda in Mesopotamia.[8]

Pakistani religious scholar Mufti Sarfraz Naeemi, of the Barelvi school, chaired a meeting of Islamic religious scholars that denounced suicide terror in 2009.[9] "Those who commit suicide attacks for attaining paradise will go to hell, as they kill many innocent people," he reportedly said.[10] Later that year, on June 12, he was himself targeted by just such a paradise-seeking Taliban bomber and killed after Friday prayers.

My childhood neighbor in Algiers, Chadly Hamza, was one of those truly kind people you gravitate toward as a kid. A consultant for the UN Development Programme who also worked to create study-abroad programs for young Algerians, he was murdered by Al Qaeda in the Islamic Maghreb, with thirty-three others, in a December 2007 suicide bombing of a UN building in Algiers.[11] The last time I heard from Hamza, as my dad called him, in 2005, he told me he had made a conscious choice to stay in Algeria to try to improve conditions, "rather than just being a consumer of development wherever I could have emigrated."

All these people of Muslim heritage fell to the fundamentalists, an immeasurable loss to their families, their countries, and the world. That is why so many know that this jihad has got to stop.

However, the scale of such losses to terrorism in Muslim majority populations is not always well understood elsewhere. In the spring of 2010, I served on an Amnesty International USA (AIUSA) task force set up to consider what the organization could do to improve its work against terrorism. I spent frustrating hours trying to convince some other members that our task was vital to many people of Muslim heritage, not something they would oppose. Ultimately, we recommended that AIUSA hold an event about the human rights of victims of terrorism around the world, to commemorate the tenth anniversary of 9/11. The board of AIUSA rejected this, in large part because they believed such an event would contribute to discrimination against Muslims. They too seemed to assume that Muslims were mostly associated with perpetrators of terrorism, not with its targets, or at least this is what the public would think. It was easier to say nothing.

During the unhappy debate on the Amnesty task force, I thought a lot about my Algerian cousin Ahcene, a retired soldier from a peasant background who could not read. In 1994, he was killed by terrorists in front of his children on the eve of *Eid el-Kebir*, one of the biggest Muslim holidays of the year. After riddling him with bullets, the fundamentalists attacked what remained of his body. His seven-year-old daughter, who threw herself on her father's remains to protect him, was covered in his blood. Though she survived, I always thought they must have killed part of her too.

You do not have to be an international lawyer to know what terrorism is and that it includes such acts. Most people can agree it is violence intentionally directed against civilians for a political or ideological purpose, or for the purpose of spreading terror. The outstanding definitional debate about who can commit it—states, non-state armed groups, "freedom fighters"—masks a political debate about when to employ the label: only against those with whom we disagree, or whenever it applies.

In any case, there is no denying that jihadist groups have purveyed widespread *terrorism* in recent decades, killing hundreds of thousands and provoking further bigotry against Muslims and counterterror abuses. It is an awful cycle I call "terror/torture."[12] It did not commence on September 11, 2001, but long before. Some will rush to say this is all justified by a range of grievances—lack of democracy, violations of human rights, military occupation. Many of those injustices are very real. However, the fundamentalist bombers often purvey equally grave injustices—or seek to—and their victims are in no way responsible for the underlying problems.

The legendary sardonic Algerian columnist Saïd Mekbel addressed a February 1994 open letter to the terrorists of Algeria, a letter that distills the rage of many people in Muslim majority societies against those who butcher in the name of Allah. "Tell me, partisan of terrorism . . . you who regularly . . . explain that terrorist acts are done . . . to—I quote—'bring down the military junta in power,' tell me how assassinating a schoolteacher in front of . . . the children in his class, when he only had a little piece of chalk in his hands, tell me . . . how this ignoble execution contributes to 'bringing down the military junta.' "[13] Ten months later, the man who asked this question was himself fatally shot by a partisan of the Armed Islamic Group while eating in a restaurant near his office.[14]

There are, of course, Muslim fundamentalist groups that do not use violence, and some that do not even condone it. There are also many others who have nothing whatsoever to do with Islam—Jewish settlers in the West Bank, for example, or Christian fundamentalist opponents of abortion in the United States—who have employed terrorism. But the Salafi jihadi groups have perfected the practice. As someone I interviewed said, "They excel in the art of terror." They have shredded *rahma* (mercy), a foundational principle of Islamic teachings. For example, Algerian fundamentalists claimed that the more the victims suffered, the wider the doors of paradise would open for their jihadi killers.[15] In other words, the terrorism was an end, not just the means.

The suffering was part of the point.

Acting in total violation of both international and Islamic humanitarian law, Muslim fundamentalist armed groups have made it seem as though suicide bombing is associated with Islam. They have blown up cafés in Morocco, churches in Cairo, the offices of the Red Crescent in Baghdad. They have used chemicals to attack girls' schools in Afghanistan. The struggle to stop this antihuman violence is one of the world's major human rights challenges.

The fact that the lamentable George W. Bush declared war on terrorism does not make it a good thing. The reality that governments have grossly abused human rights in the name of fighting terrorism does not make that fight any less important. It simply means we have to combat several forms of suffering simultaneously, rather than tolerating either one in the name of the other. These truths were confirmed to me along the way in Algiers, in Kabul, in Moscow, and in Lahore.

A LIFE OF A COWARD DOES NOT MAKE SENSE

I love Pakistan. I was there in 1996 on an Amnesty International mission. When I came down with chicken pox, the men who worked at the Pearl Continental Hotel in Peshawar took care of me as if I'd been a member of the family. I called room service daily, and the man who answered would say, "Is this Miss Karima? We're praying for you, *al Hamdulilah*." I used to hide on the balcony when the man who cleaned my room came up, because my pox-ridden face frightened even me. One day, the urbane concierge came to see me and said, "You do not have to hide. Everyone gets sick." I associate Pakistan with this kind of humanist decency, as much as any ghastly headline. When the Pearl Continental was decimated by jihadist suicide bombers in June 2009, killing seventeen, I immediately wondered what happened to the protective concierge and the prayerful cook.

When I returned in 2010, the country was riven by a bloody internal conflict against its own Taliban and myriad other extremist groups, some with close links to Al Qaeda. Across the country, more than eight thousand people had been killed in militant strikes in the prevous three years.[16] Nevertheless, the ordinary hustle and bustle in the city reminds me that one of the best forms of resistance to terrorism is to avoid doing the terrorists' work for them, to keep going about your business. My father was a firm believer in this approach. Except for occasional military checkpoints, most things seem normal in Lahore. As I travel between interviews, I see cars festooned in flowers for a wedding. Life goes on in the presence of death and death threats.

The day after witnessing the demonstration against the blasphemy laws, I visit its organizer, Diep Saeeda, in her humble seventh-floor office in what counts as a high-rise in Lahore. I find Diep at her computer in a small room with no name on the door. Down the hall from her office is a good view of the city, which looks, with its many trees, as though it would be quite beautiful if you could see through the smog.

Having labored for several decades for many seemingly lost causes—peace with India, abolition of nuclear weapons, and the defeat of fundamentalism—Diep looks exhausted. However, she shows no sign of giving up. Now forty-eight she is the founder and chair of the Institute for Peace and Secular Studies (IPSS). Much of her work has involved taking on the Pakistani security establishment. "When we organize for the nuclear rallies, people will curse, 'Why do you want to destroy the one Muslim nuclear bomb?'" She has been arrested, is regularly harassed by people she believes to be government agents, and believes herself at ongoing risk.

But today she also takes on the Taliban "because they are anti-human. They have killed one hundred thousand people in Afghanistan and Pakistan."[17] Diep grapples with the contradictions in what the Pakistani Taliban do, contradictions in stark contrast to her pacifist universalism. "I hate the killing of anyone because I believe in nonviolence. But if the Taliban targeted the Army headquarters because it was supporting America, okay that is their ideology: they hate the Army.

But the next day, they will go to the women's bazaar, explode there, and kill women doing the shopping. So, what kind of ideology is this?"

Diep stresses the lack of alternatives open to young people. "They are not enthusiastic about their future. They hate Taliban. They don't want to get into their groups. But if they are from the lower middle class families, they cannot afford to go abroad." She regrets that there are no youth resource centers in Lahore, "where young people who want to learn music, who want to paint can." On the other hand, "there are madrasas and terrorist centers in every street."

None of this is happening by accident in Pakistan. While it has both endogenous and exogenous causes at least as old as partition, Diep and many others draw a line back to the U.S. Cold War–era support for the dictatorship of Zia ul-Haq, who "Islamized" as a way of maintaining control. The rise of fundamentalism here is not just the natural by-product of Pakistan's own internal development. In its battle against the Soviet Union, during the war in Afghanistan in particular, the United States instrumentalized political Islam here. As feminist activist Neelam Hussein sees it, the country was used as an "Islamic shield against the USSR." Pakistan now, in part, reaps the terrible fruit of that unnatural crop.

So Diep and her institute have had to organize many demonstrations like the one I saw, regardless of the risk. In January 2010, she convened a rally against the Taliban. "It was immediately after the news from Swat that they were cutting off the heads of people." The picturesque Swat Valley in the Khyber-Pakhtunkwa Province, known as the "Switzerland of South Asia," saw an influx of Pakistani Taliban militants in 2007.[18] Though its people had voted for secularists, in February 2009 the Pakistani government concluded a truce with the Taliban, conceding that Swat would be ruled by an Islamist version of Sharia.[19] Thanks to the truce, the Taliban took over. This encroachment, and a series of abuses—flogging of women, killings of secularists, attacks on barbers who shaved beards—finally provoked the Pakistani Army to intervene during the second half of 2009, partially dislodging the jihadists. They subsequently returned and today continue killing. As egregious as the attack on Malala Yousafzai was, it was part of a pattern of Pakistani Taliban targeting of opponents.[20]

Despite the Taliban atrocities that were ongoing at the time of Diep's march in 2010, she faced some public opprobrium in Lahore for opposing them. "When I was distributing flyers, they would curse me. They would say, 'You are not Muslim.'" That did not stop others from joining her. She gives me a copy of the Urdu flyer that she and her sister and her daughters handed out at intersections to get people to attend. It is entitled "Peace, War, Love, and Terrorism," with X's through "War" and "Terrorism." Diep translates: "From Swat to Gaza and from Mumbai to Afghanistan, everywhere peace is in trouble. People who are responsible for this—on one side the United States and its allies—military intervention—and on the other side is the terrorism of the fundamentalists. . . . Today . . . the large majority of the population is being held hostage." By speaking against these things, those who gathered also sought to display a different face of their country. "In this critical situation, it is important for peace-loving people to raise the slogan of . . . tolerance and coexistence. . . . Let us show the world that the majority of Pakistanis . . . desire to live a peaceful life."

Five thousand came to the rally. "Rickshaw drivers, common people would come, somebody from Swat who says he had a very hard time, because of the Taliban their lives had changed, so he came with friends to the rally." They received no coverage whatsoever in the Western press. But this does not stop Saeeda and the Institute for Peace and Secular Studies. On Facebook, I can see that they organized a well-attended vigil in Lahore the day after Malala Yousafzai is shot. Diep is quoted in the international press saying, "All Pakistanis should come together and raise their voices against such acts. If they do not do this, then they should mentally prepare themselves for their own children's fate to be like Malala's."[21] In the face of such acts, the peace activist continues to speak out, entirely undaunted.

Back in 2010, I had put to Diep the question I always wanted to ask my father: "How do you keep going with the threats you face?" She says what I imagined he would have: "I believe that if I live a life of a coward, that is not going to make sense." Of course, no parent takes these risks alone. This is the hardest part for Diep. "I was upset when I was jailed and my daughter had exams, and she was sitting outside the jail all night long. That bothers me. I was a little careful when my children were young. But my children are grown up now, so I don't care." Diep Saeeda has no security guards and lives in a small house.

"If they kill me, it is an honor to be killed, instead of sealing my lips and making any compromises."

DENIAL IS NOT A RIVER IN EGYPT

Diep Saeeda and Khaled Ahmed in Lahore, and their analogues elsewhere, are very clear about what fundamentalism is doing to their societies. But many others are not. I am fascinated by the denial that swirls around Muslim fundamentalism and its violence. It pervades the contagious 9/11 conspiracy theories and the *qui-tue-qui* thesis, which conjectures that the Algerian state rather than fundamentalist armed groups murdered in the 1990s. In Pakistan when I visit, this denial is endemic.

I am told many here believe Hindus or Jews are doing the killing, not the Muslim fundamentalist armed groups. In a country like Pakistan where the Jewish population is thought to have dwindled to almost nothing,[22] where the Hindu population is 5 percent of the total 180 million and almost no Hindus whatsoever live in the areas hardest hit by terrorism, these are remarkable assertions.[23] Even though Muslim fundamentalist groups usually claim responsibility for their atrocities quite openly, others often rush in to absolve them. What does all this denial mean? How does one challenge it?

I ask the thirty-nine-year-old Pakistani documentary filmmaker and women's rights advocate Gulnar Tabassum about this in her small office at Shirkat Gah, the women's rights NGO in Lahore. She has very short, dark hair and wears a jean jacket. Gulnar grapples with an explanation for the denial, which she believes starts with identity. "The majority of Pakistanis, they are Muslims. When you talk about Islam, they say, 'We are with Islam.'" Given this starting point, they do not want to disparage their religion by standing against the fundamentalists, who claim to be advancing it. This sort of confusion underscores how useful it is for the fundamentalists to conflate their politics and popular religion. A mother who lost her son to Algeria's Armed Islamic Group once wrote to me, explaining how the fundamentalists take advantage of ignorance: "If you want to confuse an 'ordinary person,' you talk about God instead of about politics—and you have won."

Gulnar argues that this confusion is exacerbated in Pakistan by official stories and mainstream journalism aimed at obfuscating reality. "They are not getting the clear picture from the government or the propaganda agencies [of] media and newspapers." If people get confusing messages from those who are supposed to keep them informed, "they don't know who the Taliban are. Who is their enemy? And you know, it is easy for them to say, 'Oh, the Indians are doing this, Americans are doing this, and Israelis are doing this.'" The public assumes this must be true, because criticism of Muslim fundamentalist armed groups (aka "Muslims") could only be a sign that "people are against Islam."

Smoking continuously, Gulnar apportions blame for the current confusion. "Basically, this is the government's responsibility because they are not giving people a clear picture. They put them in denial." Average citizens "can't believe that any Muslim can make a suicide bomb in Pakistan and innocent people are killed."

Gulnar's most recent projects were a film called *Two Steps Forward*, about women in the peasant movement in Punjab after 2000, and another entitled *The Swollen River*, about the impact of the massive 2010 floods. During her travels, she asked ordinary people across Pakistan for their views about fundamentalist violence. "I have been in Swat and KPK for my flood film." (KPK is the Khyber Pakhtunkhwa Province, near Afghanistan.) In these at-risk zones, she asks those she interviews, "Who are the Taliban?" Their first reaction? "What Taliban? It is all American propaganda." Gulnar does not give up, though. "I put a second question to them. 'But we have suicide attacks?'" The reply she most often gets is, "You know, Indians are doing this."

During her visits to Swat while making her film about the floods, Gulnar heard many awful accounts, but these horror stories were warped by conspiracy theories and popular myths. "They told you horrendous stories about the Taliban and what they are doing in Swat," she says. "They are raping women. But the propaganda is that Hindus are doing this. I said, 'Okay, in the middle of the Taliban regime in Swat, Hindus are coming, kidnapping women and raping them. Then they throw them back to their houses. Is this possible?'" According to the Pakistan Hindu Council, there are only 474 Hindus in a population of 1.2 million in the Swat Valley. Despite such demographic impossibilities, Gulnar is assured by her interviewees that Hindus are to blame.

"One of my colleagues said, 'I met a woman who was raped. I personally talked to her. And she said the rapist was Hindu.' 'How did she know this?' I asked her. She said, 'He is not circumcised.' Then I researched and I discovered that the Mehsud tribe, they don't circumcise their people."[24] (She is referring to the tribe of Baitullah Mehsud, the late leader of the Pakistani Taliban.) According to Gulnar: "They think circumcision is not compulsory. But the propaganda is still that Hindus are doing that. People are so much in denial they just accept this." It is painful, she surmises, to contemplate that your coreligionists could be targeting your own people. "There are lots of disappointments. They can be disappointed by religion as well because jihad is very much glorified. To avoid these questions they prefer denial," Gulnar concludes. She is so concerned with this phenomenon that she wants to make a documentary film about it, featuring those injured in suicide bombings and women victims of rape in Swat who are convinced their assailants were Hindus. "Why can't they see? Or, if they are seeing, why can't they talk?"

I inquire how much of the denial has to do with a reading of the Pakistani Taliban as anti-imperialist, as fighting the United States, a justification I have heard time and again. She responds: "Al Qaeda claimed they have fight with America. Why they are doing this in Pakistan? Pakistani people, what they have done to them?" She simply does not accept that defeating imperialism is the real agenda. Instead, she insists, "This is a tactic to spread fear in people's minds." Her words echo those of Pakistani human rights lawyer Hina Jilani. In her Lahore office, up the stairs past the armed guards she must have, Jilani alleges of the fundamentalists: "They have an imperialism of their own which is very much about control and exploitation and abuse of their own people." Why would an "anti-imperialist" blow up the markets of Peshawar where local women shop? Or decimate mosque after mosque full of minority-sect Muslims?

Though they mainly kill Pakistanis, not Americans, apology for fundamentalist violence is facilitated by a festering anti-Americanism that

Gulnar Tabassum says is "spread by the media, by the government. It is a popular thing." It dovetails with a populist discourse. "They are based in surface slogans. 'America is exploitative, so we are fighting them.' 'Taliban are good people because they are fighting the huge, big power.'"

Sohail Warraich, who has long been involved in documenting human rights abuses, is a former Amnesty International researcher on Pakistan. How can we challenge the denial and the persecution complex that seem to be two of the key pillars of the problem? I asked him. "Number one: Accept that killings have taken place. Accept that whoever is taking responsibility—until proven otherwise—it's them, whatever they call themselves, rather than saying, 'No, someone else has done it.'"

More people need to say such things openly, though it is difficult. "It requires a lot of effort to actually say to people, 'Believe your eyes,'" Sohail concedes, "but we must. If you see that it was a suicide attack and the person belongs to this group, believe it. Look at what the group itself is saying." This is the application of Occam's razor to Pakistan—in fact, to all the regions I have visited. If there is violence being carried out systematically against civilians, in the absence of actual evidence to the contrary, the group that says it is doing it, whose ideology justifies it, is probably doing it. This is not to say that governments, including in Pakistan, do not commit their own atrocities. They, too, need to be held accountable. Sometimes multiple actors may collude. Nonetheless, the violence of Muslim fundamentalist armed groups, including that against Muslims, is all too real.

In 2012, I was hoping that after the Pakistani Taliban not only tried to kill Malala Yousafzai, "Daughter of the Nation," but also said openly that they did, and would do it again, this might begin to undo some of the denial. A few days afterward, I spoke to Sohail Warraich by telephone. Fresh from attending Lahore protests against the shooting, he told me that clerics were now on the defensive, and that the dreadful incident was creating space to raise these issues in a new way, by showing "the real face of militancy." It was, he said, "very encouraging to see momentum in media and political circles who are usually not clear cut about extremism." There was an immense popular outpouring of love for Malala and hatred for the Taliban across the country that could really change things. "This case has provided a catharsis of the masses for all the grievances that have been building up for years," Muhammad Amir Rana, director of the Islamabad-based Pakistan Institute for Peace Studies, told the *Guardian*.[25] However, Sohail rightly warned that denial would soon try to rear its ugly head again.

In short order, the Taliban—who were not used to getting such universally bad press at home—accused Malala of being an American spy. Members of the fundamentalist party Jamaat-e-Islami desperately accused her family of complicity with the U.S. military, tweeting a photo from their meeting with former U.S. envoy Richard Holbrooke in which they had asked the civilian diplomat for support of educational projects, but mislabeling it in Urdu as being a meeting with American military officers.[26] Ultimately, though Malala was supposedly colluding with the U.S. military, the Jamaat-e-Islami leader suggested, you guessed it, that it was in fact U.S. intelligence agents who had shot her in order to justify U.S. drone strikes. Some other right-wing commentators even excused Malala's shooting because of those drone attacks. While the civilian casualties from such strikes are a very serious matter, local commentators pointed out that U.S. drones targeting militants had likely killed three to four thousand Pakistani civilians, while the Taliban had by late 2012 deliberately killed about sixty thousand.[27]

Observing the attempts at obfuscation, horrified Pakistani editor Muhammad Arif blogged: "[W]hen Malala is fighting for her life these stone hearted people are trying to bring conspiracy theories to dilute effects of this highly sensitive issue. History would never forgive them. . . ." Safiya Aftab likewise regretted, in a *News on Sunday* article entitled "Goebbels lives on in Pakistan," that, "[e]leven years on, this nation still refuses to identify the enemy, let alone unite against it."[28] On the phone from his home village, Sohail explained that to achieve those goals of identifying the enemy and uniting against it, there needs to be "clarity of thought and action and strategy on terrorism."

I DON'T WANT TO HAVE DINNER WITH THE PROPHET

In 2003, Egypt's then-president Hosni Mubarak warned his American allies that their war in Iraq would spawn a hundred new Bin Ladens.[29]

About that, at least, he was exactly right. The illegal invasion transformed Iraq from a brutal but more secular dictatorship into a chaotic haven for fundamentalist terrorists.

When I meet Yanar Mohammed—an outspoken women's rights campaigner who founded the Organization of Women's Freedom in Iraq (OWFI)—during her summer 2011 visit to Rutgers University, she is wearing sparkly red earrings. We drink tea from paper cups while talking about Iraq's tough years. For all her strong stands, she is very approachable.

She had opposed the 2003 U.S. war, and when I first heard her speak back in 2004, she was already calling for a complete U.S. withdrawal. Simultaneously, Yanar has never once shied away from condemning Muslim fundamentalism, even in the most difficult of environments. She deplores the fact that her country now is "under the most notorious Islamic authority."[30] Her stance is not lost on Iraqi extremists themselves. After publicly protesting the Iraqi Governing Council's resolution 137—which tried to introduce Sharia into family-law decisions, and to annul all family law incompatible with Sharia—she received an e-mail message with the subject heading,

"Killing Yanar."

Opening this message in a Baghdad cybercafé, she wondered whether someone sitting anonymously in the same room had sent it. After that, Al Qaeda–linked groups threatened to blow up her offices and home. Yanar moved from one neighborhood to another to stay ahead of the bombers, but she found them all unsafe. She had to move around in a bulletproof vest that nearly doubled her girth.[31]

Still, like Diep Saeeda, Yanar Mohammed did not give up. As she had said in the past, "It is life or death for Iraqi women. If I don't do it, if other women don't do it, we are falling into this dark pit."[32] She kept fighting fundamentalism—both Sunni and Shi'a—because she could see the harm it was doing by fomenting sectarian hatred and spawning violence. "They began killing left and right. They would say we will kill everybody who is an apostate and works with the Americans, like Iraqi translators. And at that time there were no jobs!" The terrorists acted on these pledges for all to see. "They would kill a woman translator, write on her body, show her half naked and distribute her video clip. No one could cope with that."

In recent years there has been a jarring dissonance between Iraqi views of terrorism in Iraq, like Yanar's, which are mostly condemnatory, and the views of those outside—especially those of some other Arabs and some leftists elsewhere—which are sometimes surprisingly apologetic. In a 2005 article in the Arabic-language magazine *Elaph*, the journalist Nabil Charaf Eddine detailed the shock of Iraqis traveling in Egypt who watched Cairenes demonstrate in support of the Iraqi "insurgents."[33] When the Iraqis complained, they were lectured about U.S. imperialism. For Yanar Mohammed, opposition to imperialism should in no way condone indiscriminate killings of civilians by fundamentalists.

The Algerian feminist historian Anissa Hélie wrote an article called "The U.S. Occupation and Rising Religious Extremism: The Double Threat to Women in Iraq," which reflected this view in 2005, at the height of the post-Saddam killing frenzy. In it, she criticized both the U.S. military intervention and the response of the Iraqi extreme Right. She noted that in the West, "[T]here is a tendency within some leftist and feminist circles to label Muslim extremists—who kill, rape, kidnap women and girls and openly target civilians as 'the resistance.' This is highly problematic. . . . There are plenty of groups that reject the U.S. occupation yet do not engage in violence or human rights violations."[34]

Sadly, someone on the left in the West can always be counted on to attack women of Muslim heritage who raise such concerns. Corinna Mullin, a lecturer in Middle East politics at the London School of Economics, accused Hélie in an online response of Orientalism, and of "mimicking Bush."[35] Meanwhile, Iraq's fundamentalist armed groups, whom Hélie "dared" censure, were hunting gay men and blowing up the Iraqi Red Crescent, Iraqi Chaldean churches, and lines of young Iraqi men waiting to get desperately needed jobs as policemen. How could the U.S. occupation ever justify these crimes?

Yanar Mohammed tells me that because of her open criticism of fundamentalists, she has increasingly limited opportunities to speak to the media, and progressive groups in the West no longer invite her. There seems to be an unwritten rule on the Western left that women of Muslim heritage are only allowed to criticize the violence of Western men. (Of course, on the Western right, the opposite is true—they can *only* criticize Muslim men.) Why do those we call Muslims have to accept one kind of violence or the other, when, like anyone else, they are demanding better choices?

Even after all they have been through, Iraqis have not given up on those better choices. When I meet Yanar in June 2011, she is fresh from her country's version of the Arab Spring. Smiling and optimistic, she tells me that Iraqis, like Algerians, sometimes cope with fundamentalist terrorism through comedy. Laughing ruefully, she told me a terrorism joke from 2006. "A jihadi gets into a taxi, very frustrated because he can't find Americans near whom to explode himself. He can't find a good group of Iraqis to explode himself near either. So, he decides to get in a taxi and explode himself. So the taxi driver tells him, 'Please, I don't want to have dinner with the Prophet. Please do it by yourself.'"

FEAR IN THE STOMACH IN THE LAND OF THE BRAVE

Although I was in no hurry to have dinner with the Prophet either, I decided I had to go back to Afghanistan. I am drawn to this country because what happened here is inextricably linked to what happened in Algeria. Many of the worst fundamentalist killers in my father's homeland had come here to fight the so-called jihad and then brought their training home. In fact, my guesthouse in Kabul on this trip turns out to be on the same block as a former hostel for Arab jihadis. Algerians call them "Afghans," but the appalled Afghans to whom I explain this politely say, "We call them Arabs."

I am also compelled by Afghanistan because I have never seen such resilience anywhere. Despite decades of agony, Afghans endure. It is no idle boast when a sign at Kabul Airport says, "Welcome to Afghanistan. Land of the Brave."

While gearing up to come back here, I learn much that is helpful when I write about terrorism. I had been trying to understand the French-language expression *peur au ventre*, which so many Algerians used in telling me about the nineties. Literally, it means "fear in the stomach." Now I understood it exactly.

Almost no one has to live with fear in the stomach as much as a woman member of the Afghan Parliament like Fawzia Koofi. She is also the deputy speaker of its lower house and an aspiring candidate for the presidency in 2014. The Afghan Parliament building sits in a neighborhood called Karta-I Se, in western Kabul. Getting in for my appointment takes forty minutes from gate to meeting room, with multiple searches and a series of identity checks. I am asked repeatedly what I am doing here and whether Karima is my real name. Later, Fawzia Koofi apologizes profusely, but I repeat that I am glad to see the layers of protection. She and her colleagues need them.

The parliamentarian has the youthful gravitas of someone who has known danger. She is from the mountains of northeastern Afghanistan, near Badakhshan. Her skin is light against her dark hair and she wears a white jacket and a scarf with gold-colored trim. Beneath her long skirt, I glimpse open-toe pumps. Like any high-powered person elsewhere, Fawzia checks her phone constantly while answering my questions.

We talk at length about how ordinary Afghans have reacted to the emergence of suicide terrorism here, which, for all the outrages of the past, is a relatively new phenomenon. "It is strange that extremism can change the mind of people to kill themselves," she exclaims, genuinely bewildered that Afghans could do such things. There is no popular movement against terrorism by armed groups per se, she notes, but civil society groups that work for war victims generally have taken up the issue. "Everybody is against suicide attacks. The mullahs in the mosque talk against them." Unfortunately, the weight of public opinion has not yet been able to stop them.

I ask why, despite the obvious dangers, she is going to run for president in 2014. "Well," she replies, "I don't know if I'm going to survive until then." It turns out she had been invited to the dinner the previous week where another member of Parliament, Mohammed Hashim Watanwal, was killed, along with a top presidential aide. The diners were beset by two Taliban gunmen wearing suicide vests. Fortuitously, she had chosen not to go. In addition to facing such broader risks, she has also survived a direct assassination attempt.[36]

As for her presidential campaign, "I'm not running just for the sake of running. If I read my people's minds, they want change, whether it comes from a woman or a man. I had mullahs who were supporting me." She tells me one of the mullahs in her camp was asked by the BBC, "Why would you support this lady?" He replied, "In Islam, it doesn't say man or woman, it says anybody who serves you better. If they are honest, you vote for them."

In light of such endorsements, Fawzia asserts, "If I am elected, it is a success. If I am not elected, my messages are out there." Her messages to Afghans are about justice and social security. She also has a message for the world: "I want to demonstrate a different face of Afghanistan. It is not only Taliban and terrorism that this country produces."

Koofi has paid a personal price for trying to represent an alternative Afghanistan. She spends little time with her daughters, telling me flat out, "I don't have time for them. When I change clothes, that's the only time they come to my bedroom and they ask questions. I tell them, 'Can you let me change?'" Her daughters do not give up. "They say, 'Mom, after you change, you go to the guestroom and you're busy with the guests and when you come back you sleep and we don't have time to talk to you.'" Fawzia confesses, "It's true." The guests are not social visitors but often women coming to seek her help in dealing with such problems as domestic violence and divorce.

When I learn she is a widowed mother, I have to ask again how she lives with the hazards she faces. "It's not something exceptional for me. This is part of life for every Afghan, every day. If they're at home, if they're working. They are all not safe."

I try to grasp what it must do to a society for everyone to have *peur au ventre*.

Fawzia Koofi does not take the dangers she faces lightly but has a specific purpose in speaking out, come what may. "If I keep quiet and if others keep quiet, that means we accept the situation." She feels the same moral imperative to act as Diep Saeeda does in neighboring Pakistan. "My silence, another woman's silence, is an illegitimate response to extremism and fundamentalism and Taliban." In 2012, she becomes one of the leading voices pushing for pursuit of those—such as Taliban Mullah Abdul Khaliq—who orchestrated the public "execution" of a woman named Najiba for alleged adultery. Fawzia Koofi presses local authorities and U.S. military commanders alike, still a voice of conscience no matter the danger.

In addition to her civic commitment, another purpose closer to home also motivates everything Fawzia does—the future of the daughters who come to talk to their overtaxed mother when she is changing. "I'm also doing it for my daughters because I don't want them to have to struggle every day to go to school." She knows all too well what that is like. "I had to convince my family to allow me to go. My mother was every day arguing with my brothers, 'She has to go to school.' My brothers were saying, 'Well for a woman, she can read and write. That's fine. Why should she go?'"

The fact that Fawzia got an education nonetheless, made it into politics and even into Parliament, is a sign of the progress that has been possible here in spite of everything. "Now for my daughters, it's a matter of choice which school they go to. I don't want to take away that opportunity from them."

Preserving these freedoms for her daughters, for other daughters, drives her. That still does not make it easy for her children to accept her absence. "They are not happy with what I do sometimes, because I'm too busy. And in fact, I haven't had lunch yet," she concludes. Engrossed in all she has been saying, I realize it is 3 p.m. and I have kept her far too long. Fawzia Koofi has been too polite to say so.

I am reluctant to say good-bye to this impressive parliamentarian, who tells me she does not know how long she will live, who dreams of running for president because she wants better choices for Afghanistan's daughters, who will not give in to terrorism—but the driver is waiting nervously outside and she is busy. On the way back to the guesthouse, I mull over what it means for the legislature of a country to be so under threat its members must wonder whether they will survive until the next campaign. They must be separated from their constituents by layers of protection. Fawzia Koofi knows there can be a price for security precautions, however necessary. "Sometimes a strong reaction toward extremism of any kind creates another type of extremism. We need to keep the world open." It is ironic to her, given all she has risked, that, "in many airports in the world now if I show my passport, I'm Muslim and Afghan. I get an extra search."

WHY YOU RISK NOT LIVING

The chief prosecutor of Herat Province enters surrounded by four large men with four huge guns pointed downward. Maria Bashir looks small amid her guards, though she stands straight and sure among them. She wears a coat and a neat animal-print scarf and looks younger than her forty-one years. In her office, deep red carpets adorn the walls, and low tables bear plastic flowers and dishes of raisins and dried chick-peas. Maria Bashir sits at her formal glass-topped desk in the corner, on which stands an Afghan flag.

Her quiet way of speaking indicates she means business and has no need for bluster. She is the first and only woman chief prosecutor in Afghanistan. I am grateful that bodyguards fill the antechamber of her office, for the contemporaneous risk she faces is among the most significant of anyone I will interview.

"Before, I had three guards. After that the number increased to eight. Now that I have seen a lot of the difficulties, it is twenty-three. I cannot go anywhere freely which is a big change. Because of that, my life is a little interesting." It turns out "a little interesting" is a euphemism for being subjected to bomb attacks that could have killed her children. "Three years ago there was an explosion near my house, and fifteen minutes earlier my children were playing in that spot. Two of my guards were injured. One lost his leg." Maria Bashir tells me very calmly that she cannot send her children to school anymore—I learn later that their father stays at home with them. The police tell her regularly that she is being targeted by suicide attackers. To prove the point, her would-be assailants once sent an envelope to her house containing three bullets.[37]

Bashir came to work in Herat, her husband's hometown, back in the nineties, starting as an investigator in the Prosecution Office working on crimes against women. When the Taliban took over and drove women out of work, Maria Bashir started a school for girls at home. As a result, the Taliban imprisoned her husband. After their fall from power, she became an investigator again. Then, since 2007 Maria Bashir has been the chief prosecutor.

When she first started, she said, "All the people believed a woman could not do such a position. They believe that in Islam a woman cannot be a judge. So I said, 'I am not a judge. I am a prosecutor.'" Many said her office would close within a month. As they began to evaluate her work, however, Bashir feels that most people came to accept her. Today, she still focuses on violence against women, which she says is the most important area in her mandate.[38] The year before I meet her, the unit of ten lawyers Prosecutor Bashir had established to focus on gender-based violence worked on seventy-eight cases. In addition to women's cases, she investigates and prosecutes corruption—something that is dangerous everywhere, and nowhere more than here. "Fighting against corruption is a very difficult thing in Afghanistan. The people who receive bribes, they are a lot. The people who are fighting against this problem, they are less."

As a result of all of this work, the chief prosecutor is barraged with daily threats—on her phone, written threats, SMS threats—mostly from the Taliban, though she is also at risk from "smugglers, the people who receive bribes." Why does she continue? Maria Bashir says—with a smile of recognition I see before the interpreter finishes repeating my question in Dari—that this is what everybody asks. As the interpreter puts it, everyone asks, "Why you risk not living?" She answers without bravado. It is simply that a better future for the Maria Bashirs to come is, to her, worth the danger. With quietly ferocious role models like this, I am clear that the women of Afghanistan need solidarity and support, not patronizing or pity.

Given her official position, I did not want to put Bashir on the spot by inquiring what she thought of government negotiations with the Taliban, a question I put to many others. But that is exactly what she wants to address. "If we give them a place in the government, who will protect women's rights?'"

Afghan women are disappointed, she continues, that the international community seems more interested in the success of the political talks with the Taliban than in supporting women. The interpreter is

explaining, but the point is too important to leave to him. She interjects in English, urging the international community to "not forget the
promise about women's rights because now they want the peace with
Taliban." She does not mince words. "The Afghanistan government,
the international community and Americans forget women's rights.
And it's very dangerous and all the Afghan women are worried about
this." It is awful to imagine what Bashir's fate would be if the Talibs
were to regain any real power; for the last six years, she has been one of
their chief targets in this area of western Afghanistan.

Back in the United States three weeks later, I see a headline on the
Internet. An Afghan prosecutor has been assassinated. I Google desperately to find details.

Mercifully, I find she is not the victim, but, sadly, another Afghan
prosecutor named Mohammed Azam in Helmand Province has been
gunned down by two men on a motorcycle on his way to work, most
likely at the behest of the Taliban. I hear Maria's words in my head:
"The situation of the women of Afghanistan will be better. We should
pave the ground for this, even if we are killed."

JOB IN AFGHANISTAN

When I worked with Horia Mosadiq on an Amnesty International
fact-finding mission to Kandahar in 2005, I had not noticed that her
nose was a little crooked. Today, she is lead researcher on Afghanistan
for Amnesty, an organization she loves for its years of work on her country. We met again in Kabul in 2011, and in my guesthouse lounge eating
Afghan almonds, she told me her personal story. At a mere thirty-seven
years old, Horia embodies the agony of Afghanistan across the last few
decades. She survived the trials of Job and never gave up.

Originally from Herat, Horia was the daughter of an independent politician. The family moved to Kabul when he found himself
caught between the Communist government he did not want to join
and its mujahideen opponents, who extorted protection money to
spare his daughters. In the early nineties, Horia began documenting
human rights abuses. "I started writing about what I was hearing,
and what I knew myself. When I gave that to my literature teacher in

school, he said, 'My recommendation would be to keep it to yourself. Anyone instead of me, if they look at your writings, you would be in big trouble.'" I ask if she kept what the teacher told her not to share. She did, until 1993, "when our home was hit by a rocket and we lost everything."

I remember the noise of a rocket that fell not too far from where I stayed in Kabul in 1996—the worst sound I had ever heard, though it was nothing by Afghan standards. Someone far away in the United States or Germany had made the thing, had made money off of it. (Afghanistan does not manufacture rockets.) Some fundamentalist fighter on a hill above Kabul had fired it without worry about where it would land. Somewhere out there, hell had come to someone's house. In February 1993, that hell came to Horia's house.

By this time, she was studying at Kabul University and working for a news agency. The mujahideen war for the capital was in high gear. "That conflict was much worse than what we had in the '80s. In mujahideen time, all the fighting was brought inside the cities. Thousands of women were raped and disappeared." In this fraught environment, Horia's mother struggled to protect her children after their father died of cancer. At the end of their street sat a mujahideen post famous for atrocities. "Every two or three nights we could hear the scream of a young woman taken out of her home for rape or for sexual slavery. And then the family were calling for help. And no one was there to help them."

As Horia told me, the only thing that would stop the screaming was gunfire. "Then there was silence, darkness, fear, and nothing else." The Cold War was over. Afghans were of little use to the Great Powers now. The fundamentalists whom the Americans and the Pakistanis and the Saudis had armed and trained to fight the Soviet Union were unleashed against their own people. "As soon as we were hearing those screams, my mother was putting me into the chicken house. I spent countless nights there." With an international community that failed to step in, that was the only protection Afghans had—the chicken coops of Kabul.

On a Friday in February 1993, as her brothers were on the roof trying to fix the telephone line that had been knocked out by a previous rocket strike nearby, another rocket hit their house. Telling me what happened next is excruciating for Horia, and I wonder if I should turn off the recorder. But she is determined to continue. It is her description of how she found her brothers in the street that is most terrible. "At the beginning, both of them were quite yellow and there wasn't any blood. I was just looking, and suddenly I saw like bones and meats and body parts. Slowly, the blood started coming from their bodies." At first Horia and her family tried to get the boys, both still alive, to the International Committee of the Red Cross Hospital. "My youngest brother who later died, he was having that much of severe injuries that at the time I had rushed to pick him up I thought, 'Oh my God, he will just turn to pieces if I just tried to pick him up.'"

Where was the "war on terror" to stop this hell? In Afghanistan, people lived through a continuous fundamentalist terrorist attack from 1992 to 1996, followed by a Taliban reign of terror made possible by the underlying chaos. The impact on people's lives was unbelievable. A Bosnian writer once suggested, "Fiction must be plausible, reality has no such constraints."[39] If you wrote Horia's story as a screenplay, you would be told it was implausible. Ahmad Reshad Mosadiq, her thirteen-year-old brother, a straight-A student who dreamed of being a doctor, had fallen to the rockets of the mujahideen. Now her fifteen-year-old brother remained gravely injured in a hospital lacking anesthetic and bandages. Horia's mother wanted to leave Afghanistan as soon as he could be moved, but Horia feared that if she herself went into exile without her fiancé, they might never find each other again. So they married in mujahideen Kabul. In time, Horia gave birth to their first daughter. A month later, her husband was injured in another rocket attack while riding his bicycle across town.

When her husband was finally able to travel, Horia Mosadiq and her family left this Dantesque Kabul for Pakistan and then Iran, but she continued working as a journalist, returning regularly to Afghanistan. This was no easy assignment. It meant submitting to a new way of dressing for the very first time. The burqa.

"I couldn't walk. I couldn't see my way through the screens. Because I wasn't used to the burqa, I and my husband, we sat in the front seat of a car to be transported to Kabul." They were stopped at a Taliban checkpoint where the guards "started shouting at my husband what an immoral man he is, that he is allowing his wife to sit in the front seat of a car. 'You dishonored man. You don't know that we always say you should eat first, then feed your children, then feed your dog. If anything is left, then your wife should eat it. And you're bringing this bitch to sit in the front seat of the car.' "

As she recalls this Taliban hierarchy of beings, Horia's thoughts jump back to the present. "These are the people who the West want to negotiate with, who America has romanticized about sharing power with," she says sharply. Are there moderates among them, as the U.S. government has tried to suggest? "If they are moderate," she exclaims, "then why they are Taliban?"

After mujahideen rockets took her brother, after terror and exile and forced veiling in the fundamentalist hell the Cold War had made of Afghanistan, Horia has two more tales of the Taliban. "Once I was going to a shop to buy myself a piece of cloth because it was a marriage ceremony of my sister-in-law. I couldn't see the color of the cloth inside the shop and then I put my burqa off and started looking." It seems innocuous—buying fabric for a family wedding and using your eyes to check the shade. Not in Taliban Afghanistan. "Suddenly, something banged on my head and I could see just blood in my eyes. Then I was beaten so badly by an electrical cable by a Taliban, I got a broken nose and even now I think you can see here there is mark for that." Now I understand the slightly crooked nose that graces Horia's kind face. It is the trace of the Taliban.

Others bear marks of that time that are even more horrific. As Horia tells me, in 1999, in Kabul's Microrayani Square, she saw a thirteen-year-old boy holding a bunch of severed hands. "They were turned very dark blue." Those hands belonged to people who had been accused of theft and taken to Kabul Stadium for amputation. Horia remembers, "The boy shouted, 'Look, what the justice has done to the thieves. This is how the Sharia should be.' "

A few days after I hear this account, I visit Kabul's Ghazi Stadium. I stand quietly with Alem, the guide from my guesthouse, in the empty arena that is now used for sports again. In addition to amputation of hands and feet while the Qur'an was recited nearby, people were lashed here for adultery in Taliban times, and women were stoned to death.

Alem says the Talibs would go out into the city with loudspeakers and announce the punishments. People who had no TV, no radio, no entertainment, would come and watch. There are many different Muslim laws applied in many different ways, but from now on, whenever people talk about "application of the Sharia," it is hard for me not to think about this place.

The call to prayer echoes nearby. *Allahu Akbar.* Taliban supporters would shout this out after each execution. As I pause in the stadium, I cannot help wondering what a Great God might make of what is done in places like this.

THE RULE OF THE SAME PERPETRATORS WHO KILLED MY BROTHER

To say Horia Mosadiq was delighted when the Taliban were overthrown would be an understatement. She and her husband moved back to Kabul. But Horia's enthusiasm, shared by so many Afghans, quickly took its first blow in June 2002, when a traditional council was resuscitated to determine Afghanistan's transitional administration and president. The gathering was dominated by warlords who pressured other delegates. "As soon as we arrived before the emergency *loya jirga* in 2002, I noticed how Lakhdar Brahimi [special representative of the UN Secretary-General] and Zalmay Khalilzad [U.S. special presidential envoy to Afghanistan], they allowed the butchers of Afghans to join the power," Horia recounts. "Brahimi came with that famous statement that 'we cannot sacrifice peace for justice.' "[40] This was a political disappointment for many, because "it was the huge demand from the Afghan public that they wanted justice." It was also a very personal affront to those like Horia.

"We have to live under the rule of the same perpetrators who killed my brother, who are responsible for the destruction of this city. I couldn't believe that."

Horia Mosadiq does not know for sure which fundamentalists carried out the strikes that afflicted her family. Gulbuddin Hekmatyar's onetime-American-backed Hezb-e Islami might have wounded her husband. The rocket that struck down her younger brother may have been fired by Shura-e Nazar, a mujahideen coalition founded by Ahmad Shah Massoud that controlled Kabul's Television Hill then. This explains her insistence on universal accountability. To get all who may have been responsible, you have to have a wide reach.

Like Algeria's Cherifa Kheddar, Horia Mosadiq could not give up on the dream of accountability, no matter what it might cost her. Before the first presidential elections in Afghanistan in 2004, she wrote an article addressed to Hamid Karzai. "I told him, 'You have the support of 25 million. You don't need to seek support in the ring of war criminals. If you want to win the hearts of Afghans, bring justice that you promised.'" Some time afterward, "when I was leaving for my office, just by the doorstep of my residence, a man came and said, 'Stop talking about all this nonsense. Like justice or war criminals. Because no one is going to listen to you.'" The warlords wanted to be left alone right where the United States had put them—safely in power. They would not tolerate Horia's defiance. "'We are not going to shoot you to make you a hero,' the man continued, 'you just need a car accident.'" She recounts this matter-of-factly. "It was a funny story, because I was on my way to a conference organized by NATO about women living in the new security environment. . . ."

In 2007, she founded a unique coalition called the War Victims Network to buck Parliament's passage of amnesty laws by demanding justice. The network brought together four hundred survivors of war-related abuses from different time periods. Knowing their pain firsthand, Horia gave "a voice to the victims," because "when there was a discussion about human rights violations it was always the perpetrators who were justifying what they have done. The victims' voices were missing." The War Victims Network held the first-ever public demonstrations against war crimes and for accountability in Afghanistan. Horia even convinced a survivor of gang rape to appear and publicly identify herself at one such protest in 2008, at a time when the leaders of the groups who committed many of these crimes were in increasingly powerful positions. Yet again people were telling Horia Mosadiq not to show herself, this time for her protection. "I wasn't covering my face like many were telling me I should. I was believing the perpetrators should know I have no fear of them."

That year, someone tried to break into her office and her home. Someone shot at her husband's car. Luckily, he escaped. Between March and June 2008, there were three attempts to kidnap her children. "Twice I was taken at the gunpoint but they didn't kill me, they just showed me the gun." Finally, she and her family had to leave Kabul yet again.

You can take Horia out of Afghanistan, but you cannot take Afghanistan out of Horia. "I didn't want to sit silent somewhere and weep." After fighting and surviving Muslim fundamentalist violence for nearly thirty years, she continues to come here often and to document what is happening to all the Horias she left behind.

SHOCKING THE PROPHET MUHAMMAD

"I decided I should work hard for accountability of the people who don't care what's going to happen to those who they attack." Horia Mosadiq melted down her own ordeal at the hands of Afghan fundamentalists into the fuel for her fight against all who had plagued her people. She casts the net of blame beyond Afghanistan's extremist thugs to include those who used them. "As much as I go deep into the issue of fundamentalism, I can also blame the West. In 1978, as soon as the communist coup d'état happened in Afghanistan, the Western countries started supporting these mujahideen groups." The West's allies then were "the extremists who made Islam a legitimate way of killing people."

In fact, Horia tells me, the United States aided the most fundamentalist of the mujahideen. "From among the fifteen mujahideen parties, they chose to support the most extremist person, Gulbuddin Hekmatyar—the biggest recipient of the U.S. aid." She finds the outcome predictable. "Now, I'm not really surprised what's happening in Pakistan and Afghanistan." While the rise of fundamentalism was not unexpected in light of these policies, it did represent a major reversal in the course of Afghan history. "We were not an extremist society before. In the 1970s, my mom was walking on the streets of Herat with her miniskirt and no one was even looking at her." That was during the heyday of the Herat Cinema, back in an Afghanistan where short sleeves were possible. "We have forgotten this history now. My children don't know any better life than, 'Cover yourself otherwise you will be attacked.'"

The world seems ready to accept that these will be the limits of Afghan lives. "Everything is a double standard. Justice, democracy, women's rights are just words and luxuries that they cannot afford for Afghanistan." She aspires to something better. "I want my daughter to be educated. I want her to be able to walk freely on the streets." Looking ahead, she doesn't see that future. Now she thinks the United States just wants to "get rid" of her country again. "They will abandon Afghanistan, and we will go to a situation that is much worse than the 1980s and you will remember my words."

I ask what she thinks of the peace movements in the West that focus on the withdrawal of international troops and mainly protest against civilian casualties by those troops—killings she herself campaigns against. "When they talk about civilian casualties, do they know that more than twenty thousand people were killed in one week during the rule of the Taliban? Do they know that in central Afghanistan, in Yakawlang, the worst massacre happened in 2001 when thousands of men, women, and children were beheaded by the Taliban?" The Yakawlang events of January 2001 unfolded like a version of the Srebrenica massacre, but in this case both the murdered and the murderers were Muslim.[41] All adult males were rounded up. The younger men were methodically shot by firing squads; the elders were forced to load their bodies onto trucks. "In that time we didn't have any American presence," Horia reminds me. "Then why the Taliban were doing that to us?" They did not need an "anti-imperialist" excuse.

Should foreign troops stay longer? Horia wants the troops to leave in time, but "what many Afghans are fearing is the consequences of them leaving before we have a strong government and accountable national security forces capable of protecting the rights of Afghans." As much as the foreign troops have made dreadful mistakes and committed some grave crimes here, and foreign governments have a history of working *with* the fundamentalists, it is Afghanistan's past that makes her fear for its future. "Because we have the same experience when Russia left in 1989. Everything started collapsing. This time it will be even worse." The violence Horia fears in the wake of the departure of international military personnel—and of the political will of the international community likely to go with them—is that of both the so-called Northern

Alliance and the Taliban. She knows too well what it can mean to live under the thumb of such groups.

"We will have a bath of blood in this country."

Horia is taken aback that some progressives in the West still regard the Taliban as anti-imperialist. "I'm shocked some of them call Taliban the freedom fighters. I can't believe as a Muslim woman that we think that burqa is okay, the way if you want to impose Sharia it's okay." True to form, she then says something quite daring: "I can just tell them that if the Prophet Muhammad himself was alive now, he would have been shocked to see the way the fundamentalist groups are implementing Islam and Sharia on the people."

The Afghan human rights defender reminds me that the United States "owes our people not a big pardon but also a lot more. Because we Afghans were used as a human shield to defeat Russia." Americans, she thinks, must "pressure their government to pay its debt to the Afghan people, to help Afghans get rid of the fundamentalist groups." Some of what will happen now depends on Afghans themselves. But a great deal depends on choices made far away. Dr. Sima Samar, head of the Afghan Independent Human Rights Commission, warns in a speech I hear six months later: "Everyone is talking about leaving Afghanistan with dignity. But they mean their own dignity, not that of the Afghans."

The young driver who takes me to the airport when I leave Afghanistan in July 2011 plays local heavy metal on the radio. We drive through Kabul afternoon traffic while the guitars roar from the dashboard, and I say good-bye—"*Khod'hafez*"—to Afghanistan, to the schoolgirls walking determinedly with their bookbags, to the ubiquitous wedding halls, to the dust and hope and fear in the air, to all the progress they have made since I first came here in 1996. I think about what Horia Mosadiq told me about her dream for her country: "I really hope Afghanistan one day is a country where everyone can feel that they are a human being."

WHY I HATE AL QAEDA

Around the tenth anniversary of September 11, it all came back. The sense that the sky over Lower Manhattan is actively empty. The sorrow over such ghastly deaths. The equivocation by some who should know better. The wound inflicted that day on the American psyche is real, especially in the New York area, where I teach for a decade after 9/11. The toughest people I know weep when the names are read at Ground Zero each year.

On the tenth anniversary, I thought a lot about the victims, like Father Mychal Judge, a gay Franciscan priest who was a Fire Department chaplain and died in the lobby of Tower One.[42] Father Mike had ministered to AIDS patients and alcoholics and was a fan of Celtic rock band Black 47. Rushing to comfort victims of terror, he became one. Christian fundamentalist Jerry Falwell said of 9/11 a few days later that the feminists and the gays and all who tried to secularize America "helped this happen."[43] Though he subsequently apologized, Falwell clearly was unable to understand Father Mike's life or his death.

I also thought about Amenia Rasool, a Guyanan American Muslim woman who worked on the ninety-fifth floor of the World Trade Center. I first read about her in the *New York Times* remembrance section.[44] Though she had an arranged marriage, she and her husband reportedly shared domestic tasks. She worked as an accountant by day, but in the evening when her chores were done, she was said to enjoy watching taped soap operas and painting her fingernails. All of these things— women working outside the home, dramatic entertainment, and use of cosmetics—are often prohibited by Muslim fundamentalists, sometimes even on pain of death. Meanwhile, many American right-wing racists cannot conceive of a Muslim woman with such a life, nor do those who waved hateful signs in protest against the proposed Muslim community center in Lower Manhattan ("No Islamic Settlements in America") remember Amenia Rasool, even in death. She would have been "the other" to some of these Americans, but she was also "the other" for Muslim fundamentalists. Her life challenged simple narratives about what it means to be a Muslim woman in America.

On September 11, 2011, I wonder if it can really have been ten years since Amenia Rasool and Father Mike died, since nearly three thousand were killed along with them in less than two hours. To mark the occasion, I wrote a manifesto called "Why I Hate Al Qaeda." But I could not get it published. (Thankfully, it was eventually adopted by a feminist international law blog.)[45] One left-wing paper told me it was irrelevant because of the Arab Spring. Perhaps it was too off-script for me, a person of Muslim heritage, to say I hate Al Qaeda rather than just to explain how what the United States has done historically is even worse. I do speak critically of U.S. foreign policy, but not when what I am speaking about is the murder of three thousand people on a single morning by Muslim fundamentalists. While the flag-waving on the right is distasteful, the inability of some on the left and in the human rights movement to talk about Al Qaeda, to pause for a compassionate, engaged response to terrorism before rushing to criticize the government's reaction, perplexes me equally.

I want to stand with those who refuse to equivocate. With Professor Muqtedar Khan, who wrote, "[W]hat happened on September 11 will forever be a horrible scar on the history of our religion."[46] With Mehdi Hasan, who blogged, "[W]e have to declare . . . not in our name."[47] With Aziz Junejo, who denounces terrorism on the doorstep of his mosque, reminding us that "Holy Quran, in Chapter 5, verse 32, forbids the killing of any innocent person, equating it to killing the whole of humanity."[48] With Arab American journalist Ray Hanania, who calls on Muslim and Arab American organizations to denounce extremists and expel them from their organizations.[49] With the Canadian Muslim Sheema Khan, who opined, "[S]ilence is not an option in this struggle for the soul of Islam."[50]

I battled with "Why I Hate Al Qaeda" for a long time. Hatred is not a good thing. But I believe there are ideologies worth despising. As Nigerian Nobel laureate Wole Soyinka said on the International Day of Peace in 2012 with regard to a fundamentalist group responsible for the deaths of some three thousand in his home country, "We have an organization which closes down schools, shoots faculty teachers . . . and turn most of the north into an educational wasteland. How can we reach the children there? We must first get rid of Boko Haram."[51] Movements like Boko Haram and Al Qaeda are so bent on the destruction of human beings that the only possible response is to abhor them—not the individuals in them but their collective political organization and what it does.

Here are just a few of the reasons . . .

WHY I HATE AL QAEDA

September 11, 2011

To start, there are 2,975 reasons from 90 countries. An unforgettable patchwork quilt of humanity that was disappeared on a Tuesday morning ten years ago. But that is only the beginning.

I hate Al Qaeda for all the human beings they have killed—the Africans, Americans, Arabs, Asians, Europeans, agnostics, atheists, Christians, Jews, Hindus, Muslims.

I hate Al Qaeda because they have murdered thousands of Muslims while claiming to represent them, a claim they make even while bombing mosques during Ramadan. Because they make the most sacred pronouncements, like *Allahu Akbar*—God is Great—into threats, into epithets.

I hate Al Qaeda because of the Caliphate of Doom they want to build.

I hate Al Qaeda because they hate women, gays, Jews, Christians, Muslims not like them, which is most Muslims. Because they only hate. And they make me hate too.

I hate Al Qaeda for the young Algerian fiancé who bled to death in his mother's arms in Cherchell after a suicide bomber broke his fast this August; for Moustapha Akkad and his daughter Rima; for Danny Pearl, Amenia Rasool, and Father Mychal Judge, all of whom are no more because Al Qaeda is.

I hate Al Qaeda for the bombs of Baghdad, of Algiers, of Amman, of Dar es Salaam, of all the cities they have blighted like New York.

I hate Al Qaeda because they make it harder for people who look like my father to board an airplane. Because they confirmed every racist's view of Muslims. And provoked responses that confirmed every anti-American cliché.

Ten years on, I am ready to stop hating Al Qaeda. I am ready to stop Al Qaeda.

CHAPTER NINE

Sidi Bouzid Blues and the Green Wave:
Journeys through the Arab Spring and Fall

I stand in the spot where Mohamed Bouazizi had set himself on fire and unknowingly sparked what became known as the Arab Spring. All the pressures and disappointments faced by young people of modest means across the region that sometimes turn their thoughts to paradise, infuse the air in this place with a longing to truly live, to matter.

"I Burn, Therefore I am."

That was how an article in the Algerian press explained why increasing numbers of North Africans were self-immolating around the time of Bouazizi's death.[1] "I wanted them to see me die," one woman was quoted saying.[2] Those whose misery is normalized know they are only visible when they burn, though just for one awful moment. If their existential grievances remain unresolved, the ground will be ever more fertile for the fundamentalists.

How long a road of desperation is it from such a suicide to a suicide bombing?

On the March day in 2011 when I visit the southern Tunisian town of Sidi Bouzid, unemployed university graduates much like the late Bouazizi are on hunger strike in a makeshift tent near the spot where he ended it all and started it all. They have hungry eyes, and nothing else to do. I am barraged with explanations for their fast. No one talks about Allah or being Muslim. They are Tunisians. They want "bread, honor, and dignity." "*Al khobz, al sharif, wa al karama.*" "We study but we don't get work." "We need to eat." Other than the ability to stay here in a tent in the public square and express their grievances without being dragged off to Ben Ali's jails—admittedly a significant advance—these young denizens of Sidi Bouzid have seen no material benefit from the revolution yet. A twenty-two-year-old named Hocine warns, "I am ready to die."

Several others repeat this. The ghastly photo of an entirely bandaged Bouazizi dying slowly in the hospital (it took eighteen days) reminds me what an awful possibility this is. How acute must the anguish be for a twenty-six-year-old to drink gas—as I was told by people in his neighborhood he did—and then to methodically auto-combust?

Will governments in North Africa save the next generation of would-be Bouazizis? This question remains urgent for human rights across the region and central to the battle against fundamentalism, because, while Islamist movements are mostly middle-class–led, they capitalize on the anger of the disenfranchised. Will global powers and international financial institutions enable governments here to do what they must to provide these young people with an alternative to fire? Will they allow—and encourage—them to spend on social programs and the public sector? This is essential if North Africa is to kick extremism.

Though this town three hours south of Tunis is the birthplace of the North African Awakening, Sidi Bouzid feels like it was until recently a sleepy provincial capital. In the main square, men sell produce, used shoes, single eggs, and loose cigarettes from rickety carts, as Bouazizi did. But the town sleeps no more. One man's despondent act here on December 17, 2010, started a fire of such intensity that it swept across North Africa, leaving behind a new region where nothing would ever be quite the same.

When I visit, three months have passed since that December day. Ben Ali has fallen, Mubarak has fallen, Qaddhafi is on the run, and significant protests have rocked nearby Morocco and Algeria. Demonstrations have broken out from Bahrain to Yemen, all claiming roots here. Both triumph and tragedy have followed, and the long-term outcome remains unclear. But, in March 2011, Bouazizi's hometown is itself transformed. Trilingual revolutionary graffiti decorates every wall downtown. "Stand up for your right." "Stay strong, Tunisians. The world is proud of you." The earthquake of free speech unleashed a tsunami of frustrations that can at least be spoken now. Local taxi drivers picket in front of the provincial headquarters. "We are used to demonstrations now," a kid says.

I tour Bouazizi's dusty and desolate neighborhood, Hay el-nour. The houses are small, as is the gate to his family's former home. There are multiple Internet cafés. A few young women wander the streets in jeans. A twenty-nine-year-old unemployed man wearing a baseball hat is intensely frustrated with the absence of change since what he calls "*thawrat El Bouazizi*" (Bouazizi's revolution). He still has no job. He has never had a job. He probably never will. But he speaks freely. "If it was like before, we would all be in prison for talking like this."

While forcing Zine al-Abidine Ben Ali to *dégage*, as Tunisians say, or "get out," is all to the good, the future here remains unclear. Having escaped a relatively secular autocracy, are they now doomed to theocracy? Or can they break out of the so-called Islamist dilemma, which offers these as the only available alternatives? That is what I have come to find out in spring 2011, a season like no other, and what I will revisit on my return that fall.

UNVEILING ENNAHDA IN AVENUE DE LA RÉPUBLIQUE

However far North Africa may have come down the road toward theocracy since then, during that March 2011 the politics of hope hang in the clear Tunis air. I do not want to forget that spring, and so I start there, although autumn—to which I return later—will confirm my fears. You can only assess what may be lost now against the backdrop of what was won in early 2011, and of what was dreamed.

When I arrive in Tunis, it has been exactly two months since the fall of Ben Ali, or "Zinochet," as some have dubbed him (after the late Chilean dictator). Everyone is excited, and exhausted. "As happy and proud as we are, there is equally a lot of work to be done," the feminist lawyer Bochra Belhadj Hmida tells me. Tunisians freely talk politics in cafés, bars, taxis, classrooms, pastry shops, and along the walkways of the Casbah. Political discussion is as ubiquitous as the piles of garbage that have accumulated on the streets since the revolution. In this moment, the fresh smell of new politics still masks the stench of the trash.

Such civic effervescence is remarkable anywhere, but especially in a country where virtually no freedom of expression was permitted before January 14, 2011. The press was tightly controlled by the ruling party, known in Orwellian splendor as the Constitutional Democratic Rally (RCD), whose political opponents were regularly jailed and tortured. When I served as a trial observer for Amnesty International here in the 1990s, I had to carry every single document with me at all times, as my hotel room was regularly searched by Ben Ali's political police, who did not even attempt to hide evidence of their "visits." To speak safely with the lawyer in the case—the prominent rights advocate Radhia Nasraoui—she and I walked in the Casbah at night so as not to be recorded.

There was nothing strange about women walking alone after dark as Radhia and I did. Ben Ali's Tunisia was a paradoxical place—politically closed and socially open on regional standards. It was in this contradictory space that the revolution combusted, bringing new openings and new closures.

On a brisk March day in 2011, I walk across town to a meeting in the Avenue de la République, a boulevard full of clothing shops that feature haute couture and hijabs. Newsstands flutter with the new papers. There are far more women in headscarves than I had seen in the 1990s, but also lots of women in tight clothes, and young couples encircled in each other's arms. Two Tunisias share the streets.

A graying, smiling Mahmoud Ben Romdhane receives me in his political party's unembellished headquarters. I have known him since the mid-1990s, when he served on Amnesty International's highest governing body. An economist, former university professor, and longtime Ben Ali opponent, his books were sometimes banned. Now, he is trying to make Ettajdid, the secular center-left party of which he is a leader, one that can provide a credible alternative for resolving Tunisia's problems.[3] Later on, in April 2012, the party will merge with two others to create the Social Democratic Path (SDP). For now, Ettajdeed stands on its own.

Though they had long opposed the Ben Ali regime, the fundamentalists did not lead the revolution here, nor were they even supportive of it initially. Mahmoud reminds me of this when we sit down to talk. The women's rights activist Ahlem Belhadj had similarly recounted that during the revolution, the protesters did not use fundamentalist slogans. Instead, "young men carried young women on their shoulders in marches." It was "a terrain of struggle against fundamentalism, not for the fundamentalists." Islamists did not lead the first wave of the revolution in Egypt, either. Across the region, their jihads did nothing but justify dictators and close off political space for those, like Ahlem Belhadj and Mahmoud Ben Romdhane, who could offer a truly democratic alternative. Unfortunately, as Bochra Belhadj Hmida had also pointed out to me, these facts will be easily forgotten.

When I meet him that spring 2011 day, Mahmoud Ben Romdhane already suspects the fundamentalists, primarily those working in the Tunisian political party Ennahda, will try to capitalize on a revolutionary process they did not start. Ennahda understands that many Tunisians do not want Islamists in power, he thinks, "so they present themselves as a 'moderate' movement." Mahmoud finds this self-representation unconvincing. "They say they are for women's rights." But he believes they will never allow Tunisia to advance in this regard. On the other hand, his party seeks "full equality between men and women, including in inheritance," he explains. "So we will have to undertake a struggle to get Ennahda to unveil itself. We do not trust them."

Ennahda had been banned under Ben Ali and many of its members were jailed, tortured, and exiled, but they were not the only victims, Mahmoud stresses. Communists, independent women's rights advocates, professionals, trade unionists, and human rights defenders also paid a high price. Ben Romdhane tells me he saw a delegation from Amnesty International the week before my arrival. Ennahda, he argues, owes a significant debt to Amnesty, because the group defended them in Ben Ali's time. Mahmoud reminds me that the human rights groups in the West that so vigorously championed the rights of members of Ennahda during the dictatorship have a responsibility to work just as hard now to defend those who become victims under its rule.

In fact, Ben Romdhane fears the fundamentalist party's shifting positions that flow with the tide of regional politics. For example, he says that in the past Ennahda "accepted the Tunisian Personal Status Code as being within the Islamic tradition." (This law, adopted in 1956 under the late president Habib Bourguiba, outlaws polygamy and gives women the right to divorce.)[4] However, he added, "When the FIS were getting ready to take power in Algeria in the 1990s, Ennahda suddenly wanted to throw the Personal Status Code out the window."

Such stark shifts in position are worrisome, as are disparities between discourse and deed, Mahmoud points out. "Ennahda says they are against violence, but they killed. They threw acid on women's faces. Ennahda says it did not. They must openly admit what they have done and say they will never do it again."[5]

When I ask him about fundamentalist movements to the right of Ennahda, like Hizb Ut-Tahrir and Salafi groups, he does not mince words. "They are crazy. They are ignorant. They are fascist movements, really." The *Washington Post* describes the region's Salafis colorfully as "scowling men in long, black beards . . . who would like to see the strictest form of Islam applied. . . ."[6] By 2012, with Ennahda in power, Mahmoud Ben Romdhane's Ettajdid Party is speaking out vocally against those he had dubbed "fascists," who now cast an increasingly long and ugly shadow across revolutionary Tunisia. Ettajdid's March 2012 communiqué denounces "calls for violence, hatred and even death from fanatical Salafi groups . . . which have targeted Tunisian citizens of Jewish faith." Ettajdid calls on Ennahda to "react immediately and bring an end to . . . the impunity these irresponsible groups enjoy."[7] That never happens.

International pressure on the now-ruling fundamentalist party, including about the way it responds to the Salafists, is critical. As Ben Romdhane tells me, Ennahda seeks transnational legitimacy. So far, it is winning on this score, being regularly dubbed "moderate" by the *bon pensant* Western liberal press, with little discussion as to precisely what this term means.[8] It is a meaning I search for all across North Africa.

MULTITASKING WITH THE DEMOCRATIC WOMEN

When the Tunisian Democratic Women's Association (ATFD) held an unprecedented congress for equality and citizenship in March 2011, a thousand women gathered to discuss protecting—and advancing—their human rights in revolutionary Tunisia. One woman in the audience, an activist in the revolution, wept as she took the floor over having been threatened by fundamentalist youth in the Casbah after the fall of Ben Ali. They said they would create an Islamic state. That was not what she had revolted for. "Maybe in Saudi Arabia, but not here," she says she shouted back. An Algerian woman went to the microphone and urged Tunisians to learn from what happened in her country in the late eighties. Islamism was what grew most rapidly in the Petri dish of sudden democratization. They must, she urged, organize themselves very quickly against such an outcome.

Everyone agreed that there must be no going backward. The crowd at the ATFD congress that day knew their country was one of the most advanced on women's rights in the region—indeed, among all Muslim majority societies. In addition to the relatively progressive family law inherited from the Bourguiba era, access to abortion was won in 1965. Thirty-one percent of lawyers and twenty-seven percent of judges are female.[9] In this moment, Tunisian women stood both to gain and to lose. Moreover, their losses could have a knock-on effect elsewhere. If this—one of the most secular, socially liberal Arab, Muslim majority countries—were to fall to the fundos, it would be a huge symbolic victory for extremism.

A few days after the ATFD congress, Nadia Hakimi, the organization's executive director, greets me wearing casual clothes and a Tuareg necklace. As we sit in her office, appropriately located on Liberty Avenue, she is constantly interrupted in multiple languages. But we somehow manage to find time to talk about her group's work. For years under Ben Ali, the ATFD took on the dictatorship and patriarchy. The organization actively engaged during the revolution, sending women's fact-finding missions to the South, where the worst of the repression unfolded in the early weeks, and then holding a risky press conference back in the capital about their findings, with Ben Ali still in power.

With this track record, it is not surprising that Hakimi waxes more lyrical about that early phase of the revolution than anyone I meet. "People were taken in their very being. They did not sleep anymore. As soon as there was an idea, that's it. Every place became a venue for debate. It was an exceptional situation. That is what revolutions are. Exceptional situations in which human beings are in a continuous invention of who they want to be, and how they see themselves in the future."

In March 2011, Hakimi sees the ATFD's role as representing north on the Tunisian compass, showing the direction things should be heading. "The rights of women remain a priority, even in a time of revolution like this one, perhaps even more now. As soon as there is a crisis you are told women's rights must wait. 'There are other priorities.' But feminism around the world says women's rights are always a priority." Such an ordering of concerns means that just as they had fearlessly taken on Ben Ali, now they must stand up to their country's emerging fundamentalists. When I start to ask Hakimi whether she thinks Ennahda and its leader, Rached Ghannouchi, have really moderated their politics, as accepted wisdom in the West suggests, she interrupts with a mantra.

"I do not believe them. I do not believe them. I do not believe them."

Like Mahmoud Ben Romdhane, she was shocked by a recent press conference in which Ghannouchi downplayed crimes committed in the past by Ennahda members in the name of the brutality of the fallen government. "You cannot justify such crimes so easily," Hakimi says. Given her concerns, I ask what tactics she thinks can work to confront the fundamentalists now. "Fight for your ideas. Do not give up on our achievements." As the name of her organization would suggest, she is unyielding in her defense of women's rights and she is also committed to a "democratic" approach. "It is not because I disagree with someone that I must kill him or something. No. There is a way to counter them. We must be vigilant and do a lot of work."

STATES OF GRACE

On my last spring day in Tunis, I ask Alya Chammari, a human rights lawyer under Ben Ali, how she finds this post-revolutionary moment. "Is it the post-revolution?" she muses. "I hope it is still the revolution."

We drink tea at the Hotel Mechtel while her husband, longtime opposition figure Khemais Chammari, who was sentenced to five years in prison under Ben Ali and has become the Tunisian ambassador to

UNESCO, gave his own interview nearby. The air around Alya shimmers with possibility this spring. "We didn't think we would live this extraordinary moment." In Tunis, it does indeed seem in this season that anything is possible. The ex–ruling party's headquarters is now an abandoned shell littered with insulting graffiti. There are daily protests on the streets of the capital. "We could be the first state of the Global South with a Muslim majority population to install a real democracy, based on equality between men and women, based on judicial, economic, and social justice." Carthaginian Utopia—in this moment it seems attainable.

Alya Chammari is euphoric but not naïve. In this early phase, she is not in denial, like many others in and out of North Africa, about what dangers still lie ahead. She recognizes "the possibility of the confiscation of this revolution by the most retrograde currents of political Islam. Wahhabism exists in Tunisia. Salafists also. For them, the objective is to destroy the Republic and to install a Caliphate."

Nor does Chammari spare Ennahda. "They say their fundamentals are the Arab-Islamic identity and the Sharia. Democracy is in danger with these people, the rights of women also." She denounces the "strategic discourse" they use "to make us believe they have become very moderate." Alya argues that the events of International Women's Day in 2011 prove their claims untrue. "Just after March 8, when we were calling for equality in inheritance, for the freedom of Tunisian women to marry non-Muslim men, they showed their real face. They were against all these demands." Like a number of well-informed commentators I have met, Chammari is especially afraid of an alliance between members of the former ruling party and the fundamentalists. She is unequivocal. "This is the biggest danger."

I ask what strategies Tunisian feminists should employ in the face of these perils. She highlights the same one Bochra Belhadj Hmida had underscored to me. Most of all, both women want "separation of religion and law." Neither Bochra nor Alya is in an apologetic mood this March. These jurists seek not only to preserve the legal gains of Tunisian women but also to push forward. After all, it is a revolutionary moment. If not now, when exactly? "Is this a revolution or not?" Bochra demands to know. "If it is a revolution, there should be no question of going backward. So why, when we speak of women's rights, do people want to block them?"

For these reasons, Alya Chammari tells me in March 2011 she wants no reference to religion in the new constitution that will be drafted by a constituent assembly to be elected that fall. Article 1 of the old constitution stipulates that the country's "religion is Islam." However, it gives no further juridical role to religion whatsoever. Bochra says she wants equality between women and men codified in every possible way. Having just flown in from the West, where so many relativize when talking about Muslim majority countries, indulging in what Pakistani Canadian Tarek Fatah calls "the racism of low expectations,"[10] I find these lawyers' clarity and aspiration bracing. I also know how hard it will be to achieve their goals. I ask Alya Chammari whether the fundamentalists could ever accept a secular constitution.

"No. They will scream atheism. They will say we are heretics."

This does not dissuade her. She knows a secular constitution is the best way to guarantee human rights in her country, and she is willing to demand it, whatever epithets may be thrown her way and however long it may take. It is the same refusal to kowtow to "realism" that made her and her husband oppose Ben Ali all those years when they could have had a comfortable life.

Later, in March 2012, Ennahda will decide to stick with Article 1 of the old constitution for the moment and decline to push for Sharia to be codified as the source of legislation in Tunisia—a fact that is lauded in the Western press as evidence of the party's moderation. By merely raising the spectre of Sharia, however, Ennahda has succeeded in drowning out any voices, like Alya Chammari's, who would have sought to remove *any* reference to religion from the body of the constitution, a reference that is all the more frightening now with the rising power of religious parties. Morever, Maghrebi press accounts clarify that Ennahda chief Rached Ghannouchi explains to his members that some Tunisians "are not yet ready to go farther" but that "the time will come when Tunisians will see the Sharia in a better light." One journalist concludes: "They will be tempted to make new pro-Sharia advances in the future."[11]

In fact, Ghannouchi is caught on camera that same month confessing to having precisely such a strategy in a meeting with a group of Salafists (the two recordings are not leaked until October 2012). "Do not rush things," he tells the Salafist leaders. "We should present a reassuring discourse to people. . . ."[12] He points to Algeria in the 1990s as a situation in which Islamists thought they "had reached the goal and there was no turning back."[13] As Ghannouchi told his Salafist "sons and daughters," the Sharia should be applied "in increments." He even promises to amend the Personal Status Code when Islamists finally have the upper hand.[14]

Back in March 2011, Alya Chammari suggests that to forestall such a drift there has to be a clear strategy to communicate that a separation of religion and state is the only way to guarantee everyone's freedom of religion. She does not want political parties banned, or people silenced. Instead, she wants to see the fundamentalists countered by a progressive strategy of engaging youth and working on the ground in communities. However, she is not some wilting democrat ready to tolerate intolerance in the name of democracy. "The state must be the guarantor of free exercise in religious spaces, and keep others from using them for political means to install a Caliphate."

Chammari rushes to acknowledge that "Islam is our heritage." However, she rejects "all that is oppressive in Islam, and in Islamic Law which is not of divine heritage." Alya reminds me that it is everyone's right to question aspects of her own heritage, to try to take into the future that which is liberating and leave in the past that which is not. It is the only way humanity has ever advanced.

I attempt to ask Chammari which fundamentalists pose the biggest risks for revolutionary Tunisia—the obvious extremists or the so-called moderates, but, like Nadia Hakimi, she interrupts. "They are all very dangerous, all of the Islamist currents from the most radical to the most 'open.' I have no confidence in any political current founded on an interpretation of religion that is not egalitarian, and that talks about Islamic law as the essential referent." Religion, she opines, should not be used by any political party. "It belongs to everyone. No one has the right to present themselves as the spokesperson of God. You can say, 'I am conservative. I think women are below men.' Just don't say it is because you are a Muslim. My interpretation of Islam is different." She thinks the religion calls for equality.

Acutely aware of the closing window of the revolutionary moment, she wants the Left to get organized, to unify. NOW. "We are living in a state of grace. This will end soon." Alya Chammari is already clear in March 2011 about the challenge that will lie before her compatriots as fall approaches.

"We need to try to save democracy."

I leave to rush off to Tunis Carthage International Airport that March afternoon, three months after Ben Ali fled. In the departure lounge, the coffee bar with a menu offering ham sandwiches and fine Tunisian wine is right next to the prayer room. I hope it always will be.

THE TWO DOAAS

In the spring of 2011, six weeks after the fall of Hosni Mubarak, the mood in Cairo is somber, less exultant than in Tunis. The scale of Egypt is so epic, it makes everything more difficult. There are eighty-three million Egyptians waiting for the fruits of the revolution, compared with ten million Tunisians.

In Cairo, I am under the protection of "the two Doaas," as I call them. Doaa Abdelaal and I work together through the network of Women Living Under Muslim Laws (WLUML). She sends Doaa Kassem, a twenty-six-year-old who towers over me by about four inches, to look after me. When, transfixed by a throbbing demonstration, I wander away for one second in Tahrir Square, my cellphone rings instantly. My protective junior colleague asks, "Karima, where are you?"

Doaa Kassem is working then for an NGO called the Andalus Institute for Tolerance and Anti-Violence Studies. Her brief includes women's rights and youth political participation. She has been trying to increase the numbers of women in Egypt's Parliament. She has her work cut out for her. "You not only have men who are against women's participation," she laments, "but you also have women against women."

Her fight for women's rights goes on at work, in the streets, and at home. From a conservative family, the personal truly is political for Doaa

K, and the political very personal. Her four brothers "always tried to control me because I'm the honor of the family." This experience brought her to human rights, which she discovered in college: "Everybody born equal, there should be no gender discrimination—I want this."

One of her first assignments in the field was to monitor the 2005 Egyptian elections, the country's first contested presidential elections, when she was just twenty-one. While out observing the polls at 9:30 on election night, she received an angry call from one of her brothers, demanding to know where she was. When she got home, her brother insisted, "You have to obey me because I am the man here and you are a girl, and you have no option." He tried to move up her curfew to 9 p.m. She refused. Her brother slapped her.

Still, she would not give in. "I am not saying to the people that they have to struggle for their rights and in the same time, I can't struggle for my rights in the house." Her determination won over her mother and, in time, her other brothers. "There's a shift when women stand up." Still, she had to wage another battle in order to travel for work. "You have to have a man with you," her brother said. "I said, 'I have a different interpretation of the Qur'an about this. I will travel whether you accept it or not.'" Since then, she has visited the United States, Latvia, and Sweden.

The next round came when she wanted to take part in demonstrations during the revolution. Her mother was terrified of what the police might do to her. "If you go into the streets, don't talk to me. I am not your mom." Doaa K was at home in the Manyal District of Cairo on January 28, 2011, "the day which changed the whole thing." She heard loud demonstrations streaming by below on the way to Tahrir, the square named for liberation, and she watched from the balcony. "The people want to bring down the system," they called. "*As shaab yourid esqat al nitham*." Doaa did too, so she joined them, marching away from her mother.

Once in the streets, she weathered Molotov cocktails and water cannons, distributing Coca-Cola as a remedy against tear gas. As it was for many women, the revolution was a transformative moment for her. By the time we meet, however, she is decidedly focused on the morning after. "It's easy to make a revolution but it is hard to build the country after that." She is also thinking about the revolutions that have not happened yet. "The revolution changed the regime, not the mentality of people. Stop changing 'the system.' Change people's minds. If you still have the mentality that religion is everything in the world, and we have to obey anyone talking by religion, this is a disaster." She fears people will vote a certain way not because of what they believe but "because they have orders from imams and sheikhs."

The Muslim Brotherhood is "way, way, way more organized" than other political parties. "They have money. Plus they talk with religion. 'Islam is the solution.' So poor people and illiterate people are supporting them because of religion and money." Doaa K does not accept the thesis that the Muslim Brotherhood is moderate now. A devout, liberal Muslim, she was upset when a Brotherhood leader told her that if Egyptian Muslims accepted a Christian president of Egypt, they are not really Muslims. I ask her how people can challenge the Brotherhood. "Go to the streets. Go to the grassroots, the poor people and rural areas. Stop conducting seminars in hotels. Let people see you are interested in tackling their problems."

With all the battles she has fought and won, Doaa is still afraid that women's rights will face a backlash now in Egypt. "Like what happened in Afghanistan, Sudan. People voluntarily stop you and ask you why you are not veiled and stuff like that, because there are more Salafis in the streets now." Doaa covers her head and wears long skirts, but she is the most festive veiled woman I have ever seen, wearing elaborate, color-coordinated outfits in bright pink and turquoise. Her scarves match her long earrings. With her head covered like this, she says, "You can see it in people's eyes. They don't like the way you dress and your headscarf. If you are not dressed in niqab or a full veil that is longer, they are going to say bad things about you. You are not a Muslim." In the last few years, but in particular since the revolution, it is not just a question of covering your head, but how and with what and what else is still showing. "I do it in my own way, still wearing it the way I like to wear it."

Doaa Abdelaal meets me and Doaa K for lunch in a restaurant that plays Egyptian music from the fifties. Thirty-five years old, bareheaded, and middle class, Doaa A wears slacks. "I was not born a feminist. I became one," she laughs, paraphrasing Simone de Beauvoir.

Originally from Upper Egypt, Doaa A and her parents moved to Cairo in the seventies. She situates herself "in the liberal camp." Though she is ten years older than Doaa K, the revolution was no less magical for her. In keeping with her generally optimistic outlook, she estimates that about 50 percent of the protesters were women (others suggest 30 to 35 percent). These women were diverse. Some were deployed by the Muslim Brotherhood in niqabs and conservative hijabs, "as a matter of numbers," often carrying their children. But there was also a "corner for feminists, for LGBT." Doaa A told me she took lots of pictures of unveiled women to make a point, to counter the predominant media images.

Like the Tunisian women lawyers I met, Doaa Abdelaal wants what she calls "a civil constitution, a gender-sensitive constitution." Above all, she wants the constitution to guarantee equality. Then she wants to reform Egypt's family law, which the feminist Nawal El Saadawi has deemed one of the worst in the Arab world.[15] Doaa A is not in a milquetoast mood this March 2011. "If we want change, we have to fight for it. We need a high ceiling of demands so that when we compromise, we don't lose. If we introduce a moderate agenda, definitely we will get nothing." I sense her impatience.

"We cannot postpone women's issues. We cannot postpone the rights of half the population."

TAHRIR NIGHTS

At Beano's Café, near the American University of Cairo, Doaa Kassem takes me to meet her colleague Samar Hussein, who has a short pageboy haircut and wears a fitted white sweater. Active during the revolution, the twenty-three-year-old saw a child run down by a government car, and she herself was hit in the leg with a rubber bullet.

Her father, a prominent Communist, had been in and out of Mubarak's jails. Imprisoned when Samar was born, he served nine months when she was thirteen. Torture left him with a disabled hand. Knowing all too well what arrest meant here, he was reluctant at first for his daughter to participate in the January 2011 demonstrations. Eventually, the entire family went out—mom, dad, cousins. Samar was there "many days, many nights." There was no sexual harassment in the beginning, despite her father's worries. On "Tahrir nights," Samar did not sleep. "We were singing, discussing political issues." She was there on February 11, 2011, when Mubarak fell. Egypt, for her, was a sick person with respiratory problems that was hit hard on the back that day to make it inhale. "It was like breathing again."

Her father danced in the streets. Now he is worried. "He tells me: 'Your're just small kids who made a revolution, and don't know how to complete it.' Actually, I think he's right."

Now "the conservatives have even bigger spaces to move in," Samar says. During the March 19, 2011, referendum on amending the old constitution, a measure supported by many fundamentalists, "they told people, 'If you vote for yes, this means you are Muslim and you will enter paradise. If you vote no, it means that you are not Muslim, you are not going to paradise.'" They told poor women who received financial assistance from them that it would dry up if the referendum did not pass. Samar believes you cannot compete with the Brotherhood simply by using Facebook. "They have been working in the streets for thirty years."

She is concerned for women's rights but also for other rights. "If the conservative Islamists will come to power in Egypt, in this case we are all going to suffer. They are not talking only about women. They are also excluding Egypt's fifteen million Christians,[16] as well as secular and nonreligious people." Women have the most to lose, but fundamentalism is not only a women's issue. Just as the fundamentalists are getting Pakistani and Iraqi Sunnis and Shi'a to kill each other, so they are fomenting division between Muslims and Christians in Egypt. "Now, if you say that you are *almani* [secular]," human rights lawyer Dahlia Zakhary says, "it's like a crime."

So Samar Hussein is right to be worried about all these categories of people who will face increasing fundamentalist pressure. But despite our heavy discussion, her young eyes pool with this spring's light when I take her picture. I can see her father dancing in the streets on February eleventh somewhere in her smile. But I also wonder whether she will face a long struggle ahead, much as he did.

NO TO WOMEN, YES TO FGM

In the Costa Café in the Mohandseen district of Cairo, the music is loud and patrons have to shout to hear each other. In that noise, veteran women's rights activist Fatemah Khafagy tells me that during the Mubarak era she founded the gender ombudsperson's office, but then she had to battle Suzanne Mubarak to try to make it work for women. When Khafagy realized that autocracy rendered the mechanism useless, she resigned—no easy feat with Mrs. Mubarak involved. In fact, she says the government attempted to prosecute her over this. When I meet her, she is working with groups that combat religious discrimination and document the government's abuses during the revolution.

Of the overthrow of Mubarak, she says, "I never believed it was going to happen in my lifetime. I was thrilled." When the revolution started, Khafagy was determined to participate, so she worked in a friend's apartment not far from Tahrir, where they provided protesters with such needed items as blankets and a bathroom. Taking part in these events revived her. "I was so much against the regime for so many years. I paid the price for expressing it. At one point, for a few years, I was very depressed." Such "political depression," as some of my Algerian friends call it, had become common across North Africa until the start of 2011. The revolutions seemed initially to offer the antidote—political hope.

In March 2011, eight months before Egypt's parliamentary elections, Fatemah warned me about the increasing strength of the Salafis, who would surprise much of the Western media with their success at the polls that November. "They have become very active in villages, and outside of Cairo. People keep saying that Salafiya is a methodology of thinking, not a group like the Muslim Brotherhood. I'm sure that they are grouping, but they do not want us to uncover this."

On the ground, the Salafists are shifting the cultural consensus, curtailing the decades-long efforts of women's rights advocates like Fatemah Khafagy.[17] She says the Salafists are "like the Taliban," insisting that women "have to go back to their houses and should not go to school." Khafagy is outraged that "women who work on the education of girls and stopping female genital mutilation (FGM) cannot implement their projects anymore because the Salafis are telling families that education is *haram*." Such pushback on efforts to stem FGM is disastrous in a population where an estimated 96 percent of ever-married women have been subjected to the practice.[18] There have even been reports that the Muslim Brotherhood's new Freedom and Justice Party has itself organized mobile medical convoys that, among other things, promote and practice FGM in violation of Egyptian law.[19] This has sparked complaints from villagers south of Cairo, and from Egyptian human rights groups. In March 2011, Fatemah is already worried about such developments, and about how they will be spun in the increasingly Muslim Brotherhood–dominated media.[20] "We don't have the means the Brotherhood has."

A sign that Khafagy is right to be worried came on International Women's Day, March 8, 2011—in Tahrir Square itself. "It started nicely," Fatemah recalls. "We met and we were hundreds, and we walked downtown. People were giving us flowers and cards for Women's Day." Despite the call for a "million-women march," there were not enough women present, and that was a mistake, Fatemah thinks. After she and her fellow protesters arrived in Tahrir Square, they "found young men coming toward us saying awful slogans like 'Stay in your homes.'"

The absolute worst chant? "Women—no. FGM—yes."

She is not sure whether the counterdemonstrators were Salafists or from the ex-ruling party or both, but she tells me they were well organized and carried children on their shoulders. Another woman present on March 8 told me she was sure it was Salafis. They yelled at the women protesters that they were not real Egyptians but instead were foreigners, unlike the women in niqab, or "*munaqabat*," that these counterdemonstrators had brought with them. As they pushed the women protesters around that day, they accused them of being against Islam and Sharia.

Tahrir Square is normally a big tent. Not that day. "They started getting aggressive, squeezing us, and harassing some of the young," Fatemah remembers. "Actually, it was a shock. Because during the revolution, everybody was in the *midan* [square] and young women were sleeping there and the Muslim Brotherhood were accepting this."

I think of Samar Hussein's "Tahrir nights" and realize they could not be repeated.

Doaa Abdelaal was at the same International Women's Day demonstration and heard them all denounced as "the girls of Suzanne Mubarak," an insulting link to the former First Lady, who had claimed to champion women. Still, Doaa wanted to look at the glass half full. "I ran back home and e-mailed journalists: 'Please don't focus only on the harassment, because this was not the only aspect.' Under Mubarak, we wouldn't have been able to organize this march. Even if Doaa Kassem and I and a third person decided to celebrate International Women's Day with the banner in the streets, they would have sent us to state security courts under martial law. We are harassed one way or another."

What happened in Tahrir Square that day was the kickoff of a male-supremacist counterrevolution. Dahlia Zakhary told me that, twelve days later, fundamentalists in Tahrir Square—including someone from Al Qaeda head Ayman al-Zawahiri's family—were shouting that the voices of women are shameful. No matter that those women's voices were the same ones that had been raised to bring down Mubarak and make a referendum possible in the first place. At this point, Fatemah already foresees "a battle is coming."

THE SWEET-POTATO SELLER OF TAHRIR SQUARE

When I go to Tahrir Square on March 26, 2011, a mere six days after women's voices were reviled there, rival protests continue. I also find revolutionary souvenir stands hawking bright pink "I love Egypt" T-shirts. A man who sells chickpeas cooked with tomato, known here as *homos el-sham*, offers me his commentary on the scene. His stand bears a sticker inscribed "Do not forget to mention Allah." Wearing an "Egypt" pin on his lapel, he tells me his name is Yousri Mohamed Taha, and he is originally from Aswan. During the revolution, Mr. Taha closed up his stand but stayed in the square "to bring Mubarak down." The revolution has not ended, he feels. The freedom and social justice they had demanded, "you cannot achieve in two days."

I did not ask him about fundamentalism. Of his own volition, he tells me, "I am a Muslim, but we have to separate religion from politics. Religion is inside of us. All Egyptians, Christians and Muslims, must live together." That is his biggest preoccupation now. So it is no surprise the next day when Ahmed Samih, director of the Internet radio station Huriyatina (Our Freedom), tells me that ordinary Egyptians in places like Aswan, where Mr. Taha is from, care more about everyday problems—like how to get eggs—than ideology. "If we give their children a good education, good health care, they will beat the Brotherhood."

Near the souvenir stands, Doaa Kassem and I find Abdel Sabour Hassan, a thirty-seven-year-old from Upper Egypt who roasts sweet potatoes in a portable oven on a cart. He wears a dishdasha, a robe that hangs the length of his tall frame. A personal story explains why he was "totally with the revolution." Mubarak's police once confiscated a small car he owned, so he made a complaint. As a result, an officer came to his house to investigate him. When he was arrested, the sweet-potato seller asked why. "We are in a state of emergency," the policeman told him.

Hence, he was "so happy" when the revolution came. But for Mr. Hassan, like many others I meet in the square, the system they are most concerned with bringing down is the economic system, what Samar Hussein described to me as "the culture of poverty in Egypt." The sweet-potato salesman never talks about religion or Muslims, but rather about the worldly needs of regular Egyptians. "*Wallahi alatheem*," he exclaimed, "I swear to God, under the former government the prices were very high and the salaries very low." The man explains that he is nonliterate and uneducated, and there are no opportunities for people like him. He says he wants the revolution "to improve the status of people like me who sell things on the streets and suffer because we have nothing to do but this." Mohamed Bouazizi lives here in Tahrir, still waiting for change.

At the end of our discussion, I am conscious of having blocked his business, standing by his cart talking. The least I can do is buy a couple of sweet potatoes from him. He works his oven and carefully selects two. But he will not accept a single piastre. Mr. Hassan is proud to share his revolution and his wares. I say, "*Shukran Gazeelan*" (Thank you very much), feeling humbled by what Lalia Ducos, back in Blida, had called "the generosity of those who have nothing." If the revolution can improve these people's lives, which is what they expected from it, this country has a chance to escape extremism. If not, the odds are not so good, for the Muslim Brotherhood and the Salafists will take every advantage of the resulting human misery.

Not far from where the sweet-potato salesman and the chickpea vendor peddle their wares, protestors from different constituencies congregate and the revolution continues. A young man in a black and white cap stands on a makeshift stage before a crowd of four hundred chanting, *"Al shaab yourid mouhakamat Mubarak"* (The people want a trial for Mubarak). Thanks to this kind of pressure, the former president's trial for complicity in the murder of Egyptian protesters will begin later in the year, resulting in a life sentence.

As my afternoon in Tahrir wears on, the young man at the microphone shows no sign of fatigue. I see in him what human rights lawyer Dahlia Zakhary called "Tahrir Spirit." Doaa Abdelaal had also said, "The Tahrir experience created this liberated zone inside all of us." In this free space today, a gray-bearded imam named Gamal Ahmed Aallam, who was told by the Egyptian Army not to speak here today, does anyway. Wearing glasses, a blue robe, and a trim white turban, he preaches fraternity between Muslims and Christians. He denounces the Salafists. "Islam is above groups and parties. We are all children of this country." He addresses himself to Christian Egyptian youth: "We have been together to secure all, for Muslims and Christians. Christian youth are securing mosques, and vice versa, in Alexandria." Doaa Kassem tells me that in Alexandria on January 25, 2011, the first day of the revolution, Christians stood in front of Muslims to protect them from the authorities while they were praying during the demonstration. Graffiti nearby commemorates this. "Egypt: Unity," it proclaims, displaying a cross embraced by a crescent.

The imam of Tahrir continues. "We refuse and reject all people who make sectarian violence. We will meet here each Friday." The imam speaks as an Egyptian, not as a Muslim. He speaks in the name of Egypt, not in the name of God. He calls for the release of all Christian protesters who have been arrested, and he leads people in prayer for those dying in every country in the region where they are trying to get rid of dictatorships. I too want to pray with him.

His kind of God *is* great.

THE ARAB AUTUMN

Seven months later, I return to North Africa. The promising spring of 2011 has given way to an ambiguous autumn. The day after Tunisia's Constituent Assembly election gives eighty-nine of 217 seats to Ennahda, the day after Libya's transitional government next door declares the application of Sharia law and the abrogation of the law preventing polygamy, I see Alya Chammari again in Tunis. It is a rough day for North African secular feminists. One local newspaper headlines this as "Tunisia: Year Zero."

Is the grace period over? "Well, we are entering a very, very difficult period," Alya replies. But she is determined to see the election as a procedural success. "This day, the twenty-third of October, was also very important." Nevertheless, she is angry about reports she has heard about Ennahda's electoral tactics. They bought votes, she believes. They wrote the number of their electoral lists on women's arms so they would know whom to vote for and tell others inside polling stations.

Chammari is even more worried for Libyans, wondering what the application of Sharia law will mean there. "Will there be corporal punishments and hangings of women like in Saudi Arabia?" By summer 2012, Alya's fears for Libyan women become manifest in abductions of rights activists, proliferating harassment, and an ominous incident at the new Parliament's August eighth swearing-in, during which an unveiled woman presenter was heckled by a parliamentarian and asked to leave the podium.[21] When I meet with Alya in Tunis in October 2011, she wants Tunisia to succeed first and foremost for her own country's future but also to prevent what she suspects might happen in places like Libya. She says the media must speak not just of fundamentalism in "our countries" but also of all the resistance by the democratic and progressive forces.

That same evening of October 24, 2011, I spoke on the phone with Bochra Belhadj Hmida, who had not been elected to the Constituent Assembly, despite tireless campaigning. "What should women's rights advocates do now?" I query. Her answer comes in a long to-do list. "We will organize, we will become a pressure group, we will be heard about the constitution, we will not let the Constituent Assembly amuse itself by turning to Islamic Law where it concerns women's rights, we will do the maximum so there will be no regression. Even if we have to do a fifth sit-in in the Casbah."

She insists that she remains optimistic. "In the worst moments we had Ben Ali, we kept hope and we made him *dégage*. Now, we will show that we are here, we exist, and they are not the majority. They represent 30 or 35 percent—35 percent cannot impose their rules on us all." When the new government is announced after I return to the United States, Ennahda takes the key ministries of the interior, justice, and foreign affairs. But the party clearly has little interest in the economy, so that ministry goes to a secular party, Ettakatol. Why create jobs when you can cover heads? Why take on foreign debt when you can rant about polygamy?

As memories of spring fade, Kafka stalks North Africa. A prominent Ennahda woman deputy denounces single mothers, saying they need to be "taught morality" and are not suitable for "our religion."[22] An Ennahda spokesman named Samir Dilou, who has defended polygamy as a constitutional right, becomes Tunisia's first human rights minister.[23] He goes on to deplore homosexuality as "a perversion that requires medical treatment."[24] On the streets, Salafists attack nonveiled women, hurling the slogan of the revolution against them now, telling them to "*dégage*."[25] Emboldened by Ennahda's laissez-faire approach, these Salafists besiege the Manouba University campus, on the outskirts of Tunis, trying to introduce the niqab, shutting down classes and exams, threatening teachers and the dean. Ennahda does not stop them.

Alya Chammari could already see this coming back in October 2011. When my recorder is turned off, the intrepid human rights lawyer tells me that she defended Ennahda political prisoners during the Ben Ali dictatorship.

Now she asks them if they will defend her.

TEHRAN/TUNIS

On Friday, October 7, 2011, the Tunisian TV station Nessma broadcasts the film *Persepolis*, dubbed in Tunisian Arabic. The animated film, based on Marjane Satrapi's memoir about her life across Iran's recent history, depicts Islamist repression, the shattering of revolutionary dreams, sex and God. *Persepolis*, like *The Satanic Verses*, has become a bête noire of Muslim fundamentalists. So Nessma TV is besieged two days after the broadcast by enraged Salafists who take to Avenue Mohamed V, one of Tunis's main arteries, to condemn the station outside its own premises.[26] Meanwhile, in the name of defending Islam (from Muslims), they also attack the home of the TV channel's director, Nabil Karoui, terrorizing his family and employees.

Rim Saadi, a film critic who is a producer at Nessma, says showing *Persepolis* was not a courageous choice, but rather a coincidence. A local women's group had dubbed the film into Tunisian Arabic and offered it to the station for broadcast. Like many Tunisian modernists in the current environment, Saadi seems profoundly shocked by what transpired just outside her office window. "Frankly, I was not expecting this reaction. There were about five hundred to six hundred people out there, mostly men, shouting. They had a black flag and cried, 'There is no God but God, and Muhammad is his Prophet.' They chanted, 'Nessma is a depraved channel,' '*Nessma kuffar*' (Nessma are infidels). 'Close the station!'

" 'Kill them all!' "

As a film critic, Rim Saadi also tells me that, unlike me, she does not even like the film *Persepolis*. She finds it clichéd. But, she explains, "I cannot like all films. I defend it absolutely because it is a work of art. I defend the idea of creation."

The producer has been receiving death threats since the spring because of the popular debates about current events she has been hosting. Sometimes the threats are posted on Facebook, the tool of the Tunisian revolution, which is now being used to attack those who made the revolution and still dream of freedom of thought. Tunisians are going through an apprenticeship, Saadi suggests, learning how to live together because there had been no possibilities for dialogue before. "I hope we will learn in a civilized manner and not through violence." She seems quite shaken both by the threats and by the attack on station director Karoui's home.

Karoui himself makes a public apology for showing *Persepolis*. Nevertheless, he will be tried for "violating sacred values"[27] and threatened with up to three years in prison. The station owner says he hopes Tunisia will not become the Guantanamo of freedom. Witnesses who testify on his behalf are hounded and physically assaulted by Salafi mobs outside the courthouse.[28] On World Press Freedom Day, May 3, 2012, Nabil Karoui is convicted and sentenced to pay a fine of 2400 Tunisian dinars (about $1,500) for the crime of broadcasting an animated film that shows the face of God.[29] The fine is small, the symbolism of the verdict huge.

"These are the methods of Ben Ali," Rim Saadi tells me in October 2011. "It is tragic. All these martyrs, twenty-three years of national humiliation of an entire people, torture, all this to arrive here." When she tells me how her life has changed, I am truly alarmed about the new Tunisia. "I am becoming as I was during Ben Ali's time again, adopting the same mechanisms of self-protection, of social life. That is to say that I do not go out much."

Before the revolution, Nessma was strictly an entertainment channel, but when the Sidi Bouzid demonstrations first took off, the station began to break the wall of silence. For a program Rim produced, they interviewed residents of the town and even the family of Mohamed Bouazizi. This caused "an earthquake," she remembers. "We received threats from Ben Ali and from all the government ministers." The station would not be cowed then or now.

Nessma maintains its editorial line, defending women, human rights, individual liberties, an open Tunisia. "We are proud of our Arab and Muslim roots, but also Berber and African. So there is a real ideological divide and this is why we are targeted." Saadi respects the right of Ennahda to participate in politics, but as for those who attacked the station, she questions their cloak of divine legitimacy. "God has nothing to do with this. I refuse the idea that God needs these sorts of crazies to prove his existence or to protect Him with their attacks."

WINTER IN CAIRO

After I left Cairo in March 2011, I tried to stay in touch with the two Doaas and my other Egyptian friends via e-mail. There was often good reason to be concerned about them. In October 2011, six months after I absorbed Tahrir spirit with Doaa Kassem while an imam preached interfaith unity, I write to make sure they are all okay after a Christian demonstration is brutally attacked by groups of Muslims, including fundamentalists, near Tahrir. Where has the spirit gone?

Doaa Abdelaal replies on her BlackBerry and for once sounds pessimistic. She tells me that human rights lawyer Dahlia Zakhary joined the march to support the Christian protesters and injured her knees. "U know Karima," Doaa types emphatically, "I'm reaching to lose hope in people of this country." She texts me that two relatives "see that we are a muslim country and we can not agree to have churches in muslim country land." In closing, she writes, "God bless Egypt."

As what one of her friends had termed "the decade of 2011" winds down, Doaa Abdelaal and I hold a follow-up Skype. She sounds weary but resolute. She sighs a lot, and repeatedly uses the word *yani* (meaning, "that is to say") to give herself a chance to pause and think. "*Yani*, I'm honestly not sure how things will be heading. Everyone has realized there is no way back. We have to go on."

The Muslim Brotherhood's Freedom and Justice Party takes 47 percent of the seats in the first parliamentary election.[30] The Nour Party, a Salafi grouping, takes 24 percent. This gives the fundos more than two-thirds of the seats. I wonder what this will mean for the Cairo I know where women sit outside at night smoking apple tobacco in waterpipes. I look back in my notes from earlier in the year and find that Doaa Abdelaal had told me then about the Islamists, "If they get more than 20 to 30 percent of the seats, this will be a real risk, a real war." That is exactly what has happened. What now?

For her, the parliamentary election results are a big failure for the pro-democracy movement. Doaa is frustrated that liberal groups adopted a religious discourse in their campaigning, thinking that speaking the language of Islam was the best way to counter the Muslim Brotherhood. Instead, it alienated many. "Because of it they lost many supporters because people see what religion is doing." Another mistake was the decision to have many slates of liberal parties when the Islamists had only two—one for the Muslim Brotherhood's party and one for the Salafis.[31]

Still, these are not the only reasons. According to Doaa A, Saudi Arabia, the United Arab Emirates, and Kuwait poured money into Egypt's fundamentalist parties: "The percentage of money coming from these countries was way higher than the one coming from the U.S." For just one example, according to the Egyptian Justice Ministry, Ansar al Sunna al Mohamadia, a prominent Salafi group that is antiwomen and anti-Christian, received at least 296 million Egyptian pounds (nearly $49 million) from groups in Qatar and Kuwait.[32] Doaa says they used the money to open twenty-three offices across Egypt for a Salafi political party.

Later, in September 2012, in tandem with riots led by Salafi mobs over the film *Innocence of Muslims*, Salafi politicians introduce a proposal to give Al Azhar, Egypt's leading religious institution, the right to decide whether any law conforms to Islamic laws. By October 2012, they are demanding that Islamic law be the source of *all* legislation in the country.[33] Doaa A is convinced that an Islamic constitution "will not work for Egypt."

In our December 2011 Skype, she sighed as she considered the landscape. "Sometimes you cannot imagine that these are the choices. We have to create more choices, not just 'Mubarak is not there so we come back with a leader from the Muslim Brotherhood,' and that's it." She is desperate that the many other forces and voices in Egyptian society be given the space and support they need to bloom. Her words remind me of what Tunisian human rights lawyer Radhia Nasraoui had said back in March 2011: "If Tunisians made a revolution, it was so they might be free. So that rights might be respected." It was not to have different oppressors, this time with God allegedly on their side. The outcome Radhia longed for will be difficult to achieve in the face of Far Right movements like Tunisia's Salafists, who openly state: "Democracy is an impious concept . . . because its principles are based on liberties that include the right not to believe in God, which is punishable by death in Islam. . . . How can we think that an unbeliever can be the equal of a Muslim, or that a woman can be the equal of a man?"[34]

Oblivious to these threats, foreign funders have been telling women's rights groups they must be "inclusive," according to Doaa Abdelaal—that they should consult everyone, even Islamists, in their work. "People

are saying—women's groups especially—that 'we are being inclusive,'"
she complains. "I hate this word." They say, "Everyone has a right to
be at the table, but I am sorry, who is everyone? What are the values
they come with? Everyone has to put their cards on the table and say
what their values are." Will the international community—the funders,
the NGOs, the UN—dare to be half as principled as Doaa Abdelaal?
Or will they instead be "inclusive," even when it comes to those who
oppose the equality of women and religious minorities, or demand the
right to polygamy?

For example, in the Human Rights Watch World Report covering
2011, Executive Director Kenneth Roth calls on the international community to engage with Islamists in the wake of the "Arab Spring." Roth
claims that "the international community must . . . come to terms with
political Islam when it represents a majority preference. Islamist parties
are genuinely popular in much of the Arab world, in part because many
Arabs have come to see political Islam as the antithesis of autocratic
rule . . . and in part because political Islam reflects the conservative and
religious ethos of many people in the region. Ignoring that popularity
would violate democratic principles."[35] (Abuse of terror suspects might
get some popular support in the United States, too, but that seems no
reason to embrace it.)

Roth's view was an arrow through the heart of many of those I interviewed, and it sparked an outraged online petition to HRW signed
by hundreds, including women I had met across the region: Doaa
Abdelaal in Egypt; the ATFD and its president, Ahlem Belhadj, in
Tunisia; and Cherifa Kheddar in Algeria.[36] They criticized HRW's
failure to mention the Muslim Brotherhood's past abuses, and the pressure that rising "Islamism" was already placing on the rights of others.
By way of rejoinder, Roth replied to the petitioners coolly that "there
is no internationally recognized right to separate religion from the
state,"[37] a remarkable statement for him to make in these, of all times.
He compared the petitioners' stance to that of military-coup supporters and right-wing, anti-Muslim Dutch politician Geert Wilders.[38] Is
this really the best the international human rights movement had to
offer North Africans in 2012?

Human Rights Watch's positioning of fundamentalists as the

polar opposites of autocrats contrasts sharply with the viewpoint of many secularists on the ground. The Algerian satirist Chawki Amari explained in an opinion piece what he calls "[t]he convergence between headshrinking autocratic Arab nationalism and fascist-type Islamism." Their common points? "[C]ontempt for the individual . . . and an aversion to collective and individual freedoms."[39]

Refusing to choose "headshrinking autocrats" or "fascist-type Islamists," Doaa Abdelaal still hopes instead that the fundamentalists will be constrained by the realities of politics and the needs of Egyptians. "The whole infrastructure of the society is really shaking, and some of the small, faraway governorates and villages are really poor places. They need to come up with a real political solution, not about covering women's heads.

"I don't think that reciting Qur'an over a broken pipe will fix it."

IN SEARCH OF IMAGINARY REPUBLICS

In the year after the great spring of 2011, the "Green Wave" sweeps across the region with fundamentalist successes in elections from Cairo to Tunis to Rabat. Algeria's experience after October 1988, when political opening turned to Islamist surge, illustrates that it is no win for democracy when its processes are used to defeat its values. The actual political and social power of fundamentalists across the region means that the waters of social change have to be navigated with great care. This, however, is no excuse for a failure to respond to the entirely legitimate demands for democratization and justice, which remain imperative. Instead, those on the ground who champion human rights and substantive equality must fight on all fronts. There is still hope for the democratic struggle in Arab and Muslim majority countries unleashed in the spring of 2011, but the struggle against fundamentalism must be at its core.

In October 2011, when I am in Tunis, the generation that brought down Ben Ali still believes it can change the world. A young woman activist who survived severe beatings by Ben Ali's police and still has some trouble walking tells me she refuses to be pessimistic in the Arab autumn. "As long as there are progressive women, as long as there are activists, even if we do not have a lot of power, I will be optimistic, even if Ennahda takes the assembly. Even in Ben Ali's time, we were a minority, and we brought down Ben Ali. Now we must complete the job." There are some positive signs. In the spring of 2012, fundamentalist candidates are trounced in student council elections at Tunisia's universities. Even on the terrible day that Ambassador Chris Stevens is killed in Libya, for the first time a small group of young Libyans take to Al Shajara Square in Benghazi to protest against jihad. These protests spread to other parts of Libya. In a place where they may pay with their lives for doing so, young people chant: "This is the revolution of the youth—not Al Qaeda or the terrorists."[40] They actually storm the headquarters of one armed Islamist group, Ansar al-Sharia, driving it out of its base.

Algerian writer Mustapha Benfodil seemed to predict 2011 in all its contradictory glory in the manifesto he attached to his 2008 novel, *Archaeology of Chaos (Amorous)*. I heard these words in my head that year as I watched pro-democracy protesters push forward into a phalanx of police in Algiers, or return to Tahrir Square even though they had already been injured there in the past:

We need to install a climate of insurrection in this country
We need to organize a huge popular march . . .
We must celebrate the people, liberate the wonderful energy of the
   unemployed, of delinquents, losers, and the marginal.
We need . . . a revolution of every instant, of every place, of every day.

Benfodil finishes with the announcement that this cri de coeur will be published in the official journal of "the imaginary and poetic republic of Algeria," a play on the official title of the "popular and democratic" republic of Algeria.

Of course, "climates of insurrection" are unpredictable. By September 2012, leading Tunisian intellectual Yadh Ben Achour is warning, "We risk in a short time finding ourselves in a worse dictatorship than that of Ben Ali, a theocratic dictatorship."[41] Tunisian political scientist Hamadi Redissi tells an Algerian newspaper that he now doubts whether his country's Islamists would "accept the verdict of the ballot box . . . were they to ever lose an election."[42] An Ennahda leader says that strikers are "enemies of God" and should suffer the same fate as apostates.[43] Sidi Bouzid, birthplace of the Arab Awakening of 2011, is again seething with protest, now provoked by the Ennahda-dominated government's neglect. (Salafists reportedly sweep into town and attack demonstrating youth.)[44] As 2013 dawns, Al Qaeda cells are being uncovered across the country.

Meanwhile, Egypt's Islamist constitution is adopted in a flawed referendum in December 2012. Mustapha Benfodil himself travels to Tahrir Square as a correspondent for *El Watan* to cover the resulting protests there, reporting on the violence of Muslim Brotherhood thugs against journalists and antifundamentalist demonstrators. One young working-class activist had part of his ear bitten off by Islamist goons. The bodyguards of a Brotherhood leader allegedly gunned down journalist El-Husseini Abou Dhaif while he covered demonstrations against the Brotherhood's President Mohamed Morsi. Benfodil interviews a weeping twenty-seven-year-old veiled woman, Zayneb Essaghir, whose five-year-old son was knifed, she says, by the "criminal Brothers" during that same demonstration. "For her," the Algerian journalist writes, "the Brothers are a threat to women. 'They have shown their true colors by their treatment of young women who struggle in the Maydan [square]. . . . They publicly stripped and attacked one of my friends, as an example. But I warn them that the next revolution will be carried out by Egyptian women.'"[45]

In the seasons beyond the Arab Spring, it will take an unflinching, multidirectional fight against autocracy and fundamentalism, a rigorous commitment to all kinds of equality, and a very reliable political and moral compass, to find the imaginary and poetic republics of North Africa and keep them. But somewhere, they do exist. In Cairo, Doaa Abdelaal is determined to stay positive. "If I stop being optimistic, then what should I do? Just start saying that everything is ruined? We have to go on and engage more people for our cause. The world as we know it is coming to an end, and I am still hoping for the best."

CHAPTER TEN

The People of Al Qaedastan:
Voices from Northern Mali

In December 2012, the bustling Malian capital of Bamako became the last stop in my travels. In this West African city, bareheaded women ride motorbikes and thrive as street merchants. But there was also palpable tension in those crowded streets, and a significant number of those I interviewed cried while we talked about the north. In seventy-two terrible hours between March 30 and April 1, 2012, the northernmost 60 percent of Mali—roughly the size of Texas—and all its major cities, such as Gao, Timbuktu, and Kidal, fell to the rule of Al Qaeda's local affiliate and its allies. This made the territory, as CNN suggested, "al Qaeda's 'last chance' for a country."[1]

Armed fundamentalists from Algeria had already been infiltrating their southern neighbor since the 1990s, spreading their ideology and violence. Since the fall of Qaddafi in autumn 2011, many of his armed loyalists of Malian Tuareg origin had returned to the region with their weapons and joined the armed groups. Jihadists from Egypt, Nigeria, Pakistan, and beyond flocked to Mali's Afghanistan-on-the-Sahara, threatening to destabilize all of North Africa. Northern Mali became what Mauritanian historians Ciré Bâ and Boubacar Diagana call "the refuge of all the world's jihadists,"[2] dominated by Al Qaeda in the Islamic Maghreb, its offshoot MUJAO (the Movement for Unity and Jihad in West Africa), and Ansar Dine (Defenders of the Faith). "These are names that terrify," a displaced woman from Timbuktu tells me, shivering even in the heat—one of hundreds of thousands fleeing their homes in territory taken over by fundamentalist armed groups.

It is difficult to obtain extensive written documentation of atrocities, as UN Secretary-General Ban Ki-moon underscored in his November 2012 report to the Security Council.[3] Nevertheless, he reported "an evolving pattern" of executions, torture, cruel punishment, the use of child soldiers, summary executions, looting of hospitals, and sexual violence against women.[4] While in Mali, I am able to record many testimonies that corroborate such assertions about what the warriors of God did to the people of the north.

To inaugurate Jihadistan in northern Mali, the fundamentalists banned music—this in a country with one of the richest musical traditions in the world. They banned sports on TV and finally began knocking down satellite dishes altogether. They flogged people for smoking and drinking alcohol. In July 2012, they stoned an unmarried couple for adultery. "The woman fainted after the first few blows," an anonymous witness told Agence France-Presse (AFP).[5] The mother of two had been buried up to her waist in a hole in the arid ground before being pelted to death with rocks by a group of men. "This is the law of God," one Islamist chief proclaimed afterward. In a few days, we will do the same thing [again]. . . . No one can stop us."[6] A UN official reported in October 2012 that the fundamentalists had begun compiling lists of unmarried mothers.[7]

Even holy places are not safe. These self-styled "defenders of the faith" desecrated and destroyed the tombs of local Sufi saints in the city of Timbuktu. The armed groups also reportedly destroyed many—if not all—of the churches in the north, where displaced members of the small Christian minority tell me they previously felt entirely accepted. Such practices—"Al Qaeda tactics,"[8] and the extremism that demands them—are entirely alien to Malian Islam, which has a tradition of tolerance. When I visit the displaced-persons center outside of Bamako where a group of Christians from the north now dwell in misery, one man tells me that "even the Muslims do not find themselves in this Sharia. Before, we lived harmoniously in the north. Muslims and Christians. Our families together."

That openness is exactly what the jihadists seek to crush. "The fact that we are building a new country on the base of Sharia is just something the people living here will have to accept," the Islamist commissioner of Gao said in August 2012.[9] Nevertheless, even with little support from the outside world until an international intervention began in January 2013, local people have widely resisted this seventh-century mode of governance. A journalist was severely beaten by Islamist gunmen after speaking on the radio against amputations. Young people have openly demonstrated against planned amputations in Gao's Independence Square, oblivious to the blows and gunfire they faced. Despite the intense danger, so many came out to demand that limb-cutting be canceled that one man called it "a human tide."[10] Like their Algerian counterparts back in the 1990s, those who defy the Talibanization of the Sahel deserve much more attention. It is the same old story. The jihadists are a tiny minority, but they are armed to the beard and are said to be well-funded from Qatar.[11]

How could this happen in Mali despite the country's secular, democratic character and notwithstanding the hundreds of millions the United States reportedly has been spending to try to contain Islamist militants in West Africa in recent years?[12] First, the Malian government was felled by an ill-fated coup in March 2012; in its aftermath, the Malian state was dislodged from the north by a Tuareg separatist revolt. That uprising was in turn hijacked by fundamentalist armed groups. Transitional national authorities, unable to respond, simply abandoned the area's population. Meanwhile, it took nine months after the north fell for the UN Security Council to authorize ECOWAS, the fifteen-member Economic Community of West African States, to intervene militarily with a small force known as the "African-led International Support Mission in Mali."[13] However, that approval was conditional, and armed action was not envisaged before September 2013. As the international community vacillated, Islamist forces gathered strength and in January 2013 launched an offensive southward, provoking the country's president to call for assistance from France, the former colonial power. French and Malian troops rapidly ended fundamentalist rule of the region's major towns, but some of the armed men fled to the remote far north, where the battle continued, and many fear their return. Stability for the region will require a long-term commitment by the international community to support the local population. Events in Mali are in flux in 2013, but whatever happens, the lives of those who were forced to endure Islamist occupation must be recorded. Intervention came only after the population of the north had been suffering and resisting fundamentalist abuse, largely forgotten and alone, for a long, hard nine months.

WHO WILL BE MUSLIM AFTER THEY HAVE KILLED EVERYONE?

Aboubakr, twenty-eight, a computer-science student, was visiting his mother and stepfather in his hometown of Gades, in the Gao region, when "the events" of spring 2012 occurred. A group of nine terrorists in fatigues—probably from the armed group MUJAO—came to the house in a Land Rover. They killed Aboubakr's nineteen-year-old sister Fatimata, his mother Mahawa, who sold spices and vegetables in the local market, and her husband, whom Aboubakr called Tonton (Uncle) Jimmy. Tonton Jimmy was tortured first. All the while, the armed men shouted, "God is Great" and laughed. Afterward, they burned down the house for good measure. I think about this story again a few weeks after I hear it when women's human rights defender Djingarey Maiga asks rhetorically in Bamako about the fundamentalist violence afflicting her country, "Who will be Muslim after they have killed everyone?"

Aboubakr thinks his stepfather, a public employee, was deliberately targeted, but he also says their house was in a strategic location. It is not clear how or why Aboubakr survived, but he says he was beaten severely on his kidneys and his arms, which still bear scars. This young Malian refugee's eyes are sad and swollen. Still traumatized by the fundamentalist attack, he has lost all sense of time. This is common in people who have survived atrocities. The erstwhile student thinks the slaughter of his family by the armed groups happened one to two weeks after they first took the north, which would put it in about mid-April 2012, but he is not certain, and later he tells me it may have been the end of April. Saved by a buddy whose father was in the Malian army, Aboubakr fled into the desert and then was cared for by other friends until he was able to cross into Algeria, where I was able to interview him in the town of Blida in November 2012.

In the autumn chill, the bewildered Aboubakr wears flip-flops and a sweatshirt someone gave him. In Algeria, he has nothing and is unable to study or work. He sleeps in a hammam or Turkish bath at night or crashes with a Malian student he knows. Even though Blida has itself known so much terrorism in the past, some residents are welcoming but others chase him away from wherever he tries to pass his time. "Go home. Go! Go! Go!"

Though her hands are full still trying to care for Algerian victims from the nineties with limited resources, Cherifa Kheddar is so incensed by Aboubakr's story that she insists that her organization, Djazairouna, will try to assist him while he is in Blida. She knows only too well what it means to try to go on after watching armed men kill your family while chanting, *"Allahu Akbar."*

THE POPULATION IS NOT FOR THE SHARIA

Mr. Bodmar (not his real name) is a secondary-school teacher who now runs a local high school that was occupied by MUJAO, the same foreign jihadists who killed Aboubakr's family in April 2012. They announced that they had come to protect the school's premises. Instead, they quickly stole its computers, refrigerator, chairs. Given such behavior, "When they claim they are Muslims," Mr. Bodmar says, "that stuns us."

Whenever the kids would get together at school, they tended to forget the occupation. Their protective headmaster would lock them in the courtyard and constantly remind them of the jihadist presence. He was forced to separate the boys and girls in each class, something not done before in Mali, and he patrolled the students to make sure the girls were sufficiently veiled, or he knew he might be held responsible. His friends called him "MUJAO," and he loathed this monitoring duty, but he was trying to keep the school open. "Our task is to protect the schooling of those who cannot go elsewhere."

The logistical difficulties alone were stupendous. The Malian government would not refurbish the premises, for fear the armed groups would confiscate anything the school received. Moreover, Mr. Bodmar had to travel 750 miles to Bamako to obtain his salary, since the Malian bureaucracy entirely vacated the north. The risks he took were enormous—to keep his high school functioning, to keep educating girls and boys in the same classroom, to keep teaching what he termed the "republican and secular" curriculum of Malian schools in "an Islamic milieu."

"We consider ourselves under occupation," Mr. Bodmar told me. "We consider ourselves martyrs." Following the MUJAO takeover, economic activity dwindled; Gao was at a standstill. After driving out the Tuareg secessionist rebels in June 2012, it was easy for MUJAO to recruit desperate locals—especially young boys—to their ranks. Every Thursday, they held Islamic show trials in Arabic, a language most Gao residents do not speak. "Last Thursday, before I came to Bamako, there was a session of applying the Sharia on the public square. Thirteen so-called thieves—we don't know if they are thieves—were taken to the public square and beaten. Then, a stock of cigarettes and alcohol was burned publicly."

A special prison was established where "offenders" were held for weeks at a time, awaiting a public "hearing" in front of the so-called Islamic tribunal. "If you don't follow their rules, there are punishments," Mr. Bodmar explained. "A hundred blows. Eighty blows. Smokers are imprisoned, those who drink alcohol, the same." The fundamentalists focused on teaching the predominantly Muslim population of Gao how to be Muslim. As with Al Shabaab in Somalia's recent past or the Taliban in Afghanistan's, their morality brigade (Al Hisbah) patrolled the city, checking to see who was not wearing a sufficient veil, whose telephone sinned with a musical ringtone. Speaking to a woman in the street was an offense, and this ban caused so much terror that Mr. Bodmar said men would flee in fear if they simply saw a woman. In Algiers, I had met a young smoker named Youssouf, who quit Gao to avoid being flogged for his habit, after watching people whipped in front of his local mosque. According to Youssouf, some were even killed in Gao for taking part in a public wedding procession. He reminded me what a change this was for the people of northern Mali. "Before, we went out. We had no money, but we lived well."

On November 29, 2012, just before I arrive in Mali, thirty women in Gao reportedly were whipped for failing to wear the right kind of veil.[14] (The women had their heads covered, just not "correctly.") A contact of journalist Abdoulaye Guindo was so outraged by this incident that he risked his life to get the news out to him by phone; Guindo reported the story in the Malian newspaper *Procès-Verbal*. The thirty female denizens of the town had been busted by Al Hisbah and taken to the municipality, where each reportedly received ten lashes in front of a crowd. Guindo pointed out that even though the women were chastised for insufficient covering, their backs were forcibly bared during their public scourging. Afterward, their husbands had to buy Islamist-approved headgear for their wives to don before they could be released.

Mr. Bodmar attended many such public punishments, in order to accurately document the fundamentalist atrocities committed in his city and identify their victims. He and the aid group he risked his life to work with tried to provide such victims with psychological and health services afterward. However, this meant Mr. Bodmar had to watch repeated floggings of his fellow citizens, unable to do anything but observe and absorb the horror. He even had to see what it looks like when a "convict" has his foot hewn off. "This takes place on the public square. Usually, adults don't go. But little kids sometimes go." One day, five alleged thieves were brought out before the crowd and tied to chairs before his eyes. What seems to have spooked Mr. Bodmar the most was that the condemned men did not struggle. "I do not know what they gave these men. They did not scream when they cut off their feet." This was no surgical procedure. "They do it in an archaic way. Cut. Cut. Cut." Sawing back and forth with his arm, he demonstrated the slow process. One victim told the Algerian newspaper *El Watan* afterward, from the hospital room in Gao where he was detained by the men of Ansar Dine: "I will be obliged to hide myself in order to live. My life is over." Another lamented, "It is finished. I will never work again."[15]

In addition to the limb-cutting, there were also cases where people were beaten publicly with leather straps until they bled. "Flogging happen[ed] every day and everywhere," according to Abdoulaye Guindo in December 2012. These punishments, which became especially violent when the victim resisted, as Mr. Bodmar explained, also traumatized those who watched, especially the children.

Feeling as though I were back in Kabul Stadium, I asked Mr. Bodmar what it could possibly be like to witness such things in the city of his birth. "This disgusts us, but ours is the disgust of the weak. So, we are very angry at the Malian state, and at our elders. It is not possible that they amputate people's limbs, and meanwhile people are sitting here and bickering. This repulses us. Sometimes we fall into skepticism, into doubt. We give ourselves over to God." He stopped speaking. There really is no way to convey the impact of seeing the Prophet of his religion reduced to the claimed patron saint of mutilators. Finally, he tried again. "No one can stand it, but it is imposed on us. Those of us who attend, we cry." The small man was nearly crying even as he said this.

"We cannot stand it."

In such a climate, the population of Gao was divided on the subject of an armed intervention to rescue them, according to Mr. Bodmar. "Some say even if we perish, we want war, because we have suffered and we can't take it anymore. Children with weapons impose rules and conditions. It hurts. And you have no force to defend yourself, so you want the sky to fall on everyone." But, there were also concerns among the population-to-be-liberated. "There are others who fear for their lives, their goods, their families, their futures. They do not want an intervention."

Yet most of those I meet from the north had decided by late 2012, as the women's rights activist Rokia Bah told me, that "the risks of non-intervention are 10,000 times worse than the risks of intervention." A young refugee from Gao put it like this: "We do not want war, but if these people don't leave us alone, we have to fight them."

For his own part, Mr. Bodmar worried that the Malian military alone would be incapable of dislodging the armed groups and was in favor of an international intervention, but he was also terribly nervous about what it could do to his already devastated hometown. "What will be our fate in the case of an intervention? What will we become? Syria? Libya? That is the question we pose to the world." With all these caveats, was he sure he wanted outside forces to intervene? He clarified that he wanted a well-organized military operation that spares the civilian population. He could not see any other option. I think of Mr. Bodmar's dilemma when French bombs fall around Gao in January 2013.

In fact, from his point of view, international intervention had already begun in Gao before the French showed up—but on the side of the fundamentalists. The local Islamic "commissioner" was Egyptian, he told me. Other armed rulers in Gao, "Abu This and Abu That," as he termed these loathed foreign jihadis who all use noms de guerre, are Pakistani, Nigerian. He feared that if the international response to their aggression was delayed, there would be "many deaths, much suffering, many difficulties" in the interim in Gao. "How can we live if this situation continues? Will they continue to beat us, to amputate our limbs? This cannot continue. We want to be free."

Local and international opponents of intervention advocated negotiation with at least some of the rebel groups as an alternative. As for Mr. Bodmar, he worried that "the negotiations are not possible because of the attitude of these people. They think they are doing this for God. It is not to please anyone. They are willing to die for the mission of God rather than giving up the Sharia." Yet their imagined Islamic mode of governance was utterly alien to the indigenous people of Gao. Mr. Bodmar pronounced the word "*Sshha-ria*" deliberately, and with great intensity. As a practicing Muslim, he said it with utter rejection because it was the label used by local terrorists imposing the unforgiveable— with knives, rocks, whips, guns, and hijacked divine sanction—on ordinary believers like him. "The population is not for the Sharia," he stressed. "Do you understand?" I heard this again and again in Mali, in the words of people from Timbuktu, Gao, and Bamako, from Muslims and Christians, from women and men, from ordinary people like my driver, who drinks beer and goes to the mosque on Friday, and from pious activists of the Muslim women's movement. The preservation of Mali's tradition of secularism remains essential for so many here. "Mali is not a Muslim country," a women's rights activist opined. "It is a secular country. We cannot have a secular state in the south and Sharia in the north."

Meanwhile, even in Bamako, Mali's capital, where Mr. Bodmar and I talked, many feared the presence of Islamist terrorists. A conference that I was to attend, organized by COREN, a network of people from the north, was canceled during my visit, reportedly due to fears of a terror attack. A mosque in the city was supposedly training young jihadis. "There is no security here or there," Mr. Bodmar reflected. "I don't know where there is security. So I would rather stay there," he concluded about remaining in Gao. (He would return there the day after we met.) I asked why he was willing to take the risks he did.

"My presence creates hope for my students. I cannot kill this hope."

Ten days after I interviewed him, the day after the UN Security Council authorized possible armed action in northern Mali, another two alleged thieves were taken to Gao's public square to have limbs chopped off. Mr. Bodmar may have had to watch again. Eight more such theocratic amputations were threatened. "This is the law of God and no one can keep us from imposing it," announced a MUJAO spokesman.[16]

I WILL NOT NEGOTIATE MY LIBERTY

"The Sharia means women suffer the most," Mr. Bodmar had said. "First, by the obligatory wearing of the veil. And the revenue-generating activities of women, selling things in the market, have become impossible because they are prohibited from going out. You have to stay in the house." Bibata Maiga Guindo, a sixty-seven-year-old woman who fled Mr. Bodmar's hometown, told me that MUJAO had even banned women swimming in the river there, a common practice in the heat of northern Mali.

As in Algeria in the 1990s, those who sought to police morality in northern Mali also carried out gang rapes. It is a paradox the perpetrators found entirely manageable. A displaced sixty-two-year-old retired teacher from Timbuktu, who heads an association of Muslim women, told me she heard about this from relatives on the phone every week. A woman "given" in marriage to one armed Islamist would end up forced to have sex with all his comrades. The retired teacher, wrapped in a green-and-black-patterned scarf, sighed: "If they were real people of Sharia, I would be pleased to see them in my city, but they do everything except what is in Sharia."

Another displaced women's rights activist from Timbuktu, whom I will call Fatimata Cissé, confirmed these reports in her testimony before a gathering of women from across Mali. Finding public speaking difficult, she started and stopped several times. But, determined to get the word out, she propelled herself onward in nervous French: "I want to tell you about the suffering of our sisters." The fundamentalists,

Fatimata asserted, have raped more than fifty women in the city of Timbuktu alone. Girls, sometimes younger than fifteen, were forced into marriages with fundamentalist men who offered large sums of money, and then ten to fifteen armed grooms would take advantage of the nuptials to stage their own wedding nights.

A new women's prison, established in the premises of the Banque Malienne de Solidarité in Timbuktu, was run, Fatima said, by MUJAO and Ansar Dine. Women were sent there for inappropriate attire or for other "moral infractions." Members of the female half of the population were watched everywhere they went, she explained, to the point where many women no longer went out at all. This Muslim woman, who got up in the middle of the meeting where I met her to pray in the corner of the room, concluded: "With this Sharia, we cannot survive."

Women continued to resist, to reject, to revolt as best as they could. In October 2012, hundreds went out and marched in the streets of Timbuktu against the new diktats, until gunfire ended their protest. "They impose veils on us and now we are hunted like bandits for not wearing them," one protester named Cissé Touré reportedly told Reuters.[17] Small daily struggles continued. A distinguished Bamako-based physician, originally from Timbuktu, told me in December 2012 that she heard from medical colleagues living in Gao that young people were still defiant.

Tamate, a feisty Tuareg woman lawyer from the Kidal region, wearing a long blue boubou, told me she could not bear to go back to Islamist-occupied Kidal, "where my freedoms would be taken back to antiquity. They will tell me who to talk to, how to dress." Her own mother is an elected official, the first woman president of a local council. Though Tamate was frightened by the prospect of war at the end of 2012 when we met, and favored negotiations, she also saw limits to dialogue with Ansar Dine, which then controlled her home region. "My liberty—I will not negotiate it. It is up to me and only up to me."

TIMBUKTU DOES NOT DESERVE THIS, TIMBUKTU IS EVERYTHING

Among the cities that came under fundamentalist fiefdom in northern Mali was the cultural capital of the classical Sahel: Timbuktu. While its name has come to mean the middle of nowhere in English, it is anything but that. Founded about 1105 AD, the city attracted tens of thousands of students from around the world in its heyday; under Islamist rule, its schools were closed. Timbuktu houses some hundreds of thousands of significant historical manuscripts—"gold in words," as an expert has termed them—in its myriad libraries.[18] The exact fate of the manuscripts remains unclear. It seems as if most survived the Islamist occupation of the city despite militants torching part of the Ahmed Baba Institute, the city's most important library, before fleeing in January 2013. Local librarians and ordinary people seem to have hidden most of the precious texts in their homes—under floors and in secret rooms—saving them from the Islamists, as the Bactrian Gold of Afghanistan had been saved from the mujahideen. Still, at least two thousand manuscripts are believed destroyed. One European scholar long ago noted that Timbuktu's cultural treasures are so precious that "some day we will correct our classical Greek and Latin texts against the manuscripts that are preserved there."[19] This is no ordinary town that came under jihadi dominion. Making their kind of jihad in Timbuktu was nothing short of declaring war on Islamic history itself.

In addition to being famous for its precious written treasure, Timbuktu is known as "the city of 333 saints," whose tombs are shrines for local people. So it was a terrible shock to them when Ansar Dine began knocking down these mausoleums with hammers and pickaxes in the summer of 2012. For the fundamentalists, the veneration of saints, practiced for centuries by Muslims across North Africa, is idolatrous.

The Bamako-based physician from Timbuktu whom I interviewed explained to me that every family in her hometown, including her own, has saints among their ancestors, and those esteemed figures are buried in the cemeteries near their relatives' graves. Her own father's tomb was located next to the mausoleum of such a saint. When the saint's tomb was destroyed by the armed groups, her father's grave was also desecrated by the warriors of God. "How can people who dare to say they are Muslims, who say they have come for jihad, dare to touch things which are so important for Muslims? But we are so powerless. What can we do?" After her father's final resting place was attacked, her sister cried all day. "I said, 'What does that do?'"

The doctor's sister, a round-faced, thirty-four-year-old sociologist, fled Timbuktu a few months before I met her, after seeing an armed man chasing people with a belt in the market and beating women vendors. "We do not want the Sharia in Timbuktu," she insisted. "I say this as a Muslim. . . . You cannot say to a believer that I know better than you, and you must do what I want you to do." Timbuktu, as she described it, "is a truly religious city. I do not know how we can be reproached." In fact, the local imams and marabouts stood against the fundamentalists, while the armed men in turn tried to dictate their newfangled "Islam" to these local clergymen. "They attack even the imams. They go to mosque with arms at prayer time."

Exiled from her beloved home in the north, the sociologist repeated through her tears: "I have no life. I have no life." Having left her home behind so that her five children might be able to continue their schooling, she sold hair-care products to pay her kids' school fees. Her husband went back and forth to Timbuktu, trying to protect their home.

After her flight, another sister was arrested for speaking to a male cousin on the streets of Timbuktu near their family home. (They were discussing the risqué subject of salary-disbursement difficulties during the occupation.) Taken to the women's prison, she was kept in such total darkness "she could not see her own hand in front of her face." After this incident, she still refused to quit Timbuktu, but she avoided leaving the house as much as possible. The entire female population was effectively in prison. "There is a general psychosis," in the sociologist's words.

Praying for the success of negotiations, the sociologist knew there were things that remained nonnegotiable for her. With a nervous laugh, she said, "Really, I am Muslim. But I cannot return and live in Timbuktu under the Sharia." She was also terrified of the ethnic tensions that could arise later from the fact that those with lighter skin are now associated with fundamentalists by many darker-skinned people who were often the targets of fundamentalist violence. Though she is darkskinned, her family, like many others, is mixed through marriage; her sister-in-law hails from Algeria, and she wonders how they will all be able to live together safely in a future Timbuktu.

Her legendary hometown is also her own West African Kansas, and she longed to be able to click her heels and return there. "We want to go home. There we know we are alive. Timbuktu is everything. It is a city that represents everything. Everyone must do what they can to liberate the north." From hundreds of kilometers away, she, like so many displaced by the fundamentalist occupation, followed events back home closely through regular calls to family and friends. Each abuse of her city and its people wounded her, even in Bamako. "It was desolation after the mausoleums were destroyed. Everyone was crying. But God is Great. We are still here. There are times when I have hope. And sometimes when I speak about this, it makes me sick. Sometimes I lose hope and I say, 'We will not recover Timbuktu for twenty years.'"

A week after I left Mali, on December 23, 2012, Ansar Dine destroyed three more sacred shrines there. "Not a single mausoleum," proclaimed the head of Ansar Dine, "will remain in Timbuktu."[20] Such men must never again be allowed to rule the "city of 333 saints."

A Baby Cries at Qalandia Checkpoint: Opposing Injustice in the Struggle against Muslim Fundamentalism

For the tenth anniversary of the 9/11 attacks, I asked my students to read about the plethora of absurd conspiracy theories about that day. *Popular Mechanics* magazine has used science to disprove many of them.[1] In an essay explaining his epic battle with the "truthers" who advocate such views, the magazine's editor, James B. Meigs, quoted a reader's post: "Some people are open to any possibility, and honestly examine all evidence in a rational manner to come to a conclusion, followed by a moral evaluation. Others start with a desire for a specific moral evaluation, and then work backwards assembling any fact that supports them, and dismissing any fact that does not."[2]

I did go into this project with a preexisting moral evaluation of fundamentalism based on many years of examining the evidence, and I stand by that entirely. It was confirmed and reinforced by stories I heard, people I met, time and again from Cairo to Kabul. However, I take seriously the concerns expressed in the *Popular Mechanics* post. I never want to brush aside anything complicated or off-message. The world is messy and defies simple paradigms. That is what the fundamentalists cannot tolerate, but their opponents must.

I think the trouble that some human rights advocates have gotten into, when writing about Algeria or when writing about the "war on terror," is that the "Islamist victims" to whom they spoke conformed to their preexisting narrative—the state is bad (whether the United States, the Algerian state, or others) and the Islamists are persecuted. As a result, they did not ask other questions, or look for what was left out. Why do that when what they found confirmed what they wanted to say? I want to avoid that trap.

So, I want also to convey the stories I heard about what counterterrorism, what a putative battle against fundamentalism has sometimes done to the human rights of people of Muslim heritage. Too often, governments have done nothing to stop fundamentalists, failing to protect human rights as required by international law. But sometimes they have done the wrong things, also violating international law. Governments around the world battling Muslim fundamentalist opponents—or claiming to—have arbitrarily arrested and tortured thousands.[3] They have killed both indiscriminately and in a targeted way. They have stifled civil liberties, curtailed nonviolent political activism by people across the political spectrum, and engaged in religious and ethnic profiling. They too have bombed and killed the innocent, though often claiming that was not their intent. While I support an effective and thorough political struggle against fundamentalism, I do not support grave abuses in the name of that struggle. As prominent Arab American international lawyer Cherif Bassiouni rightly wrote back in the late eighties, in an article about the cycle of terrorism and counterterrorism, "Every form of violence is potentially terror-inspiring to its victim. . . ."[4]

The battle against fundamentalism is a critical fight for human rights as well as one that has to be guided by human rights. Omar Belhouchet, the Algerian newspaper editor who survived an attempt on his life by fundamentalist armed groups, underscored that even the "suppression of those carrying weapons must be done according to the laws." There is both an ethical and a strategic cost for doing otherwise. For one thing, as Russian human rights activist Gregory Shvedov says of repression by Russian security forces in Chechnya, "When you are killing religiously motivated people, you are motivating more of them." Responding as a human rights advocate in such a context is, I think, a matter of multi-directionality, of being able to recognize and take on multiple threats to rights simultaneously. I have no patience with voices on the left who think there is no need to vigorously combat extremism or terrorism and that force should never be used, nor with those on the right who think the rules should not apply when you do and that the war paradigm is always acceptable.

A right-of-center U.S. legal blog excerpted some of my criticisms of the first Awlaki lawsuit brought by the Center for Constitutional Rights. While they were intrigued by my challenge to the leftists who chose to represent the now late Al Qaeda ideologue's interests, I did not make them happy either. "[B]efore folks on the right become too enthusiastic about Professor Bennoune's critical perspective on the al-Aulaki suit, they might want to take into account her concluding remarks . . . in which she appears to equate the U.S. government's use of targeted killing with [Al Qaeda in the Arabian Peninsula's] use of terrorism."[5] To support this claim, the blog cites something I said to Mark Tran of the *Guardian*: "We have to oppose death lists of the US government but we also have to oppose calls for assassination by the likes of Awlaki. We have to find a way to navigate between Scylla and Charybdis."[6] I did not equate the two. In Greek mythology, Scylla and Charybdis were very different kinds of monsters; one had to avoid both to find safe passage.

I cannot do justice here to the abuses perpetrated in the fight against Muslim fundamentalism. That is not the main focus of this book, but it has been the major focus of the leading international human rights groups and much of the Western Left with regard to this entire issue. My narrative fills in gaps in theirs because they rarely say anything about what fundamentalism itself means for rights. Human rights law itself in fact requires the state to both respect and ensure rights, to defend its population from assaults by non-state fundamentalist groups but not to violate rights in doing so.

Many treaties, such as the International Covenant on Civil and Political Rights, explicitly prohibit the misuse of their guarantees for the purpose of threatening human rights themselves.[7] For example, the right to political participation is not a license to work freely for a totalitarian system that seeks to deny the rights of others.[8] Failure to acknowledge this undermines those who are peacefully battling extremism on the ground. It makes human rights a simple procedural device capable of facilitating totalitarianism. While some important work has been done by some international rights groups on related abuses—like that of Human Rights First on blasphemy laws[9]—the international human rights movement has all too often failed to grasp what is at stake in the fight against fundamentalism. "The international human rights organizations have been my enemies for thirty years," says one Algerian feminist activist. Global rights groups "are not balanced between the two," affirms Dalila Djerbal from the Wassila Network for women's rights in Algeria, referring to their positioning between government abuses and those by fundamentalist non-state actors in many countries like her own. On the front lines, many local human rights defenders try to strike that very delicate balance.

Tunisian human rights lawyer Radhia Nasraoui openly declares she is an atheist and tells me she ate ice cream during Ramadan as a girl. She remains committed to a democratic Tunisia where there is "room for everyone." "As long as people respect the rules of democracy, we cannot forbid them from being politically active. But once they threaten the rules of democracy, it is expected that we should defend it." While she represented many Islamist political detainees throughout Ben Ali's time, she recently became one of the lawyers for Nessma TV when Nabil Karoui was prosecuted for broadcasting *Persepolis*. "Just as we fought the dictatorship, we will fight any other party that will try to take away our rights," she told me in March 2011.

Nasraoui is all for vigilance but opposes a security-based approach to fundamentalism. "That is what Ben Ali did." She insists that one has to keep talking to people in order to learn to respect one another. She keeps conversing with the young Salafists she once represented who are now out of prison. "I tell them they must understand that they are not the holders of truth. They must accept that others may not agree with them. I think it is better to proceed in this manner to avoid excesses."

Senegalese historian Penda Mbow, who has received repeated death threats for her progressive way of teaching Islamic history, tells me in Dakar that the best strategy for fighting fundamentalism is democracy: "Real democracy with social justice. The fight against corruption. Respect for the rule of law. These are the most important antidotes to fundamentalism."

I HOPE MY SON DIED RIGHT AWAY

One of those whose testimony would remind me to center the rule of law in my argument was Nassera Dutour. Though I thought of her as someone largely on the other side of the debate, her story would turn out to be an integral part of the one I am trying to tell. Nassera heads SOS Disparus, the Algerian Association of the Families of the Disappeared (at the hands of the state) from the 1990s.

As a Spanish virtual memorial for this category of Algerian disappeared says, "In the name of the antiterrorist fight, in response to assassinations, rapes, torture, massacres and kidnapping carried out by the armed Islamist groups, the Algerian security forces were guilty of multiple abuses and disappeared thousands after arresting them."[10] This is unquestionably true. Some who vanished during that time may have been involved with the fundamentalist armed groups, and it is important to be honest about that, even if it can never justify a forced disappearance. However, many were simply ordinary people in the wrong place at the wrong time, especially after 1994. Unfortunately, unlike the Spanish memorial, many international human rights groups largely forgot how the Islamist abuses fueled the state atrocities. Neither justifies the other, but to understand what was happening in Algeria, you have to consider both. Nassera's odyssey and Adnane Bouchaïb's go together.

Principled universalists, Cherifa Kheddar (a victim of fundamentalist armed groups) and Cherifa Bouatta (a key documenter of their crimes) told me I had to meet Nassera Dutour, who had lost her son to the Algerian state's war against terrorism. I thought of Nassera's organization as the darling of the large international human rights NGOs that emphasized this paradigm of abuse in Algeria by the state in the 1990s to the virtual exclusion of everything else. But this in no way diminished the weight of the story Nassera would tell me. I could not disappear what she said because it threatened to wrinkle my own neatly pressed thesis.

A collage of headshots adorns the walls of the offices of SOS Disparus, rows of somber faces of those who were picked up by the authorities in the 1990s during the fight against jihadism and never seen again. In a fast, airy French, Nassera tells me the history of her organization, which is a collective of families, rather like Soumoud. Back in the late nineties, she had worked in France to bring families of the disappeared together and to take them around Europe to raise awareness about the issue. She subsequently returned to Algeria and traveled the country to meet families of disappeared people far from the capital, rallying them and protesting publicly in Algiers, despite bans on doing so.

Today, SOS Disparus, like Djazairouna, is one of Algeria's most active human rights groups. It receives far more international support than Djazairouna and has a small, bustling office off Didouche Mourad Street in downtown Algiers. She and her colleagues try to do too many things, Nassera laughs. They have organized demonstrations and workshops and collected testimonies and information in eight thousand cases, submitting many of these to the United Nations.

I ask how many people disappeared at the hands of the Algerian state while it was fighting the fundamentalists in the nineties. She does not know for sure but believes that some of the numbers advanced by human rights lawyers such as Ali Yahia Abdennour back then (around eighteen thousand) were too high. The official Ad Hoc Commission in charge of the question of disappearances, Nassera explains, determined that at least six thousand people had vanished at the hands of the state.[11] However, even today, SOS Disparus continues to receive new cases that are posted on its website—somebody's lost brother, somebody's missing son.

Just as with Adnane Bouchaïb, I only manage to ask Nassera about her own loss after we have been talking for half an hour. While it was Adnane's father who vanished, it was Nassera's child who did. The sole sign of strain she reveals when explaining what happened is that she talks even faster, much as Cherifa did when narrating the deaths of her brother and sister at the hands of the Armed Islamic Group. Like Cherifa, Nassera persists, telling me everything, or at least all she knows.

She herself does not know how the story ends.

January 30, 1997. Nassera Dutour's son, Amine Amrouche, was twenty-one. Like many young people, he would spend a lot of time in the bathroom in the morning, concerned about his appearance. That day his uncle, Nassera's brother, evicted Amine from the one bathroom they all shared, and he has felt terrible about it ever since. Exactly what happened next is not clear. Nabbed on his way to return videos, pushed into a white Nissan carrying three men in suits, Amine was later spotted in the Baraki police station, near where he lived with his grandmother. And he was never seen again.

So, Nassera Dutour's search began. She assumed the men in the car were agents of the DRS, the Department for Information and Security, Algeria's notorious internal intelligence agency, which was heavily involved in the fight against fundamentalist terrorism—but which also terrorized. She received various reports of Amine's arrest, of his presence in a few detention facilities. Then nothing.

Nassera was told there had been a terrorist attack and several murders by fundamentalists in the area the same day Amine disappeared. A police officer's family had had their throats cut. Amine seems to have been rounded up with many other men following those crimes. Through a connection, Dutour managed to see the local police commissioner. Right away he told her: "We arrested lots of people on January thirtieth, but not your son." Nassera said, "This is a joke. You have not even asked me my son's name. How do you know you have not arrested him?" The commissioner then asked for the name, which she told him. He replied instantly: "We arrested 130 people that day. But not your son."

With disdain in her soft voice, she repeats the words she used at the time. "You told me you carried out 130 arrests between Thursday and Saturday. How do you remember all their names?" He answered, "I interrogate them all." The commissioner was proud of himself, she says.

I apologize for making her again recount what she must be asked to tell all the time. "I am glad to tell the story," Nassera corrects me, "because sometimes I forget the details. I should write about it but when I am alone at home, I cannot. It reminds me of too many memories."

Like Adnane, her story has terrible ellipses. There is no ending. "To really be able to mourn," Nassera says quickly, "you must know they are dead." Instead, she and the families she works with are left piecing together rumors and secondhand fragments of what might have befallen those they love, those whose pictures cover the wall behind her in the SOS Disparus office. Based on the patchwork quilt of this half-information, she thinks her son may have been taken to the Beni Messous Military Base. But she does not know for sure. She may never know. In the trailer for a film about her, *Song for Amine*, Nassera explains that for years she waited for his knock at the door, thought she heard his voice in the street, saw his face everywhere. It is a kind of torture.

At one point, she tells me she believes she knows whether her son is dead or alive, but she does not want to specify because her mother, Amine's doting grandmother, would be upset. An older woman with her head wrapped in a gauzy scarf, Fatima Yous sits at protests holding a picture of her handsome young grandson, along with a sign:

"Don't worry, my little Amine. I will look for you my whole life."

A huge hole was blown through an entire generation full of promise, both by the extensive fundamentalist terrorism and by the smaller-scale but very grave and sometimes indiscriminate violence of the state fighting against it. I do not equate them, or justify either because of the other. International human rights groups highlighted the violence of the state and ignored many of the stories I was told in the Triangle of Death. However, that does not mean I can ignore Nassera Dutour's story.

After recounting the sighting of Amine at the Beni Messous base, she continues, "I do not know if he was taken somewhere else or if he died there. This is the terrible question we ask ourselves all the time. When I hear testimony about the torture then, I hope that my son died fast. Right away. In the first twenty-four hours even. And did not suffer."

This grim hope is akin to the dream of the journalists, my dream for my father, that if they had to die at the hands of the fundamentalists, it would be over quickly. It was one thing to hope for this prospectively but quite another to have to live with that hope when the person is already gone, and you may never know whether he died quickly or not.

Amine's story is a gift of memory given to me by his mother, like the stories shared in the Triangle of Death. This particular account reminds me to be very clear that I support an effective and robust political struggle against fundamentalism, but not one that disregards the rule of law. While I hold the Algerian fundamentalist armed groups and their awful violence at least partially responsible for the harsh response of the Algerian state, the state too must be held accountable. Nassera says that for her the discovery of the depth of government violence during the dark decade was a shock. "I never imagined that there was so much violence. On the part of the terrorists, yes. I knew that. But on the side of the state, what I discovered was horror." That familiar word again.

The horror recounted in this book is no justification for what happened to Amine and others like him. Many of the victims have come to understand that. Today, Nassera works in a surprising coalition with Adnane Bouchaïb and Cherifa Kheddar against the amnesty given by the Algerian government to all the perpetrators—whether they killed for the armed fundamentalist groups or for the state. Initially, there seems to have been suspicion all around. Of Cherifa Kheddar, Nassera recalls, "She thought we were the families of terrorists and we thought they were working with the state." As it turns out, neither was true. The victims on both sides wanted many of the same things, most of all an accounting.

Their relationship began to thaw at a dinner at a foreign embassy, where a diverse group of victims discussed the national reconciliation. Ali Merabet, the president of Soumoud, said he was ready to forgive, but he wanted the truth. Cherifa said she had no right to forgive on behalf of the victims. "This hit me," Nassera remembers, "that she said something I would have said."

Now they organize meetings together and publicize their demand for a truth commission, though it is never easy. Some of this cooperation was facilitated by Amine's grandmother, who not only lost her grandson to the state but also was attacked by fundamentalist thugs in the street—representing in one person the spectrum of the Algerian drama of the 1990s.

At the end of our meeting, I am again floored by Nassera's decency. She has just shared her most painful life experience, yet she is somehow concerned about me.

"I am sorry to tell you such things."

THE MOST DANGEROUS PLACE IN EUROPE

"The people I hate most are Dagestanis," a masked member of Russia's Far Right confesses in a documentary shown at the Russian Union of

Journalists (RUJ) conference I attend in Moscow in December 2010. People from the Caucasus are frequently targets of prejudice and even violence in Moscow, including during rioting that takes place while I am there. As in Algeria and many other places I visited, the rise of Muslim fundamentalism presents a significant human rights crisis across their region, but so do the "counterterrorist" actions of the authorities, who have often used this issue to justify their own transgressions. All told, this makes for a perplexing, entangled, and deadly reality.

Biyakay Magomedov is the lawyer for *Chernovik*, an outspoken independent newspaper based in Makhachkala, the capital of Dagestan. Wearing a pinstripe suit and navy tie, he has a shock of jet-black hair. *Chernovik* seeks to expose corruption and human rights abuses in this violence-plagued Russian republic on the Caspian Sea—"the most dangerous place in Europe"[12]—whose multiethnic population of 2.9 million is 90 percent Muslim. As a result of their forthrightness and choice of topics, the paper's journalists are regularly assaulted by thugs likely associated with local officials, often incited by claims they are aiding the radical Islamic groups.

Dagestan has seen unrelenting strife between fundamentalist fighters and Russian security forces—what the BBC dubs "the worst militant violence in the North Caucasus."[13] Shops that sell alcohol are blown up; headmasters who ban the hijab are gunned down. Nearly eight hundred people were killed here in 2010 and 2011 alone.[14] A significant part of the violence is Muslims killing Muslims. Since the 1990s, when the war in neighboring Chechnya spilled across Dagestan's borders, Wahhabi-linked militants have been growing in influence. Much of the population here was traditionally Sufi, but increasing numbers of young people are turning to the more radical Salafism they regard as free of state control. Rampant corruption and disenfranchisement fan the flames of their fanaticism.

A great deal of the violence swirls around the police. Biyakay puts forward a figure of a hundred policemen killed in Dagestan every year for the last decade. Chernovik has a video of a wounded cop lying on the street bleeding, with passersby taking photos on their mobile phones rather than helping him. The lawyer seems both horrified by and understanding of the popular reaction. The police are "no angels," he says. "If you are accused of the humiliation of men's dignity, taking off their clothes and making them sit on bottles and filming and putting on the Internet, for Caucasian men, this is unacceptable." These are the kinds of allegations of police torture his paper takes so many risks to report.

Magomedov is critical of fundamentalism and not defensive about my questions on this topic, as some others here have been. "I see Afghan-istan, and the result of fundamentalism there." He explains what this example means to him in words that are picturesquely translated for me. "I do not want to live in times minus 700 years." The journalist is clearly too modern for that.

Nevertheless, in December 2010, Biyakay Magomedov believes that *radicalism*—the term used most often in Dagestan, is growing in his home republic, "because young people see justice only through Mus-lim understanding, not through democratic institutions." This is due to the impunity afforded high officials involved in killings. "The Kremlin does nothing." He regrets that "radicalism and terrorism" are presented in Russia "as if that appeared with no reason, but it is like resistance to broken human rights." Unfortunately, this "resistance" seems merely to lead to the "breaking" of other rights. This conundrum reminds me that my father once termed Muslim fundamentalism "a disease mas-querading as a cure."[15]

When I meet Biyakay, I also meet Ali Kamalov, head of the Dagestan branch of the Russian Union of Journalists, who was nearly beaten to death by the flunkies of an oligarch in 1996. He believes the troubles in Dagestan stem in part from denials of the rule of law: "Since civil laws are not implemented, and do not work, religion takes the part of poli-tics." If the force of the law were stronger, "religion would be relegated to the personal field." His own near-murder was never investigated. It is a harrowing landscape in which he finds himself between the state on the one hand and "religious people who call to go back to a dark yester-day" on the other. Very concerned about what he calls "the Islamization of Dagestan," and an increasing rejection of science, which he considers to be un-Islamic, he says the terrorists are "the enemy of society."

In 2008, Biyakay Magomedov was involved in organizing a series of meetings against this very terrorism and the "illegal behavior of the police," as well as in favor of the constitution. But he was disappointed at the low turnout and thinks that what is really needed to change Dagestan is public protest. When an important prosecutor's son was kidnapped, his wife asked Biyakay for help. "Why didn't you go to the streets with us against kidnapping?" he asked her. People only really understand terrorism when it happens to them, Biyakay regrets.

At the time I see him in Moscow, Magomedov was being prosecuted along with some colleagues for allegedly promoting extremism by criticizing in print the human rights practices of the Dagestan police. He faced up to two years in prison as a result of antiextremism legislation that seems to be used selectively to pursue critics of government policy.[16] The charges stem from *Chernovik* articles claiming that the authorities' brutal antiterrorism measures have contributed to the fundamentalist boom. Having been publicly labeled a militant sympathizer, Biyakay feels greatly under threat. "All the time, I'm thinking about my life and every day I choose a different way to the house. I don't want to be beaten and killed." When he asked officials for protection, it was denied. Following an appearance in court in which he testified against the deputy police minister, this official told him, "I will kill you. You will disappear."

"Very often, I think of quitting out of fear for my child and wife, but I think if I quit and give up, what will happen?"

Magomedov and his colleagues were acquitted, and a few months later Biyakay became the editor-in-chief of his newspaper. Six months after that, his boss, Khadjimurad Kamalov—Ali Kamalov's relative and *Chernovik*'s founder and owner—was gunned down right outside the paper's offices. The slain man's name had appeared several years earlier on anonymous death lists of "militants' helpers," though no one knows for sure whether this was connected to his death.[17] He was also outspoken about human rights abuses by the authorities in Dagestan.

I hope Biyakay has not yet run out of alternate routes home.

THIS YEAR IN JERUSALEM

I went to Palestine and Israel in December 2010 for the same reason that I interviewed Nassera Dutour. I did not want to make any of this too easy. I also do not want this book to be misunderstood or used for purposes for which it was not intended, like justifying human rights abuses or, specifically, the policies of the Israeli government toward Palestinians.

On my last day in the West Bank, I go to Ramallah to interview Dr. George Giacaman, the Birzeit University professor who directs Muwatin, the Palestinian Institute for the Study of Democracy. Its office has just reopened after the New Year, and it is still quiet and cold.

With his tweed jacket and spectacles, Dr. Giacaman looks just like a stereotypical university professor anywhere. He tells me about the difficult strategic dilemmas Palestinian secularists face. Israeli occupation is the primary political issue in the minds of many in the West Bank, and this sometimes leads to postponing the fight with Hamas. "Once you have a state, it is easier to make choices." Nonetheless, he is concerned about the Hamas social agenda, which he characterizes as "repressive." The Algerian in me worries about the impact of the "postponement" of the social debate, but the strategic options on offer to Palestinian secularists are almost all undesirable.

Ironically, Giacaman tells me, polls show increasing support for Hamas in the West Bank, where the Palestinian Authority is in charge, and decreasing support in Gaza, where Hamas runs the show.[18] The big question in people's minds is: "What are the alternatives?" This question has been on the table in nearly every country I have visited. If the Palestinian Authority is not able to make progress toward a political solution that ameliorates living conditions for its people, in a few years, Giacaman argues, "We will be in a very dire situation."

For him, the "stigma of terrorism," as repeatedly applied to Palestinians, is useful for Israel. "Any form of resistance is described as terrorism, not only targeting civilians," something he is unequivocally against. On the other hand, he says, "When Israel targets civilians, this is not called terrorism." Undoubtedly, one of the most useful ways to support secularists like him in the battle against fundamentalists is to be evenhanded about the Palestinian-Israeli conflict. Double standards alienate people from the concepts of justice and reason.

George Giacaman is my final interlocutor on this leg of the trip. I am leaving saddened by the burgeoning Jewish settlements that increasingly engulf East Jerusalem and suffocate hopes for a two-state solution, by the obliviousness of many ordinary Israelis to living conditions for Palestinians literally a stone's throw away, and by the rise in conservatism and fundamentalism in some Palestinian circles. Taken together, one can only wonder what the future holds for the peoples here. Israeli journalist Anat Saragusti tells me a Palestinian intellectual she interviewed predicted that in coming years both moderate Israelis and moderate Palestinians will depart in increasing numbers, leaving behind a conflict dominated by fundamentalists on all sides. Abu Hassan, the guide who took me to Hebron, told me something similar. As we walked through Hebron's Old City—now occupied by five hundred fanatical Jewish settlers and the four thousand Israeli soldiers who protect them at the expense of two hundred thousand Palestinians—he warned that if there is no resolution, another intifada is coming.

He fears it will be the Al Qaeda intifada this time.

So I want Dr. George Giacaman to tell me there is still hope here. His organization has declared the beginning of a third intifada that is nonviolent and globalized, involving divestment campaigns, pursuit of Israeli officials alleged to have committed war crimes, and peaceful protests. To avoid the uprising Abu Hassan warns about, it is imperative that such nonviolent endeavors succeed in ending the conflict.

Contemplating all of this in that quiet office in Ramallah, I suddenly realize my time is getting tight and I must head back to Jerusalem and then to Tel Aviv's Ben Gurion Airport. As I ride back across Ramallah, I keep thinking about something Dr. Giacaman had said: "If there had been success toward establishing a Palestinian state, Hamas probably would not have won the elections."

When I reach Ramallah's main bus station, the taxi driver tells me there is an *azma*, a crisis. A rally is taking place for Fatah anniversary day, which celebrates the founding of the largely secular ruling party in the West Bank, and there are buses everywhere. The town has become a snarled nationalist traffic jam. So the driver takes me back to the Qalandia checkpoint, where I can cross the Wall. As the crow flies, the airport is only about twenty-eight miles from where I am, but it is a million miles away thanks to what is called "separation." There is still theoretically plenty of time before my flight, but here anything can happen.

Near the checkpoint, I bid the driver *maasalama* (go in peace), and set out on foot. I am told to board a bus, manned by a heavily bearded Arab driver, that is parked by the side of the road. We wait, trapped. No one knows what is happening or why. When we learn we must all alight and walk across the checkpoint, I begin to worry. We flow out into the weak December sunshine and are told by Israeli soldiers to enter a cage-like area blocked in the front. Even women with small children have to get off the bus today. A pack of us waits—many women in hijab, a few women with heads bare, children, older men. It is cold and windy and we do not know how long we will be stuck here.

A tiny peasant woman wearing a long embroidered dress stands beside me, holding a shrieking baby. The woman explains to me and a couple squashed with us that her baby is sick and she is trying to take her to the hospital in Jerusalem. Even the cold gusts of wind cannot drown out the baby's desperate bleating as her mother attempts to comfort her, to rewrap her in a blanket. We all try to allow the mother to go ahead of us, but, trapped ourselves, we have no privilege to yield.

A struggle breaks out ahead where people are trying to get into the mysterious automatic turnstile that is our only outlet. Controlled remotely by the Israeli soldiers manning the checkpoint, it opens without warning and then stops just as suddenly. An old Palestinian man and a younger one have begun to shout at each other. The more senior man says the youth thinks he is better than others because he is trying to go around. Being trapped does not nourish humanism.

As I wait in the cold air at Qalandia, I think about all the checkpoints I have crossed here. I held my breath when we battled to get the New Generation School's kids across to Jerusalem. But I also got stuck at unofficial Muslim checkpoints at the Haram al-Sharif. On the day I helped Terry Boullata take the schoolchildren to the puppet show, we also took them to one of Islam's holiest sites, which most of them had never seen. (Once there, they promptly ate potato chips on the steps.) Though the name on the passport I was forced to show is Karima, the guards did not believe I was of Muslim heritage, and they refused to let me in. Terry was livid, and, ever the activist, she finally got the head guard to admit me by shouting at him that my grandfather was a martyr of the Algerian revolution. The world is full of checkpoints policed by many kinds of fundamentalists. Luckily, there are also many kinds of checkpoint challengers.

Marieme Hélie-Lucas had described such people well in eulogizing our friend Rhonda Copelon. A legendary Jewish feminist human rights lawyer, Rhonda took on the human rights establishment to represent the victims of Algeria's fundamentalist armed groups against FIS spokesman Anouar Haddam.[19] Hélie-Lucas's description is apt for so many I met along the way. "I like such 'traitors,'" she wrote, like "the Women in Black in Israel fighting against the occupation of Palestine. . . . I respect people who are capable of standing alone, against their own people, for what they believe is right." They are indeed the most antifundamentalist of all.

I think of Tanya Rosenblit—"the Rosa Parks of Israel"—a Jewish woman who absolutely refused to move to the back of a gender-segregated Israeli bus when told to do so in December 2011 by a group of ultra-Orthodox Jewish men who kept the bus from moving.[20] Her battle was all too similar to that of some I met on my journey.

I also think of Mahdi Abdul Hadi, the distinguished Palestinian policy expert who told me he had been seated next to a religious figure, a sheikh, at a meeting on Palestinian negotiating strategy back in the nineties and had ordered a glass of wine with his dinner. "You cannot drink wine with me," the sheikh said. Mahdi replied, "Then go to your room and have your dinner, or take another table." The sheikh insisted he wanted to sit with Abdul Hadi to discuss a document. Abdul Hadi said fine, but he was going to have his glass of wine nonetheless, which the sheikh ultimately tolerated. Sadly, in December 2010, Mahdi Abdul Hadi told me, "Today, I cannot dare to order a glass of wine in the presence of a sheikh in a public restaurant." It sounds like a small thing, but, as Mahdi said, "It is serious."

I have plenty of time to think about all of this, and to stew about missing my afternoon plane, while waiting at the Qalandia checkpoint. I finally get through its phantom turnstile after forty minutes, but it could just as easily have taken four hours. I learn the meaning of "freedom of movement" that day. Looking back, I often wonder whether the crying baby made it to the hospital, whether she survived. And if so, what kind of life will she have, caught between Hamas and the Israeli government?

There are very real security issues for Israelis, and some Israeli children have also died at the hands of Palestinian bombers—most often sent by Muslim fundamentalists—who have blown themselves up on civilian buses, unconscionably. Not enough Arabs, Arab Americans, Palestinians, and their supporters have condemned these crimes for which there is no excuse, just as not enough supporters of Israel have spoken out against the human impact of the Wall. But you cannot treat an entire population in this illegal way and expect liberal values to thrive.

Meanwhile, the Israeli government misuses the issue of fundamentalism as a way of whitewashing its own harsh policies, conduct that in turn only stokes more fundamentalism. When Israeli prime minister Benjamin Netanyahu takes the stage at the UN General Assembly in September 2011 and rails about the "insatiable crocodile of militant Islam,"[21] while seeking to block Palestinians from admission to the world body, it only undermines the people I have met and narrows the space for this book to be heard.

Palestine does become a non-member observer state at the United Nations in 2012, though real statehood and the rights that accompany it remain elusive. While Muslim fundamentalists grossly misuse this cause as a rallying cry, the real struggle for a free, democratic, secular Palestine alongside Israel remains central to a just peace and to the defeat of all the region's fundamentalists.

At the end of my trip to Israel and Palestine, I carve in my notes a mantra: "Nothing I write should ever be used to justify what I have seen here."

Raise Your Voice While Singing Is Still Possible

It has been twenty years since the knock on my father's door that set me on the path to writing this book. Globally, the danger of fundamentalism is now perhaps even greater than it was then. Fundamentalist social ideas are proliferating within societies like Algeria, as feminist scholar Cherifa Bouatta tells me. But it must not be said that there are no Muslims who speak out, that people of Muslim heritage are not doing anything to take on extremism. Such assertions are simply untrue. Undoubtedly more can, should, and must be done—especially by those of us living safely and securely in diasporas. The president of Pakistan's Supreme Court Bar Association, Asma Jahangir, who has long risked her life to challenge extremism, contradicts the claim that we cannot speak openly in the diasporas because of bigotry. "There won't be racism," she assures me, "if you come out and speak the truth."

As Penda Mbow, the Islamic history scholar I met in Dakar exhorted, young Muslims in America must "join hands with those Muslims who love their religion and are completely against violence, to work for a world that is more peaceful, more just, more equal." This solidarity needs to be extended across the spectrum to those among believers and nonbelievers, practicing Muslims as well as atheists, agnostics, and freethinkers of Muslim heritage, and the religious minorities who live with them, who work together against fundamentalism. "[T]he free-thinkers have been trying very hard . . . within the Arab world, . . ." my father, Mahfoud Bennoune, emphasized not long after 9/11. He was deeply frustrated that there was not more international interest in their work. "[W]ho gives a damn about what Arab intellectuals say?"[1] We *must* give a damn.

Those who do speak out need and deserve both support and a hearing, something they too infrequently receive. As Pakistani sociologist Farida Shaheed, the UN's independent expert on culture, tells me in her office in Lahore, "The greatest support would be for the alternative voices to be heard wherever they are."

Often when people mouth platitudes about Islam-religion-of-peace, my eyes glaze over. Have they slept through the last few decades? But that cliché does have a basis in truth that must not be forgotten. I think again about the words of Penda Mbow in Dakar about the divide in Muslim cultures: "One must recognize the Islam that I studied. That Islam of the Abbassids had a prodigious culture, development of the arts, of letters, of beauty. It is this Islam that I know. But, the Islam which inspires fear, which oppresses women, that Islam which is *against*, which wants to impose the Sharia, this is not that Islam."

In Karachi, women's rights activist Nuzhat Kidvai said, "The practice of Islam is what shows what Islam is. And if that is violent or that is unjust, then that is what Islam has become." It is that kind of "practice" that must be opposed. She told me about her recent TV debate with a mullah about crimes against women. He was lecturing her about Islam-religion-of-peace. Her retort? "I don't need to be told how peaceful Islam is. I know Islam. I want to know about you, your practice and how that is peaceful." The best way to defend Islam is to display that peaceful practice, and to defend those who do. This requires an unabashed challenge of fundamentalism.

What can be done now to turn back the tide of extremism? In Kabul, outspoken former Afghan parliamentarian Malalai Joya tells me that she wants us all to work together to magnify our efforts. "Let's raise our voice together against these fundamentalists," she exclaims. I imagine an unstoppable chorus of all the people I have met. These people need to be able to work together across borders the way their fundamentalist opponents do. They need to not feel isolated or marginal, as Said Bit-soev in Moscow and Nighat Khan in Lahore and so many others told me they did. But this requires resources and structures.

As Marieme Hélie-Lucas views it, "There is individual resistance. That is not the problem. But the conditions are not there for it to move to a higher level, a truly political level." "We need more networks of solidarity and reflection," Chahla Chafiq urges. "There are many good things being done, but they do not converge." As the liberal Libyan politician Mahmoud Jibril told a journalist, "The parties claiming to represent political Islam do not have more supporters than we do. They are just better organized."[2] Hélie-Lucas identifies some of the things the heterogeneous antifundamentalist forces need in order to get orga-nized: "Lots of money, our own newspapers, radio, TV." However, she knows there are other problems to be faced. Those doing the kind of work she does are almost unrecognized internationally. "We have no voice outside. Who wants our revolution? No one."

When I asked many of those I met what they thought should be done around the world to support them, I received a range of answers: "clearly support secular feminist groups and the principle of universal rights"; "support actions taken on the ground to counter fundamental-ist indoctrination"; "openly support those who defend the separation of religion and politics"; "provide financial assistance to such forces so as to enable them to network"; "give them visibility"; "unpack the myth of the 'moderate Islamist'—especially when it comes to the rights of women, freedom of expression, and freedom of religion—a myth that gives great support to the fundamentalists." Many wanted the United States to take a long look at its own policies that had promoted fundamentalism—whether collaborating with the Saudi government, financing fundamentalist groups in Afghanistan, or violating inter-national law in our own treatment of Muslim majority populations in places like Iraq.

Without a doubt, the single most important development would be widespread popular mobilization against fundamentalism, like that which ultimately happened in Algeria in the 1990s and then emerged in Pakistan in the immediate aftermath of the targeting of Malala Yousafzai. There are some encouraging signs: In Afghanistan, students protested the renaming of their campus after a mujahideen leader,[3] and women took to the streets after a sixteen-year-old rape victim received a hundred lashes.[4] Tunisian women's demonstrations actually defeated a proposal to make women "complementary" to men rather than equal in the new constitution. In Mali, people banded together to try to meet the humanitarian needs of their compatriots living under jihadist occupation.[5] Niger's president himself called on Nigeriens to "mobilize as a single person" following the October 2012 kidnapping, presumably by Al Qaeda in the Islamic Maghreb, of local aid workers fighting malaria among children.[6] "Who would dare claim," he asked, "that the perpetrators of such acts may really be called Muslims?"

As the widowed hairdresser back in Blida had explained to me, this kind of opposition has to develop organically from within populations. But it can be thoughtfully bolstered from without by like-minded supporters. In Afghanistan, Horia Mosadiq tells me, "I think we should support civil society groups, women's right groups, and the groups that are able to speak out against fundamentalists. Not the groups that are supporting fundamentalists." Empowering civil society is not a strategy that has really been tried in combating Muslim extremism. The West has mostly empowered autocrats, or worked with that oxymoronic category of "moderate" fundamentalists. Local governments supposedly battling "the Islamists" have often constrained liberal civil society any way they could because they are more afraid of its democratic spirit than of fundamentalism. Liberal civil society groups often face insurmountable political and material obstacles. In 2011, after operating for ten years, Algeria's Sidi Moussa sewing club closed its doors. The organizers are still seeking the funds to reopen.

The fact that the fundamentalist message sometimes comes through so clearly is more a matter of having the resources to amplify it, rather than of its actually representing the dominant popular view. Many Americans might be surprised that Horia Mosadiq would argue that Afghans are basically antifundamentalist, "even if you go to the most underprivileged part of Afghanistan." In academia, I often hear claims that the Islamists represent ordinary people, and their opponents are simply elite. Conversely, Horia argues, "We have so many liberal Muslims, so many liberal Muslim scholars. Why are they not given the chances to go to the public to talk to the people and to give them the messages that the fundamentalists have removed even from the Islamic textbooks?" Antifundamentalist voices are at the ready, but they are rarely the ones with the loudspeakers. That must change.

THE INSTITUTE OF LEARNING

Every time I ask people what the solution is to the problem of fundamentalism, every time in every country, the first answer is always education—whether in Pakistan, Egypt, or Niger. On the outskirts of Herat, Afghanistan, I visit an organization that is putting that thesis to the test, the Afghanistan Institute of Learning (AIL). Founded in 1995 by Dr. Sakena Yacoobi, a partner in Mahnaz Afkhami's Women's Learning Partnership, they train teachers and students. "Education is the key of all success and progress in the country," AIL's program director, a Mr. R., tells me. For him, the relationship is linear. If you provide education, people "don't go to the fundamentalist side." Dr. Yacoobi stresses: "If you really want to bring democracy, you must educate the people." This is the only way to introduce the critical thinking that is vital to challenging fundamentalism. Think of it as the "war on ignorance."

It is no accident that the Algerian fundamentalists carried out a massive campaign against the country's schools, burning the buildings and threatening the pupils, nor that fundamentalists in many other countries I visited had targeted education in one way or another, either destroying girls' schools as in Pakistan, or speaking out against girls' education as Egyptian Salafists do, or trying to influence the content of education nearly everywhere. In the wrong hands, as Aïssatou Cissé reminded me in Senegal, education can become a tool of fundamentalist indoctrination. After all, the word *Taliban* means "the students." Even Tunisian Ennahda Party leader Rached Ghannouchi told the Salafists in his country to focus on education as a means for gradually taking over their society.

When I am in Herat, I visit one of the AIL schools that is committed instead to a tolerant and liberating kind of learning, where boys and girls study together, even though they sit on opposite sides of the classroom. It is electric to sit on the floor in this class in a poor neighborhood, surrounded by kids learning English with books in their laps. A smiling young woman teacher wearing a loose scarf on her head and trousers writes on the rickety whiteboard, patiently explaining the difference between "these" and "those." Back in Taliban days, 170 students, mostly girls, would sneak into this building to learn at a clandestine school, coming from 6 a.m. to 10 a.m. They would come in one by one so as not to be a recognizable student body. Now, when they look into my camera, it is unadulterated hope I see in their eyes.

What will happen to these boys and girls, to their young woman teacher, if the Taliban return to power in Herat?

The woman who directs this school was also in charge during Taliban rule. Twice, she was arrested for this work, as there was a checkpoint nearby. The school director said she was willing to take the risk because she believes in education. Her gamble is paying off in real lives; some of the students from that time are teachers, and some have even studied at the university. "I tried to make their future," she explains. That is what it is all about—building a decent future with possibilities for enlightenment, opportunity, and joy on this side of paradise.

Security is one of the biggest challenges for AIL's schools. Another is lack of sufficient funds. Given the limited funding provided to critical programs like hers, Dr. Yacoobi says she has a question for the international community: "Do they really want change or not?"

WHY DID THEY DIE?

I think back to all the victims and opponents of terrorism of Muslim heritage whom I met along my journey. I think of the depth of the suffering of the survivors, of the obstacles they have all surmounted to stand against that terrorism, and of how little recognition or aid they have received.

Iranian rights activist Roya Boroumand was undoubtedly right. Had more people outside criticized fundamentalism and its violence— whether in Iran, Algeria, or Afghanistan—and worked against its causes, fewer people inside would have been killed. It is still true. Had more people supported the peaceful, progressive antifundamentalists when they came under fire, there could have been, could still be a different outcome. In any case, those resisting would at least feel the embrace of international solidarity from people like them elsewhere with the same liberal values, something many of them, including my father, did not experience during the worst of times.

The annals I have recorded have taught me many things. One is that there can be no successful strategy to combat terrorism that does not include a commitment to ending the relentless fundamentalist attacks on civilians in Muslim majority contexts. That is not a residual, tolerable violence that can be allowed to simply go on because it is happening somewhere else, while we try to stop attacks on "us." Any bifurcation of the violence that befalls Afghans or Somalis or Pakistanis or Iraqis or Algerians, and that which befalls Westerners, at the hands of Muslim fundamentalist terrorists, is immoral and strategically nonsensical. These violences are intertwined, their victims equally deserving of safety.

Nor can we trade acquiescence to human rights abuses for protection from the fundamentalists. As Roya and Ladan Boroumand have written, "[T]he denigration of human rights marks the spot where the internal war on Muslim society meets the terrorist war against the West."[7] These things, too, are inextricably linked. For the Boroumands, there is an ongoing correlation between "terror against the West" and "tyranny against Muslims."

But we should focus not only on fundamentalist violence, because the problem is also the discriminatory and hateful ideology that underlies it, the yeast that makes its beer. The Western response in places like Afghanistan, and even in Britain, has often been to seek fundamentalist allies against terrorism, to oppose only fundamentalist terrorism (especially when it targets Westerners) and not fundamentalism itself, to think that one can find a nonviolent extremism with which one can coexist. This is the critical error that gives rise to such oxymoronic constructs as the "moderate Taliban" the United States allegedly can use against Al Qaeda. In Algeria, Cherifa Kheddar maintains, "We cannot defeat terrorism by an anti-terrorist battle without doing the anti-fundamentalist battle."

Similarly, Jamil Omar, a former trade unionist and secretary of Pakistan's Awami Jamhouri Forum, who was facing such persistent threats when I met him in 2010 that he tried not to spend too much time near colleagues because he might endanger them, believes that the core task is "challenging fundamentalist thought." He knows "it's not an easy struggle." But he also knows there is no other way forward. "Muslim societies, in Algeria, in Pakistan, will only come of age when they are willing to challenge fundamentalism" and reclaim their "rational, secular, golden past."

I try to fathom the depth of the determination shared with me by people like Cherifa Kheddar and Jamil Omar and so many others who have stood against fundamentalist terrorism even when the world was not watching. Afghan women's rights defender Mary Akrami puts this into words: "I just say that one day I came to this world. One day I'm going. I'm sure that if something happened to me, after a few days people will forget me." Sadly, she may be right.

I think of all of those who have died defying extremism without receiving international fanfare and accolades. Or those whose stories fill these pages and have passed away since I began my research, like Rafi Peer Theatre Workshop director Faizan Peerzada, who was unexpectedly felled by a heart attack in Lahore in December 2012, or nurse Malika Rouabah, who died alone in Blida at the beginning of 2012, after almost fifteen years as a paraplegic. These losses are distilled in a poem by the Algerian writer Lazhari Labter, an extract of which was published by RAFD in the program for its International Women's Day event on March 8, 2005:

> *You will ask yourself . . .*
> *Why did they die*
> *All those dead that you know*
> *And also all those dead*
> *That you had never seen . . .*
> *You will go from cemetery to cemetery*
> *You will bow before the graves of friends*
> *And also of those nameless dead*
> *You will speak to them*
> *And you will say . . .*

Why did you die?
And it is the wind that will answer you
By blowing harder
And harder still.[8]

As I have written this book, I have found myself going figuratively from cemetery to cemetery, from the Triangle of Death to Ground Zero, bowing before the graves of so many as I lean over my laptop. I have tried to speak to them, as Labter describes it, late at night when their fates kept me awake, tried to understand why and how they died, who was responsible, and who tried to stop it. I think I have learned much toward an answer to these questions, about how we could better go about preventing any more from joining the dead that we know and the dead that we have never seen. But sometimes, the scale of the losses, the size of the ongoing challenge, makes me feel as if it is the wind that has answered me, by blowing harder and harder still.

Yet, I feel no right to despair when those who are and have been on the frontlines do not give up. I asked many I met if they were optimistic about the fight against Muslim fundamentalism now. I loved Aziz Smati's answer: "I hope so." In his wheelchair, he remained defiant. "During ten years they didn't succeed, so I don't think they ever will. Algeria will never become an Islamist country." To prove the point, Aziz kept producing culture even after being shot for doing so.

Like Aziz Smati, my father drew optimism from the fact that Algeria did not collapse into an Islamic state in the 1990s. "The fundamentalists," he told me, looking far ahead at their prospects for political survival, ultimately "are condemned to disappear because they oppose not only hope but also love."[9] Even after illness attacked Mahfoud Bennoune's voice, he continued giving public lectures, explaining what fundamentalists were doing to his beloved Algeria, touring the United States with the Quakers' Africa Peace Tour, telling students to sit close and keeping his water bottle at the ready. Even when he could barely speak, he would not stop speaking out.

Franco-Algerian community organizer Mimouna Hadjam, who works in a tough Parisian *banlieue* troubled by growing fundamentalism, is similarly resolute. She feels that those progressives who oppose Muslim fundamentalism must simply keep working, must "explain, write, testify and get others to do so. What else can we do? They are much stronger than we are." Though she claims she is a prudent pessimist, she ultimately concedes, "I still have hope anyway."

Doaa Abdelaal writes to me from Cairo shortly after the June 2012 election of Mohamed Morsi as the first Muslim Brotherhood president of Egypt. She says she is "still optimistic although I had some down moments in the last couple of months. As I keep saying, as a researcher I am living my golden moments, but as an activist, I am living in very dark ones." Still, she cannot resist finishing her sentence with this clause: "And I keep smiling."

Mahnaz Afkhami thinks the jury is still out: "Sometimes, it looks like we're wining. Sometimes it looks like we're losing." There are positive developments, such as when a secular, liberal, centrist party trounces the Muslim Brotherhood in Libya's first post-Qaddafi parliamentary election in July 2012.[10] And, at the end of 2012, the Sixth Abu Dhabi Film Festival is full of films "attacking religious extremism": from Algeria's *Perfumes of Algiers* to the Kuwaiti movie *Tora Bora*, made by director Walid Al Awadi, who openly announces, "I am against the Taliban . . . and I believe in a secular state."[11] But sometimes the victories seem few and far between. Nevertheless, an Afghan woman activist, who preferred to retain anonymity due to her security problems, gives me what I tell her is the single best answer to the question about prospects.

"Optimism is key to survival."

CODA: THE IMAM COUGHS

The Karachi Marriott features a mosque right at the entrance. When I walk by during Friday services, the imam coughs repeatedly into the loudspeaker while giving his sermon. I am struck by the importance of the cough. It is a very human reminder of the temporal. The imam coughs. It has become my motto. Admitting the human source of what we do and choose, admitting our own fallibility and flaws and those of our constructs, being open to questioning—all are essential to fighting fundamentalism. So I must concede that there are things I may have gotten wrong in this book, or that diverse readers may disagree with. I cough too. At the very least, my aim has been to ask people to rethink this issue by transmitting voices they may not have heard before.

There are, however, things about which I am certain.

One is that women's rights must be the nonnegotiable centerpiece of the struggle against fundamentalism. They are not an acceptable bargaining chip in the "war on terror" or any other pseudoattempt to contain jihadism. To unpack the heart of that ideology, one must be absolutely committed to women's full equality and not tolerant of an exemption for "Muslim women" from the human category that includes everyone else. "There should be no discrimination in the Mosques of God," exclaims Nigerien Haja Salamatou Traoré, who has made the pilgrimage to Mecca. In Senegal, Dr. Fatou Sow correctly points out that the process of achieving equality between the sexes is at the heart of political debates about the transformation of contemporary societies.[12]

Another thing of which I am certain is that time is of the essence.

In October 2011, I spent a day with two young Tunisians meeting other women activists in Sfax, an industrial town three hours southeast of Tunis. Though we were there to talk about the Constituent Assembly elections, the topic we heard the most about—from women trade unionists, businesswomen, women candidates—was the rising threat of fundamentalism since the revolution. In the car on the way back to Tunis late at night, as I talked this over with my two young traveling companions, the voice of Egyptian superstar Mohamed Mounir burst out of the radio with one of my favorite songs, *"Alli Soutak."* The song is from the soundtrack of the greatest antifundamentalist musical of all time, *Al Maseer* (Destiny), directed by the late Egyptian auteur Youssef Chahine. The 1997 film tells the story of Andalusian Muslim philosopher Ibn Rushd's twelfth-century struggle against the Muslim extremists of his day.

In the best scene, musicians and dancers, who used to be friends with a young man who has been brainwashed by a fundamentalist cult, try to win him back. While men and women dance together, the women's hair swinging freely, Mohamed Mounir's character, Marwan the

Bard, sings: "Raise your voice. Raise your voice in song. Singing is still possible."[13] Still possible, for now. Marwan the Bard will be murdered by fundamentalists before film's end, though his words live on, as relevant now as in twelfth-century Andalusia.

Mohamed Boukhobza, the prominent Algerian sociologist whose terrible murder twenty years ago preceded the fateful knock on my father's door by one sad week, knew just how high the stakes were. If a culture of progress is not allowed to develop and flourish, if states do not enable such development, religion will fill the space. Boukhobza stressed that the problem was not religion per se, but rather its use for ideological ends. Ultimately, he believed there was a fork in the road that had to be faced, with no intermediate alternative available. In his last interview, reprinted the day after he was killed in 1993 by Algeria's fundamentalists, he insisted: "The choice is simple: modernity or death."[14]

Boukhobza's final message is also a reminder of the need to sometimes be uncompromising in facing off with fundamentalism. The attempts by some governments, by some academics, by some in civil society, and even by some Western feminists to accommodate some Muslim fundamentalist views about things like equality and the role of religion in public life help advance Islamist goals and undermine the people whose efforts are chronicled in this book.

When I returned to Algiers in November 2012 on my last research trip for this book, I was able to locate some of the final writings of Salah Chouaki, a left-wing educator gunned down by the fundamentalists in 1994. He was crystal clear about the danger of such concessions. Back in March 1993, just a few months before Boukhobza's assassination and eighteen months before his own, Chouaki published an article that is as pertinent today as the day he wrote it. It is entitled "Compromise with Political Islam is Impossible." According to Chouaki, "there is an unresolvable contradiction between support for the idea of a modern society and the belief . . . that it is possible to 'domesticate' the totalitarian monster of fundamentalism. . . . The best way to defend Islam is to put it out of the reach of all political manipulation. . . . The best way to defend the modern state is to put it out of the reach of all exploitation of religion for political ends."[15]

One more thing about which I am entirely certain is that speaking out in support of those in this book who today continue to express views similar to Chouaki's is a moral imperative. I think of words written by O.Z. in the rubble of Tahar Djaout Press House in Algiers on the night of February 11, 1996. I carry my copy of that day's papers with me now as a reminder of what is at stake, and of the need for courage. "Hush up the truth, hush up the crime," O.Z. wrote in figurative "red ink," and "you give fundamentalism tremendous power, the power of eradicating a people in silence."[16] Whether the eradication is physical (as in the case of Algeria in the 1990s, Afghanistan, Iran, and elsewhere) or cultural, or social, whether it is eradication of artists and their work, cultural space, journalists and their writing, or women's freedom, at the end of this journey O.Z.'s warning written that fateful day rings in my ears.

The time to raise our voices is now.

Notes

NOTE: Unless otherwise indicated, all translations of cited materials were done by the author.

INTRODUCTION

1. "Homage à Djilali Liabes: Des temoignages émouvants," *El Watan*, March 18, 2003, 5.

2. This title denotes religious scholars or leaders; sometimes it is an honorific and on other occasions it indicates that the person has completed advanced studies of Islam.

3. "Libye: Des mausolées musulmans détruits par des islamistes," *Le Monde*, August 25, 2012, http://www.lemonde.fr/libye/article/2012/08/25/libye-des-mausolees-musulmans-detruits-par-des-islamistes_1751418_1496980.html.

4. Rick Gladstone, "Anti-American Protests Flare Beyond the Mideast," *New York Times*, September 14, 2012, http://www.nytimes.com/2012/09/15/world/middleeast/anti-american-protests-over-film-enter-4th-day.html.

5. Mehdi Bsikri, "Tentatives de marche avortées à Alger," *El Watan*, September 15, 2012, 2.

6. Faycal Métaoui, "Yasmina Khadra: La violence est la faillite du bon sens," *El Watan Weekend*, September 28, 2012, 6.

7. "Mali Islamist Radicals Raze more Timbuktu Shrines," Canadian Broadcasting Corporation News (CBC News), July 2, 2012, http://www.cbc.ca/news/arts/story/2012/07/02/mali-timbuktu-unesco.html.

8. Faith Karimi, "Fear Grows as Mali Extremists Compile List of Unmarried Mothers," CNN.com, October 13, 2012, http://www.cnn.com/2012/10/12/world/africa/mali-women-lists/index.html?utm_source=feedburner&utm_medium=feed&utm_campaign=Feed%3A+rss%2Fcnn_world+(RSS%3A+World).

9. "Destruction of Ancient Timbuktu Shrines a 'War Crime,'" Al Arabiya News, July 1, 2012, http://english.alarabiya.net/articles/2012/07/01/223879 .html.

10. Amel Blidi, "Le Mali est le banc d'essai de la stratégie à long terme d'AQMI," *El Watan*, August 29, 2012, 2.

11. "Mali Jihadists Threaten North Africa," UPI, July 9, 2012, http://www.upi .com/Top_News/Special/2012/07/09/Mali-jihadists-threaten-North-Africa/ UPI-11941341858614/.

12. Amie Ferris Rotman, "Bomb Kills Head of Women's Affairs in Afghan East," Reuters, July 13, 2012, http://www.reuters.com/article/2012/07/13/ us-afghanistan-women-assassination-idUSBRE86C0JO20120713.

13. Tom Peter, "Afghanistan's Test Case: NATO Handover in Laghman Province," *Christian Science Monitor*, July 19, 2011, http://www.cs monitor.com/World/Asia-South-Central/2011/0719/Afghanistan-s-test- case-NATO-handover-in-Laghman-Province.

14. Gilles Dorronsoro, *Waiting for the Taliban in Afghanistan* (Washington, DC: Carnegie Endowment for International Peace, 2012).

15. "FAQ," 2 Million Friends for Peace in Afghanistan, accessed October 4, 2012, http://www.2millionfriends.org/#!faq.

16. "Pakistan: Murder of School Headmaster and Human Rights Defender Mr Zarteef Afridi," Front Line Defenders, December 16, 2011, http://www .frontlinedefenders.org/node/16917.

17. Salman Rashid, "Zarteef Afridi: Hero of Jamrud," *Express Tribune*, December 9, 2011, http://tribune.com.pk/story/304186/zarteef-afridi-hero-of-jamrud.

18. "If Malala Survives, We Will Target Her Again: Taliban," *Express Tribune*, October 9, 2012, http://tribune.com.pk/story/449070/national-peace- award-winner-malala-yousufzai-injured-in-firing-incident/.

19. "Malala, militante de 14 ans, survit par miracle à une attaque des talibans," *Le Monde*, October 9, 2012, http://www.lemonde.fr/asie-pacifique/article/ 2012/10/09/malala-militante-de-14-ans-survit-par-miracle-a-une-attaque- des-talibans_1772632_3216.html.

20. "Qatar Embraces Wahhabism," Middle East Online, December 18, 2011, http://www.middle-east-online.com/english/?id=49555.

21. "Des islamistes menacent des athlètes des JO," Associated Press, August 14, 2012, http://www.20min.ch/ro/news/monde/story/Des-islamistes-menacent- des-athletes-des-JO-28414758.

22. Cited in Karima Bennoune, "S.O.S. Algeria: Women's Human Rights Under Siege," in *Faith and Freedom: Women's Human Rights in the Muslim World*, ed. Mahnaz Afkhami (Syracuse: Syracuse University Press, 1995), 184, 201.

23. Marieme Hélie-Lucas, "What Is Your Tribe? Women's Struggles and the Construction of Muslimness," in *Dossier 23–24*, ed. Harsh Kapoor (London: Women Living Under Muslim Laws (WLUML), 2001), 49, 54.

24. Hassan Rachik, "National & Global Islam: The Use and Meaning of the Notion of 'Moroccan Islam'" (paper presented at "From Colonial Histories to Post-Colonial Societies: Placing the Maghrib at the Center of the Twentieth Century," University of Michigan, Ann Arbor, April 6–7, 2009), 13.

25.   WLUML, *Knowing Our Rights: Women, Family, Laws and Custom in the Muslim World* (London: WLUML, 2006), 28.

26.   Sheik Yusuf al-Qaradawi, "Homosexuals Should Be Punished like Fornicators but their Harm Is Less When Not Done in Public," Al Jazeera TV, June 5, 2006, available at Memri TV Monitoring Project, http://web.archive.org/web/20061002054147/http://www.memritv.org/Transcript.asp?p1=1170.

27.   Salma El Wardany, "U.S. Embassy Calls Out Muslim Brotherhood Over Twitter," Bloomberg News, September 13, 2012, http://www.businessweek .com/news/2012-09-13/u-dot-s-dot-embassy-calls-out-muslim-brotherhood-over-twitter.

28.   William Wan, "Muslim Brotherhood Officials Aim to Promote Moderate Image in Washington Visit," *Washington Post*, April 3, 2012, A1.

29.   Monica Marks, "Can Islamism and Feminism Mix?" *New York Times*, October 26, 2011, http://www.nytimes.com/2011/10/27/opinion/can-islam ism-and-feminism-mix.html.

30.   Tariq Ramadan, "Whither the Muslim Brotherhood?" *New York Times*, February 8, 2011, http://www.nytimes.com/2011/02/09/opinion/09iht-edrama dan09.html?Pagewanted=all.

31.   Sally Steenland, "Setting the Record Straight on Sharia: An Interview with Intisar Rabb," Center for American Progress, March 8, 2011, http:// www.americanprogress.org/issues/religion/news/2011/03/08/9263/setting-the-record-straight-on-sharia/.

32.   "Protesters Descend on Ground Zero for Anti-Mosque Demonstration," CNN International, June 7, 2010, http://edition.cnn.com/2010/US/06/06/ new.york.ground.zero.mosque/index.html.

33.   Ron Scherer, "Is New York Cabbie Stabbing Result of 'Anti-Muslim Hysteria?'" *Christian Science Monitor*, August 26, 2010, http://www.csmonitor .com/USA/Society/2010/0826/Is-New-York-cabbie-stabbing-result-of-anti-Muslim-hysteria.

34.   Alan M. Dershowitz, *Why Terrorism Works: Understanding the Threat* (New Haven, CT: Yale University Press, 2002).

35.   See, e.g., discussion of this issue in Steve Hendricks, *A Kidnapping in Milan: The CIA on Trial* (New York: W. W. Norton, 2010).

36.   Jeanne Favret-Saada, "La liberté d'expression comme ressource terroriste," *ResPUBLICA*, September 21, 2012, http://www.gaucherepublicaine.org/ respublica/la-liberte-dexpression-comme-ressource-terroriste/4952.

37.   See the extensive documentation of this phenomenon in Meredith Tax, *Double Bind: The Muslim Right, the Anglo-American Left and Universal Human Rights* (New York: Centre for Secular Space, 2012).

38.   See Richard Kerbaj, "Amnesty International Is 'Damaged' by Taliban Link," *Sunday Times*, February 7, 2010, http://www.thesundaytimes.co.uk/sto/news/ world_news/article197042.ece. Amnesty International's official response to these concerns is found in Claudio Cordone, "Amnesty International Response to the Sunday Times," Amnesty International, http://livewire.amnesty .org/2010/02/14/amnesty-international-response-to-the-sunday-times/.

39.   CagePrisoners, the organization with which he works, defends the rights only

of detainees in the context of the "War on Terror," including many Salafi jihadists convicted in fair trials. The organization also offers a platform for the most extreme views. For example, it had invited Anwar al-Awlaki to address its Ramadan fundraising dinner in 2008 and 2009. See Fahad Ansari, "Beyond Guantanamo—Review of CagePrisoners Fundraising Dinner," CagePrisoners, http://www.cageprisoners.com/articles.php?id=30493. The Quilliam Foundation has charged that CagePrisoners has "[a]cted as a conduit between convicted extremists such as Abu Hamza [a well-known Al Qaeda and Armed Islamic Group supporter then imprisoned in the U.K. and since extradited to the U.S.] and their supporters and sympathizers outside prison. . . ." James Brandon, *Unlocking Al-Qaeda: Islamist Extremism in British Prisons* (London: Quilliam Foundation, 2009).

40. On the significance of this network of bookshops, see Chetan Bhatt, "The 'British Jihad' and the Curves of Religious Violence," *Ethnic and Racial Studies 33* (2010): 49–50.

41. The *Guardian* reported in November 2001 that a "photocopy of a money transfer in sterling asking a London branch of the Pakistani firm Union Bank to credit an account in Karachi held by a man named Moazzam Begg" was among the documents discovered when "a secret toxins and explosives laboratory operated by Arab fighters at an al-Qa'ida military training camp near the eastern Afghan city of Jalalabad" was raided during the U.S. invasion of Afghanistan. See Rory McCarthy, "Inside Bin Laden's Chemical Bunker," *Guardian*, November 17, 2001, 3. Such reports should at least be investigated.

42. *Global Petition to Amnesty International: Restoring the Integrity of Human Rights, Human Rights for All*, February 13, 2010, http://www.human-rights-for-all.org/spip.php?article15.

43. Claudio Cordone, "Amnesty International's response to 'The Global Petition to Amnesty International, Restoring the Integrity of Human Rights,'" Amnesty International, February 28, 2010, http://www.human-rights-for-all .org/IMG/pdf/Claudioletter-2.pdf.

44. Shaykh Anwar al-Awlaki, "May Our Souls Be Sacrificed For You!" *Al Qaeda Inspire*, summer 2010, http://azelin.files.wordpress.com/2010/06/aqap-inspire-magazine-volume-1-uncorrupted.pdf.

45. Brian Stelter, "Cartoonist in Hiding After Death Threats," *New York Times*, September 17, 2010, A14.

46. See, e.g., http://salsa.democracyinaction.org/o/1170/images/WORLD_CANT_WAIT-1.pdf.

47. Karima Bennoune, "Why I Spoke Out on Anwar al-Awlaki," *Guardian*, November 19, 2010, http://www.guardian.co.uk/commentisfree/cifamerica/2010/nov/19/human-rights-usa?INTCMP=ILCNE TTXT3487.

48. "Al Aulaqi v. Panetta: Synopsis," Center for Constitutional Rights, accessed September 4, 2012, http://www.ccrjustice.org/targetedkillings.

49. Kavita M. Ramdas, "Violence Against Women Is No Rationale for Military Violence," *Huffington Post*, August 5, 2010, http://www.huffingtonpost.com/kavita-n-ramdas/violence-against-women-is_b_672387.html.

50.   Salah Chouaki, "Quels sont les enjeux de la crise?," *Le Matin*, August 31, 1994, 6.

51.   "Islamic Scholar Tariq Ramadan on the Growing Mideast Protest and 'Islam & the Arab Awakening,'" *Democracy Now.org*, September 13, 2012, http://www .democracynow.org/2012/9/13/islamic_scholar_tariq_ramadan_on_the.

52.   Liess Boukra, *Le Djihadisme: l'Islam à l'épreuve de l'Histoire* (Algiers: Les éditions APIC, 2009), 255.

53.   Ahmed Rashid, *Taliban: Militant Islam, Oil and Fundamentalism in Central Asia* (New Haven, CT: Yale University Press, 2001), 129–30.

54.   M.B., "RAFD: Rassemblement sur le lieu de l'attentat," *El Watan*, February 4, 1995, 2.

CHAPTER ONE

1.   "Pakistan Security Report 2010," Pak Institute for Peace Studies, January 2011.

2.   Khadija Ghazi, "Bomb blasts are killing the culture," *All Voices*, November 23, 2008, http://www.allvoices.com/contributed-news/1857453-bomb-blasts-are-killing-the-culture.

3.   "Pakistan Arts-Lovers Defy Taliban Stage Fright," One Minute World News: BBC News Online, July 27, 2009, http://news.bbc.co.uk/2/hi/south_ asia/8170803.stm.

4.   Sonya Rehman, "When All Hell Broke Loose at the World Performing Arts Festival," *Sonya Rehman's Archive*, November 27, 2008, http:// sonyarehman.wordpress.com/2008/11/27/when-all-hell-broke-lose-at-the-world-performing-arts-festival.

5.   Afnan Khan, "Performing Arts Festival Cancelled Due to Lack of Security," *Daily Times*, November 13, 2009, http://www.dailytimes.com.pk/default .asp?page=2009%5C11%5C13%5C story_13-11-2009_pg7_28.

6.   In June 2012, allegations of financial corruption were made against the Rafi Peer Theatre Workshop by a newspaper called *Pakistan Today*, reporting on their loss of USAID funding for a Pakistani version of *Sesame Street*. The organization denied the charges and threatened to sue the paper for defamation. See Fasih Ahmed, "Pakistan Loses Urdu Language Sesame Street," *Newsweek*, June 18, 2012, http://www.thedailybeast.com/newsweek/2012/06/17/ pakistan-loses-urdu-language-sesame-street.html. Whatever the truth of these allegations, which remain unverified, this in no way calls into question the artistic merit of RPTW's work under very difficult circumstances. Moreover, some Pakistani commentators have suggested that USAID raised these concerns to get out of its contract with the theatre company. See "USAID Sullies Sesame Street, Henson Family and Rafi Peer Theater & Creates a Diplomatic Nightmare for the State Department across Art for Children World," posting by Jawad, August 18, 2012, http://alchemya.com/wordpress2/2012/08/ usaid-the-real-case-against-rafi-peer-theater/.

7.   Al-Muhajabah, "Fiqh of Music," *Al-Muhajabah Islamic Pages*, http://www .muhajabah.com/music-fiqh.htm.

8. Mufti Ebrahim Desai, "Is it Permissible to Listen to Islamic Songs with the Sound of Music in the Background?" Muslim Salvation Organization, November 15, 2010, http://muslimsalvationorganization.webs.com/apps/forums/topics/show/3750230-all-kinds-of-musical-instrument-and-drum-including.

9. For the definitive account of the Danish cartoons of the Prophet Muhammad, see Jeanne Favret-Saada, *Comment produire une crise mondiale avec douze petits dessins* (Paris: Les Prairies Ordinaires, 2007).

10. Riaz Khan, "Pakistani Protests of Anti-Muslim Film Turn Deadly," Associated Press, September 21, 2012, http://news.yahoo.com/pakistani-protests-anti-muslim-film-turn-deadly-152509346.html.

11. Michael Georgy and Qasim Nauman, "Pakistani Girls Defy Taliban School Bombings," Reuters, November 16, 2011, http://www.reuters.com/article/2011/11/16/us-pakistan-taliban-schools-idUSTRE7AF0GP20111116.

12. See Omer Alvie, "Drama Queens," *Olive Ream*, April 29, 2007, http://www.theoliveream.com/2007/04/29/drama-queens/.

13. "Punjab Minister Zill-e-Huma Shot Dead," *The News*, February 21, 2007, http://www.thenews.com.pk/TodayPrintDetail.aspx?ID=6000&Cat=13&dt=2/21/2007.

14. Shahid Nadeem, "Bulha," in *Selected Plays* (New York: Oxford University Press, 2009), 270.

15. Ibid., 251.

16. Rina Saeed Khan, *Friday Times* (Lahore), July 4, 2003.

17. "Bulha," 268.

18. "Mujahid," Ajoka Theatre Online, http://www.ajoka.org.pk/ajoka/mujahid.asp.

19. Hamid Baroudi, *Caravan to Baghdad* (Hoggar Music, 1991, cassette tape) (translated from Arabic by Samia Benkherroubi and Karima Bennoune).

20. Louisa Ait-Hamou, "Women's Struggle against Muslim Fundamentalism in Algeria: Strategies or a Lesson for Survival?" in *Warning Signs of Fundamentalism*, ed. Ayesha Imam (London: WLUML, 2004), 117.

21. "Middle East, North Africa: 1990–1999," Free Musepedia: History of Music censorship, January 1, 2001, http://www.freem_use.org/sw20664.asp.

22. H.B., "Aziz Smati victim d'un attentat," *El Watan*, February 15, 1994, 3.

23. Redouane Zizi, "Aziz Smati victim d'un attentat," *Le Matin*, February 15, 1994, 1.

24. The video for the song *"Ouech dek yal qadi"* is available at http://imow.org/wpp/stories/viewStory?language=fr&storyid=1328.

25 See Abderrahmane Hakkar, "Pour que nul l'oublie: Les deux soeurs Rachida et Houria Hammadi sont mortes pour l'Algérie," *Le Journal des Infos*, March 20, 2010, http://lavoixdesmartyrsdelaplume.over-blog.com/article-pour-que-nul-n-oublie-les-deux-soeurs-rachida-et-houria-hammadi-sont-mortes-pour-l-algerie-47049852.html. There are divergent accounts of this event, but this one seems to be the most accurate and complete. Houria's nickname was Meriem.

26. Mustapha Benfodil, *Zarta!* (Algiers: Barzakh, 2000), 208.

27. Ghania Lassal, "71,500 diplômés ont quitée le pays: Fuite des cerveaux," *El Watan*, April 18, 2011, 4 (citing the research of Ahmed Guessoum).

28. Asma Guenifi, *Je ne pardonne pas aux assassins de mon frère* (Paris: Riveneuve éditions, 2011), 51.

29. "Last Words of a Doomed Editor," *Independent*, February 1, 1995.

30. "Je Rêve, Rêvons Ensemble d'une Algérie Nouvelle," *The Algerian Speaker*, http://www.kassaman.com/article-je-reve-revons-ensemble-d-une-algerie-nouvelle-74319068.html.

31. David Heiden, "Literacy and Public Health," *Western Journal of Medicine* 176, no. 3 (May 2002): 216.

32. "Obituary: Mohamed Said [*sic*] Barre," *Independent*, January 3, 1995.

33. See, e.g., Abdisalam Issa-Salwe, *Cold War Fallout: Boundary Politics and Conflict in the Horn of Africa* (London: Haan Publishing, 2000).

34. UNESCO, *Education for All Global Monitoring Report 2006: Literacy for Life* (Paris: UNESCO, 2005), 196–97. According to UNESCO, the literacy rate increased to 20 percent after the first year of the campaign; Professor Ahmed believes it soared much higher by campaign's end.

35. See Writenet, *Somalia: Civil War, Intervention and Withdrawal* 1990–1995 (Geneva: UNHCR, 1995).

36. Mohammed Ibrahim, "No Music on Radios in Somalia, Militants Say," *New York Times*, April 14, 2012, A15.

37. Said Salah Ahmed, "When the Art Died," unpublished poem, 2008 (translated from Somali by Said Salah Ahmed).

38. Lee Ferran, "Theater Explosion Kills Several in Mogadishu," ABC News, April 4, 2012, http://abcnews.go.com/Blotter/al-shabaab-claims-theater-explosion-kills-mogadishu/story?id=16070499.

39. Ricahrd Burton, *First Footsteps in East Africa* (New York: Dover Publications, 1987), 81.

40. This quote, attributed to Canadian writer Margaret Laurence, is cited in Mohamed Diriye Abdullahi, *Culture and Customs of Somalia* (Westport, CT: Greenwood Press, 2001), 75.

41. "Somalia: 'Planned Infiltration' of Security Forces by Al Shabaab—Sources," *Garowe Online*, September 27, 2012, http://allafrica.com/stories/201209270688.html.

CHAPTER TWO

1. "Death toll rises in Karachi suicide attack," CNN World, December 28, 2009, http://articles.cnn.com/2009-12-28/world/pakistan.blasts_1_ashura-imam-hussein-shiites?_s=PM:WORLD.

2. Mohammad Farooq, "Karachi Killings: Pakistan's Largest City Reels after 51 Killed in 5 Days," *Huffington Post*, October 10, 2012, http://www.huffingtonpost.com/2010/10/20/karachi-killings-pakistan_n_769259.html.

3. "Karachi CID Building Hit by Bomb and Gun Attack," BBC News South Asia, November 11, 2010, http://www.bbc.co.uk/news/world-south-asia-11737402.

4. See, e.g., Saeed Shah, "Mainstream Pakistan Organisations Applaud Killing of Salmaan Taseer," *Guardian*, January 5, 2011, 17.

5. Richard Covington, "Lost & Found: Ancient Gold Artifacts from Afghanistan Hidden for More than a Decade Dazzle in New Exhibition," *Smithsonian*, http://www.smithsonianmag.com/arts-culture/lost-and-found-afghan .html.

6. Nancy Hatch Dupree, "Museum Under Siege," *Archaeology*, April 20, 1998, http://www.archaeology.org/online/features/afghan/.

7. Frederick Hiebert, *Afghanistan: Hidden Treasures from the National Museum, Kabul* (Washington, DC: National Geographic, 2008), 37.

8. Dupree, "Museum Under Siege."

9. Ibid.

10. Amir Shah, "Taliban: Ancient Buddha Statues to Be Destroyed," Associated Press, February 26, 2001, http://www.beliefnet.com/Faiths/Islam/2001/03/ Taliban-Ancient-Buddha-Statues-To-Be-Destroyed.aspx?p=1.

11. "Ancient Buddha Statues Smashed in Afghanistan," CBC News, March 3, 2011, http://www.cbc.ca/news/world/story/2001/03/03/buddha_statues 010303.html.

12. Francesco Francioni and Federico Lenzerini, "The Destruction of the Buddhas of Bamiyan and International Law," *European Journal of International Law* 14, no. 4 (2003): 619.

13. "Ancient Buddha Statues Smashed in Afghanistan."

14. Paul Watson, "Taliban Took an Ax to Antiquities," *Los Angeles Times*, November 22, 2001, A, 1, 1.

15. "Ancient Buddha Statues Smashed in Afghanistan."

16. "US Grants $5m for Expansion of Afghan Museum," Tolo News, March 15, 2011, http://afghanistannewscenter.com/news/2011/march/mar162011 .html#9.

17. Omara Khan Massoudi, "Who Is the Museum Director?" in *Kabul: A City at Work*, http://www.kabulatwork.tv/chapter/masters-and-servants/the-museum-director-pages/.

18. Ibid.

19. Paul Clammer, *Afghanistan* (Footscray, Australia: Lonely Planet, 2007), 134.

20. Suheir Daoud, "The Price of Teaching Satrapi in the Palestinian Occupied Territories" (paper presented at "The Left in Palestine/The Palestinian Left," Brunei Gallery, School of Oriental and African Studies, London, February 2010); Suheir Daoud, "Teaching Satrapi in the Palestinian Occupied Territories," *Al-Jabha Haifa*, February 21, 2010 [Arabic].

CHAPTER THREE

1. Comment made at "Terrorism & War" (Brecht Forum Event), New York, May 15, 2003.

2. "Update Sudan: Flogging Sentence Dropped and Fine Paid against Hussein's Will," WLUML, July 9, 2009, http://www.wluml.org/node/5429.

3. Aïssatou Cissé, "Les Histoires de Nafi et de Khadija: Bande dessinée!" WLUML, June 2011, http://www.wluml.org/node/7264.

4. Souleymane Faye, "Percée des femmes à l'Assemblée nationale," Inter Press Service, July 12, 2012, http://ipsinternational.org/fr/_note.asp?id news=7122.

5. On foreign funding see, e.g., Erin Augis, "Jambaar or Jumbax-out? How Sunnite Women Negotiate Power and Belief in Orthodox Islamic Femininity," in *New Perspectives on Islam in Senegal: Conversion, Migration, Wealth, Power and Femininity*, eds. Mamadou Diouf and Mara Leichtman (New York: Palgrave Macmillan, 2009), 215.

6. "Female Genital Mutilation, Fact Sheet No. 214," World Health Organization, February 2012, http://www.who.int/mediacentre/factsheets/fs241/en/.

7. "Female Genital Mutilation and Other Harmful Practices, Prevalence of Female Genital Mutilation," World Health Organization, accessed August 24, 2012, http://www.who.int/reproductivehealth/topics/fgm/prevalence/en/index.html.

8. "23 year old Woman Sentenced to Death by Stoning for Adultery," African Centre for Justice and Peace Studies, July 13, 2012.

9. "Maldives Teenage Girl Faces Lashing for Pre-marital Sex," Agence France Presse, September 4, 2012, http://www.google.com/hostednews/afp/article/ALeqM5j2ri6fc78RW_SCBe-LoGTtpiHGfg?docId=CNG.4dcb93b63d1fec1c2743d9ba7e043b1b.981.

10. Feriel Lalami, *Les Algériennes contre le code de la famille* (Paris: Les Presses de Sciences Po, 2012).

11. Marieme Hélie-Lucas, "Bound and Gagged by the Family Code," in *Third World, Second Sex,* vol. 2, ed. Miranda Davies (London: Zed Press, 1987), 11.

12. "What Is Women Living Under Muslim Laws?" WLUML, http://www.wluml.org/node/5408.

13. Marieme Hélie-Lucas, "WLUML 'Heart and Soul,' Transcribed from the Plan of Action, Dhaka 1997," WLUML, http://www.wluml.org/sites/wluml.org/files/Heart%20and%20 Soul_Marieme%20Helie-Lucas.pdf.

14. Marieme Hélie-Lucas, "In the Name of Democracy—What Secularists and Women Have to Lose in the Tunisian Elections," Secularism is a Women's Issue, October 22, 2011, http://www.siawi.org/article2624.html.

15. Marieme Hélie-Lucas, "Honour the Dissenters," Secularism is a Women's Issue, October 10, 2012, http://www.siawi.org/article4176.html.

16. BAOBAB for Women's Human Rights, untitled informational pamphlet, *The Name*: *"BAOBAB for Women's Human Rights,"* 2.

17. Ayesha Imam, "Women's Reproductive and Sexual Rights and the Offense of Zina in Muslim Laws in Nigeria," in *Where Human Rights Begin: Health, Sexuality and Women in the New Millennium*, ed. Wendy Chavkin and Ellen Chesler (New Brunswick, NJ: Rutgers University Press, 2005), 65.

18. Gunnar J. Weimann, *Islamic Criminal Law in Northern Nigeria* (Amsterdam: Amsterdam University Press, 2010), 77.

19. Ayesha M. Imam, "Reaction to Whipping of Bariya Bagaza [*sic*]—BAOBAB," accessed October 8, 2012, http://www.presbyterian.ca/ministry/justice/urgent actions/urgentactionsarchives/bariya.

20. DIMOL, *Guide sur les Droits des Femmes et d'Enfants* 7 (2009).

21. Rukmini Callimachi, "In Niger, Child Marriage Rises Due to Hunger," Associated Press, September 16, 2012, http://news.yahoo.com/niger-child-marriage-rise-due-hunger-130108726.html.

22. Michelle Nicholas, "In high heels, headscarves, Afghan women protest harassment," Reuters, July 14, 2011, http://www.reuters.com/article/2011/07/14/us-afghanistan-women-protest-idUSTRE76D3WJ20110714.

23. For an Afghan critique of the "myth that there's a correlation between the hijab and a low incidence of sexual harassment," see Josh Shahryar, "The Myth of How the Hijab Protects Women against Sexual Assault," *Women Under Siege*, posting of September 6, 2012, http://www.womenundersiegeproject.org/blog/entry/the-myth-of-how-the-hijab-protects-women-against-sexual-assault

24. "Chay Magazine issues a call for submissions," WLUML, accessed August 24, 2012, http://www.wluml.org/node/4619.

25. Junaid Jahangir, "Pakistan, Islam and Homosexuality," *Chay Magazine*, May 8, 2009, http://www.chaymagazine.org/religion/173-pakistan-islam-and-homosexuality.

26. MH Tarrar, "The cure for what ails you," *Chay Magazine*, June 10, 2009, http://www.chaymagazine.org/homosexuality-2009-oct/193-the-cure-for-what-ails-you.

27. See Pakistan Penal Code (Act XLV of 1860), Article 377, http://www.pakistani.org/pakistan/legislation/1860/actXLVof1860.html.

28. Nicholas Kristof, "Bush and the UN Population Fund," *New York Times*, June 26, 2008, http://kristof.blogs.nytimes.com/2008/06/26/bush-and-the-un-population-fund/.

29. "Brave Saudi Arabian Woman Confronts Religious Police Officer Harassing Her," *Huffington Post*, May 25, 2012, http://www.huffingtonpost.com/2012/05/25/brave-saudi-woman-confronts-police_n_1546375.html.

30. "Saudi Police 'Stopped' Fire Rescue," BBC News Online, May 15, 2002, http://news.bbc.co.uk/2/hi/middle_east/1874471.stm.

31. Amnesty International, "Saudi Arabia: Flogging: 24 Filipino Workers, Names Unknown," AI Index: MDE 23/11/96, October 3, 1996, http://195.234.175.160/en/library/asset/MDE23/011/1996/en/135089d3-eadd-11dd-b22b-3f24cef8f6d8/mde230111996en.html.

32. Henry Steiner et al., *International Human Rights in Context Law, Politics, Morals* (Oxford: Oxford University Press, 2000), 615–18.

33. Thoraya Ahmed Obaid, Mills College (California), 114th Commencement Address, May 11, 2002, http://www.unfpa.org/public/news/pid/3746.

34. For further discussion, see "Saudi Time Bomb? Interview: Vali Nasr," *Frontline*, October 25, 2001, http://www.pbs.org/wgbh/pages/frontline/shows/saudi/interviews/nasr.html.

35. For a discussion of the issue without provision of specific statistics, see Council on Foreign Relations, *Terrorist Financing: Report of an Independent Task*

Force Sponsored by the Council on Foreign Relations (New York: Council on Foreign Relations, 2002). "For years, individuals and charities based in Saudi Arabia have been the most important source of funds for al-Qaeda; and for years, Saudi officials have turned a blind eye to this problem. . . . Saudi nationals and charities were previously the most important sources of funds for the [Afghan] mujahideen . . ." (p. 8). Ahmed Rashid documents official Saudi funding of the Afghan mujahideen to the tune of US$4 billion, as well as unofficial and "charity" assistance, followed by Saudi support of the Taliban, and separate streams of funding for madrasas in many locations. Rashid, *Taliban*, 197, 201, 90.

36. Mills College Commencement Address.

37. Albert Chaïbou, "Editorial: Pour un consensus fort," *Alternative*, September 2010, 1.

38. Mahfoud Bennoune, *Les Algériennes: Victimes d'une Société Néopatriarcale* (Algiers: Editions Marinoor, 1999).

39. Mona Eltahawy, "Why Do They Hate Us?" *Foreign Policy*, May/June 2012, http://www.foreignpolicy.com/articles/2012/04/23/why_do_they_hate_us.

40. Mills College Commencement Address.

41. Palestinian Centre for Human Rights, "Israeli Offensive on Gaza Stopped Following 8 Days of Attacks," November 22, 2012.

42. Taghreed El-Khodary, "For War Widows, Hamas Recruits an Army of Husbands," *New York Times*, October 30, 2008, A8.

43. Sarah A. Topol, "Gaza Summer Camp War," *Slate*, July 27, 2010, http://www.slate.com/articles/news_and_politics/dispatches/2010/07/gazas_summer_camp_war.html.

44. Ashley Bates, "Sorry, Hamas, I'm Wearing Blue Jeans," *Mother Jones*, December 16, 2010, http://www.motherjones.com/politics/2010/12/gaza-hamas-asma-al-ghoul.

45. See, e.g., "Gaza support for Hamas waning," PRI: *The World*, January 26, 2012, http://www.theworld.org/2010/01/gaza-support-for-hamas-waning/.

46. "At Rally in Gaza, PFLP Calls for Palestinian Unity," *Haaretz* (via DPA), December 11, 2010, http://www.haaretz.com/news/diplomacy-defense/at-rally-in-gaza-pflp-calls-for-palestinian-unity-1.330087.

47. A successful doctoral thesis by Sheikh Mohamed Mustapha Rashed at Al Azhar, one of the world centers of Islamic learning, made this very point. See Ahmad Alkhamisi, Facebook posting of May 10, 2012 (on file with the author).

48. Leila Boucli, "Voile: Symbole ou Acte Individuel," *Revue des droits de l'Enfant et de la Femme* (January–March 2008): 16.

49. Conseil Européens des Fatwas et de la Recherche, fatwa no. 6, in *Recueil de Fatwas, Série No. 1, Avis Juridiques Concernant Les Musulmans d'Europe* (2002), 74.

50. Joe Tacopino, "Al Jazeera Walk-out: Five Female Journalists Quit Over Offensive Remarks," *Daily News* (New York), June 1, 2010, http://articles.nydailynews.com/2010-06-01/news/27065937_1_al-jazeera-female-journalists-dress-code.

51. "New Egyptian TV Channel to Only Feature Fully Face-veiled Women," Ahram online, July 5, 2012, http://english.ahram.org.eg/News/46968.aspx.

52. Henry Meyer and Heidi Couch, "Harrods Sees profit from Islamic fashion as Qatar takes control," Bloomberg, July 12, 2010, http://www.bloomberg.com/news/2010-07-12/harrods-sees-profits-in-islamic-fashion-as-qatari-owners-showcase-abayas.html.

53. See, e.g., Chahdortt Djavann, *Bas les voiles!* (Paris: Gallimard, 2003).

54. See Joan Scott, "Symptomatic Politics: The Banning of Islamic Headscarves in French Public Schools," *French Politics, Culture & Society* 23, no. 3 (2005): 106; Joan Scott, *The Politics of the Veil* (Princeton, NJ: Princeton University Press, 2007); Joan Scott, Presentation at panel on "Veiling and the Law," Yale Law School (October 31, 2007) (notes on file with the author).

55. Wassila Tamzali, "Chères amies féministes françaises, je vous écris d'Alger," in *Revue des droits*, 18; Scott, *Politics of the Veil*, 18.

56. Adele Wilde-Blavatsky, "When Anti-Racism Becomes Anti-Woman: The "Privileging" of Race above Gender," *Huffington Post*, May 1, 2012, http://www.huffingtonpost.co.uk/adele-tomlin/race-above-gender-when-anti-racism-becomes-anti-woman_b_1460469.html.

57. Wassyla [sic] Tamzali, *Une femme en colère: Lettre d'Alger aux Européens désabusés* (Algiers: Éditions Sedia, 2010), 139.

58. Karima Bennoune, "Secularism and Human Rights: A Contextual Analysis of Headscarves, Religious Expression and Women's Equality Under International Law," *Columbia Journal of Transnational Law* 45, no. 2 (2007): 426.

59. Charlene Gubash, "As Morsi Takes Symbolic Oath, Many Fear the Islamization of Egyptian Society," NBC News, June 30, 2012, http://worldnews.nbcnews.com/_news/2012/06/29/12484697-as-morsi-takes-symbolic-oath-many-fear-the-islamization-of-egyptian-society?lite.

CHAPTER FOUR

1. Ghania Oukazi, "Hier, l'horreur," *El Watan*, February 12, 1996, 2.

2. "Omar Belhouchet, Algeria," International Press Institute, http://www.freemedia.at/index.php?id=517.

3. Ahmed Ancer, *Encre Rouge* (Algiers: Al Khabar, 2001), 156.

4. Omar Belhouchet, "Carnage à Alger," *El Watan*, February 12, 1996, 1.

5. Oukazi, "Hier, l'horreur."

6. A. L. Chabane, "Les autres victims de la barbarie," *El Watan*, February 12, 1996, 2.

7. S.B., "On ne combat pas le terrorisme avec des arbalettes," *El Watan*, February 12, 1996, 3.

8. Naïm B., "Un people face à la barbarie intégriste," *El Watan*, February 12, 1996, 4.

9. Salima Tlemcani, "Le 11 février 1996, une voiture piégée explose devant la maison de la presse d'Alger," *El Watan*, February 11, 2006, 2.

10. Oukazi, "Hier, l'horreur."

11. C.D., "Des décombres, de la poussière et des larmes . . .," *El Watan*, February 12, 1996, 3.

12. Oukazi, "Hier, l'horreur," 132.

13. "Protecting the Lives of Journalists," Office of the High Commissioner for Human Rights, http://www.ohchr.org/EN/NewsEvents/Pages/Protecting thelivesofjournalists.aspx.

14. Ancer, *Encre Rouge*, 152.

15. "Protecting the Lives of Journalists."

16. Nora Boustany, "Journalism: Algeria's Fatal Profession," *Washington Post*, March 23, 1995, A20.

17. See, e.g., F.M. "On Assassine nos mères," *Le Matin*, January 10, 1994 (copy on file with the author).

18. See, e.g., Sidi Aich, "Les citoyens disent non au terrorisme," *El Watan*, January 8, 1994, 1.

19. One of the court cases against Omar Belhouchet in the early nineties resulted from investigative reporting about Health Ministry mismanagement of public funds. Boustany, "Journalism: Algeria's Fatal Profession."

20. For example, it ran the annual report of Amnesty International on Algeria in full in its May 26, 1992, edition, followed by a heated debate about the report (see, e.g., H.N., "Qu'a fait Amnesty International?" *El Watan*, June 6, 1992, 9) and a rejoinder from the vice president of the Algerian section of AI, who would later become a critic himself. Daho Djerbal, "A propos de 'crimes à motivation politique,'" *El Watan*, June 6, 1992, 9.

21. Mahfoud Bennoune, "Lettre ouverte à Monsieur Anouar Haddam (Porte-parole de l'ex-FIS et des groupes terroristes aux États-Unis)," *El Watan*, September 16, 1995, part 1, 7; Mahfoud Bennoune, "Lettre ouverte à Monsieur Anouar Haddam (Porte-parole de l'ex-FIS et des groupes terroristes aux États-Unis)," *El Watan*, September 17, 1995, part 2, 7.

22. Mahfoud Bennoune, "Comment l'intégrisme a produit un terrorisme sans précédent," *El Watan*, November 6, 1994, part 1, 7; Mahfoud Bennoune, "Comment l'intégrisme a produit un terrorisme sans précédent," *El Watan*, November 7, 1994, part 2, 7; Mahfoud Bennoune, "Comment l'intégrisme a produit un terrorisme sans précédent," *El Watan*, November 8, 1994, part 3, 7.

23. Benfodil, *Zarta!*, 216.

24. Mustapha Benfodil, "Avec les semeurs de miel à Si Mustapha," *El Watan*, January 2, 2011, 6.

25. Mustapha Benfodil, *Les Borgnes* (2007 play; unpublished). This is taken from his English translation attached to the French-language version of his press release, "Parce que l'art n'est pas une langue de bois," WLUML, April 6, 2011, http://www.wluml.org/node/7090.

26. See Réseau Wassila, *Algérie: Le viol des femmes par les terroristes: Un crime contre l'humanité* (Algiers: SARP, 2005).

27. Mustapha Benfodil, "Because Art Is Free to Be Impolite," About.com, April 6, 2011, http://middleeast.about.com/od/algeria/qt/Mustafa-Benfodil-censorship.htm.

28. Rasha Salti, in conversation with Nancy Adajania, "Translation, Treason,

Transfiguration: The Biennale as an Agent of Political Consciousness," *Take on Art*, June 13, 2012, http://takeonart.wordpress.com/2012/06/13/translation-treason-transfiguration-the-biennale-as-an-agent-of-political-conscious ness/.

29. Salima Tlemcani, "Scènes d'horreur à Birtouta," *El Watan*, November 8, 1994, 1.

30. Salima Tlemcani, "Carnage de Birtouta, Deux members de la famille libérés," *El Watan*, November 9, 1994, 1.

31. This figure is confirmed in "Maghreb Egalité: Les Maghrébines entre violences symboliques et violences physiques: Algérie, Maroc, Tunisie," Collectif 95, Annual Report 1998–1999, http://www.retelilith.it/ee/host/maghreb/htm/magh.htm.

32. For testimonies from victims, see Zazi Sadou, "Le martyre des femmes violées," *El Watan*, June 24, 1995, 1.

33. Instead, they downplayed the issue or mentioned it in passing. In 1996, Human Rights Watch suggested that "common criminals" might be responsible. *World Report 1996: Algeria*, Human Rights Watch, http://www.hrw.org/reports/1996/WR96/MIDEAST-01.htm#P137_26320. Amnesty International regularly referred to "claims" about these rapes, while asserting government abuses as confirmed. In 2004, in a shadow report to the UN CEDAW committee, it noted that "*[h]undreds* of women and girls have *reportedly* been subjected to sexual violence by armed groups during the internal conflict." "Algeria: Briefing to the Committee on the Elimination of Discrimination Against Women," Amnesty International, December 2004, AI Index: MDE 28/011/2004, 12 (emphasis added).

34. "Group: Al-Qaida's N. African Arm Claims 32 Attacks," *Guardian*, September 1, 2011, http://www.guardian.co.uk/world/feedarticle/9826143.

35. Salima Tlemcani, "Deux bombes humaines pour ébranler l'Armée," *El Watan*, August 28, 2011, 3.

36. Khaled Ahmed, "Islamic Rejectionism and Terrorism," in *Religious Revivalism in South Asia*, ed. Imtiaz Alam (Lahore, Pakistan: Free Media Foundation, 2006), 45, 46.

37. Ahmed, "Islamic Extremism in Pakistan," in *Religious Revivalism in South Asia*, 51.

38. Ibid., 73.

39. Amir Mir, "Who Killed Syed Saleem Shahzad?" *Asia Times*, June 4, 2011, http://www.atimes.com/atimes/South_Asia/MF04Df03.html.

40. See Committee to Protect Journalists, "46 Journalists Killed in Pakistan since 1992/Motive Confirmed," accessed October 13, 2012, http://cpj.org/killed/asia/pakistan/.

41. For an example of this sort of argument, see e.g., Doug Bandow, "Terrorism: Why They Want to Kill Us," *Huffington Post*, July 1, 2010, http://www.huffingtonpost.com/doug-bandow/terrorism-why-they-want-t_b_631942.html.

42. Muqtida Mansoor, "The Fragile State," *The Daily Express* (Urdu), November 29, 2010 (translated from Urdu by Muqtida Mansoor).

43. Slimane Zéghidour, "Interview with Ali Ben [*sic*] Hadj: The Realm of Islam," *Politique Internationale* 49 (1990): 163.

44. Note that casualty figures cited are widely divergent. See "Chechens and Russians: Victories, Defeats, and Losses," Carnegie Endowment for International Peace, June 4, 2012, http://www.carnegieendowment.org/2010/06/04/chechens-and-russians-victories-defeats-and-losses/2h8a (citing a figure of about forty-eight thousand), and "Chechen Official Puts Death Toll for 2 Wars at up to 160,000," *New York Times*, August 16, 2005, http://www.nytimes.com/2005/08/15/world/europe/15iht-chech.html.

45. See Svante E. Cornell, "The War in Chechnya: A Regional Time Bomb," *Global Dialogues* 7, no. 3,4 (Summer/Autumn 2005): 1.

46. Svante Cornell, "The War Against Terrorism and the Conflict in Chechnya: A Case for Distinction," *The Fletcher Forum of World Affairs* 27, no. 2 (Summer/Fall 2003): 167, 179.

47. "'You Dress According to Their Rules': Enforcement of an Islamic Dress Code for Women in Chechnya," Human Rights Watch, March 10, 2011, 2, 5.

48. Anna Nemtsova, "I Do Not Want Independence," *Newsweek*, October 24, 2010, http://www.thedailybeast.com/newsweek/2010/10/24/ramzan-kadyrov-talks-about-chechnya-s-future.html.

49. "'You Dress According to Their Rules,'" 9–15.

50. Ibid., 7.

51. Cornell, "The War Against Terrorism and the Conflict in Chechnya," 2.

52. Ibid.

53. Maxim Stepenin and Marat Isaev, "Mufti became a citizen: Chechnya is now facing a civil war," *Kommersant*, June 17, 2000, http://www.memo.ru/hr/hotpoints/N-Caucas/ch99/000617/k0617b.htm (translated from Russian by Svetlana Svistunova).

54. Luiza Orazaeva and Elena Khrustaleva, "Mufti of Kabardino-Balkaria Anas Pshikhachev Struggled with Extremism and Illegal Persecution of Muslims," *Caucasian Knot*, December 17, 2010, http://www.eng.kavkaz-uzel.ru/articles/15577/.

55. Ibid.

56. "Grozny Residents Tell about Unknown Persons 'Hunting' for Girls without Headscarves," *Caucasian Knot*, June 9, 2010, http://www.eng.kavkaz-uzel.ru/articles/13583.

57. "'You Dress According to Their Rules,'" 7.

CHAPTER FIVE

1. Djermoune Nadir, "Chadli Bendjedid et l'impasse du capitalisme algérien," Europe Solidaire sans Frontières, October 9, 2012, http://www.europe-solidaire.org/spip.php?article26614.

2. Abed Charef, *Octobre: un chahut de gamins?* (Algiers: Lapohomic, 1990). See also *Cahier noir d'Octobre* (Algiers: Comité national contre la torture, 1989).

3. See "Maghreb Egalité: Les Maghrébines entre violences symboliques et violences physiques: Algérie, Maroc, Tunisie."

4. Hélie-Lucas, "What Is Your Tribe?"

5. Ibid.

6. See, e.g., Hassan Zenati, "Algerians Converge on Capital for Anti-Islamist Protest March," Agence France Presse, January 2, 1992, WestLaw; and Ricardo Ustarroz, "At Least 300,000 People March for Democracy in Algiers," Agence France Presse, January 2, 1992, WestLaw. Moreover, regarding the first round of the elections in which the FIS did well, Ustarroz also notes: "Fresh elections for many of the seats won by the fundamentalists may have to be held because of complaints of ballot rigging and other irregularities in 140 constituencies."

7. A thorough explanation of the underpinning of such violence in the ghastly ideology of Salafi-jihadi terror groups can be found in Chetan Bhatt, "The Virtues of Violence and the Arts of Terror" (forthcoming, 2013).

8. M. Bennoune, "Comment l'intégrisme a produit un terrorisme sans précédent," part 3.

9. Published by presidential decree (05-278), August 14, 2005. The enabling legislation was 06-01 of February 28, 2006. See discussion in George Joffé, "National Reconciliation and General Amnesty in Algeria," *Mediterranean Politics* 13 (2008): 213–28.

10. Nassima Oulebsir, "Monde musulman: Le calvaire des non-jeûneurs," *El Watan Weekend*, August 10, 2012, 9.

11. Mahfoud Bennoune, "Ébauche d'une histoire sociale du triangle de la mort (part 1)," *El Watan*, February 25, 1999, 9.

12. Ibid.

13. Mahfoud Bennoune, "Ébauche d'une histoire sociale du triangle de la mort (part 4)," *El Watan*, March 1, 1999, 11.

14. Boukra, *Le Djihadisme*, 7.

15. See the accounts in Souâd Belhaddad, *Algérie: Le Prix de l'Oubli 1992–2005* (Paris: Flammarion, 2005), and her mention of "oscillating" casualty figures. Ibid., 11.

16. See "Repression and Violence Must End," Amnesty International, October 1994, MDE 28/08/94, 6. ("In many cases it is impossible to know with certainty who carried out the killings and why.") One of the most egregious examples is a campaign publication: "Algeria: A Human Rights Crisis," Amnesty International, AI Index: MDE 28/36/07. Through repeated use of circumstantial evidence, it blames the 1997 massacres on the Algerian government without any suggestion whatsoever of the involvement of fundamentalist armed groups.

17. For Algerian scholarly documentation of jihadist violence and the organizational structure that enabled it, see Abdelhamid Boumezbar and Azine Djamila, *L'Islamisme Algérien: De la genèse au terrorisme* (Algiers: Chihab Éditions, 2002).

18. "Those who deserve to die," Agence France Presse, available at http://www.library.cornell.edu/colldev/mideast/3gia.htm.

19. A. Nabila, "Nacer Ouari, La voix des sourds-muets s'est tue," *El Watan*, February 4, 1995, 1.

20. Cited in Lamine Chikhi, "On veut tuer l'algérie intelligente: faut-il 'rentrer dans les tranchées?'" *Liberté*, June 23, 1991, 2.

21. Mustapha Benfodil, *Les six derniers jours de Bagdad: Journal d'un voyage de guerre* (Algiers: Casbah Éditions and Éditions SAEC-Liberté, 2003), 47.

22. Joffé, "National Reconciliation and General Amnesty in Algeria."

23. H.Z., "Eradicateurs?" *Le Matin*, February 16, 1994, 5.

24. Note, e.g., the insulting tone of Jean-Paul Mari, "Cris de femme: la guerre d'Algérie," *Le Nouvel Observateur*, May 11, 1995, http://www.grands-reporters.com/spip.php?page=imprimersans&id_article=389&nom_site=Grands%20Reporters&url_site=http://www.grands-reporters.com.

25. "Second Optional Protocol to the International Covenant on Civil and Political Rights, aiming at the abolition of the death penalty," December 15, 1989, A/RES/44/128, Article 2(1).

CHAPTER SIX

1. Rick Atkinson, "Killing of Iranian Dissenters: 'Bloody Trail Back to Tehran,'" *Washington Post*, November 21, 1993, A1.

2. Ibid.

3. Lahouari Addi, *L'Algérie et la démocratie: Pouvoir et crise du politique dans l'Algérie contemporaine* (Paris: Découverte, 1994).

4. Atkinson, "Killing of Iranian Dissenters," citing a *German Federal Criminal Office* report on Iranian state killings in Berlin in 1992 (emphasis added).

5. Anne Applebaum, "A Web Witness to Iranian Brutality," *Washington Post*, January 20, 2006, A17.

6. Ayatollah Ruhollah Khomeini, "Speech of June 15, 1981," in *Sahifeh Imam: Compilation of the Writings of Imam Khomeini*, vol. 14, eds. Mansoor Sana'i and Mansoor Limba (Tehran: Institute for the Compilation and Publication of Imam Khomeini's Work, 1999), 462.

7. Steven M. Nadler, *Spinoza: A Life* (Cambridge, UK: Cambridge University, 1999), 5. Quoted language is from the *cherem* (censure) itself.

8. Hannah Arendt, *Responsibility and Judgment* (New York: Schocken Books, 2003), 17.

9. Ibid.

10. Benedict (Baruch) Spinoza, "Freedom of Thought and Speech," in *The Philosophy of Spinoza*, ed. Joseph Ratner (New York: Modern Library, 1927), 53.

11. These are the last recorded words of Ehsan Fattahian, reportedly executed in November 2009, as translated orally (from Farsi) by Roya Boroumand.

12. Arendt, *Responsibility and Judgment*, 33.

13. Ladan Boroumand and Roya Boroumand, "Terror, Islam, and Democracy," *Journal of Democracy* 13, no. 2 (2002): 10.

14. "Iran Opposition says 72 People Killed in Vote Protest," Agence France Presse, September 3, 2009, http://www.google.com/hostednews/afp/article/ALeqM5iaWYtGitSBRRBJkDanoZ1gwP4DBA.

15. "This Day in World History, October 10, 680 CE: Hussein ibn Ali Killed at Karbala," Oxford University Press, accessed August 24, 2012, http://blog .oup.com/2011/10/hussein/.

16. *Islamic Republic's Penal Code of Iran* (as amended November 28, 1991), Article 110 (*Iran Penal Code*).

17. "Witness Statement of Kourosh Sehati," Iran Human Rights Documentation Center, accessed August 24, 2012, http://www.iranhrdc.org/english/ publications/witness-testimony/3171-witness-statement-kourosh-sehati .html?p=1.

18. Ibid.

19. D. Parvaz, "Notebook: 16 Days in Evin Prison," *Frontline* (Tehran Bureau), January 25, 2012, http://www.pbs.org/wgbh/pages/frontline/tehranbureau /2012/01/notebook-16-days-in-evin-prison.html.

20. "Witness Statement of Kourosh Sehati," 6.

21. Ibid., 10.

22. Mahnaz Afkhami, "At the Crossroads of Tradition and Modernity: Personal Reflection," *SAIS Review* 20, no. 2 (Summer–Fall 2000): 87.

23. Women's Learning Partnership, "Iran Obstructs Women's Access to Education, Moves Closer to Segregating University Classes and Bars Women's Entry to Certain Majors," August 16, 2012, http://www.learningpartnership .org/lib/iran-obstructs-women%E2%80%99s-access-education-moves-closer-segregating-university-classes-and-bars-wom.

24. See the analysis in Janet Afary and Kevin B. Anderson, *Foucault and the Iranian Revolution: Gender and the Seductions of Islamism* (Chicago: University of Chicago Press, 2005).

25. "Iran—One Million Signatures Campaign—4th Anniversary Analysis," One Million Signatures Campaign, http://www.npr.org/templates/story/story .php?storyId=112150486http://www.1millionchange.info/english/spip .pho?article751.

26. Noushin Ahmadi Khorasani, *Iranian Women's One Million Signatures Campaign for Equality: The Inside Story* (Baltimore: Women's Learning Partnership, 2009), 101.

27. Ibid.

28. For details of arrests, see Human Rights First, "One Million Signatures Campaign Timeline," accessed October 14, 2012, http://www .humanrightsfirst.org/our-work/human-rights-defenders/iran/one-million-signature-campaign-timeline/.

29. "Iranian Women Fight Polygamy Proposal," *Womensphere*, February 2, 2010, http://womensphere.wordpress.com/2010/02/02/iranian-women-fight-polygamy-proposal/.

30. Anthony Faiola, "Dissident Iranians Find Refuge in Turkey," *Washington Post*, February 15, 2010, A8.

31. Monica Garmsey, "Death of a Teenager," *Guardian*, July 27, 2006, http:// www.guardian.co.uk/media/2006/jul/27/iran.broadcasting.

32. *Iran Penal Code*, Section 113.

33. Soheila Vahdati, "Asieh's Eyes," *Iranian.com*, October 16, 2007, http://www.iranian.com/main/2007/asieh-s-eyes.

34. Vahdati, "Asieh's Eyes."

35. Asieh Amini, "The Island," translated and reprinted in Vahdati, "Asieh's Eyes."

36. Ibid.

CHAPTER SEVEN

1. Andrea Elliott, "A Call to Jihad, Answered in America," *New York Times*, July 12, 2009, AA1.

2. Eli Saslow, "Muslim Activist in Minnesota Struggles as One-Man Counter against Lure of Terrorism," *Washington Post*, July 10, 2011, A1.

3. "Muslim Activist in Minnesota Struggles."

4. A similar account is reflected in "Statement of Osman Ahmed on Behalf of the Victim Families Whose Children Have Been Recruited and Kidnapped to Somalia Before the United States Senate Committee on Homeland Security and Governmental Affairs," Committee on Homeland Security and Governmental Affairs, March 8, 2009. Osman Ahmed, another of Burhan's uncles, testified that "[p]ublic threats were issued to us at Abubakar as-Saddique for simply speaking with CNN and *Newsweek*."

5. "A Call to Jihad, Answered in America."

6. See debate detailed in updates to "Rep. Peter King: There Are 'Too Many Mosques in this Country,'" *Politico*, September 19, 2007, http://www.politico.com/blogs/thecrypt/0907/Rep_King_There_are_too_many_mosques_in_this_country_.html.

7. See, e.g., William Wan, "Hearings on Muslims Trigger Panic," *Washington Post*, January 24, 2011, A1.

8. See, e.g., Elise Foley, "Keith Ellison Tears Up at Hearing on Muslim-American 'Radicalization,'" *Huffington Post*, March 10, 2011, http://www.huffingtonpost.com/2011/03/10/keith-ellison-tears-up-muslim-hearings_n_833981.html.

9. Allie Shah and James Walsh, "Somalis Take to the Street to Protest Group's Actions," *Star Tribune* (Minneapolis–St. Paul), June 12, 2009, 05B.

10. "CAIR Claims 2 Metro Somali Leaders are Anti-Muslim," MyFox9 (Minneapolis), November 8, 2011, http://www.freerepublic.com/focus/f-news/2805302/posts.

11. "Ore. Bombing Suspect Wanted 'Spectacular Show,'" MSN, November 27, 2010, http://www.msnbc.msn.com/id/40389899/ns/us_news-security/t/ore-bomb-suspect-wanted-spectacular-show.

12. Ibid.

13. Malkhadir Muhumed, "Somalia: Al Shabab Aid Ban Will Bring Disaster, Groups Warn," *Huffington Post*, November 29, 2011, http://www.huffingtonpost.com/2011/11/29/Somalia-al-shabaab-ban_n_1119356.html.

14. Gabriel Gatehouse, "Defections Put Militant Group Al-Shabaab on the Run

in Somalia," BBC News Magazine, June 8, 2012, http://www.bbc.co.uk/news/magazine-18364762.

15. Slightly different numbers of indictments have been reported in relation to these events, all of which are close to nineteen. "Ohio Man Admits Fundraising Help for Somalia Terror Group al-Shabab," MSNBC, February 7, 2012, http://www.msnbc.msn.com/id/46291809/ns/us_news-crime_and_courts/t/ohio-man-admits-fundraising-help-somalia-terror-group-al-shabab/#.UD0VdGjOxgt.

16. Somali American Elders Press Release, Minneapolis, September 1, 2010 (on file with the author).

17. Mathilde Aarseth, "World Cup Fatwa," *Jihadica* (Documenting the Global Jihad), June 17, 2010, http://www.jihadica.com/world-cup-fatwa/, citing a fatwa originally posted at http://tawhed.ws/FAQ/display_question?qid=2256.

18. His financial troubles were detailed in Saslow, "Muslim Activist in Minnesota Struggles."

19. Ibid.

20. Quoted in ibid.

21. Cited in ibid.

22. Laura Yuen, "Jury Finds Minn. Man Guilty in al-Shabab Trial," Minnesota Public Radio, October 18, 2012, http://minnesota.publicradio.org/display/web/2012/10/18/news/al-shabab-trial-verdict-guilty/.

23. Census data released in October 2011 suggest that there are thirty-two thousand people of Somali descent in Minnesota. "State Somali Population Continues to Grow," *Minnesota Daily*, October 30, 2011, http://www.mndaily.com/2011/10/27/state-somali-population-continues-grow. The figure of twenty-five recruits is cited in Yuen, "Jury Finds Minn. Man Guilty in al-Shabab Trial." The figure of forty comes from Majority Investigative Report, "Al Shabaab: Recruitment and Radicalization within the Muslim American Community and the Threat to the Homeland," Committee on Homeland Security, July 27, 2011, 2.

24. See Laura Yuen, "Local Somalis Condemn Suicide Bombing in Homeland," Minnesota Public Radio, December 13, 2009, http://minnesota.publicradio.org/display/web/2009/12/13/somali-rally/.

25. For updated information on the case, see Laura Bashraheel, "Hamza Kashgari's Poem from Prison," *Saudi Gazette*, August 21, 2012, http://www.saudigazette.com.sa/index.cfm?method=home.regcon&contentid=20120821133666.

26. Hussein Ibish, "Muslims must speak up against the Kashgari scandal," *Ibishblog*, February 21, 2012, http://ibishblog.com/article/2012/02/21/muslims_must_speak_against_kashgari_scandal.

27. See "Family Income Distribution (Overview)," Somali Justice Advocacy Center, http://www.somaliadvocacy.net./Income%20Distribution%20(Overview).php.

28. Elliott, "A Call to Jihad."

29. Cited in "Muslim Activist in Minnesota Struggles."

30. See Abdi Guled, "Militants Say Suicide Bomber Was Somali-American, *Arab News*, June 2, 2011, http://www.arabnews.com/node/379452.

CHAPTER EIGHT

1. "Year End Results: Terrorists Kill Twice as Many in 2010 in Lahore," *Express Tribune*, December 27, 2010, http://tribune.com.pk/story/95306/ year-end-results-terrorists-kill-twice-as-many-in-2010-in-lahore/.

2. Waqar Gillani and Salman Masood, "Suicide Bombers in Pakistan Kill Dozens of Shiites," *New York Times*, September 1, 2010, A17.

3. See "Pakistan: Shirkat Gah Joins Protests against Killing of Ahmedis in Lahore and Karachi," WLUML, June 3, 2010, http://www.wluml.org/node/6372.

4. Ibid.

5. "Al Qaida revendique 131 attaques commises en Irak Durant le Ramadan," Agence France Presse, accessed October 4, 2012, http://reunion.orange.fr/ news/monde/al-qaida-revendique-131-attaques-commises-en-irak-durant-le-ramadan,631281.html.

6. Scott Helfstein, Nassir Abdulla, and Muhammad al-Obaidi, "Deadly Vanguards: A Study of al-Qa'ida's Violence Against Muslims," Occasional Paper Series: Combating Terrorism Center at West Point (December 2009): 10.

7. Ibid.

8. "Moustapha Akkad, 75, Who Produced Religious and Horror Films, Is Dead," *New York Times*, November 12, 2005, A13.

9. See "Pakistan Security Report 2009," Pakistan Institute for Peace Studies, January 2010, 21.

10. "Anti-Taliban Views Cost Mufti Naeemi His Life," *Daily Times*, June 13, 2009, http://www.dailytimes.com.pk/default.asp?page=2009/06/13/story_ 13-6-2009_pg13_5.

11. Note that there are diverse estimates of casualties. I cite the figure given in Jill Carroll, "Algeria Bombing Prompts Question: Can Al Qaeda Spread across North Africa?" *Christian Science Monitor*, December 14, 2007, http://www .csmonitor.com/2007/1214/p07s02-wome.html.

12. Karima Bennoune, "Terror/Torture," *Berkeley Journal of International Law* 26, no. 1 (2008): 1–61.

13. Saïd Mekbel, "Mesmar J'ha: Dis-moi," *Le Matin*, February 16, 1994, 24.

14. "Saïd Mekbel," Committee to Protect Journalists, accessed August 24, 2012, http://cpj.org/killed/1994/said-mekbel.php.

15. M. Bennoune, "Comment l'intégrisme a produit un terrorisme sans précédent (part 1)."

16. I am citing the statistics of the Pakistan Institute for Peace Studies from 2008 to 2010: http://san-pips.com/. Note that casualty figures for recent violence in Pakistan are controversial and divergent.

17. There are almost no statistics that count the totality of such killings. However, exhaustive review of NGO, press, and UN reports on Pakistan and Afghanistan suggest Diep Saeeda's figure is in the ballpark.

18. "Times Topics: Swat Valley," *New York Times*, accessed August 24, 2012, http://topics.nytimes.com/top/news/international/countriesandterritories/pakistan/northwest-pakistan/swat_valley/index.html.

19. Susanne Koelbl, "Bowing Down to the Taliban," *Der Spiegel Online*, February 21, 2009, http://www.salon.com/2009/02/25/koelbl/.

20. Zia ur Rehman, "Where Killing Comes Easy," *The News on Sunday*, January 15, 2012, http://jang.com.pk/thenews/jan2012-weekly/nos-15-01-2012/dia.htm#2.

21. "Malala Yousafzai: Reward Offered for Arrest of Attackers," BBC News Online, October 10, 2012, http://www.bbc.co.uk/news/world-asia-19901277.

22. Huma Imtiaz, "In Search of the Jews of Karachi," *Express Tribune*, February 3, 2011, http://tribune.com.pk/story/113103/in-search-of-the-jews-of-karachi/.

23. "Population of Hindus in Pakistan," Pakistan Hindu Council, accessed August 24, 2012, http://www.pakistanhinducouncil.org/hindupopulation.asp.

24. For confirmation of this, see Christine Fair, "Under the Shrinking U.S. Security Umbrella: India's End Game in Afghanistan," *Washington Quarterly* 34, no. 2 (Spring 2011): 184.

25. Jon Boone, "Taliban Threaten Journalists over Malala Yousafzai Coverage," *Guardian*, October 15, 2012, http://www.guardian.co.uk/world/2012/oct/15/taliban-threaten-journalists-malala-yousafzai.

26. Robert Mackey, "After a Bullet in the Head, Assaults on a Pakistani Schoolgirl's Character Follow," *The Lede* (blog), *New York Times*, October 16, 2012, http://thelede.blogs.nytimes.com/2012/10/16/after-a-bullet-in-the-head-assaults-on-a-pakistani-schoolgirls-character-follow/.

27. Muhammad Arif, "Attack on Malala Yousufzai," *Financial Daily*, October 15, 2012, http://www.thefinancialdaily.com/NewsDetail/153365%20.aspx.

28. Safiya Aftab, "Goebbels Lives On in Pakistan," *The News on Sunday*, October 14, 2012, http://www.sacw.net/article2925.html.

29. "Conflict Will Create 100 Bin Ladens, Warns Egyptian President," *Guardian*, March 31, 2003, 4.

30. Amy DePaul, "First Victims of Freedom," *Guernica*, May 1, 2007, http://www.guernicamag.com/interviews/the_black_glove/.

31. Graham Usher, "Mother Iraq," *Al Ahram Weekly On-line*, February 26, 2004, http://weekly.ahram.org.eg/2004/679/re9.htm.

32. Lucinda Marshall, "'Our Lives are Worse Now': Yanar Mohammed Talks about the Impact of the US Occupation on the Lives of Iraqi Women," *Dissident Voice*, http://www.dissidentvoice.org/June04/Marshall0621.htm.

33. Nabil Charaf Eddine, "A force de louer la 'résistance irakienne,'" *Elaph*, reprinted in *Courrier International* (July 13–20, 2005): 32.

34. Anissa Hélie, "The U.S. Occupation and Rising Religious Extremism: The Double Threat to Women in Iraq," *Znet*, June 24, 2005, http://www.zcommunications.org/the-u-s-occupation-and-rising-religious-extremism-by-anissa-h-lie.

35. See Corinna Mullin, "Reply to Anissa Hélie's 'The U.S. Occupation and Rising Religious Extremism: The Double Threat to Women in Iraq,'" *Znet*, July 12, 2005, http://www.zcommunications.org/reply-to-anissa-helies-the-u-s-

occupation-and-rising-religious-extremism-the-double-threat-to-women-in-iraq-by-corinna-mullin.

36. Yalda Hakim, "Afghan Women Who Fight for Freedoms," *The Australian*, September 25, 2012, http://www.theaustralian.com.au/news/world/afghan-women-who-fight-for-freedoms/story-e6frg6so-1226480544161.

37. Sean Carberry, "Afghan Women Fear Backsliding on Key Gains," NPR, August 27, 2012, http://www.npr.org.2012/08/27/158522519/afghan-women-fear-backsliding-on-key.gains.

38. In late 2012, Maria Bashir faced scrutiny for her office's prosecution of women for "moral crimes" under Afghan law, as reported by Graham Bowley, "Afghan Prosecutor Faces Criticism for Her Pursuit of 'Moral Crimes,'" *New York Times*, December 28, 2012, http://www.nytimes.com/2012/12/29/world/asia/afghan-prosecutor-faces-attacks-over-her-pursuit-of-moral-crimes.html?pagewanted=all&_r=0. Heather Barr of Human Rights Watch told the *Times* it was fair to question Bashir's record on this score, while Manizha Naderi of Women for Afghan Women insisted that "[t]he law is the problem, and not Maria Bashir."

39. I first heard this quote, attributed to an anonymous Bosnian writer, in a long-lost documentary from the 1990s. A similar assertion was later made in Stewart Brand, *The Clock of the Long Now: Time and Responsibility* (New York: Basic Books, 1999), 115.

40. See Michael Hughes, "No Peace Without Justice and Equality in Afghanistan," *Huffington Post*, November 1, 2010, http://www.huffingtonpost.com/michael-hughes/no-peace-without-justice_b_776810.html.

41. "Interim Report of Special Rapporteur on Human Rights in Afghanistan," September 26, 2001, UN Doc. No. A/56/409, 8–11.

42. See Jennifer Senior, "The Firemen's Friar," *New York Magazine*, November 12, 2001, http://nymag.com/nymetro/news/sept11/features/5372/.

43. Cited in Austin Carty, "Jerry Falwell 9/11 Remarks: A former Liberty University Student Reflects," *Huffington Post*, September 13, 2011, http://www.huffingtonpost.com/austin-carty/jerry-falwell-911-remarks-reflection_b_960571.html.

44. "Amenia Rasool: Dining as a Twosome," in "A NATION CHALLENGED: PORTRAITS OF GRIEF: THE VICTIMS; Weight Lifting, the French Horn and a Woman Who Didn't Do Shoes," *New York Times*, October 16, 2001, B11.

45. For the full original version, see Karima Bennoune, "Why I Hate Al Qaeda," *IntLawGrrls,* September 11, 2011, http://www.intlawgrrls.com/2011/09/why-i-hate-al-qaeda.html.

46. Muqtedar Khan, "Muslims Condemn Israel but Ignore Their Own Crimes," *Telegraph*, November 17, 2001, http://www.telegraph.co.uk/news/worldnews/1362668/Muslims-condemn-Israel-but-ignore-thier-own-crimes.html.

47. Mehdi Hasan, "Why Muslims Must Speak Out against Terrorism," *New Statesman*, July 5, 2010, http://www.newstatesman.com/blogs/mehdi-hasan/2010/07/muslims-terrorism-condemn.

48. Aziz Junejo, "Muslims Are Obliged to Denounce Terrorism," *Seattle Times*, August 6, 2005, B5.

49. Ray Hanania, "Arabs, Muslims Need Stronger Stand against Extremists," *Daily Herald* (Arlington Heights, IL), October 2, 2005, Section 1, 8.

50. Sheema Khan, "Silence Is not an Option in the Struggle for Islam's Soul," *Globe and Mail*, January 12, 2011, A23.

51. Becky Bergdahl, "Nobel Laureate Calls for Armed Intervention in Nigeria," Inter Press Service, September 24, 2012. According to Agence France Presse, Boko Haram killed nearly three thousand people in Nigeria between 2009 and late 2012. "Nigeria: au moins 31 morts dans une série d'attaques attribuées à Boko Haram," Agence France Presse, October 20, 2012, http://www.courrier international.com/depeche/newsmlmmd.33a4bd699ea17ae224dbd7fca0 d77b18.8e1.xml.

CHAPTER NINE

1.   Chawki Amari, Mélanie Matarese, Ramdane Koubabi, Ghellab Smail, "I Burn, Therefore I Am [*Je Brûle, donc Je Suis*]," *El Watan*, January 21, 2011, 3.

2.   Ibid.

3.   The party's home page is http://ettajdid.org/spip.php?article680.

4.   See Mounira M. Charrad, "Tunisia in the Forefront of the Arab World: Two Waves of Gender Legislation," *Washington and Lee Law Review* 64, no. 4 (Winter 2008): 1513.

5.   Some of Ennahda's violent history is recounted in Joshua Hammer, "In a Worried Corner of Tunis," *New York Review of Books*, October 27, 2011, 24.

6.   Edward Cody, "Egypt's Fundamentalist Salafists Rise in Wake of Mubarak's Fall," *Washington Post*, March 27, 2011, A8.

7.   "Communiqué 2012-03-26 du Mouvement Ettajdid," March 28, 2012, http:// ettajdid.org/spip.php?article680.

8.   See, e.g., Marks, "Can Islamism and Feminism Mix?"

9.   Sanja Kelly and Julia Breslin, *Women's Rights in the Middle East and North Africa: Progress Amid Resistance* (New York: Freedom House, 2010), 490.

10. Stuart Laidlaw, "Struggling to Find a Moderate Voice," *Toronto Star*, May 5, 2007, L10.

11. Seif Soudani, "Tunisie: Au pied du mur, Ennahdha céde sur l'ex article 1," *Le courier de l'Atlas*, March 26, 2012, http://www.lecourrierdelatlas .com/232526032012Billet-Tunisie-Au-pied-du-mur-Ennahdha-cede-sur-l-ex-article-1.html.

12. Roua Khlifi and Adam Le Nevez, "Secret Video Reveals Ghannouchi's Vision for Islam in Tunisia," Tunisia Live, October 11, 2012, http://www.tunisia-live.net/2012/10/11/secret-video-reveals-ghannouchis-vision-for-islam-in-tunisia/.

13. Ibid.

14. Mourad Sellami, "Ghannouchi, sur la défensive, lâche sur l'atteinte au sacré," *El Watan*, October 13, 2012, 10.

15. Jerome Socolovsky, "Egypt Protests Level Playing Field for Women," Voice of

America, February 8, 2011, http://www.voanews.com/content/egypt-protest-leveling-the-playing-field-for-women-115591364/172704.html.

16. The size of Egypt's Christian population is a topic of controversy, with estimates varying from about five million up to the figure cited here. An Egyptian official in 2012 indicated that there is no "definitive data on the number of Egyptian Christians currently residing in the country. . . ." Al-Masry Al-Youm, "Official Number of Egyptian Christians Unknown, Says CAPMAS," *Egypt Independent*, June 14, 2012, http://www.egyptindependent.com/news/official-number-egyptian-christians-unknown-says-capmas.

17. Cody, "Egypt's Fundamentalist Salafists Rise in Wake of Mubarak's Fall."

18. Fatma El-Zanaty and Ann Way, "Egypt Demographic and Health Survey 2005," Cairo: Ministry of Health and Population, National Population Council, El-Zanaty and Associates, and ORC Macro.

19. Mohamed Abdel Salam, "Egypt's Brotherhood Mobile FGM Convoys Condemned by Women's Groups," Bikyamasr, May 14, 2012, http://www.bikyamasr.com/68750/egypts-brotherhood-mobile-fgm-convoys-condemned-by-womens-group/.

20. Such domination is increasing. See "Egypt: Newspaper Editor Detained, Muslim Brotherhood Take Control of State Media," Reporters sans Frontières, August 23, 2012, http://allafrica.com/stories/201208240256.html.

21. Amena Raghei, "Women in Libyan Public Life: A Seismic Shift," Muftah, September 12, 2012, http://muftah.org/women-in-libyan-public-life-a-seismic-shift/.

22. Kouichi Shirayanagi, "Ennahda Spokeswoman Souad Abderrahim: Single Mothers Are a Disgrace to Tunisia," Tunisia Live, November 9, 2011, http://www.tunisia-live.net/2011/11/09/ennahda-spokeswoman-souad-abderrahim-single-mothers-are-a-disgrace-to-tunisia/.

23. Yasmine Ryan, "Tunisia: Women's Rights Hang in the Balance," Al Jazeera, August 20, 2011, http://www.aljazeera.com/indepth/features/2011/08/201181617052432756.html.

24. Farah Samti, "Human Rights Minister Refuses to Retract Homophobic Comments," Tunisia Live, March 2, 2012, http://www.tunisia-live.net/2012/03/02/human-rights-minister-refuses-to-retract-homophobic-comments/.

25. Giuliana Sgrena, "Tunisia: Women Fearful of Islamists' Rise," Inter Press Service, November 14, 2011, http://www.ipsnews.net/2011/11/tunisia-women-fearful-of-islamistsrsquo-rise/.

26. "Tunisians Riot over Animated Film 'Persepolis,'" CBS News, October 14, 2011, http://www.cbsnews.com/2100-202_162-20120697.html.

27. Asma Ghribi, "Trial of Nabil Karoui, Owner of Nessma TV for Broadcasting Persepolis Last October," Tunisia Live, January 22, 2012, http://www.tunisia-live.net/2012/01/22/trial-of-nabil-karoui-owner-of-nessma-tv-for-broadcasting-persepolis-last-october/.

28. "Des journalistes et intellectuels aggressés par des salafistes devant le palais de justice," Leaders, January 23, 2012, http://www.leaders.com.tn/article/des-journalistes-et-intellectuels-agresses-par-des-salafistes-devant-le-palais-de-justice-jebali-promet-des-sanctions?id=7508.

29. "Tunisia: TV Chief Fined Over a Film," *New York Times*, May 4, 2012, A7.

30. "Egypt's Islamist Parties Win Elections to Parliament," BBC News Middle East, January 21, 2012, http://www.bbc.co.uk/news/world-middle-east-16665748.

31. On September 19, 2012, ten left-wing parties took a step to rectify this error, banding together to form the Democratic Revolutionary Coalition. Randa Ali, "Egypt's Left Launches 'Democratic Revolutionary Coalition,'" *Al Ahram*, September 19, 2012, http://english.ahram.org.eg/News/53304.aspx.

32. "Five Salafi Organization Officials Referred to Trial in Foreign Funding Case," *Egypt Independent*, March 14, 2012, http://www.egyptindependent.com/news/five-salafi-organization-officials-referred-trial-foreign-funding-case.

33. "Egypt's Salafists Are Pushing for Islamic Law to Be the Source of All Legislation in the Country," *Al Ahram*, October 16, 2012, http://english.ahram.org.eg/NewsContent/1/64/55755/Egypt/Politics-/Egyptian-Salafists-demand-increased-role-for-Shari.aspx.

34. Imed Bensaied, "Pour nous, salafistes, la démocratie est un concept impie," France 24, September 28, 2012, http://www.france24.com/fr/20120928-tunisie-salafistes-temoignages-islamisme-radical-religion-reportage-ennahda.

35. Kenneth Roth, "Time to Abandon the Autocrats and Embrace Rights," in *Human Rights Watch World Report 2012* (New York: Human Rights Watch, 2012).

36. "Support Separation Between Religion and State: A Petition to Human Rights Watch," *Centre for Secular Space*, February 9, 2012, http:/www.centreforsecularspace.org/?q=campaigns/open-letter-kenneth-roth-human-rights-watch.

37. This is a conservative reading of international human rights law. By way of contrast, see Jeroen Temperman, *State–Religion Relationships and Human Rights Law: Towards a Right to Religiously Neutral Government* (Leiden: Martinus Nijhoff Publishers, 2010).

38. "Women and Islam: A Debate with Human Rights Watch," *New York Review of Books Blog*, accessed August 24, 2012, http://www.nybooks.com/blogs/nyrblog/2012/feb/23/women-islam-debate-human-rights-watch/.

39. Chawki Amari, "Le puits des autocrates," *El Watan*, February 13, 2012, 32.

40. Amira Al Hussaini, "Libya: Sorry Chris, Benghazi Couldn't Protect You," *Global Voices*, September 12, 2012, http://globalvoicesonline.org/2012/09/12/libya-sorry-chris-benghazi-couldnt-protect-you/.

41. Hassane Zerrouky, "Tunisie, la démocratie confisquée," *Le Soir d'Algérie*, September 6, 2012, http://www.lesoirdalgerie.com/articles/2012/09/06/article.php?sid=138788&cid=26.

42. Mourad Sellami, "Hamadi Redissi: La situation désastreuse ne peut qu'entraîner une tension sociale grandissante," *El Watan Weekend*, October 19, 2012, 9.

43. Christopher Barrie, "Tunisia: Al-Nahda's Failures Lead Sidi Bouzid to Rise Again," *Al Akhbar English*, August 17, 2012, http://english.al-akhbar.com/node/11211.

44. See, e.g., "En Tunisie, des centaines de Salafistes attaquent un quartier de Sidi Bouzid," Agence France Presse, August 23, 2012, http://www.libera

tion.fr/monde/2012/08/23/en-tunisie-des-centaines-de-salafistes-attaquent-un-quartier-de-sidi-bouzie_841446.

45. Mustapha Benfodil, "Le discours de Morsi et l'oreille mutilée de Sayed Ahmed," *El Watan*, December 30, 2012, 13.

CHAPTER TEN

1. Katarina Hoije, "Islamists: two stoned to death for committing adultery in Mali," CNN.com, August 3, 2012.

2. Doumbi-Fakoly, Hamidou Magassa, Ciré Bâ, and Boubacar Diagana, *L'Occupation du Nord du Mali* (Paris: L'Harmattan, Bamako: La Sahelienne, 2012), 47.

3. *Report of the Secretary-General on the Situation in Mali*, November 29, 2012, S/2012/894, para. 25.

4. Ibid., paras. 21–25.

5. "Mali unwed couple 'stoned to death,'" Al Jazeera.com, July 30, 2012.

6. AFP, "Nord-Mali: première amputation d'une main par les islamistes," *El Watan*, August 9, 2012.

7. Faith Karimi, "Fear grows as Mali extremists compile list of unmarried mothers," CNN.com, October 13, 2012.

8. "Mali unwed couple 'stoned to death.'"

9. Cited in "Islamists: two stoned to death for committing adultery in Mali."

10. "Malian youth, Islamists clash over planned amputation," Reuters, July 8, 2012.

11. See, e.g., William Lloyd-George, "The Man Who Brought the Black Flag to Timbuktu," *Foreign Policy*, October 22, 2012.

12. Vicki Huddleston, "Why We Must Help Save Mali," *New York Times*, January 14, 2013, http://www.nytimes.com/2013/01/15/opinion/why-we-must-help-save-mali.html?_r=0.

13. UN Security Council Resolution 2085, December 20, 2012, S/RES/2085(2012).

14. Abdoulaye Guindo, "30 femmes fouettées pour non port du voile 'réglementaire,'" *Procès-Verbal*, December 2, 2012, 7.

15. "Les Maliens subissent la loi de Ançar Eddine: au pavillon des amputés à Gao," *El Watan.com*, September 30, 2012.

16. "Mali: nouvelles amputations après un feu vert sous condition à une force armée," Agence France Presse, December 22, 2012.

17. "Mali: Islamists Fire on Women Defending Their Rights," *Morning Star Online*, October 7, 2012.

18. Jean-Michel Djian, *Les Manuscrits de Tombouctou: Secrets, mythes et réalités* (Paris: Éditions JCLattès, 2012), 17.

19. Félix Dubois, quoted in *Les Manuscrits de Tombouctou*, 35.

CHAPTER ELEVEN

1. David Dunbar et al., *Debunking 9/11 Myths: Why Conspiracy Theories Can't Stand Up to the Facts* (New York: Hearst Books, 2006).

2. James B. Meigs, afterword to *Debunking 9/11 Myths*.

3. See, e.g., "Assessing Damage, Urging Action: Report of the Eminent Jurists Panel on Terrorism, Counter-terrorism and Human Rights," International Commission of Jurists, accessed August 24, 2012, http://www.ifj.org/assets/docs/028/207/3e83flc-fbfc2cf.pdf. Unfortunately, notwithstanding its title, this important 2009 report says very little about the threat from terrorism.

4. M. Cherif Bassiouni, "A Policy-Oriented Inquiry into the Different Forms and Manifestations of 'International Terrorism,'" in *Legal Responses to International Terrorism: US Procedural Aspects*, ed. M. Cherif Bassiouni (Dordrecht, Netherlands: Martinus Nijhoff, 1988).

5. Robert Chesney, "Dissent from a CCR Board Member Regarding the al-Aulaki Suit," *Lawfare*, November 15, 2010, http://www.lawfareblog.com/2010/11/dissent-from-a-ccr-board-member-regarding-the-al-aulaki-suit-and-a-curious-response-from-ccrs-executive-director/.

6. Cited in Mark Tran, "Legal Challenge to U.S. Assassination Policy Divides Rights Groups," *Guardian*, November 15, 2010, http://www.guardian.co.uk/world/2010/nov/15/us-assassination-policy-rights-awlaki.

7. Article 5 of the ICCPR stipulates that "[n]othing in the present Covenant . . . impl[ies] . . . any right to engage in any activity . . . aimed at the destruction of any of the rights and freedoms recognized herein. . . ."

8. For further discussion, see Karima Bennoune, "Remembering the Other's Others: Theorizing the Approach of International Law to Muslim Fundamentalism," *Columbia Human Rights Law Review* 41 (2010), 692–97.

9. See, e.g., Human Rights First, *Blasphemy Laws Exposed: The Consequences of Criminalizing 'Defamation of Religion'* (New York: Human Rights First, March 2012).

10. "Mémorial des disparus en Algérie," accessed August 24, 2012, http://www.memorial-algerie.org/?q=fr/node/3319.

11. See *Commission of Inquiry: Algeria*, United States Institute of Peace, Truth Commissions Digital Collection, accessed January 15, 2013, http://www.usip.org/publications/commission-algeria.

12. Lucy Ash, "Dagestan—The Most Dangerous Place in Europe," BBC News Magazine, November 23, 2011, http://www.bbc.co.uk/news/magazine-15824831.

13. "Dagestan Russia Blasts: At Least 12 Dead in Makhachkala," BBC News Europe, May 4, 2012, http://www.bbc.co.uk/news/world-europe-17947301.

14. Ilya Arkhipov, "Russian Suicide Blast Kills Muslim Leader in Dagestan Region," *Businessweek*, August 28, 2012, http://www.bloomberg.com/news/2012-08-28/russian-suicide-blast-kills-muslim-leader-in-dagestan-region.html.

15. See Karima Bennoune, "A Disease Masquerading as a Cure": Women, Fundamentalism and Human Rights in Algeria (interview with Mahfoud Bennoune), in *Nothing Sacred: Women Respond to Religious Fundamentalism and Terror*, ed. Betsy Reed (New York: Thunder's Mouth Press/Nation Books, 2002), 75.

16. "Alert: Dagestan Court Acquits 'Chernovik' Journalists," Committee to

Protect Journalists, May 19, 2011, http://cpj.org/2011/05/dagestan-court-acquits-chernovik-journalists.php.

17. Karina Gadjieva, "Last Article by Khadjimurad Kamalov, Assassinated in Dagestan, Was on Election of the Head of Gunib District," *Caucasian Knot*, December 16, 2011, http://www.eng.kavkaz-uzel.ru/articles/19361/.

18. For an update to such views, see "Poll No. 39," Palestinian Center for Policy and Survey Research, March 17–19, 2011, http://www.pcpsr.org/survey/polls/2011/p39efull.html.

19. See Karima Bennoune, "The Paradoxical Feminist Quest for Remedy: A Case Study of Jane Doe v. Islamic Salvation Front and Anouar Haddam," *International Criminal Law Review* 11 (2011), 579–87.

20. Revital Blumenfeld, "Israeli Woman Refuses ultra-Orthodox Dictate to Move to Back of Bus," *Haaretz*, December 18, 2011, http://www.haaretz.com/print-edition/news/israeli-woman-refuses-ultra-orthodox-dictate-to-move-to-back-of-bus-1.402021.

21. "Full Transcript of Netanyahu Speech at UN General Assembly," *Haaretz*, September 24, 2011, http://www.haaretz.com/news/diplomacy-defense/full-transcript-of-netanyahu-speech-at-un-general-assembly-1.386464.

CONCLUSION

1. Cited in "A Disease Masquerading as a Cure," 89.

2. Mourad Sellami, "Prise de conscience en Libye: La société civile s'organise contre les djihadistes," *El Watan*, September 12, 2012, 12.

3. Rod Nordland, "Discontent Over a Name," *The Hindu*, October 18, 2012, http://www.thehindu.com/opinion/op-ed/discontent-over-a-name/article4006598.ece.

4. Will Jordan, "Protests Have Been Held in Afghanistan over the Public Flogging of a 16-Year-Old Girl," Al Jazeera, September 25, 2012, http://www.aljazeera.com/video/asia/2012/09/201292513949172636.html.

5. "Mali Women Protest against Veil," News24, October 7, 2012, http://www.news24.com/Africa/News/Mali-women-protest-against-veil-20121007.

6. "Après le rapt de cinq humanitaires: Le président du Niger appelle à la mobilisation générale," *El Watan*, October 18, 2012, 11.

7. Roya and Ladan Boroumand, "Terror, Islam, and Democracy."

8. Lazhari Labter, "Les déshumains ou complainte d'un pays de longue peine," in *Yasmina ou les sept pierres de mon collier d'amour* (Algiers: Éditions Barzakh, 2001).

9. Cited in "A Disease Masquerading as a Cure," 89.

10. Rana Jawad, "Libya Election Success for Secularist Jibril's Bloc," BBC News, July 18, 2012, http://www.bbc.co.uk/news/world-africa-18880908.

11. Fayçal Métaoui, "Le cinéma arabe s'attaque à l'extrémisme religieux," *El Watan*, November 30, 2012, 16–17.

12. Fatou Sow, "Religion et Politique: Renégocier avec les religieux" (paper presented at conference: "Le féminisme face aux défis du multiculturalisme," Rabat, Morocco, October 21–25, 2008).

13. Mohamed Mounir, Alli Soutak, *Al Maseer* soundtrack. Released by EMI–Arabia, 1999, as *Le Destin* (original soundtrack).

14. "La Modernité ou la Disparition, M'hamed Boukhobza à Alger Rep.," *Alger Républicain*, June 23, 1993, 2.

15. Salah Chouaki, "Le compromis avec l'islamisme politique est impossible," *El Watan*, March 15, 1993, 2.

16. O.Z., "Discours qui tuent, discourse qui mentent," *Le Matin*, February 12, 1996.

Acknowledgments

This volume is only seeing the light of day because, at every destination along the way, people took the project to heart and invested their time in it. I am deeply grateful to them all.

The first person I have to thank is Rutgers-Newark Law School Dean John Farmer, who believed in this idea from the start and generously introduced me to Flip Brophy, my agent, to whom I am profoundly grateful for always making me feel I could actually do this. Alane Mason, my editor, put so much care and countless hours into making this a better book.

I thank Samia Allalou, Zazi Sadou, Malika Zouba, and Said Nemsi for their warm hospitality and for answering my endless questions, and my friend S.M. for all her help. In Niger, my research was only possible because of the help of Aminata Daouda Hainikoye and Zeinabou Hadari. Gita Sahgal inspired me to speak out as she does. Sharon Swartz got me packed and kept me organized, which is not easy. Melanie Grund was the most loyal and thoughtful reader. Kari Busch always cheered me on. Rhonda Copelon was a great inspiration during her life, and I felt her spirit with me on the road. Ariane Brunet put me in touch with all the right people in Tunisia. Doaa Kassem watched over me in Tahrir Square and beyond, and Doaa Abdelaal made time for this when she did not have time. Abdulwahid Qalinle at the University of Minnesota Law School made my work in Minneapolis possible with his expert help and hospitality. My research in Russia could only be carried out because of the support of journalists Nadia Azhgikhina and Svetlana Svistunova. Farida Shaheed and the staff at Shirkat Gah in Lahore helped me immeasurably, as did the Malkani family in Karachi, the inimitable Nuzhat Kidvai, and Sabeen Mahmud. Horia Mosadiq kindly shared contacts, her precious time, and her insight. My research in Mali was enabled by Djingarey Maiga, and Dr. A in Bamako.

I also thank the network of Women Living Under Muslim Laws (WLUML), CODESRIA, the Urgent Action Fund for Women's Human Rights, Gender Concerns–International, the ATFD, SOS Disparus, the Women's Learning Partnership, the Centre for Secular Space, as well as Nassera Dutour, Omar Belhouchet, Fatima Bendriss from *El Watan*'s documentation department who painstakingly collected all of my father's articles, Yasmina and Ourida Chouaki, Fatma-Zohra Kheddar, Souhila Aissa, Giuliana Sgrena, Yofi Tirosh, Anissa Hélie, Akila Ouared, Amine Khene, Kheira Dekkali, Fayza L, Wahiba and family for their warm welcome, Professor Fatou Sow, Aïssatou Cissé, Hamid Baroudi, Lazhari Labter, Said Salah Ahmed, Madeeha Gauhar and Shahid Nadeem, Salil Tripathi, Chetan Bhatt, Meredith Tax, Hassina Neekzad, Alia Hogben, Sadia Abbas, Denise Scarfi, Rachel Salzman, Kathleen Brandes, Mahnaz Afkhami, Ouessina Alidou, Codou Bop, Ayesha Imam, Harsh Kapoor, Pragna Patel, Pamela Wu, Cecilia Bailliet, Diane Amann, the late Greg Finger for his profound decency, ABC Visa Service, my Rutgers research assistants Natalae Anderson, Jennifer Berman, Herman Marcia, Moraa Onyonka, Chris Royal, Emily Button, and especially superstar Team Bennoune leader Mary Orsini, for her incredible contributions to the research. At Rutgers, I should also thank former chancellor Steve Diner for recognizing my work and Helene Wright for facilitating it. My new boss, UC Davis Dean Kevin Johnson, has already done so much to further my research. Most of all, I am deeply appreciative of every single person who granted me an interview.

There is a group of people without whom there would simply be no book, including my adopted aunt and uncle Lalia and Selim/Jean-Paul Ducos, who made their home mine whether in Blida, Algiers, or Paris and never wanted me to thank them for anything; the amazing Cherifa Kheddar and the whole family at Djazairouna, who entrusted me with their stories and honored me with their welcome and assistance; and Marieme Hélie-Lucas, who has never ceased inspiring me and goading me to keep doing this work. Terry Boullata has been "my hero" for nearly twenty-five years and made my work in Palestine possible. Mustapha Benfodil generously encouraged me and offered so much help and inspiration. Roya Boroumand met me once and then devoted several full days to working with me (and endured all my follow-up questions), for which I am truly grateful. Sohail Warraich, my Lahore "air traffic controller," kindly shared his considerable expertise and contacts and time. Human rights goddess Donna Guest watched my back.

I would also like to thank all the drivers who got me from place to place, a job that was rarely easy in a world of few marked addresses. They sometimes gave me great political insights along the way. Likewise, I send heartfelt gratitude to my cherished Muse, who nourished me in cyberspace during these travels.

Absentminded professor's caveat: If I forgot anyone, please know that I appreciated everything you did! Standard academic caveat: All remaining shortcomings are the sole responsibility of the author.

I am most appreciative of the support and understanding of friends in the United States, in Algeria, and on many continents, some of whom I have not seen for a long time because I was working on this project and others whom I have been lucky to meet because of it. In particular, I have been deeply touched by N.I.'s unflagging solidarity, which kept me going on difficult days.

This book was really inspired by two people: my late grandmother, Elizabeth Sutton, who taught me how to read and so much else, and my father, Mahfoud Bennoune, one of the bravest people I ever met. Finally, there are simply no words adequate to thank my beautiful mother for every gift she has given me.

INDEX